As featured in Book of the Year choices:

'My choice this year is, without any doubt, Antony Beevor's *Stalingrad*, a magnificent winter tapestry . . . it reads like an accessible novel rather than the superb history book which it really is' Dirk Bogarde, *Daily Telegraph*

'I want to add to the many laurels that have crowned *Stalingrad* by Antony Beevor. This superb work of narrative history (all of human despair, and also of heroism is there) chilled the marrow of my bones, even though read at high summer' Antonia Fraser, *Sunday Times*

'Antony Beevor's *Stalingrad* is superb: a gripping and dispassionate account of alternating folly and endurance' Nicholas Shakespeare, *Daily Telegraph*

'I have recently read and been hugely impressed by *Stalingrad* by Antony Beevor' Ben Elton, *Sunday Telegraph*

'*Stalingrad* is distinguished not only for its exhaustive research and sheer narrative drive, but for its portrayal of the ordinarily human during one of the most atrocious battles of the century' Colin Thubron, *Sunday Teleraph*

'A brilliantly researched *tour de force*' Sarah Bradford, *Sunday Times*

'*Stalingrad* by Antony Beevor is the best battle history for many years – balanced, dramatic, dreadful' Robert Conquest, *The Times Literary Supplement*

'*Stalingrad* by Antony Beevor cannot fail to leave one moved' Victoria Mather, *Daily Mail*

'Revealing, profound and thoroughly unputdownable, *Stalingrad* is an extraordinary achievement which transcends its genre' Vitali Vitaliev, *Daily Telegraph*

STALINGRAD

Antony Beevor

PENGUIN BOOKS

PENGUIN BOOKS

Published by the Penguin Group
Penguin Books Ltd, 80 Strand, London WC2R 0RL, England
Penguin Putnam Inc., 375 Hudson Street, New York, New York 10014, USA
Penguin Books Australia Ltd, 250 Camberwell Road, Camberwell, Victoria 3124, Australia
Penguin Books Canada Ltd, 10 Alcorn Avenue, Toronto, Ontario, Canada M4V 3B2
Penguin Books India (P) Ltd, 11 Community Centre, Panchsheel Park, New Delhi – 110 017, India
Penguin Books (NZ) Ltd, Cnr Rosedale and Airborne Roads, Albany, Auckland, New Zealand
Penguin Books (South Africa) (Pty) Ltd, 24 Sturdee Avenue, Rosebank 2196, South Africa

Penguin Books Ltd, Registered Offices: 80 Strand, London WC2R 0RL, England

www.penguin.com

First published by Viking 1998
Published in Penguin Books 1999
The open market edition published 2001

7

Set in Monotype Ehrhardt
Typeset by Rowland Phototypesetting Ltd, Bury St Edmunds, Suffolk
Printed in England by Clays Ltd, St Ives plc

Contents

Contents

Contents

vii

List of Illustrations

SECTION ONE

SECTION TWO

PHOTOGRAPHIC ACKNOWLEDGEMENTS

I am particularly grateful to the Arkhiv Muzeya Panorami Stalin-gradskoy Bitvi (the Archive of the Panoramic Museum of the Battle of Stalingrad) in Volgograd for providing illustrations 10, 14, 18, 19 and 20.

Helmut Abt Verlag, *Bis Stalingrad*, Alois Beck: 6
AKG London: 24, 30
Archive Photos, London: 12, 15
Bundesarchiv, Koblenz: 2, 21
Getty Images, London: 1, 3, 17, 22, 23, 25
Imperial War Museum, London: 4, 5, 8, 9, 11, 26, 28, 29, 31
Methuen & Co Ltd, *Paulus and Stalingrad: A Life of Field Marshal Paulus*, Walter Goerlitz: 13
Private collection: 27
Topham Picturepoint, Edenbridge, Kent: 16
Westdeutsches Verlag, *Das Oberkommando der Wehrmacht Gibt Bekannt*, Martin H. Sommerfeldt: 7

List of Maps

Preface

'Russia', observed the poet Tyuchev, 'cannot be understood with the mind.' The Battle of Stalingrad cannot be adequately understood through a standard examination. A purely military study of such a titanic struggle fails to convey its reality on the ground, rather as Hitler's maps in his Rastenburg *Wolfsschanze* isolated him in a fantasy-world, far from the suffering of his soldiers.

The idea behind this book is to show, within the framework of a conventional historical narrative, the experience of troops on both sides, using a wide range of new material, especially from archives in Russia. The variety of sources is important to convey the unprecedented nature of the fighting and its effects on those caught up in it with little hope of escape.

The sources include war diaries, chaplains' reports, personal accounts, letters, NKVD (security police) interrogations of German and other prisoners, personal diaries and interviews with participants. One of the richest sources in the Russian Ministry of Defence central archive at Podolsk consists of the very detailed reports sent daily from the Stalingrad Front to Aleksandr Shcherbakov, the head of the political department of the Red Army in Moscow. These describe not only heroic actions, but also 'extraordinary events' (the commissars' euphemism for treasonous behaviour), such as desertion, crossing over to the enemy, cowardice, incompetence, self-inflicted wounds, 'anti-Soviet agitation' and even drunkenness. The Soviet authorities executed around 13,500 of their own soldiers at Stalingrad – equivalent to more than a whole division of troops. The main challenge, I soon realized, was to try to balance the genuine self-sacrifice of so many Red Army soldiers with the utterly brutal coercion used against waverers by the NKVD special departments (which very soon afterwards became part of SMERSH – counter-espionage).

The barely believable ruthlessness of the Soviet system largely, but not entirely, explains why so many former Red Army soldiers fought on the German side. At Stalingrad, the Sixth Army's front-line divisions contained over 50,000 Soviet citizens in German uniform. Some had been brutally press-ganged into service through starvation in prison camps; others were volunteers. During the final battles, many German reports testify to the bravery and loyalty of these 'Hiwis', fighting against their own countrymen. Needless to say, Beria's NKVD became frenzied with suspicion when it discovered the scale of the disloyalty.

The subject is still taboo in Russia today. An infantry colonel with whom I happened to share a sleeping compartment on the journey down to Volgograd (the former Stalingrad), refused at first to believe that any Russian could have put on German uniform. He was finally convinced when I told him of the Sixth Army ration returns in the German archives. His reaction, for a man who clearly loathed Stalin for his purges of the Red Army, was interesting. 'They were no longer Russians', he said quietly. His comment was almost exactly the same as the formula used over fifty years before when Stalingrad Front reported on 'former Russians' back to Shcherbakov in Moscow. The emotions of the Great Patriotic War remain almost as unforgiving today as at the time.

The whole story of folly, pitilessness and tragedy is revealing in a number of unexpected ways. On the German side, the most striking aspect does not lie so much in the overt issue of Wehrmacht involvement in war crimes, still so hotly debated in Germany today. It lies in the confusion of cause and effect, especially the confusion between political beliefs and their consequences. German troops in Russia – as so many letters written from Stalingrad reveal – were in complete moral disarray. The objectives of subjugating the Slavs and defending

Europe from Bolshevism through a pre-emptive strike proved counter-productive, to say the least. To this day, many German survivors still see the Battle of Stalingrad as a clever Soviet trap into which they had been enticed by deliberate withdrawals. They consequently tend to view themselves as the victims rather than the instigators of this disaster.

One thing, however, is unarguable. The Battle of Stalingrad remains such an ideologically charged and symbolically important subject that the last word will not be heard for many years.

A good deal of the time spent researching this book might well have been wasted and valuable opportunities missed if it had not been for the help and suggestions of archivists and librarians. I am particularly grateful to: Frau Irina Renz at the Bibliothek für Zeitgeschichte in Stuttgart; Herr Meyer and Frau Ehrhardt at the Bundesarchiv-Militärarchiv in Freiburg; Frau Stang and other members of the staff of the Militärgeschichtliches Forschungsamt library in Potsdam; Valery Mikhailovich Rumyantsev of the Historical Archive and Military Memorial Centre of the Russian Ministry of Defence and the staff of the Central Archive of the Ministry of Defence at Podolsk; Doctor Kyril Mikhailovich Andersen, the Director of the Russian Centre for the Conservation and Study of Documents of Contemporary History in Moscow; Doctor Natalya Borisovna Volkova, the Director of the Russian State Archive of Literature and the Arts; and Doctor Dina Nikolaevna Nohotovich at the State Archive of the Russian Federation.

I owe an incalculable amount to Dr Detlef Vogel, in Freiburg, who was a vital help in numerous ways at the beginning of my research and also lent me his collection of German and Austrian *Stalingradbünde* veterans' publications. Doctor Alexander Friedrich Paulus kindly gave me permission to consult the papers of his grandfather, General-feldmarschall Friedrich Paulus, and provided copies of subsequent family contributions to the subject. Professor Doctor Hans Girgensohn, the Sixth Army pathologist in the Stalingrad encirclement or *Kessel*, was most patient in explaining the details of his work and findings there, and the background to the deaths of besieged German soldiers from hunger, cold and stress. Ben Shepherd kindly explained the latest research into battle stress during the Second World War. I am also most grateful for the observations of Kurt Graf von Schweinitz on strategy at Stalingrad, as well as for his comments on the implications of military terminology used in signals in November 1942.

For advice on Russian sources and other suggestions, I am indebted to Doctor Catherine Andreev, Professor Anatoly Aleksandrovich Chernobaev, Professor John Erickson, Doctor Viktor Gorbarev, Jon Halliday, Colonel Lemar Ivanovich Maximov of the Russian Ministry of Defence's Historical Branch, and Yury Ovzianko. I also owe a great deal to those who put me in touch with survivors of Stalingrad in both Russia and Germany, or who helped and looked after me so generously in both countries: Chris Alexander, Leopold Graf von Bismarck, Andrew Gimson, Major Joachim Freiherr von Maltzan, Gleb and Harriet Shestakov, Doctor Marie-Christine Gräfin von Stauffenberg and Christiane van de Velde.

In Volgograd I owed much to the kind assistance of Doctor Raisa Maratovna Petrunyova, the Vice-Rector of Volgograd University, and her colleagues, Professor Nadezhda Vasilevna Dulina, the Director of Historical and Cultural Studies, Galina Borisovna of the History department, and Boris Nikolaevich Ulko, the Director of the University Museum, as well as Nikolay Stepanovich Fyodortov, chairman of the Volgograd District Committee of War Veterans, and Lieutenant-Colonel Gennady Vasilevich Pavlov.

Translations from the Russian are by Doctor Galya Vinogradova and Lyubov Vinogradova, whose assistance in negotiations over access to archives offered a model of skilled diplomacy, persistence and good humour. Their contribution, to say nothing of their friendship, helped transform the whole project.

I am most grateful to those participants and eyewitnesses who were prepared to devote so much time and effort to recalling the past. A number very generously lent me unpublished manuscripts, letters and diaries. Their names – three others preferred not to be identified – are listed with the References, after the Appendices.

This book would never have come about if it had not been for Eleo Gordon of Penguin, whose idea it was, and also Peter Mayer in the

United States and Hans Ewald Dede in Germany, whose enthusiasm and support for the project right from the start made the research possible. I have been particularly blessed by having Andrew Nurnberg as literary agent, adviser and friend.

My greatest thanks, as always, are due to Artemis Cooper, my wife and editor of first resort, who was such a help during my months abroad when she had more than enough work of her own.

Part One

'THE WORLD WILL HOLD
ITS BREATH!'

Map 1 **OPERATION BARBAROSSA,**
JUNE – DECEMBER 1941

.... Front line, 4 December 1941
—·—·— International boundaries

1

The Double-Edged Sword of Barbarossa

Saturday, 21 June 1941, produced a perfect summer's morning. Many Berliners took the train out to Potsdam to spend the day in the park of Sans Souci. Others went swimming from the beaches of the Wannsee or the Nikolassee. In cafés, the rich repertoire of jokes about Rudolf Hess's flight to Britain had given way to stories about an imminent invasion of the Soviet Union. Others, dismayed at the idea of a much wider war, rested their hopes upon the idea that Stalin would cede the Ukraine to Germany at the last moment.

In the Soviet Embassy on the Unter den Linden officials were at their posts. An urgent signal from Moscow demanded 'an important clarification' of the huge military preparations along the frontiers from the Baltic to the Black Sea. Valentin Berezhkov, the first secretary and chief interpreter, rang the German Foreign Office on the Wilhelm-strasse to arrange a meeting. He was told that Reichsminister Joachim von Ribbentrop was out of town, and that Staatssekretär Freiherr von Weizsäcker could not be reached by telephone. As the morning passed, more and more urgent messages arrived from Moscow demanding news. There was an atmosphere of repressed hysteria in the Kremlin as the evidence of German intentions mounted, adding to more than eighty warnings received over the previous eight months. The deputy head of the NKVD had just reported that there were no fewer than 'thirty-nine aircraft incursions over the state border of the USSR' during the previous day. The Wehrmacht was quite shameless in its preparations, yet the lack of secrecy seems only to have confirmed the idea in Stalin's convoluted mind that this must all be part of a plan by Adolf Hitler to extract greater concessions.

The Soviet ambassador in Berlin, Vladimir Dekanozov, shared Stalin's conviction that it was all a campaign of disinformation, originally started by the British. He even dismissed the report of his own military attaché that 180 divisions had deployed along the border. Dekanozov, a protégé of Lavrenty Beria, was yet another Georgian and a senior member of the NKVD. His experience of foreign affairs had gone little beyond interrogating and purging rather more practised diplomats. Other members of the mission, although they did not dare express their views too forcefully, had little doubt that Hitler was planning to invade. They had even sent on the proofs of a phrase book prepared for invading troops, which had been brought secretly to the Soviet consulate by a German Communist printer. Useful terms included the Russian for 'Surrender!', 'Hands up!', 'Where is the collective farm chairman?', 'Are you a Communist?', and 'I'll shoot!'

Berezhkov's renewed telephone calls to the Wilhelmstrasse were met by the statement that Ribbentrop 'is not here and nobody knows when he will return'. At midday, he tried another official, the head of the political department. 'I believe something is going on at Führer headquarters. Very probably everybody's there.' But the German Foreign Minister was not out of Berlin. Ribbentrop was busy preparing instructions to the German Embassy in Moscow, headed 'Urgent! State Secret!' Early the next morning, some two hours after the invasion began, the ambassador, Count Friedrich Werner von der Schulenburg, was to convey to the Soviet government a list of grievances to serve as the pretext.

As the Saturday afternoon in Berlin turned to evening, the messages from Moscow grew increasingly frantic. Berezhkov rang the Wilhelmstrasse every thirty minutes. Still no senior functionary would accept his call. From the open window of his office, he could see the old-fashioned Schutzmann helmets of the police guarding the embassy. Beyond them, Berliners were taking a Saturday evening stroll on the Unter den Linden. The polarity between war and peace had a bewildering air of unreality. The Berlin–Moscow express was about to pass through the waiting German armies and cross the frontier as if nothing were amiss.

In Moscow, the Soviet Foreign Minister, Molotov, summoned Count von der Schulenburg to the Kremlin. The German ambassador, after overseeing the destruction of the embassy's secret papers, set off for the meeting called for half past nine. When challenged with the evidence of German preparations, he did not admit that an invasion was about to take place. He simply expressed his astonishment that the Soviet Union could not understand the situation and refused to answer any questions until he had consulted Berlin.

Schulenburg, a diplomat of the old school who believed in Bismarck's dictum that Germany should never make war on Russia, had good reason to be astonished by the Kremlin's ignorance. Over two weeks before, he had invited Dekanozov, then back in Moscow, to a private lunch and warned him of Hitler's plans. The old count clearly felt absolved from any loyalty to the Nazi regime after the Führer had blatantly lied to him, claiming to have no designs against Russia.* But Dekanozov, astonished at such a revelation, immediately suspected a trick. Stalin, reacting in the same way, exploded to the Politburo: 'Disinformation has now reached ambassadorial level!' Stalin was certain that most warnings had been '*Angliyskaya provokatsiya*' – part of a plot by Winston Churchill, the arch-enemy of the Soviet Union, to start a war between Russia and Germany. Since Hess's flight to Scotland, the conspiracy had grown even more complicated in his mind.

Stalin, who had refused to accept the possibility of an invasion until that Saturday afternoon, still remained terrified of provoking Hitler. Goebbels, with some justification, compared him to a rabbit mesmerized by a snake. A succession of reports from frontier guards told of tank engines being warmed up in the woods across the border,

---

* Hitler had his revenge in the end. Schulenburg, chosen in 1944 by the July plotters as their Foreign Minister after the planned assassination at Rastenburg, was hanged by the Nazis on 10 November of that year.

of German army engineers constructing bridges across rivers and removing barbed-wire entanglements in front of their positions. The commander of the Kiev Special Military District warned that war would begin in a matter of hours. Reports arrived that in Baltic ports, German ships had suddenly stopped loading and sailed for home. Yet Stalin, the totalitarian dictator, still could not come to terms with the idea that events might be outside his control.

That night, after long discussions in his study with senior commanders of the Red Army, Stalin agreed to the dispatch in code of a signal to all military-district headquarters in the West. 'In the course of 22–23 June 1941, sudden attacks by the Germans on the fronts of Leningrad, Baltic Special, Western Special, Kiev Special and Odessa Military Districts are possible. The task of our forces is not to yield to any provocations likely to prompt major complications. At the same time troops . . . are to be at full combat readiness, to meet a possible surprise blow by the Germans and their allies.' The navy and some senior officers in the Red Army had quietly ignored Stalin's orders against mobilization. But for many units, the warning order, which did not go out until after midnight, arrived too late.

In Berlin, Berezhkov had given up any hope of getting through to Ribbentrop's office as the night wore on. Suddenly, at around three in the morning, the telephone beside him rang. 'Herr Reichsminister von Ribbentrop', announced an unfamiliar voice, 'wishes to see representatives of the Soviet government at the Foreign Office in the Wilhelmstrasse.' Berezhkov explained that it would take time to wake the ambassador and order a car.

'The Reichsminister's motor car is already waiting outside your embassy. The Minister wishes to see Soviet representatives immediately.'

Outside the embassy, Dekanozov and Berezhkov found the black limousine waiting at the kerb. An official of the foreign ministry in full uniform stood beside the door, while an SS officer remained seated beside the driver. As they drove off, Berezhkov noted that, beyond the Brandenburg Gate, dawn was already spreading a glow in the sky above the trees of the Tiergarten. It was midsummer's morning.

When they reached the Wilhelmstrasse, they saw a crowd of people outside. The entrance with its wrought-iron awning was lit by camera lights for newsreel crews. Pressmen surrounded the two Soviet diplomats, momentarily blinding them with the flashbulbs of their cameras. This unexpected reception made Berezhkov fear the worst, but Dekanozov appeared unshaken in his belief that Germany and Russia were still at peace.

The Soviet ambassador, 'barely five feet tall, with a small beak nose and a few strands of black hair plastered across a bald pate', was not an impressive figure. Hitler, when he first received him, had him flanked by two of his tallest SS guards to emphasize the contrast. Yet the diminutive Georgian was dangerous to those in his power. He had been known as the 'hangman of Baku' from his repressive activities in the Caucasus following the Russian civil war. In the Berlin embassy, he had even had a torture and execution chamber constructed in the basement to deal with suspected traitors in the Soviet community.

Ribbentrop, while waiting for them to arrive, paced up and down his room 'like a caged animal'. There was little sign of the 'statesmanlike expression which he reserved for great occasions'.

'The Führer is absolutely right to attack Russia now,' he kept repeating as if trying to convince himself. 'The Russians would certainly themselves attack us, if we did not do so.' His subordinates were convinced that he could not face the prospect of destroying what he saw as his most important achievement, the Molotov–Ribbentrop Pact. He may also have started to suspect that Hitler's reckless gamble could turn into the greatest disaster in history.

The two Soviet representatives were shown into the Reichsminister's huge office. An expanse of patterned parquet floor led to the desk at the far end. Bronze statuettes on stands lined the walls. As they came close, Berezhkov was struck by Ribbentrop's appearance. 'His face was scarlet and bloated, his eyes were glassy and inflamed.' He wondered if he had been drinking.

Ribbentrop, after the most perfunctory of handshakes, led them to a table to one side where they sat down. Dekanozov started to read a statement requesting reassurances from the German government, but Ribbentrop broke in to say that they had been invited to attend a meeting for very different reasons. He stumbled through what amounted to a declaration of war, although the word was never mentioned: 'The Soviet Government's hostile attitude to Germany and the serious threat represented by Russian troop concentrations on Germany's eastern frontier have compelled the Reich to take military counter-measures.' Ribbentrop repeated himself in different ways, and accused the Soviet Union of various acts, including the military violation of German territory. It suddenly became clear to Berezhkov that the Wehrmacht must have already started its invasion. The Reichsminister stood up abruptly. He handed over the full text of Hitler's memorandum to Stalin's ambassador, who was speechless. 'The Führer has charged me with informing you officially of these defensive measures.'

Dekanozov also rose to his feet. He barely reached to Ribbentrop's shoulder. The full significance sank in at last. 'You'll regret this insulting, provocative and thoroughly predatory attack on the Soviet Union. You'll pay dearly for it!' He turned away, followed by Berezhkov, and strode towards the door. Ribbentrop hurried after them. 'Tell them in Moscow', he whispered urgently, 'that I was against this attack.'

Dawn had broken by the time Dekanozov and Berezhkov climbed into the limousine for the short ride back to the Soviet Embassy. On the Unter den Linden, they found that a detachment of SS troops had already cordoned off the block. Inside, members of the staff, awaiting their return, told them that all their telephone lines had been cut. They tuned the wireless to a Russian radio station. Moscow was an hour ahead of German summer time, so there it was now six o'clock on the morning of Sunday, 22 June. To their amazement and consternation, the news bulletin concentrated on increased production figures for Soviet industry and agriculture. It was followed by a keep-fit broadcast. There was no mention of the German invasion. The senior NKVD and GRU (military intelligence) officers in the embassy immediately proceeded to the top floor, a restricted area sealed off with reinforced steel doors and steel-shuttered windows. Secret documents were fed into the special quick-burning ovens, installed in case of emergency.

*

8

In the Russian capital, the anti-aircraft defences had been alerted, but the bulk of the population still had no idea of what was happening. Members of the *nomenklatura* ordered into their offices felt paralysed from a lack of guidance. Stalin had not spoken. No dividing line between 'provocation' and full-scale war had been defined and nobody knew what was happening at the front. Communications had collapsed under the onslaught.

The hopes of even the most fanatic Kremlin optimist were crumbling. Confirmation was received at 3.15 a.m. from the commander of the Black Sea Fleet of a German bombing raid on the naval base of Sevastopol. Soviet naval officers could not help thinking of the surprise Japanese attack against Port Arthur in 1904. Georgy Malenkov, one of Stalin's closest associates, refused to believe the word of Admiral Nikolay Kuznetsov, so he telephoned again himself in private to check that it was not a trick by senior officers to force the Leader's hand. At half past five – two hours after the assault began on the western frontiers – Schulenburg had delivered Nazi Germany's declaration of war to Molotov. According to one person present, the old ambassador had spoken with angry tears in his eyes, adding that personally he thought Hitler's decision was madness. Molotov had then hurried to Stalin's office, where the Politburo was assembled. Stalin, on hearing the news, apparently sank into his chair and said nothing. His succession of obsessive miscalculations offered much material for bitter reflection. The leader most famed for his ruthless trickery had fallen into a trap which was largely of his own making.

The news from the front was so catastrophic over the next few days that Stalin, whose bullying nature contained a strong streak of cowardice, summoned Beria and Molotov for a secret discussion. Should they make peace with Hitler, whatever the price and humiliation, just like the Brest-Litovsk deal in 1918? They could give up most of the Ukraine, Belorussia and the Baltic States. The Bulgarian ambassador, Ivan Stamenov, was later summoned to the Kremlin. Molotov asked him if he would act as intermediary, but to their astonishment he refused. 'Even if you retreat to the Urals,' he replied, 'you'll still win in the end.'

*

The vast majority of the population in the hinterland of the Soviet Union knew nothing of the disaster which had befallen their country. As befitted a day of rest, the centre of Moscow was empty. Admiral Kuznetsov, the chief of naval staff, reflected on the peaceful scene in his car on the way to the Kremlin. The population of the capital 'still did not know that a fire was blazing on the frontiers and that our advance units were engaged in heavy fighting'.

Finally, at midday on 22 June, Molotov's voice, not Stalin's, emerged from the wireless. 'Today at four o'clock in the morning, German troops attacked our country without making any claims on the Soviet Union and without any declaration of war.' His statement gave little detail. 'Our cause is just,' he concluded woodenly. 'The enemy will be beaten. We will be victorious.'

Molotov's choice of words was uninspired and his delivery awkward, but this announcement created a powerful reaction throughout the Soviet Union. The city of Stalingrad on the Volga may have been far from the fighting, but this did not diminish the effect. 'It was as if a bomb had fallen out of the sky, it was such a shock,' remembered a young female student. She promptly volunteered as a nurse. Her friends, especially Komsomol (Communist Youth) members, began collections for the war effort.

Reservists did not wait for mobilization orders. They reported at once. Within half an hour of Molotov's speech, the reservist Viktor Goncharov set out from home for the centre, accompanied by his old father, whom he assumed was coming to see him off. His wife, working out at the Stalingrad tram park, could not get back to say goodbye. He had no idea that his father, an eighty-one-year-old Cossack who had 'fought in four wars', was planning to come along to volunteer. But old Goncharov was furious when the staff at the centre rejected him.

In Stalingrad Technical University, near the huge Stalingrad tractor factory, students put up a large map on the wall, ready to mark with flags the advance of the Red Army into Germany. 'We thought', said one, 'that with a huge, decisive blow we'd smash the enemy.' Countless newsreels of tank production and aviation achievements had convinced them of the Soviet Union's immense industrial and military strength.

The images had proved doubly impressive in a country which, until recently, had been technologically backward. In addition, the domestic omnipotence of the Stalinist system made it appear unshakeable to those inside it. 'Propaganda fell on a well prepared soil,' acknowledged another of the Stalingrad students. 'We all had this powerful image of the Soviet state and therefore of the country's invincibility.' None of them imagined the fate that awaited the Soviet Union, even less the one in store for the model city of Stalingrad, with its engineering plants, municipal parks and tall white apartment blocks looking across the great Volga.

2

'Nothing is Impossible for the German Soldier!'

During that night of 21 June, the diplomats in Berlin and Moscow could only guess at what was happening along the frontier that separated them. Never had foreign ministries been so redundant. Some 3,050,000 German troops, with other pro-Axis armies bringing the total to four million men, awaited the invasion of the Soviet Union from Finland to the Black Sea. 'The world will hold its breath!' Hitler had declared at a planning session several months before. The ultimate objective was 'to establish a defence line against Asiatic Russia from a line running from the Volga river to Archangel'. The last industrial area left to Russia in the Urals could then be destroyed by the Luftwaffe.

It was the shortest night of the year. Wireless silence was maintained for the many hundreds of thousands of troops hidden in the birch and fir forests of East Prussia and occupied Poland. Artillery regiments which had arrived in the eastern frontier regions weeks before, ostensibly to prepare for manoeuvres, were well prepared. In East Prussia, the gun teams, wearing old clothes borrowed from local civilians, had brought forward reserves of shells on farm carts and camouflaged them next to pre-selected fire positions. Most soldiers believed the stories that this exercise was all part of a huge diversion to cover preparations for the invasion of Britain.

At nightfall, when orders were issued, the German Army was left in no doubt. The guns were stripped of their camouflage, or hauled out from hiding places in barns. They were then hitched to teams of horses, to half-tracks or to artillery tractors, with masked headlights, and towed out to their fire positions. Forward observation officers went ahead with the infantry to within a few hundred yards of the frontier posts occupied by the Soviet border guards.

Some officers in second-wave divisions toasted the coming operation with vintage Champagne and Cognac brought from occupied France. A few glanced again through the memoirs of General de Caulaincourt, to whom Napoleon had said on the eve of his invasion in 1812: *'Avant deux mois, la Russie me demandera la paix.'* Some, trying to imagine what lay ahead, leafed through copies of the phrase book which Dekanozov's embassy had sent to Moscow with so little effect. A number read the Bible.

Soldiers had built fires in their camouflaged encampments to keep away the mosquitoes. Accordion players struck up sentimental songs. While a few sang, others stayed with their thoughts. Many dreaded crossing the frontier into the unknown land of which they had heard only terrible things. Officers had warned them that if they slept in Russian houses, they would be bitten by insects and catch diseases. Many laughed, however, at comrades who wanted to cut all their hair off as a precaution against lice. In any case, most of them believed their officers when they said that there would be no need to worry about winter quarters. In the 24th Panzer Division, for example, Captain von Rosenbach-Lepinski is said to have told his motorcycle reconnaissance battalion: 'The war with Russia will last only four weeks.'

Such confidence was, in many ways, understandable. Even foreign intelligence services expected the Red Army to collapse. The Wehrmacht had assembled the largest invasion force ever seen, with 3,350 tanks, around 7,000 field guns and over 2,000 aircraft. The German Army had improved its level of motor transport with French army vehicles; for example, 70 per cent of the trucks in the 305th Infantry Division, another division to perish at Stalingrad the following year, came from France. Yet the Wehrmacht, although famed for its Blitzkrieg, also depended on over 600,000 horses to tow guns, ambulances and ration wagons. With the vast majority of the infantry divisions on their feet, the overall speed of advance was unlikely to be much faster than that of the Grande Armée in 1812.

Many officers had mixed sensations. 'Our optimism was tremendous after the rather easy victories in Poland, in France and in the Balkans,' recounted the commander of the first panzer company to reach the Volga at Stalingrad fourteen months later. But, as one of those who had just read Caulaincourt, he had 'bad feelings about the enormous space of Russia'. It also seemed rather late in the year 'to start such an ambitious campaign'. Operation Barbarossa had been planned to begin on 15 May. The delay of over five weeks, often blamed entirely on Hitler's Balkan campaign, was in fact influenced by many other factors, including the exceptionally heavy spring rains, the inability of the Luftwaffe to prepare forward airfields in time, and the allocation of motor transport to divisions.

That evening, regimental officers were told of certain 'special orders' affecting the conflict ahead. They included 'collective measures of force against villages' in areas of partisan activity and the 'Commissar Order'. Soviet political officers, Jews and partisans were to be handed over to the SS or the Secret Field Police. Most staff officers, and certainly all intelligence officers, were told of Field Marshal von Brauchitsch's order of 28 April, laying down ground rules for relations between army commanders and the SS Sonderkommando and security police operating in their rear areas. Their 'special tasks' would form part of 'the final encounter between two opposing political systems'. Finally, a 'Jurisdiction Order' deprived Russian civilians of any right of appeal, and effectively exonerated soldiers from crimes committed against them, whether murder, rape or looting. The order signed by Field Marshal Keitel on 13 May justified this on the grounds 'that the downfall of 1918, the German people's period of suffering which followed and the struggle against National Socialism – with the many blood sacrifices endured by the movement – can be traced to Bolshevik influence. No German should forget this.'

When Lieutenant Alexander Stahlberg was privately warned of the 'Commissar Order' by his cousin, Henning von Tresckow, later one of the key members of the July Plot, he burst out: 'That would be murder!'

'The order is just that,' agreed Tresckow. Stahlberg then asked where it had come from. 'From the man to whom you gave your oath,' answered his cousin. 'As I did,' he added with a penetrating look.

A number of commanders refused to acknowledge or pass on such instructions. They were generally those who respected the traditional ethos of the army and disliked the Nazis. Many, but not all, were from military families, now a fast-diminishing proportion of the officer corps. The generals were the ones with the least excuse. Over 200 senior officers had attended Hitler's address, in which he left no doubts about the war ahead. It was to be a 'battle between two opposing world views', a 'battle of annihilation' against 'bolshevik commissars and the Communist intelligentsia'.

The idea of *Rassenkampf*, or 'race war', gave the Russian campaign its unprecedented character. Many historians now argue that Nazi propaganda had so effectively dehumanized the Soviet enemy in the eyes of the Wehrmacht that it was morally anaesthetized from the start of the invasion. Perhaps the greatest measure of successful indoctrination was the almost negligible opposition within the Wehrmacht to the mass execution of Jews, which was deliberately confused with the notion of rear-area security measures against partisans. Many officers were affronted by the Wehrmacht's abandonment of international law on the *Ostfront*, but only the tiniest minority voiced disgust at the massacres, even when it became clear that they belonged to a programme of racial extermination.

The degree of ignorance claimed after the war by many officers, especially those on the staff, is rather hard to believe in the light of all the evidence that has now emerged from their own files. Sixth Army headquarters, for example, cooperated with SS Sonderkommando 4a, which followed in its tracks almost all the way from the western frontier of the Ukraine to Stalingrad. Not only were staff officers well aware of its activities, they even provided troops to assist in the round-up of Jews in Kiev and transport them to the ravine of Babi Yar.

What is particularly hard to assess in retrospect is the degree of initial ignorance at regimental level about the true programme, in which perhaps the cruellest weapon of all was to be starvation. Few officers saw the directive of 23 May, which called for the German armies in the east to expropriate whatever they needed, and also to send at least seven million tons of grain a year back to Germany; yet it should not have been hard to guess its basic outline, with the orders to live off the land. Nazi leaders had no illusions about the consequences for civilians deprived of the Ukraine's resources. 'Many tens of millions will starve,' predicted Martin Bormann. Goering bragged that the population would have to eat Cossack saddles.

When the illegal Barbarossa orders were prepared, in March 1941, it was General Franz Halder, the chief of staff, who bore the main responsibility for the army's acceptance of collective reprisals against civilians. As early as the first week in April 1941, two opponents of the regime, the former ambassador Ulrich von Hassell and General Ludwig Beck, were shown copies of these secret orders by Lieutenant-Colonel Helmuth Groscurth, who was to perish soon after the surrender at Stalingrad. 'It makes one's hair stand on end', wrote Hassell in his diary, 'to learn about measures to be taken in Russia, and about the systematic transformation of military law concerning the conquered population into uncontrolled despotism – indeed a caricature of all law. This kind of thing turns the German into a type of being which had existed only in enemy propaganda.' 'The army', he subsequently noted, 'must assume the onus of the murders and burnings which up to now have been confined to the SS.'

Hassell's pessimism was justified. Although a few army commanders were reluctant to distribute the instructions, several others issued orders to their troops which might have come straight from Goebbels's office. The most notorious order of all came from the commander of the Sixth Army, Field Marshal von Reichenau. General Hermann Hoth, who was to command the Fourth Panzer Army in the Stalingrad campaign, declared: 'The annihilation of those same Jews who support Bolshevism and its organization for murder, the partisans, is a measure of self-preservation.' General Erich von Manstein, a Prussian guards officer admired as the most brilliant strategist of the whole of the Second World War, and who privately admitted to being partly Jewish, issued an order shortly after taking over command of the Eleventh Army in which he declared: 'The jewish-bolshevik system must be rooted out once and for all.' He even went on to justify 'the necessity of harsh measures against Jewry.' There was little mention of this in his post-war memoirs, *Lost Victories.*

The acceptance of Nazi symbols on uniform and the personal oath of allegiance to Hitler had ended any pretence that the army remained independent from politics. 'The generals followed Hitler in these circumstances', Field Marshal Paulus acknowledged many years later in Soviet captivity, 'and as a result they became completely involved in the consequences of his policies and conduct of the war.'

In spite of all the Nazis' attempts to reshape the German Army, it was not as monolithic at regimental level in June 1941 as some writers have made out. The difference in character between a Bavarian, an East Prussian, a Saxon, and above all an Austrian division, would be remarked upon immediately. Even within a division from a particular region, there could be strong contrasts. For example, in the 60th Motorized Infantry Division, which was later trapped at Stalingrad, many young officers in its volunteer battalions came from the Technische Hochschule in Danzig, and were caught up in the heady atmosphere of the city's return to the Fatherland: 'For us,' wrote one of them, 'National Socialism was not a Party programme but the very essence of being German.' On the other hand, the officers in the division's reconnaissance battalion, 160 Aufklärungs-Abteilung, a sort of mechanized yeomanry cavalry, came mainly from East Prussian landowning families. They included Prince zu Dohna-Schlobitten, who had served in the Kaiser's Garde du Corps in the Ukraine in 1918.

The 16th Panzer Division was firmly in the tradition of the old Prussian Army. Its 2nd Panzer Regiment, which spearheaded the dash to Stalingrad the following summer, was descended from the oldest Prussian cavalry regiment, the Great Elector's Life Guard Cuirassiers. The regiment had so many members of the nobility that few were addressed by their military rank. 'Instead of Herr Hauptmann or Herr Leutnant', one of their tank crewmen remembered, 'it was Herr Fürst or Herr Graf'. The regiment had suffered such low losses in the Polish and French campaigns that its peacetime identity remained virtually untouched.

Traditions from an earlier age offered an advantage. 'Within the regiment', observed an officer from another panzer division, 'it was safe to talk. Nobody in Berlin could joke like us about Hitler.' Officer conspirators on the general staff were able to talk about deposing Hitler, even to uncommitted generals, without risking denunciation to the Gestapo. Dr Alois Beck, the Catholic chaplain of 297th Infantry Division, was convinced that 'of the three Wehrmacht services, the army was the least influenced by National Socialist ideology'. In the Luftwaffe, those who disliked the regime remained silent. 'You could not entirely trust any German in those days,' said a lieutenant in the 9th Flak Division who was captured at Stalingrad. He dared to talk freely with only one fellow officer, who had once admitted in private that the Nazis had exterminated a mentally ill cousin of his.

One historian has pointed out that although 'the Wehrmacht should not be regarded as a homogeneous entity', the degree to which its different elements were 'willing to participate in a war of extermination against the Soviet Union, be it as an anti-Russian, anti-Bolshevik, or anti-Jewish crusade, is an area of research that needs to be pursued'. Prince Dohna, with the 60th Mechanized Infantry Division, was 'shocked by my own callousness', when he reread his diary many years later. 'Today it seems impossible to understand that I could have allowed myself to have been caught up unprotesting in this megalomania, but we were dominated by the feeling of being part of a tremendous war machine, which was rolling irresistibly to the east against Bolshevism.'

At 3.15 a.m. German time, on 22 June, the first artillery barrages began. Bridges over rivers were seized before the NKVD border guards reacted. The guards' families, who lived at the frontier posts, died with them. In some cases, demolition charges had been removed earlier by silent raiding parties. German commando groups from the 'Sonderverband Brandenburg' (named after their barracks on the edge of Berlin) were already to the rear of Russian frontier units, cutting telephone lines. And since late April, small teams of anti-Communist Russian and Ukrainian volunteers had been infiltrated with radio sets. As early as 29 April, Beria had been informed of three groups of spies caught crossing the border with radio sets. Those taken alive, had been 'handed over to the NKGB for further interrogation'.

The first sign of dawn on 22 June appeared ahead of the infantry on the eastern horizon as point units facing water obstacles clambered into assault boats. Many infantry regiments, as they advanced the last few hundred yards to their start lines, could hear waves of bombers and fighters approaching from behind. Gull-winged Stukas, flying at a lower altitude, were off in search of tank parks, headquarters and communications centres behind the lines.

A Red Army engineer officer at 4th Army headquarters was awoken by the sound of massed aero engines. He recognized the sound from the Spanish Civil War, in which he had served as an adviser. 'The bombs were falling with a piercing shriek,' he recorded. 'The army headquarters building we had just left was shrouded in smoke and dust. The powerful blasts rent the air and made our ears ring. Another flight appeared. The German bombers dived confidently at the defenceless military settlement. When the raid was over, thick black pillars of smoke billowed up from many places. Part of the headquarters building was in ruins. Somewhere a high-pitched, hysterical female voice was crying out.'

The main Luftwaffe effort was directed against the Red Army's aviation regiments. Pre-emptive sorties over the next nine hours destroyed 1,200 Soviet aircraft, the vast majority on the ground. Messerschmitt pilots could hardly believe their eyes when, banking over aerodromes, instantly recognizable from photoreconnaissance, they glimpsed hundreds of enemy planes neatly lined up at dispersal beside the runways. Those which managed to get off the ground, or arrived from airfields further east, proved easy targets. Some Soviet pilots who either had never learned aerial combat techniques or knew that their obsolete models stood no chance, even resorted to ramming German aircraft. A Luftwaffe general described these air battles against inexperienced pilots as infanticide.

The panzer divisions, with the engines of their tanks and half-tracks running, heard little except through their headphones. They received the order to advance as soon as the infantry had secured the bridges and crossings. The task of the panzer formations was to cut through and then encircle the bulk of the enemy's army, trapping it in a *Kessel*, or cauldron. This is how the Wehrmacht planned to destroy the Red Army's fighting strength, then advance virtually unopposed on its three major objectives: Leningrad, Moscow and the Ukraine.

Army Group North under Field Marshal Ritter von Leeb was primarily responsible for the advance from East Prussia into the Baltic States to secure the ports, and then on to Leningrad. Army Group Centre under Field Marshal Fedor von Bock was to follow Napoleon's route to Moscow once it had encircled the main concentrations of the Red Army in its path. Brauchitsch and Halder were deeply disturbed, however, when Hitler decided to weaken this central thrust, in order to bolster what they saw as subsidiary operations. The Führer believed that once he seized the agricultural wealth of the Ukraine and the Caucasian oilfields, the Reich's invincibility was guaranteed. Army Group South under Field Marshal Gerd von Rundstedt, soon supported on his right by a small Hungarian army and two Romanian armies, was entrusted with this task. The Romanian dictator, Marshal Ion Antonescu, had been delighted when told of Operation Barbarossa ten days before its launch. 'Of course I'll be there from the start', he had said. 'When it's a question of action against the Slavs, you can always count on Romania.'

On the anniversary of Napoleon's proclamation from his imperial headquarters at Wilkowski, Hitler issued a long justification of the breakdown of relations with the Soviet Union. He turned the truth inside out, claiming that Germany was threatened by 'approximately 160 Russian divisions massed on our frontier'. He thus started the 'European crusade against Bolshevism' with a shameless lie to his own people and to his own soldiers.

3

'Smash in the Door and the Whole Rotten Structure Will Come Crashing Down!'

Seldom had an attacker enjoyed such advantages as the Wehrmacht in June 1941. Most Red Army and frontier units, having been ordered not to respond to 'provocations', did not know how to react. Even beyond the twelfth hour, Stalin still desperately hoped for a last chance of conciliation and was reluctant to allow his troops to strike back. An officer entering the office of Colonel-General D. G. Pavlov, the commander of the central front, heard him yelling in nervous exasperation down the telephone as yet another front-line commander reported German activity on the border: 'I know! It has already been reported! Those at the top know better than we!'

The three Soviet armies stretched out along the frontier on Stalin's orders never stood a chance and their tank brigades behind were destroyed by air attack before they had a chance to deploy. The great eighteenth-century citadel of Brest-Litovsk, the town where the Kaiser's general staff had inflicted such a humiliating *Diktat* on Lenin and Trotsky in 1918, was surrounded in the first few hours. Army Group Centre's two panzer groups, commanded by Generals Hoth and Guderian, surrounded large Soviet forces in two rapid encirclements. Within five days their forces had joined up near Minsk, some 200 miles from the border. More than 300,000 Red Army soldiers were trapped and 2,500 tanks destroyed or captured.

In the north, striking out of East Prussia across the river Niemen, the Fourth Panzer Group smashed through the Russian line with ease. Five days later, General von Manstein's LVI Panzer Corps, advancing almost fifty miles a day, was nearly halfway to Leningrad and had secured the crossing of the river Dvina. This 'impetuous dash', Manstein wrote later, 'was the fulfilment of a tank commander's dream'.

The Luftwaffe, meanwhile, had continued to annihilate Red Army aviation. By the end of the second day of fighting, it had increased its score to two thousand aircraft destroyed. The Soviet Union could build fresh aircraft and train new pilots, but that immediate 'infanticide' of aircrew crushed morale for a long time. 'Our pilots feel that they are corpses already when they take off,' a squadron officer admitted to a commissar fifteen months later at the height of the battle of Stalingrad. 'This is where the losses come from.'

In the south, where Soviet forces were strongest, the German advance was much less rapid. General Kirponos had managed to establish a defence in depth, rather than line his armies along the frontier. But although his divisions inflicted quite heavy casualties on the Germans, their own losses were infinitely greater. Kirponos rushed his tank formations into battle before they could deploy effectively. On the second day, 23 June, General Ewald von Kleist's First Panzer Group came up against Soviet divisions equipped with the monster KV tank, and for the very first time, German crews saw the T-34 tank, the best general-purpose tank developed in the Second World War.

The reduction of the southern front between the Pripet Marshes and the Carpathian mountains took much longer than expected. Field Marshal von Reichenau's Sixth Army found itself continually harassed by Russian forces cut off in the wooded swampland to its left. Reichenau wanted prisoners executed as partisans, whether or not they still wore uniform. Red Army units also shot their German captives, especially Luftwaffe pilots who had baled out. There were few opportunities for sending them to the rear, and they did not want them to be saved by the enemy advance.

In Lvov, the capital of Galicia, the NKVD slaughtered political prisoners to prevent their release by the Germans. Its savagery was no doubt increased by the atmosphere of suspicion and chaos in the city, with drunkenness and looting. Lvov was subjected not only to aerial bombing, but also to sabotage by German-organized groups of Ukrainian nationalists. The mood of violent fear had been fuelled just before the invasion by jibes from the non-Russian population: 'The Germans are coming to get you.'

Hitler's conviction that the Soviet Union was a 'rotten structure' that would come 'crashing down' was shared by many foreign observers and intelligence services. Stalin's purge of the Red Army, which had begun in 1937, was fuelled by an inimitable mixture of paranoia, sadistic megalomania and a vindictiveness for old slights dating back to the Russian civil war and the Russo-Polish War.

Altogether, 36,671 officers were executed, imprisoned or dismissed, and out of the 706 officers of the rank of brigade commander and above, only 303 remained untouched. Cases against arrested officers were usually grotesque inventions. Colonel K. K. Rokossovsky, later the commander who delivered the *coup de grâce* at Stalingrad, faced evidence purportedly provided by a man who had died nearly twenty years before.

The most prominent victim was Marshal Mikhail Tukhachevsky, the leading advocate of mobile warfare. His arrest and execution also represented the deliberate destruction of the Red Army's operational thinking, which had encroached dangerously upon Stalin's preserve of strategy. Former imperial army officers under Tukhachevsky had been developing a sophisticated theory of 'Operational Art' based on 'the study of the relationship between mass firepower and mobility'. By 1941, this was a treasonous heresy, which explained why few Red Army generals had dared to mass their tanks effectively against the German threat. Even though most of the purged officers were reinstated, the psychological effect had been devastating.

Two and a half years after the purge began, the Red Army presented a disastrous spectacle in the Winter War against Finland. Marshal Voroshilov, Stalin's old crony from the 1st Cavalry Army, displayed an astonishing lack of imagination. The Finns outmanoeuvred their opponents time after time. Their machine-gunners scythed down the massed Soviet infantry struggling forward through the snowfields.

Only after deploying five times as many men as their opponents, and huge concentrations of artillery, did the Red Army begin to prevail. Hitler had observed this lamentable performance with excitement.

Japanese military intelligence took rather a different view. It was about the only foreign service which did not underestimate the Red Army at this time. A series of border skirmishes on the Manchurian frontier, which culminated in the battle at Khalkin-Gol in August 1939, had shown what an aggressive young commander, in this case the forty-three-year-old General Georgy Zhukov, could achieve. In January 1941, Stalin was persuaded to promote Zhukov to Chief of the General Staff. He was therefore right at the centre when, on the day after the invasion, Stalin set up a supreme general-staff headquarters, under its old tsarist name of *Stavka*. The Great Leader then appointed himself Commissar of Defence and Supreme Commander of the Soviet Armed Forces.

In the first days of Barbarossa, German generals saw little to change their low opinion of Soviet commanders, especially on the central part of the front. General Heinz Guderian, like most of his colleagues, was struck by the readiness of Red Army commanders to waste the lives of their men in prodigious quantities. He also noted in a memorandum that they were severely hampered by the 'political demands of the state leadership', and suffered a 'basic fear of responsibility'. This combined with bad coordination meant that 'orders to carry out necessary measures, counter-measures in particular, are issued too late'. Soviet tank forces were 'insufficiently trained, and lacked intelligence and initiative during the offensive'. All of this was true, but Guderian and his colleagues underestimated the desire within the Red Army to learn from its mistakes.

The process of reform was not, of course, easy or rapid. Stalin and his placemen, especially senior commissars, refused to acknowledge that their political interference and obsessive blindness had caused such disasters. Front and army commanders had been hamstrung by the Kremlin's militarily illogical instructions. To make matters worse, the 'dual command' system of commissars approving orders was reinstituted on 16 July. The political controllers of the Red Army tried to escape their responsibility by accusing front-line commanders and their staff officers of treason, sabotage or cowardice.

General Pavlov, the commander of the central part of the front, and the general yelling down the telephone that those at the top knew better what was going on, was not saved by having followed orders. Accused of treason, he became the most prominent victim to be executed in this second round of the Red Army purges. The paralysing atmosphere in headquarters can be imagined. A sapper expert in mines, who arrived at a command centre accompanied by NKVD border guards because they knew the area, was greeted by expressions of terror. A general babbled pathetically: 'I was with the troops, and I did everything – I am not guilty of anything.' Only then did the sapper officer realize that, on seeing the green tabs of his escort, these staff officers had thought that he had come to arrest them.

During this hysteria of deflected blame, the groundwork for reorganization began. Zhukov's *Stavka* directive of 15 July 1941 set down 'a number of conclusions' following 'the experience of three weeks of war against German fascism'. His main argument was that the Red Army had suffered from bad communications and overlarge, sluggish formations, which simply presented a 'vulnerable target for air attack'. Large armies with several corps 'made it difficult to organize command and control during a battle, especially because so many of our officers are young and inexperienced'. (Even if the purges were not mentioned, their shadow was impossible to forget.) 'The *Stavka*', he wrote, 'therefore believes it is necessary to prepare to change to a system of small armies consisting of a maximum of five or six divisions.' This step, when eventually introduced, greatly improved the rapidity of response, largely by cutting out the corps level of command between division and army.

The biggest mistake made by German commanders was to have underestimated 'Ivan', the ordinary Red Army soldier. They quickly found that surrounded or outnumbered Soviet soldiers went on fighting when their counterparts from western armies would have surrendered. Right from the first morning of Barbarossa, there were countless cases of extraordinary courage and self-sacrifice, although not perhaps as many as there were of mass panic, but that was largely due to the confusion. The defence of the citadel of Brest-Litovsk is the most striking example. German infantry occupied the complex after a week of heavy fighting, but some Red Army soldiers held out for almost a month from the initial attack without any resupply of ammunition or food. One of the defenders scratched on a wall: 'I am dying but do not surrender. Farewell Motherland. 20/VII–41'. This piece of wall is still reverently preserved in the Central Museum of the Armed Forces in Moscow. What is not mentioned is that several of the wounded Soviet soldiers captured in the citadel managed to survive Nazi prisoner-of-war camps until liberated in 1945. Instead of being treated as heroes, they were sent straight to the Gulag by SMERSH, following Stalin's order that anyone who had fallen into enemy hands was a traitor. Stalin even disowned his own son, Yakov, captured near Vitebsk on 16 July.

As the chaos on the Russian side lessened during the summer, the resistance became more dogged. General Halder, who at the beginning of July had felt that victory was at hand, soon felt less certain. 'Everywhere the Russians fight to the last man,' he wrote in his diary. 'They capitulate only occasionally.' Guderian also admitted that Russian infantrymen were 'nearly always stubborn in defence', and added that they showed skill in fighting at night and in forests. These two advantages, above all night-fighting, were to prove far more important than the Germans realized.

The German commanders had believed that no society run by political terror could defend itself against a determined attack from outside. The warm welcome from civilians convinced many Germans that they would win. Devout Ukrainians, who had suffered one of the most terrifying man-made famines in history, greeted the arrival of military vehicles with black crosses as symbolic of a new crusade against the anti-Christ. But Hitler's plans of subjugation and exploitation could only strengthen the 'rotten structure', by forcing even those who loathed the Stalinist regime to support it.

Stalin and the apparatus of the Communist Party quickly recognized the need to shift their rhetoric away from Marxist-Leninist clichés. The phrase 'the Great Patriotic War' appeared in a headline in the first issue of *Pravda* to appear after the invasion, and Stalin himself soon took up this deliberate evocation of 'the Patriotic War' against Napoleon. Later that year, on the anniversary of the October Revolution, he went on to invoke the distinctly unproletarian heroes of Russian history: Alexander Nevsky, Dmitry Donskoy, Suvorov and Kutuzov.

The preservation of Stalin's personal reputation was greatly helped by the political ignorance of the majority of the population. Few outside the *nomenklatura* and the well-connected intelligentsia linked him directly with the refusal to acknowledge the threat from Germany and the disasters of late June. Stalin, in his broadcast of 3 July, did not, of course, take any of the blame. He addressed the people as 'brothers and sisters', and told them that the Motherland was in great danger, with the Germans advancing deep into the Soviet Union. On balance, this admission strengthened the mood of the country with its unprecedented frankness, because until then the official communiqués had spoken only of heavy losses inflicted on the enemy. It was nevertheless a great shock to many, such as the students of Stalingrad technical university, waiting to mark the advance of Red Army troops into Germany with flags on their wall-map. When the 'shocking and incomprehensible' advance of the Wehrmacht became clear, the map was hurriedly taken down.

Whatever one may think about Stalinism, there can be little doubt that its ideological preparation, through deliberately manipulated alternatives, provided ruthlessly effective arguments for total warfare. All right-thinking people had to accept that Fascism was bad and must be destroyed by any means. The Communist Party should lead the struggle because Fascism was totally devoted to its destruction. This form of logic is captured in Vasily Grossman's novel, *Life and Fate*. 'The hatred Fascism bears us', declares Mostovskoy, an old Bolshevik who had fallen foul of Stalinism, 'is yet another proof – a far-reaching proof – of the justice of Lenin's cause.'

Political arguments were, however, of secondary importance for the majority of the population. Their real stimulus came from a visceral patriotism. The recruiting poster, 'The Motherland Calls!', showed a typical Russian woman holding the military oath and backed by a sheaf of bayonets. Although unsubtle, it was deeply effective at the time. Huge sacrifices were expected. 'Our aim is to defend something greater than millions of lives,' wrote a young tank commander in his diary exactly a month after the invasion. 'I am not speaking about my own life. The only thing to be done is to lose it to some advantage for the Motherland.'

Four million people volunteered or felt obliged to volunteer for the *opolchentsy* militia. The waste of lives was so terrible, it is hard to comprehend: a carnage whose futility was perhaps exceeded only by the Zulu king marching an *impi* of his warriors over a cliff to prove their discipline. These untrained soldiers, often without weapons and many still in civilian clothes, were sent against the Wehrmacht's panzer formations. Four militia divisions were almost completely annihilated before the siege of Leningrad had even begun. Families, ignorant of the incompetence and chaos at the front, with drunkenness and looting, or NKVD executions, mourned almost without criticism of the regime. Anger was reserved for the enemy.

Most acts of bravery from that summer never came to light, having disappeared with the death of witnesses. Some of the stories, however, did emerge later, partly because a strong feeling of injustice grew in the ranks that the deeds of many brave men were not being acknowledged. For example, a letter was found on the body of a Surgeon Maltsev at Stalingrad expressing his need to testify to the courage of a comrade during the terrible retreat. 'Tomorrow, or the day after tomorrow, a big battle will take place,' he had written, 'and I will probably be killed, and I dream that this account will be published so that people will learn of the feats performed by Lychkin.'

Tales of bravery offered little compensation at the time. By mid-July, the Red Army was in a desperate position. In the first three weeks of fighting it had lost 3,500 tanks, over 6,000 aircraft, and some two million men, including a significant proportion of the Red Army officer corps.

The next disaster was the battle round Smolensk, during the second half of July, in which several Soviet armies were trapped. Although at least five divisions escaped, some 300,000 Red Army prisoners were still taken by the beginning of August. Over 3,000 tanks and 3,000 guns were also lost. Many more Soviet divisions were then sacrificed, one after the other, to prevent Field Marshal von Bock's panzer divisions seizing the rail junctions of Yelnaya and Roslavl and sealing another pocket. Some historians, however, argue convincingly that this delayed the German advance at a crucial moment, with important consequences later.

In the south, Field Marshal von Rundstedt's army group, now supported by Romanians and Hungarians, took 100,000 prisoners from the divisions trapped in the Uman pocket early in August. The advance into the Ukraine across the open, rolling prairie with sunflowers, soya beans and unharvested corn, seemed unstoppable. The greatest concentration of Soviet forces, however, lay round the Ukrainian capital of Kiev. Their commander-in-chief was another of Stalin's cronies, Marshal Budenny, with Nikita Khrushchev as chief commissar, whose main responsibility was the evacuation of industrial machinery to the east. General Zhukov warned Stalin that the Red Army must abandon Kiev to avoid encirclement, but the Soviet dictator, who had just told Churchill that the Soviet Union would never give up Moscow, Leningrad and Kiev, lost his temper and removed him from his position as Chief of the General Staff.

Once Rundstedt's mobile forces had finished at Uman, they continued, veering to the south of Kiev. The First Panzer Group then swung north, joining up with Guderian's divisions, whose sudden strike down from the central front took the Soviet command by surprise. The danger of a terrible trap became plain, but Stalin refused to abandon Kiev. He only changed his mind when it was far too late. On 21 September, the encirclement battle of Kiev ended. The Germans claimed a further 665,000 prisoners. Hitler called it 'the greatest battle in world history'. The Chief of the General Staff, Halder, on the other hand, called it the greatest strategic mistake of the campaign in the east. Like Guderian, he felt that all their energies should have been concentrated on Moscow.

The advancing invaders, overrunning one position after another, suffered a confusion of emotions and ideas as they gazed with a mixture of disbelief, contempt and also fear on the Communist enemy, who had fought to the last. The piles of corpses seemed even more dehumanized when charred, and with half their clothes stripped from them by the force of a shell blast. 'Look closely at these dead, these Tartar dead, these Russian dead,' wrote a journalist attached to the German Army in the Ukraine. 'They are new corpses, absolutely brand-new. Just delivered from the great factory of the *Pyatyletka* [five-year plan]. They are all the same. Mass-produced. They typify a new race, a tough race, these corpses of workers killed in an industrial accident.' Yet, however compelling the image, it was a mistake to assume that the bodies before them were simply modern Communist robots. They were the remains of men and women who, in most cases, had reacted to a sense of patriotism that was somehow both spiritual and visceral.

4

Hitler's Hubris:
The Delayed Battle for Moscow

'The vastness of Russia devours us,' wrote Field Marshal von Rundstedt to his wife just after his armies had successfully completed the Uman encirclement. The moods of German commanders had started to swing between self-congratulation and unease. They were conquering huge territories, yet the horizon seemed just as limitless. The Red Army had lost over two million men, yet still more Soviet armies appeared. 'At the outset of the war', General Halder wrote in his diary on 11 August, 'we reckoned on about 200 enemy divisions. Now we have already counted 360.' The door had been smashed in, but the structure was not collapsing.

By mid-July, the Wehrmacht had lost its initial momentum. It was simply not strong enough to mount offensives in three different directions at once. Casualties had been higher than expected – over 400,000 by the end of August – and the wear and tear on vehicles far greater than predicted. Engines became clogged with grit from the dust clouds, and broke down constantly, yet replacements were in very short supply. Bad communications also took their toll. The railway tracks, which were a slightly broader gauge, had to be relaid, and instead of the highways marked on their maps, the armies found dirt roads which turned to glutinous mud in a brief summer downpour. In many marshy places German troops had to build their own 'corduroy roads' of birch trunks laid side to side. The further they advanced into Russia, the harder it was to bring supplies forward.

Panzer columns racing ahead frequently had to stop through lack of fuel.

The infantry divisions, which composed the bulk of the army, were marching 'up to forty miles a day' (but more usually around twenty), their jackboots roasting in the summer heat. The *Landser*, or infantry-man, carried about fifty-five pounds of equipment, including steel helmet, rifle, ammunition and entrenching tool. His canvas and leather pack contained mess tin, canteen, an Esbit field stove, a combined spoon and fork in aluminium, rifle-cleaning kit, spare clothes, tent pegs and poles, field dressing, sewing kit, razor, soap and Vulkan Sanex condoms, even though carnal relations with civilians were officially forbidden.

The infantry was so tired trudging forwards in full kit that many fell asleep on the march. Even the panzer troops were exhausted. After servicing their vehicles – track-maintenance was the heaviest work – and cleaning their guns, they had a quick wash in a canvas bucket in a vain attempt to shift the ingrained dirt and oil from their hands. Their eyes swollen from fatigue, they then shaved, blinking into a mirror temporarily attached to a machine-gun mounting. The infantry tended to refer to them as '*die Schwarze*' because of their black overalls. War correspondents described them as 'the knights of modern warfare', but their dust-choked vehicles broke down with monotonous regularity.

The frustrations provoked quarrels between commanders. A majority – General Heinz Guderian was the most outspoken – despaired of Hitler's diversions. Moscow was not only the capital of the Soviet Union, they argued, it was also a major centre for communications and the armaments industry. An attack on it would also draw in surviving Soviet armies to their final destruction. The Führer, how-ever, kept his generals in order by exploiting their rivalries and disagreements. He told them that they knew nothing of economic matters. Leningrad and the Baltic had to be secured to protect essential trade with Sweden, while the agriculture of the Ukraine was vital to Germany. Yet his instinct to avoid the road to Moscow was partly a superstitious avoidance of Napoleon's footsteps.

Army Group Centre, having secured Smolensk and encircled the Soviet armies beyond it at the end of July, was ordered to halt. Hitler sent most of Hoth's panzer group northwards to help the attack on Leningrad, while 'Panzerarmee Guderian' (the new designation was a typical Hitlerian sop to a disgruntled but necessary general) was diverted southwards to act as the upper jaw of the great Kiev encirclement.

Hitler changed his mind again early in September when he at last agreed to Operation Typhoon, the advance on Moscow. Yet more time was lost because Hoth's panzer divisions were still engaged in the outskirts of Leningrad. The forces for Operation Typhoon were not finally ready until the very end of September. Moscow lay just over 200 miles away from where Army Group Centre had been halted, and little time remained before the period of autumn mud, and then winter. When General Friedrich Paulus, Halder's chief planner for Barbarossa, had raised the question of winter warfare earlier, Hitler had forbidden any mention of the subject.

Hitler in the *Wolfsschanze* used to gaze at the operations map showing the huge areas notionally controlled by his forces. For a visionary who had achieved total power in a country possessing the best-trained army in the world, the sight induced a sense of invincibility. This armchair strategist never possessed the qualities for true generalship, because he ignored practical problems. During the brief campaigns in Poland, Scandinavia, France and the Balkans, resupply had at times been difficult, but never an insuperable problem. In Russia, however, logistics would be as decisive a factor as firepower, manpower, mobility and morale. Hitler's fundamental irresponsibility – a psychologically interesting defiance of fate – had been to launch the most ambitious invasion in history while refusing to gear the German economy and industry for all-out war. In hindsight, it seems more like the act of a compulsive gambler, subconsciously striving to increase the odds. The horrific consequences for millions of people seemed only to strengthen his megalomania.

Field Marshal von Bock had under his command one and a half million men, but his panzer divisions were weakened by the lack of replacement tanks and spare parts. When he assembled his commanders on the eve of the offensive, he set 7 November (the anniversary of the Russian Revolution) as the deadline for surrounding the Soviet capital. The ambitious Bock longed to be known as the conqueror of Moscow.

The *Stavka*, meanwhile, had been expecting a German offensive against Moscow ever since Army Group Centre had halted in mid-August. Stalin had sent General Yeremenko to organize armies into a new Bryansk Front, while two other fronts, Western and Reserve, were prepared to protect the capital. Yet in spite of these precautions, Yeremenko's forces were taken by surprise when, early on the morning of 30 September, Guderian's panzer *Schwerpunkte* struck their southern flank out of an autumnal mist. The sun soon broke through, making a warm, clear day, ideal for the offensive. The Germans had nothing to fear from the air. At that moment, less than five per cent of Red Army aviation in European Russia still survived.

During the first days of October, the offensive went perfectly for the Germans, with the panzer groups and Field Marshal Kesselring's Second Air Fleet working closely together. Yeremenko asked the *Stavka* for permission to withdraw, but no permission was given. On 3 October, Guderian's point units on the right reached the city of Orel, 125 miles behind Yeremenko's lines. Surprise was complete. As the leading panzers raced up the main street past trams, passers-by waved to them, assuming they were Russian. The Red Army had not even had time to prepare charges to blow up the important arms factories. On 6 October, Yeremenko and his staff narrowly escaped capture by German tanks soon after midday. All communications were lost. In the chaos of the following days, Marshal Budenny, supposedly commanding the Reserve Front, even lost his headquarters, and Yeremenko, who was badly wounded in the leg, had to be evacuated by air.

Soviet leaders in the Kremlin at first refused to acknowledge the scale of the threat. On 5 October, a fighter pilot reported a column of German panzers a dozen miles in length, advancing rapidly up the road to Yukhnov, not much more than a hundred miles from Moscow. Even when another pilot was sent out on reconnaissance and confirmed the report, the *Stavka* still refused to believe it. A third pilot was sent out, and he too confirmed the sighting. This did not stop Beria from wanting to arrest and interrogate their commander as a 'panic-monger', but it finally succeeded in galvanizing the Kremlin.

Stalin called an emergency session of the State Defence Committee. He also ordered General Zhukov, who had brutally invigorated the defence of Leningrad, to fly back immediately. After Zhukov had seen the chaos for himself, Stalin instructed him to reorganize the remnants from the disaster into a new western front. Every available unit was thrown in to hold some sort of line until the *Stavka* reserves could be deployed. With Moscow itself now at risk, over one hundred thousand men were mobilized as militia and a quarter of a million civilians, mostly women, were marched out to dig anti-tank ditches.

The first snow fell on the night of 6 October, then promptly melted, turning roads to thick mud for twenty-four hours. Bock's panzer groups still managed to achieve two large double encirclements, one by Bryansk itself and the other round Vyazma on the central route to Moscow. The Germans claimed to have cut off 665,000 Red Army soldiers and to have destroyed or captured 1,242 tanks – more than in the whole of Bock's three panzer groups.

'What a great satisfaction it must be for you to see your plans maturing so well!' wrote Field Marshal von Reichenau to General Paulus, his former chief of staff, and soon to be his successor as the commander-in-chief of the Sixth Army. But groups of Russian soldiers, although surrounded and unsupplied within the pockets, fought on almost until the end of the month. 'Strong-point after strong-point has to be captured individually,' Paulus heard from a divisional commander. 'As often as not, we cannot get them out even with flame-throwers, and we have to blow the whole thing to bits.'

Several German panzer divisions also encountered a new form of unconventional weapon during this fighting. They found Russian dogs running towards them with a curious-looking saddle holding a load on top with a short upright stick. At first the panzer troops thought that they must be first-aid dogs, but then they realized that the animals had explosives or an anti-tank mine strapped to them. These 'mine-dogs', trained on Pavlovian principles, had been taught to run under large vehicles to obtain their food. The stick, catching against the underside, would detonate the charge. Most of the dogs were shot before they reached their target, but this macabre tactic had an unnerving effect.

It was, however, the weather which rapidly became the Wehrmacht's worst hindrance. The season of rain and mud, the *rasputitsa*, set in before the middle of October. German ration lorries frequently could not get through, so single-horse farm carts, known as *panje* wagons (*panje* was Wehrmacht slang for a Polish or Russian peasant), were commandeered from agricultural communities for hundreds of miles around. In some places, where no birch trunks came to hand to make a 'corduroy road', the corpses of Russian dead were used instead as 'planks'. A *Landser* would often lose a jackboot, sucked from his leg in the knee-deep mud. Motorcyclists could only advance in places by getting off to haul their vehicles through. Commanders, who never lacked for manpower to push their staff cars through a boggy patch, wondered how anybody could make war in such conditions. All of them, however, feared the freeze that would soon follow. Nobody forgot that every day counted.

The German advance formations struggled on as best they could. In the centre, on 14 October, 10th Panzer Division and the SS *Das Reich* Division reached the Napoleonic battlefield of Borodino in rolling countryside with woods and rich farmland. They were only seventy miles from the western edge of Moscow. On the same day, 100 miles north-west of the capital, 1st Panzer Division took the town of Kalinin, with its bridge over the Volga, and severed the Moscow–Leningrad railway line. Meanwhile, on the southern flank, Guderian's panzers swung up past Tula to threaten the Soviet capital from below.

The progress of the three-pronged attack on Moscow threw the Soviet leadership into panic. On the night of 15 October, foreign embassies were told to prepare to leave for Kuybyshev on the Volga. Beria started evacuating his headquarters too. The NKVD interrogators took their most important prisoners with them. They included senior officers who, although desperately needed at the front, were still being beaten to a pulp in the search for confessions. Three hundred other prisoners were executed in batches in the Lubyanka.

At the end of the month, however, Stalin told the chief of the NKVD to halt what Beria himself called his 'mincing machine'. The Soviet dictator was more than willing to go on shooting 'defeatists and cowards', but for the moment he had tired of Beria's conspiracy fantasies, describing them as 'rubbish'.

Stalin demanded accurate reports from the front, but anyone who dared to tell him the truth was accused of panic-mongering. He found it hard to hide his own disquiet. He suspected that Leningrad would fall, so his first consideration was how best to extricate the troops to help save Moscow. His lack of concern for the starving population was as callous as that of Hitler.

There was only one encouraging development at this time. Red Army divisions from the Manchurian frontier were already starting to deploy in the region of Moscow. Two of the first Siberian rifle regiments to arrive had in fact faced the SS *Das Reich* at Borodino a few days before, but it would take several weeks to transport the bulk of the reinforcements along the Trans-Siberian railway. The key Soviet agent in Tokyo, Richard Sorge, had discovered that the Japanese planned to strike south into the Pacific against the Americans, not against the Soviet Far East. Stalin did not entirely trust Sorge, but this time his information had been confirmed by signals intercepts.

On the morning of 16 October, Aleksey Kosygin, the deputy chairman of Sovnarkom, the Council of Peoples' Commissars, entered its building to find the place abandoned. Papers had been scattered by draughts, doors were left open, and telephones rang in empty offices. Kosygin, guessing that the callers wanted to check whether the leadership had left the capital, ran from desk to desk trying to answer them. Even when he picked up the receiver in time there was silence at the other end. Only one important official dared to identify himself. He asked bluntly whether Moscow would be surrendered.

At Stalin's crisis meeting in the Kremlin on 17 October with Molotov, Malenkov, Beria and Aleksandr Shcherbakov, the new chief of the Red Army political department, plans were discussed for mining factories, bridges, railways, roads and even that Stalinist showpiece, the Moscow Metro. No public announcement was made about the evacuation of the remaining ministries to Kuybyshev, but news spread with astonishing rapidity, considering the penalties for defeatist talk. Stories circulated that Stalin had been arrested in a Kremlin coup, that German paratroopers had dropped in Red Square and other enemy troops had infiltrated the city in Soviet uniform. The fear that the capital was about to be abandoned to the enemy provoked thousands to try to get out, storming trains in stations. Food riots, looting and drunkenness turned many minds to the chaos in 1812 which led to the burning of Moscow.

Stalin had considered leaving, but changed his mind. It was Aleksandr Shcherbakov, 'with his impassive Buddha face, with thick horn-rimmed glasses resting on the tiny turned-up button of a nose', wearing 'a plain khaki tunic with only one decoration on it – the Order of Lenin', who announced on Moscow Radio Stalin's decision to remain.

A state of siege was declared on 19 October. Beria brought several regiments of NKVD troops into the city to restore order. 'Panic-mongers' were shot along with looters, and even drunkards. In the popular mind, there was only one test of whether the city would be defended or abandoned: 'Was the military parade [for the anniversary of the Revolution] going to take place on Red Square?' The people of Moscow seemed to provide the answer themselves, rather than wait for their leader to speak. Rather like the defence of Madrid exactly five years before, the mood suddenly turned from one of mass panic to one of mass defiance.

Stalin, with his uncanny instinct, soon realized the symbolic importance of the parade in Red Square, even if Lenin's mummified corpse had been evacuated to a safer place. Molotov and Beria at first thought the idea crazy, with the German Luftwaffe in easy striking distance, but Stalin told them to concentrate every anti-aircraft battery available round the capital. The cunning old impresario was planning to borrow the best-dramatized touch from the siege of Madrid, when on 9 November 1936 the first international brigade of foreign volunteers had paraded up the Gran Vía, to the populace's wildly enthusiastic but mistaken cheers of '*Vivan los rusos!*' They had then marched straight on through the city, to face Franco's Army of Africa on its western edge. In Moscow, Stalin decided, reinforcements for Zhukov's armies would march through Red Square, past the saluting base of Lenin's mausoleum, and straight on to face the invader. He knew the value that newsreel footage of this event would have when distributed round the world. He also knew the right response to Hitler's speeches. 'If they want a war of extermination', he growled on the eve of the anniversary parade, 'they shall have one!'

The Wehrmacht was by now severely handicapped by the weather. Bad visibility hampered the 'flying artillery' of the Luftwaffe. Field Marshal von Bock's armies, forced to halt at the end of October for resupply and reinforcement, were spurred on by desperation to finish off the enemy before the real winter came.

The fighting in the second half of November was relentless. Regiments on both sides were reduced to fractions of their former numbers. Guderian, having found himself blocked by strong resistance at Tula, south of Moscow, swung further round to the right. On the left flank, Hoth's panzers pushed forward to cross the Moskva–Volga canal. From one point north of Moscow, German troops could see through their binoculars the muzzle flashes of the anti-aircraft batteries round the Kremlin. Zhukov ordered Rokossovsky to hold the line at Kryukovo with the remains of his 16th Army. 'There can be no further falling back,' he ordered on 25 November. Rokossovsky knew that he meant what he said.

Russian resistance was so determined that the weakened German forces slowed to a halt. At the end of November, in a last-ditch attempt, Field Marshal von Kluge sent a large force straight up the main road to Moscow, the Minsk Chaussée, along which Napoleon's troops had marched. They broke through, but numbing cold and the suicidal resistance of Soviet regiments blunted their attack.

Guderian and Kluge, on their own initiative, began to withdraw their most exposed regiments. Guderian took the decision sitting in the Tolstoy house of Yasnaya Polyana, with the grave of the great writer covered by snow outside. They wondered what would happen next along the whole central front. The deep German salients either side of Moscow were vulnerable, but the desperation and shortages of the troops they had been fighting convinced them that the enemy had also been fought to a standstill. They never imagined that the Soviet leadership was secretly massing fresh armies behind Moscow.

Winter had arrived in full force, with snow, bitter winds, and temperatures dropping below minus twenty degrees centigrade. German tank engines were frozen solid. In the front line, the exhausted infantrymen dug bunkers to shelter from the cold as much as from enemy bombardment. The ground had started to freeze so hard that they needed to light big fires on it first, before attempting to dig. Headquarters staffs and rear echelons occupied peasant houses, expelling Russian civilians into the snow.

Hitler's refusal to contemplate a winter campaign meant that his soldiers suffered terribly. 'Many of the men are going about with their feet wrapped in paper, and there is a great dearth of gloves,' wrote the commander of a panzer corps to General Paulus. Except for their coal-scuttle helmets, many German soldiers were by now hardly recognizable as members of the Wehrmacht. Their own close-fitting, steel-shod jackboots simply hastened the process of frostbite, so they had resorted to stealing the clothes and boots of prisoners of war and civilians.

Operation Typhoon may have inflicted huge casualties on the Red Army, but it cost the smaller Wehrmacht irreparable losses in trained men and officers. 'This is no longer the old division,' wrote the chaplain of 18th Panzer Division in his diary. 'All around are new faces. When one asks after somebody, the same reply is always given: dead or wounded.'

Field Marshal von Bock was forced to acknowledge at the beginning of December that no further hope of 'strategic success' remained. His armies were exhausted and the cases of frostbite – which reached over 100,000 by Christmas – were rapidly outstripping the numbers of wounded. But any hope that the Red Army was also incapable of further attack was suddenly shattered, just as the temperature fell to minus twenty-five degrees centigrade.

The Siberian divisions, including many ski-troop battalions, formed only a part of the counter-attack force prepared secretly on *Stavka* orders. New aircraft and squadrons from the Far East had been assembled on airfields to the east of Moscow. Some 1,700 tanks, mainly the highly mobile T-34, whose unusually broad tracks coped with the snow and ice far better than German panzers, were also ready for deployment. Most Red Army soldiers, but far from all, were equipped for winter warfare, with padded jackets and white camouflage suits. Their heads were kept warm with *ushanki*, round fur caps with ear flaps at the side, and their feet with large *valenki* (felt boots). They also had covers for the working parts of their weapons and special oil to prevent the action from freezing.

On 5 December, General Koniev's Kalinin Front attacked the outer edge of the German's northern salient. Salvoes of *Katyusha* rockets fired from multiple launchers, which German soldiers had already nicknamed Stalin organs, acted as the terrifying heralds of the onslaught. The following morning, Zhukov threw in the 1st Shock Army, Rokossovsky's 16th Army, and two others against the inner side of the salient. To the south of Moscow, Guderian's flanks were also attacked from different directions. Within three days, his lines of communication were gravely threatened. In the centre, continual attacks prevented Field Marshal von Kluge from diverting troops from his Fourth Army to help the threatened flanks.

For the first time, the Red Army enjoyed air superiority. The aviation regiments brought up to aerodromes behind Moscow had protected their aircraft from the cold, while the weakened Luftwaffe, operating from improvised landing strips, had to defrost every machine by lighting fires under its engines. The Russians enjoyed a harsh satisfaction at the abrupt change in fortunes. They knew the retreat would be cruel for the ill-clad German soldiers struggling back through blizzards and the frozen snowfields.

The conventional counter-attacks were greatly aided by raids causing panic and chaos in the German rear. Partisan detachments, organized by officers of NKVD frontier troops sent behind enemy lines, attacked from frozen marshes and the forests of birch and pine. Siberian winter-warfare battalions from the 1st Shock Army appeared suddenly out of the haze: the only warning was the hiss of their skis on the snow-crust. Red Army cavalry divisions also ranged far into the rear, mounted on resilient little Cossack ponies. Squadrons and entire regiments would suddenly appear fifteen miles behind the front, charging artillery batteries or supply depots with drawn sabres and terrifying war-cries.

The Soviet plan of encirclement rapidly became clear. In ten days, Bock's armies were forced to pull back anything up to a hundred miles. Moscow was saved. The German armies, ill-equipped for winter warfare, were now doomed to suffer in the open.

Events elsewhere had also been momentous. On 7 December, the day after the main counter-attack started, the Japanese had attacked Pearl Harbor. Four days later Hitler announced, to the cheers of the Greater German Reichstag housed in the Berlin Kroll Opera, that he had declared war on the United States of America.

During that second week of December, a savagely exultant Stalin became convinced that the Germans were on the point of disintegration. Reports of their line of retreat, with scenes of abandoned guns, horse carcasses and the bodies of frozen infantrymen half-covered in drifting snow, tended to encourage the idea of another 1812. There had also been outbreaks of panic in the German rear. Support troops, whose vehicles often became unusable in the terrible conditions, were shaken by unexpected attacks far behind the lines. Visceral fears of barbarous Russia surged inside them. They felt very far from home.

Stalin was obsessed with the opportunity, and fell into Hitler's mistake of believing in the power of the will, while discounting the reality of insufficient supplies, bad transport and exhausted troops. His ambition knew no bounds as he gazed at the *Stavka* 'decision-map'. He demanded much more than an extension of the counter-attacks against Army Group Centre. On 5 January 1942, Stalin's plans for a general offensive were fully set out at a joint meeting of the *Stavka* and the State Defence Committee. He wanted major offensives in the north to cut off the besiegers of Leningrad, and also in the south – back into the lost territories of the Ukraine and the Crimea, an idea strongly encouraged by Marshal Timoshenko. Zhukov and others who tried to warn of the dangers failed utterly.

*

The Führer, also preoccupied by thoughts of 1812, had issued a stream of orders against any retreat. He was convinced that, if they held out through the winter, they would break the historical curse on invaders of Russia.

His intervention has long been the subject of debate. Some argue that his resolution saved the German Army from annihilation. Others believe that his demands to hold ground at any cost led to terrible and unnecessary losses in trained men which Germany could not afford. The retreat never really risked becoming a rout, if only because the Red Army lacked the communications, the reserves and the transport needed to continue the pursuit. Hitler, however, was convinced that his strength of will in the face of defeatist generals had saved the whole *Ostfront*. This was to have disastrous consequences at Stalingrad the following year, bolstering his obstinacy to a perverse degree.

The fighting became increasingly chaotic, with front lines swirling in different directions on the map as Stalin's general offensive deteriorated into a series of flailing brawls. Several Soviet formations became cut off as they broke through the German front with insufficient support. Stalin had underestimated the capacity of German troops to recover from a reverse. In most cases, they fought back ferociously, well aware of the consequences of being caught in the open. Commanders on the spot assembled scratch units, often including support personnel, and bolstered their defences with whatever armament was available, especially flak guns.

North-west of Moscow, at Kholm, a force 5,000 strong led by General Scherer held out, resupplied by parachute drops. The much larger Demyansk *Kessel*, with 100,000 men, was resupplied by Junkers 52 transports painted white for camouflage. Over 100 flights a day, bringing in a total of 60,000 tons of supplies and evacuating 35,000 wounded, allowed the defenders to hold out against several Soviet armies for seventy-two days. The German troops were half-starved when finally relieved at the end of April, yet the conditions for Russian civilians trapped in the pocket were infinitely worse. Nobody knows how many died. They had nothing to eat save the entrails of the horses slaughtered for the soldiers. Yet this operation determined

Hitler in his belief that encircled troops should automatically hold on. It was part of the fixation which greatly contributed to the disaster at Stalingrad less than a year later.

Stalin's callous abandonment of General Andrey Vlasov's 2nd Shock Army, cut off in marshes and forests a hundred miles north-west of Demyansk, did not, however, serve as a warning to Hitler, even after the embittered Vlasov surrendered and, throwing in his lot with the Germans, agreed to raise an anti-Stalinist Russian army. As if to offer a curious dramatic balance, the commander of the relief force at Demyansk, General Walther von Seydlitz-Kurzbach, turned against Hitler after being captured at Stalingrad. Then, in September 1943, as will be seen, he volunteered to raise 'a small army from prisoners of war' to be air-landed in the Reich to start an uprising. It was a proposal which the suspicious Beria did not take up.

With troops in the open at temperatures sometimes dropping to minus forty degrees centigrade, Hitler's almost superstitious refusal to order winter clothing had to be remedied. Goebbels quickly managed to mask the truth. An appeal to the population at home provided newsreel footage of national solidarity, with women handing over fur coats, even winter-sports champions bringing in their skis for the *Ostfront*. The response encouraged Hitler to declaim over lunch at the *Wolfs-schanze*: 'The German people have heard my call.' But when the clothes started to arrive towards the end of December, soldiers tried them on with cynical amusement or wonder. The garments, clean and sometimes smelling of mothballs, created a strange impression on the lice-plagued recipients. 'You could see the sitting room with the sofa,' wrote a lieutenant, 'or the child's bed, or perhaps the young girl's room from which they came. It could have been on another planet.'

Sentimental thoughts of home were not just a form of escapism from their world of vermin and filth, but also from an environment of escalating brutality in which conventional morality had become utterly distorted. German troops, most of them, no doubt, loving fathers and sons at home, indulged in a sort of sick war tourism in Russia. An order had to be circulated which forbade the 'photographing of executions of [German] deserters', events which had greatly increased with the sudden decline in morale. And executions of partisans and Jews in the Ukraine – to judge from the audience shown in the pictures – attracted an even greater throng of amateur photographers in Wehrmacht uniforms.

A German officer described how shocked he and his soldiers had been when Russian civilians had cheerfully stripped the corpses of their fellow countrymen. Yet German soldiers were taking clothes and boots from living civilians for themselves, then forcing them out into the freezing wastes, in most cases to die of cold and starvation. Senior officers complained that their soldiers looked like Russian peasants, but no sympathy was spared for the victims robbed of their only hope of survival in such conditions. A bullet might well have been less cruel.

During the retreat from Moscow, German soldiers seized any livestock and food supplies on which they could lay their hands. They ripped up floorboards in living rooms to check for potatoes stored underneath. Furniture and parts of houses were used for firewood. Never did a population suffer so much from both sides in a war. Stalin had signed an order on 17 November ordering Red Army units – aviation, artillery, ski-troops and partisan detachments – to 'destroy and burn to ashes' all houses and farms for up to forty miles behind the German lines to deny the enemy shelter. The fate of Russian women and children was not considered for a moment.

The combination of battle stress and the horrors of war increased the suicide rate among German soldiers. 'Suicide in field conditions is tantamount to desertion', troops were warned in one order. 'A soldier's life belongs to the Fatherland.' Most shot themselves when alone on sentry duty.

Men would pass the long, dark nights thinking of home and dreaming of leave. *Samizdat* discovered by Russian soldiers on German bodies demonstrates that there were indeed cynics as well as sentimentalists. 'Christmas', ran one spoof order, 'will not take place this year for the following reasons: Joseph has been called up for the army; Mary has joined the Red Cross; Baby Jesus has been sent with other children out into the countryside [to avoid the bombing]; the Three Wise Men could not get visas because they lacked proof of

Aryan origin; there will be no star because of the blackout; the shepherds have been made into sentries and the angels have become Blitzmädeln [telephone operators]. Only the donkey is left, and one can't have Christmas with just a donkey.'*

The military authorities were concerned that soldiers going home on leave would demoralize the home population with horror stories of the *Ostfront*. 'You are under military law', ran the forceful reminder, 'and you are still subject to punishment. Don't speak about weapons, tactics or losses. Don't speak about bad rations or injustice. The intelligence service of the enemy is ready to exploit it.'

One soldier, or more likely a group, produced their own version of instructions, entitled 'Notes for Those Going on Leave'. Their attempt to be funny reveals a great deal about the brutalizing effects of the *Ostfront*. 'You must remember that you are entering a National Socialist country whose living conditions are very different to those to which you have become accustomed. You must be tactful with the inhabitants, adapting to their customs and refrain from the habits which you have come to love so much. *Food*: Do not rip up the parquet or other kinds of floor, because potatoes are kept in a different place. *Curfew*: If you forget your key, try to open the door with the round-shaped object. Only in cases of extreme urgency use a grenade. *Defence against Partisans*: It is not necessary to ask civilians the password and open fire on receiving an unsatisfactory answer. *Defence against Animals*: Dogs with mines attached to them are a special feature of the Soviet Union. German dogs in the worst cases bite, but they do not explode. Shooting every dog you see, although recommended in the Soviet Union, might create a bad impression. *Relations with the Civil Population*: In Germany just because somebody is wearing women's clothes does not necessarily mean that she is a partisan. But in spite of this, they are dangerous for anyone on leave from the front. *General*: When on leave back in the Fatherland take care not to talk about the paradise existence in the Soviet Union in case everybody wants to come here and spoil our idyllic comfort.'

---

* 'I do not understand,' a Red Army intelligence officer has written at the bottom of the translation. 'Where does this come from?'

A certain cynicism even emerged over medals. When a winter-campaign medal was issued the following year, it quickly became known as the 'Order of the Frozen Flesh'. There were more serious cases of disaffection. Field Marshal von Reichenau, the commander-in-chief of the Sixth Army, exploded in rage just before Christmas on finding the following examples of graffiti on the buildings allotted for his headquarters: 'We want to return to Germany'; 'We've had enough of this'; 'We are dirty and have lice and want to go home'; and 'We didn't want this war!' Reichenau, while acknowledging that 'such thoughts and moods' were evidently the 'result of great tension and deprivation', put full responsibility on all officers for the 'political and moral condition of their troops'.

And while a small group of well-connected officers led by Henning von Tresckow plotted to assassinate Hitler, at least one Communist cell was at work in the ranks. The following appeal in 'Front Letter No. 3' to set up 'soldier committees in each unit, in each regiment, in each division' was found by a Russian soldier in the lining of the greatcoat of a German soldier. 'Comrades, who is not up to his neck in shit here on the Eastern Front? . . . It is a criminal war unleashed by Hitler and it is leading Germany to hell . . . Hitler must be got rid of and we soldiers can do this. The fate of Germany is in the hands of people at the front. Our password should be "Away with Hitler!" Against the Nazi lie! The war means the death of Germany.'

The dynamics of power during total war inevitably strengthened state control even further. Any criticism of the regime could be attacked as enemy-inspired propaganda, and any opponent could be portrayed as a traitor. Hitler's ascendancy over his generals was unchallenged and they became the scapegoats for the former corporal's obsessions. Those commanders who disagreed with his policy of holding on at all costs in December 1941 were removed. He forced Brauchitsch to retire and appointed himself commander-in-chief instead, on the grounds that no general possessed the necessary National Socialist will.

The German Army managed to re-establish a firm defence line east of Smolensk, but its eventual destruction had become virtually certain. We can now see, with the benefit of hindsight, that the balance of power – geopolitical, industrial, economic and demographic – swung decisively against the Axis in December 1941, with the Wehrmacht's failure to capture Moscow and the American entry into the war. The psychological turning point of the war, however, would come only in the following winter with the battle for the city of Stalingrad, which, partly because of its name, became a personal duel by mass proxy.

Part Two

BARBAROSSA RELAUNCHED

5

General Paulus's First Battle

The curious chain of events which brought General Friedrich Paulus to command the Sixth Army began with Hitler's angry disappointment towards the end of 1941. And a year later, a very similar frustration would lead to the disaster which befell Paulus and his divisions.

In November 1941, while the world's attention was focused on the approaches to Moscow, the situation in the eastern Ukraine had fluctuated wildly. At the climax of Army Group South's advance, the leading divisions of Kleist's First Panzer Group reached Rostov-on-Don on 19 November in driving snow. The following day, they seized the bridge over the great river, the last barrier before the Caucasus. But the Soviet commander, Timoshenko, reacted quickly. The left flank of the German spearhead was weakly guarded by Hungarian troops, and a thrust there, combined with counter-attacks across the frozen Don, soon forced Kleist back.

Hitler was furious, having just exulted in the illusion that both Moscow and the Caucasian oilfields lay within his grasp. To make matters worse, this was the first withdrawal by the German Army during the Second World War. He refused to believe that Field Marshal von Rundstedt lacked the strength and the supplies, and he refused to accept that Kleist should be permitted to pull back his troops, many of them badly frost-bitten, to the line of the river Mius.

Rundstedt indicated on 30 November that if confidence no longer existed in his leadership, then he wished to be relieved of his command.

Early the next morning, Hitler dismissed him. He ordered Reichenau, the commander of the Sixth Army, to take over and halt the withdrawal immediately. This, Reichenau attempted – or pretended – to do. A few hours later, a shamelessly short time, he sent a message to Führer headquarters with the information that withdrawal behind the Mius had become inevitable. Reichenau, an overactive bulldog of a man whose apoplectic expression was heightened by his monocle, did not endear himself to Rundstedt, who later described him as a 'roughneck who used to run around half naked when taking physical exercise'.

On 3 December, the Führer flew down to the Ukraine in his Focke-Wulf Condor to find out what had happened. He first spoke to Sepp Dietrich, the commander of the SS *Leibstandarte* Division. Dietrich, to Hitler's astonishment, supported Rundstedt's decision to withdraw.

Both Rundstedt and Reichenau had their headquarters at Poltava, where Charles XII of Sweden, the first modern invader of Russia, had been defeated by Peter the Great in 1709. Hitler made his peace with Rundstedt, who had not yet departed. It was agreed that the old field marshal should still return home, although now it would be for sick leave. Nine days later, he received a cheque for RM250,000 from the Führer as a birthday present.

Hitler, still slightly suspicious of Reichenau, at first insisted that he remain commander-in-chief of the Sixth Army as well as of Army Group South. But over dinner, while the Führer carefully chewed his millet and pumpkin and potato puffs, Reichenau argued convincingly that he could not run two headquarters at once. He recommended that General Paulus, his former chief of staff, should take over the Sixth Army. Hitler assented, although without much enthusiasm. Thus, on New Year's Day 1942, Paulus, who had never even commanded a division or corps, found himself catapulted up the army list to the rank of General of Panzer Troops. Five days later, he became commander-in-chief of the Sixth Army, just after Timoshenko launched a major, but ill-coordinated, offensive towards Kursk.

Friedrich Wilhelm Paulus came of Hessian yeoman stock. His father had risen from the post of bookkeeper in a reformatory to become the Chief Treasurer of Hesse-Nassau. The young Paulus had applied to join the imperial navy in 1909, but was refused. A year later, the army's enlargement offered an opening. Paulus, almost certainly feeling at a social disadvantage in the Kaiser's army, was obsessed with his turnout. His contemporaries called him '*der Lord*'. In 1912, he married Elena Rosetti-Solescu, the sister of two brother officers, members of a Romanian family with princely connections. She disliked the Nazis, but Paulus, who had joined the Freikorps in the fight against bolshevism after the First World War, most probably shared Reichenau's admiration of Hitler.

As a company commander in the 13th Infantry Regiment, the tall and fastidious Paulus was competent yet uninspired when compared with Erwin Rommel, the commander of the machine-gun company. Unlike Rommel, a robust leader prepared to ignore his superiors, Paulus possessed an exaggerated respect for the chain of command. His work as a staff officer was conscientious and meticulous. He enjoyed working late at night, bent over maps, with coffee and cigarettes to hand. His hobby was drawing scale-maps of Napoleon's campaign in Russia. He later appeared to his son's brother officers in the 3rd Panzer Division as 'more like a scientist than a general, when compared to Rommel or Model'.

Paulus's good manners made him popular with senior officers. He even got on well with that rumbustious thug Reichenau, when he became his chief of staff in August 1939. Their teamwork impressed other senior officers during the first year of the war, in which their most memorable moment was taking the surrender of King Leopold of the Belgians. Not long after the conquest of France, General Halder summoned Paulus to Berlin to work as chief planner on the general staff. There, his most important task lay in evaluating the options for Operation Barbarossa. Once the invasion was well under way, Reichenau asked Halder to let him have his chief of staff back again.

Paulus's 'fantastic leap' to army commander, as friends described it in letters of congratulation, was marred exactly a week later. On 12 January 1942, his patron, Field Marshal von Reichenau, went for his morning run at Poltava. The temperature was twenty degrees below zero. Reichenau felt unwell during lunch, and suddenly collapsed from a heart attack. Hitler, on hearing the news, ordered Dr Flade, the Sixth Army's senior medical officer, to bring him straight back to Germany. The unconscious Reichenau was strapped to an armchair fastened inside the fuselage of a Dornier.

The pilot insisted on landing at Lemberg to refuel, but he crash-landed some distance from the field. Doctor Flade, despite a broken leg, fired signal flares to attract help. By the time the party finally reached the hospital in Leipzig, Reichenau was dead. Flade reported to Paulus afterwards that the ill-omened crash had been almost like a film. 'Even his field marshal's baton had been broken in two.' Hitler ordered a state funeral, but did not attend. He gave Rundstedt the distinction of representing him.

Although Paulus's rather aloof manner made him appear cold, he was more sensitive than many generals to the well-being of his soldiers. He is also said to have cancelled Reichenau's order of 10 October 1941, encouraging the 'severe' treatment of Jews and partisans, yet when the Sixth Army reached Stalingrad, its Feldgendarmerie was apparently given the task of arresting Communist activists and Jews to hand them over to the SD Sonderkommando for 'punitive measures'.

Paulus certainly inherited a heavy legacy. From the very start of Barbarossa, the massacres of Jews and gypsies had been deliberately mixed in, whenever possible, with the execution of partisans, mainly because the phrase *'jüdische Saboteure'* helped to cloud the illegality of the act and to bolster the notion of a 'judeo–bolshevik' conspiracy. The definition of partisan and saboteur was soon widened far beyond the terms of international law, which permitted a death sentence only after a proper trial. In an order of 10 July 1941, Sixth Army headquarters warned soldiers that anyone in civilian clothes with a close-cropped head was almost certain to be a Red Army soldier and should therefore be shot. Civilians who behaved in a hostile fashion, including those who gave food to Red Army soldiers hiding in woods, were also to be shot. 'Dangerous elements', such as Soviet officials, a category which extended from the local Communist Party secretary and collective-farm manager to almost anyone employed by the government, should, like commissars and Jews, be handed over to the Feldgendarmerie or the SD-Einsatzkommando. A subsequent order called for 'collective measures' – either executions or the burning of villages – to punish sabotage. According to the evidence of SS-Obersturmführer August Häfner, Field Marshal von Reichenau himself gave the order early in July 1941 for 3,000 Jews to be shot as a reprisal measure.

The behaviour of many soldiers in Army Group South was particularly gruesome. Reichenau's Sixth Army headquarters issued the following order on 10 August 1941: 'In various places within the army's area of responsibility, organs of the SD, of the Reichsführer's SS and chiefs of the German Police have been carrying out necessary executions of criminal, bolshevik and mostly Jewish elements. There have been cases of off-duty soldiers volunteering to help the SD with their executions, or acting as spectators and taking photographs.' It was now forbidden for any soldiers, 'who have not been ordered by a superior officer', to take part in, to watch or to photograph any of these executions. Later, General von Manstein's chief of staff passed the message to the *Offizierkorps* of the Eleventh Army in the Crimea that it was 'dishonourable for officers to be present at the execution of Jews'. German military logic, in another of its distortions of cause and effect, does not appear to have acknowledged the possibility that officers had already shamed themselves by furthering the aims of a regime capable of such crimes.

Occasionally atrocities were halted, but not for long. On 20 August, chaplains from the 295th Infantry Division informed Lieutenant-Colonel Helmuth Groscurth, the chief of staff, that ninety Jewish orphans in the town of Belaya Tserkov were being held in disgusting conditions. They ranged from infants up to seven-year-old children. They were to be shot, like their parents. Groscurth, the son of a pastor and a convinced anti-Nazi, had been the Abwehr officer who, that spring, had secretly passed details of the illegal orders for Barbarossa to Ulrich von Hassell. Groscurth immediately sought out the district commander and insisted that the execution must be stopped. He then contacted Sixth Army headquarters, even though Standartenführer Paul Blobel, the head of the Sonderkommando, warned Groscurth that he would report his interference to Reichsführer SS Himmler.

Field Marshal von Reichenau supported Blobel. The ninety Jewish children were shot the next evening by Ukrainian militiamen, to save the feelings of the Sonderkommando.

Groscurth wrote a full report which he sent direct to headquarters Army Group South. Appalled and furious, he wrote to his wife: 'We cannot and should not be allowed to win this war.' At the first opportunity, he went on leave to Paris to see Field Marshal von Witlzleben, one of the leading members in the anti-Hitler movement.

The massacre of the innocents in Belaya Tserkov was soon dwarfed by a far greater atrocity. Following the capture of Kiev, 33,771 Jews were rounded up in the last days of September, to be slaughtered by Sonderkommando 4a and two police battalions in the ravine of Babi Yar outside the city. This '*Gross-Aktion*' was once again entirely within the Sixth Army's area of responsibility. Reichenau, along with certain key officers from his headquarters who attended the town commandant's planning conference on 27 September 1941, must have known their fate in advance, even if the soldiers detailed to assist in the round-up may have been taken in by the cover story of 'evacuation'. Soviet Jews did not imagine what awaited them. They had little idea of Nazi anti-Semitism, because under the Molotov–Ribbentrop pact, no criticism of National Socialist policies had been published. The town commandant in his proclamation posters had also lulled suspicions with the instruction: 'You should bring with you identity papers, money and valuables as well as warm clothing.' The Sonderkommando, which had expected 5,000–6,000 Jews, was astonished to find that more than 30,000 had turned up.

Field Marshal von Reichenau's notorious order to the Sixth Army of 10 October 1941, which was supported by Field Marshal von Rundstedt, quite clearly makes the Wehrmacht chain of command jointly responsible for atrocities against Jews and civilians in the Ukraine. 'In this eastern theatre of war, the soldier is not only a man fighting in accordance with the rules of war, but also the ruthless standard-bearer of a national ideal and the avenger of all the bestialities perpetrated on the German peoples. For this reason the soldier must fully appreciate the necessity for the severe but just retribution that must be meted out to the subhuman species of Jewry.' Their duty was to 'free the German people forever from the Jewish-Asiatic threat'.

Reprisal burnings and executions did not end with Reichenau's death and Paulus's arrival. For example, on 29 January 1942, some three weeks after the new commander-in-chief of Sixth Army took over, the village of Komsomolsk near Kharkov with 150 houses was burned to the ground. During this operation, eight people were shot and two children, presumably so terrified that they stayed hidden, were burned to death.

German soldiers were bound to mistreat civilians after nearly nine years of the regime's anti-Slav and anti-Semitic propaganda, even if few of them consciously acted at the time out of Nazi values. The nature of the war produced emotions that were both primitive and complex. Although there were cases of soldiers reluctant to carry out executions when ordered, most natural pity for civilians was transmuted into an incoherent anger based on the feeling that women and children had no business to be in a battle zone.

Officers preferred to avoid moral reflection. They concentrated instead on the need for good military order. Those who still believed in the rules of war were often horrified at the conduct of their soldiers, but instructions to respect procedures had little effect. 'Interrogations should end with the release of the prisoner, or putting the prisoner in a camp,' emphasized an order from the 371st Infantry Division. 'Nobody should be executed without the order of the officer in charge.'

They also despaired at the scale of looting. Few soldiers offered to pay the locals for livestock and produce, mainly because the German government refused to provide adequate rations. 'The Landsers go to vegetable gardens and take everything,' a company commander in the 384th Infantry Division wrote in his diary later that summer, during the advance to Stalingrad. 'They even take household items, chairs and pots. It's a scandal. Severe prohibitions are published, but the ordinary soldier hardly restrains himself. He is forced into such conduct by hunger.' The effects were particularly serious in a country of such extreme climate as Russia. The plundering of food reserves condemned the civil population to death by starvation when winter came. Even honey-making became impossible, because the sugar needed to keep bees alive during the winter was seized.

The terrible truth, which very few officers could bear to recognize, was that the army's tolerance or support for the Nazi doctrine of a 'race war' on the eastern front, exempt from normal military and international law, was bound to turn it into a semi-criminal organization. The failure of generals to protest demonstrated a total lack of moral sensibility, or of moral courage. Physical courage was unnecessary. The Nazis, in the earlier stages of the Russian campaign, would not have dared to do anything worse to a senior officer who objected than remove him from his command.

Hitler's ability to manipulate generals was uncanny. Although most generals in the Sixth Army were not convinced Nazis, they were nevertheless loyal to Hitler, or certainly pretended to be. For example, a letter written on 20 April would be dated 'Führer's Birthday' and proclamations were signed 'Long Live the Führer!' But it was perfectly possible for a general to keep his independence and his career unharmed, using military rather than political exhortations. General Karl Strecker, the commander of XI Corps and an unashamed old warhorse, made a point of never acknowledging the regime. He signed proclamations to his soldiers: 'Forward with God. Our belief is in victory. Hail my brave fighters!' More important, he personally countermanded illegal orders from above, on one occasion driving from unit to unit to make sure that officers understood him. He chose Groscurth as his chief of staff and, together, they were to direct the last pocket of resistance at Stalingrad, loyal to their own sense of duty, but not to the Führer.

Contrary to all rules of war, surrender did not guarantee the lives of Red Army soldiers. On the third day of the invasion of the Ukraine, August von Kageneck, a reconnaissance troop commander with 9th Panzer Division, saw from the turret of his reconnaissance vehicle, 'dead men lying in a neat row under the trees alongside a country lane, all in the same position – face down'. They had clearly not been killed in combat. Nazi propaganda, simultaneously provoking both atavistic fears and hate, incited soldiers to kill as much out of the former as the latter, yet at the same time it also reminded them that they were brave German soldiers. This produced a powerfully destructive combination, for it is the attempt to control the outward signs of cowardice which produces the most violent reaction of all. The greatest fear that Nazi propaganda encouraged among troops was a fear of capture. 'We were afraid,' Kageneck acknowledged, 'afraid of falling into the hands of the Russians, no doubt thirsty for revenge after our surprise attack.'

Officers with traditional values were even more appalled when they heard of soldiers taking pot-shots at the columns of Soviet prisoners trudging to the rear. These endless columns of defeated men, hungry and above all thirsty in the summer heat, their brown uniforms and fore-and-aft *pilotka* caps covered in dust, were seen as little better than herds of animals. An Italian journalist, who had seen many columns, wrote: 'Most of them are wounded. They wear no bandages, their faces are caked with blood and dust, their uniforms are in rags, their hands blackened. They walk slowly, supporting one another.' The wounded generally received no medical assistance, and those who could not march or who collapsed from exhaustion were shot. Soviet soldiers were not allowed to be transported in German military transport in case they infected it with lice and fleas. It should not be forgotten that 600 Soviet prisoners of war were gassed in Auschwitz on 3 September 1941. This was the first experiment there with Zyklon B.

For those who reached prisoner-of-war camps alive, the chance of survival turned out to be not much better than one in three. Altogether, over three million Red Army soldiers out of 5.7 million died in German camps from disease, exposure, starvation and ill-treatment. The German Army itself, not the SS nor any other Nazi organization, was responsible for prisoners of war. Its attitude was reminiscent of Kaiser Wilhelm II's remark in 1914 that the 90,000 Russian prisoners captured at Tannenberg 'should be left to starve'.

On the southern front, a German camp at Lozovaya, overrun by Timoshenko's January advance, revealed appalling conditions, with Red Army prisoners dying 'of cold, of starvation, of brutal maltreatment'. Yury Mikhailovich Maximov of the 127th Rifle Division, captured in the autumn of 1941, was one of those taken to Novo-Aleksandrovsk. The so-called camp there had no huts, just open ground with a barbed-wire fence. The 18,000 men were fed from twelve cauldrons in which odd hunks of horseflesh were boiled. When the guards on duty gave the order to come forward to receive food, sub-machine-gunners shot down anybody who ran. Their corpses were left there for three days as a warning.

German officers at the front wanted prisoners to be better treated for practical reasons. 'Their information on enemy numbers, organization and intentions may give us more than our own intelligence services can provide,' read an instruction from the chief intelligence officer of the 96th Infantry Division. 'Russian soldiers', he added, 'respond to interrogation in a naive way.' The OKW propaganda department at the same time issued orders that Russian desertion must be encouraged to save German lives. But intelligence staffs at the front knew well that this could 'work only if promises made to deserters are kept'. The trouble was that they were usually treated just as badly as any other prisoners.

Stalin's dislike of international law had suited Hitler's plan for a war of annihilation, so when the Soviet Union proposed a reciprocal adherence to the Hague convention less than a month after the invasion, its note was left unanswered. Stalin did not usually believe in observing such niceties, but the ferocity of the German onslaught had shaken him.

Within the Red Army, there was no formal equivalent to the illegal orders issued to the Wehrmacht, but members of the SS, and later other categories such as camp guards and members of the Secret Field Police, were almost certain to be shot after capture. Luftwaffe pilots and panzer crews also risked lynching, but on the whole the shooting of prisoners was random rather than calculated, while acts of wanton cruelty were localized and inconsistent. The Soviet authorities desperately wanted prisoners, especially officers, for interrogation.

For partisans, including Red Army detachments, hospital trains were regarded as legitimate targets, and few pilots or gunners spared ambulances or field hospitals. A doctor with the 22nd Panzer Division observed: 'My ambulance had a machine-gun mounted on top and a red cross on the side. The red cross symbol was a farce in Russia, and served only as a sign for our own people.' The worst incident took place on 29 December 1941, when a German field hospital was overrun at Feodosia on the Crimean coast. Soviet marine infantry, many of them apparently drunk, killed about 160 German wounded. A number of them had been thrown out of the windows, others were taken outside, soaked in water and left to freeze to death.

The occasional, primitive atrocity committed by Red Army soldiers during the first eighteen months – there would almost certainly have been more if they had not been retreating so rapidly – prompted many Germans to make comparisons with the Thirty Years War. A truer link, however, would have been to the Russian civil war, one of the cruellest of twentieth-century conflicts, which Hitler's crusade against bolshevism had reignited. But as the war progressed, Russian outrage and a terrible desire for revenge was fired much more by news of German acts in the 'occupied territories': villages burned to the ground in reprisals, and civilians starved, massacred or deported to work camps. This impression of genocide against the Slavs aroused, along with the desire for revenge, a pitiless determination not to be beaten.

General Paulus did not take over the Sixth Army at an easy moment, and he was probably more shaken by Reichenau's death than he showed. His first experience of senior command in January 1942 coincided with Stalin's ill-judged general offensive, following the Red Army's success round Moscow. In fact, it was a difficult time for all German forces on the southern front. General von Manstein's Eleventh Army in the Crimea had not yet managed to seize Sevastopol, and a surprise attack by Red Army troops from the Caucasus at the end of December had taken the Kerch peninsula. Hitler, apoplectic with rage, had the corps commander, General Count von Sponeck, court-martialled.

Paulus moved Sixth Army headquarters forward to Kharkov, Marshal Timoshenko's objective. The temperature had dropped to thirty degrees below zero, sometimes lower. German transport by rail and road was frozen solid, and horse-drawn carts could provide only the barest rations.

Timoshenko's plan had been to cut off the industrial region of the Donbas and seize Kharkov in a huge encirclement, but only the southern part of the pincer had managed to pierce the German lines. This had been a successful thrust, taking a salient nearly sixty miles deep. But the Red Army lacked the resources and fresh troops, and after two months of bitter fighting, their attacks ground to a halt.

The Sixth Army held on, yet Paulus was uneasy. Field Marshal von Bock, whom Hitler had reluctantly appointed to command Army Group South, did not disguise his feeling that he had been overcautious in counter-attacking. Paulus kept his command, with the support of his protector, General Halder. His chief of staff, Colonel Ferdinand Heim, was moved instead. In his place came Colonel Arthur Schmidt, a slim, sharp-featured and sharp-tongued staff officer from a Hamburg mercantile family. Schmidt, confident of his own abilities, put up many backs within Sixth Army headquarters, although he also had his supporters. Paulus relied greatly on his judgement, and as a result he played a large, some say an excessive, role in determining the course of events later that year.

In the early spring of 1942, the divisions that were to perish at Stalingrad took little interest in staff gossip. Their immediate concerns were replenishment and rearmament. It said much for the professional resilience of the German Army (and much less for its sense of self-preservation) that memories of the terrible winter were virtually effaced as soon as spring and new equipment arrived. 'Morale was higher again,' remembered one commander, whose company at last had a full complement of eighteen tanks. 'We were in a good state.' They were not even greatly disturbed by the fact that even the long-barrelled version of the Panzer Mark III had only a 50-mm gun, whose shell often failed to penetrate Soviet tanks.

Although no announcement had been made within divisions, everyone knew that a major offensive would not be long in coming. In March, General Pfeffer, the commander of the 297th Infantry Division, said half-jokingly to a captain who was reluctant to be sent back to France for a battalion commander's course: 'Just be happy that you're getting a break. The war will last long enough and be terrible enough for you to get a good taste of it.'

On 28 March, General Halder drove to Rastenburg to present the plans demanded by the Führer for the conquest of the Caucasus and southern Russia up to the Volga. He did not suspect that in Moscow, the *Stavka* was studying Timoshenko's project for a renewed offensive in the area of Kharkov.

On 5 April, the Führer's headquarters issued orders for the campaign to bring 'final victory in the East'. While Northern Army Group, with Operation Northern Light, was planned to bring the siege of Leningrad to a successful conclusion and link up with the Finns, the main offensive – Operation Siegfried, renamed Operation Blue – would take place in southern Russia.

Hitler was still convinced of the Wehrmacht's 'qualitative superiority over the Soviets', and saw no need for reserves. It was almost as though his removal of the army-group commanders had also effaced all memory of the recent failures. Field Marshal von Bock, the most rapidly reappointed, doubted that they had the strength to seize, let alone hold, the Caucasian oilfields. He feared that the Soviet Union was not running out of reserves as the Führer's headquarters so firmly believed. 'My great concern – that the Russians might pre-empt us with their own attack –' he wrote in his diary on 8 May, 'has not diminished.'

That same day, Bock welcomed General Walther von Seydlitz-Kurzbach, who had broken the Demyansk encirclement. Seydlitz, an artilleryman, was a descendant of Frederick the Great's brilliant cavalry general, known in his youth for galloping between the sails of a windmill in full swing, but most famous for the great victory of Rossbach in the Seven Years War, where his massed squadrons carried the day. Walther von Seydlitz was also impulsive and, like his ancestor, he was also doomed to ill fortune and an embittered old age. Seydlitz had arrived that afternoon by air from Königsberg, where he had snatched a few days' leave with his wife, before taking over command of LI Corps under Paulus. When he and his wife had said goodbye at the airfield, they never imagined, 'that it was a farewell for almost fourteen years'.

Seydlitz went forward to Kharkov the next day. The city, he found,

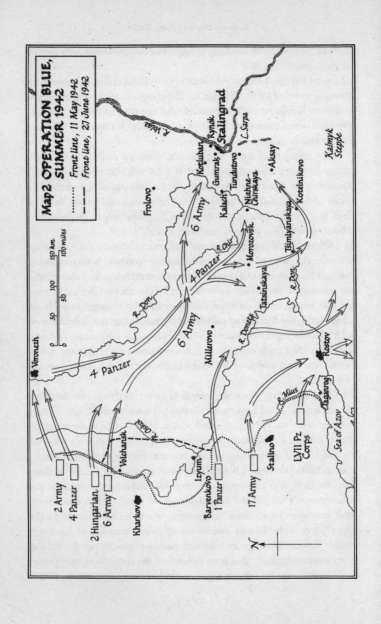

Map 2 OPERATION BLUE, SUMMER 1942

.... Front line, 11 May 1942
- - - - - Front line, 27 June 1942

0   50   100   150 km.
0   50   100 miles

R. Volga

Stalingrad
Rynok
Koluban
Gumrak
Kalach
Tundutowo
L. Sarpa
Nizhne-Chirskaya
Aksay
Kalmyk
Steppe
Kotelnikovo
Tsimlyanskaya
Frolovo
6 Army
4 Panzer
R. Chir
Morozovsk
R. Don
Tatsinskaya
R. Don
6 Army
Millerovo
R. Donets
Rostov
Voronezh
4 Panzer
2 Army
4 Panzer
2 Hungarian
6 Army
Kharkov
Volchansk
R. Oskol
Izyum
Barvenkovo
1 Panzer
Stalino
17 Army
R. Mius
Taganrog
LVII Pz Corps
Sea of Azov

N

had not been seriously damaged when captured. 'The buildings mainly date from tsarist times, except for a new university in bombastic Stalinist style, and a huge American-built tractorworks. In the centre almost everything is built of brick, while further out, houses are made of wood.' In his new corps, he found that he had two Austrian divisions, the 44th Infantry Division, successor to the old Habsburg Hoch- und Deutschmeister regiment, and General Pfeffer's 297th Infantry Division.

On 10 May, Paulus submitted to Field Marshal von Bock his draft plans for Operation Fridericus, the elimination of the Barvenkovo salient gained by Timoshenko during the January offensive. Bock's fears of a Russian attack proved correct even sooner than he had feared. Timoshenko had assembled 640,000 men, 1,200 tanks and nearly a thousand aircraft. On 12 May, six days before the scheduled start of Operation Fridericus, the Red Army launched twin attacks from around Volchansk and from the Barvenkovo salient to cut off Kharkov. Bock warned Paulus not to counter-attack too hurriedly or without air support, but Soviet tank brigades broke through the front of General Walther Heitz's VIII Corps and by that evening, Russian tank units were a dozen miles from Kharkov.

Next morning, Bock realized that the enemy breakthrough round Volchansk was more serious than he had realized. Paulus's Sixth Army received a heavy battering from different directions. In seventy-two hours of fighting, much of it in heavy rain, sixteen battalions were destroyed. Paulus was convinced that a holding action, giving ground where necessary, was the only solution. Bock, however, had other ideas. He persuaded Halder to convince Hitler that a bold counter-attack with Kleist's First Panzer Army could transform a setback into victory. The Führer, who lived for such moments, immediately recognized the opportunity. Claiming the idea for his own, he galvanized Kleist into moving his First Panzer Army rapidly into position to strike at the enemy's southern flank. He ordered the Luftwaffe to concentrate every available attack group to pin down Timoshenko's formations until Kleist was ready.

Kleist struck at the southern side of the Barvenkovo salient before dawn on 17 May. By midday, his spearhead had advanced ten miles, even though his panzer divisions had to engage the T-34 at close range, otherwise their 'shells bounced off like fireworks'.

That evening, Timoshenko signalled Moscow, pleading for reinforcements to stop Kleist. According to Zhukov, Timoshenko did not warn Moscow that his armies were likely to be encircled, but the chief commissar of the front, Nikita Khrushchev, claimed that Stalin persistently refused to allow them to withdraw from danger. (This later formed one of his indictments of Stalin during his famous denunciation in 1956 at the XX Party Congress.) Finally, on 19 May, Timoshenko called off the offensive, with Stalin's agreement, but it was too late.

Bock decided that the moment had come for Paulus to attack from the north to seal the trap. The fighting which resulted, a gradual compression of over a quarter of a million Soviet troops, led to unusual situations. According to a senior NCO in the 389th Infantry Division, his grenadier regiment found itself in a merciless battle with what he described as a 'bandit battalion' of women soldiers, commanded by a redhead. 'The fighting methods of these female beasts showed itself in treacherous and dangerous ways. They lie concealed in heaps of straw, and shoot us in the back when we pass by.'

Just as the ring was closing, part of the 2nd Panzer Regiment and some mechanized artillery found themselves cut off at nightfall within the massed Russians. Their commander was the legendary Hyazinth Graf von Strachwitz, known as the 'Panzer-Kavallerist'. The forty-nine-year-old Strachwitz, a renowned cavalryman in the First World War – his troop had been so far to the front in the advance of 1914 that they had seen Paris in the distance – still retained the dark moustache and the dashing good looks of a 1920s film star. More important, he had not lost the uncanny nose for danger which had made his reputation as a lucky commander.

As this small force from 16th Panzer Division had no idea of the situation around them when darkness fell, Strachwitz ordered a hedgehog defence until daybreak. Just before first light, he took Captain Baron Bernd von Freytag-Loringhoven, who was one of his squadron commanders, and two of the artillery officers up a small hill, ready to look around. As the four officers were focusing their binoculars, Strachwitz suddenly grabbed Freytag-Loringhoven by the arm and dragged him down the slope. He shouted a warning to the two gunners, but they were not quick enough. Both were killed by a shell from a Russian battery on another small hill. Strachwitz, wasting no time, ordered the drivers to start up, and the tanks and vehicles charged in a body out of the vast arena, to rejoin the rest of the division.

Red Army soldiers fought back bitterly for more than a week during humid spring weather. They made desperate charges – sometimes with arms linked – at the German lines at night, but the trap was firm and they were massacred in their thousands under the curiously dead light of magnesium flares. The bodies piled in front of the German positions testified to their suicidal bravery. The survivors wondered if they would ever get out. One unknown Russian soldier trapped in the pocket wrote on a scrap of paper how, watching 'the German searchlights playing on the clouds', he wondered if he would ever see his sweetheart again.

Less than one man in ten managed to escape. The 6th and 57th Armies, caught in the 'Barvenkovo mousetrap', were virtually annihilated. Paulus and Kleist's armies had secured nearly 240,000 prisoners, 2,000 guns and the bulk of Timoshenko's tank force. Their own losses were not much more than 20,000 men. Congratulations arrived from all quarters. Paulus found himself fêted in the Nazi press which, reluctant to praise reactionary aristocrats, made much of his modest family origins. The Führer awarded him the Knight's Cross and sent a message to say that he fully appreciated 'the success of the Sixth Army against an enemy overwhelmingly superior in numbers'. Schmidt, Paulus's chief of staff, argued in later years that the most influential effect of this battle was on Paulus's attitude towards Hitler. The Führer's decision to back the ambitious counter-attack convinced Paulus of his brilliance and of the superior ability of OKW to judge the strategic situation.

Ironically in the circumstances, Paulus also received an unusually emotional letter of appreciation from Major Count Claus von Stauffenberg of the general staff, who had stayed as his companion during part of the battle. 'How refreshing it is', wrote Stauffenberg, 'to get away from this atmosphere to surroundings where men give of their best without a thought, and give their lives too, without a murmur of complaint, while the leaders and those who should set an example quarrel and quibble about their own prestige, or haven't the courage to speak their minds on a question which affects the lives of thousands of their fellow men.' Paulus either did not notice, or more likely he deliberately ignored, the coded message.

Paulus was clearly reluctant to examine Hitler's faults, yet after the way the plans for Barbarossa had been changed at the Führer's whim the previous year, he should have been able to assess the real danger for field commanders. Hitler, intoxicated with the notion of his own infallibility, and profiting from almost instant communications with their headquarters, would try, godlike, to control every manoeuvre from afar.

6

'How Much Land Does a Man Need?'

Early on 1 June, Hitler took off from the airfield near Rastenburg in his personal Focke-Wulf Condor for the headquarters of Army Group South at Poltava. The subject of the conference was the great summer offensive. He was in an exhilarated mood when he greeted Field Marshal von Bock and his senior commanders, including Kleist of First Panzer Army, Hoth of Fourth Panzer Army and Paulus of Sixth Army. The senior Luftwaffe officer present was Colonel-General Baron Wolfram von Richthofen.

Richthofen, a cousin of the 'Red Baron', whose squadron he had joined in 1917, was a hard-faced man, both intelligent and arrogant. His record of ruthlessness spoke for itself. He had commanded the Condor Legion in Spain, when the technique of carpet-bombing was invented and had been directly responsible for the destruction of Guernica in 1937, an event which came to symbolize the horror of modern war. It was Richthofen's VIII Air Corps which destroyed Belgrade in April 1941, killing 17,000 civilians: an act for which his commander-in-chief, General Alexander Löhr, was executed after the war by the Yugoslavs. The following month, during the invasion of Crete, Richthofen's aircraft reduced the Venetian architecture of both Canea and Heraklion to rubble.

During the conference, Hitler hardly mentioned Stalingrad. As far as his generals were concerned it was little more than a name on the map. His obsession was with the oilfields of the Caucasus. 'If we don't take Maikop and Grozny,' he told his generals, 'then I must put an end to the war.' At that stage, the only interest in Stalingrad was to eliminate the armaments factories there and secure a position on the Volga. The capture of the city itself was not considered necessary.

The first phase of Operation Blue was to capture Voronezh. The second was to trap the bulk of the Soviet forces in a great pincer movement west of the Don. The Sixth Army would then move towards Stalingrad to secure the north-east flank, while Kleist's First Panzer Army and the Seventeenth Army would occupy the Caucasus. After Bock had finished his presentation, Hitler spoke. He made it all sound so simple. The Red Army was finished after the winter fighting, and the victory at Kharkov had again confirmed German supremacy. So certain was Hitler of success in the south, that as soon as Sevastopol fell, he planned to send Manstein's Eleventh Army northwards. He even told Manstein about his dream of sending armoured columns through the Caucasus into the Middle East and India.

Before Operation Blue could start in earnest, two lesser offensives had to be performed to straighten the front and prepare the start-line, with bridgeheads across the river Donets. On the afternoon of 5 June, as a last treat, many officers and soldiers from the Sixth Army went to the Kharkov ballet. The unpaid dancers had been kept alive through the winter on Wehrmacht rations. That day, they danced *Swan Lake* and the packed audience, sweating in their *feldgrau* uniforms, greatly enjoyed their interpretation of Prince Siegfried's tragedy, trapped by the wicked Rothbart. (This curious conjunction of two code-names – Siegfried, the original name for Operation Blue, and Rothbart, the German equivalent of Barbarossa – was entirely coincidental.) After the performance, the audience hurried back to their units. On that hot moonless night, leading elements from the Sixth Army started to move north-eastwards to the Volchansk sector.

On 10 June, at two in the morning, companies from the 297th Infantry Division began to cross the Donets by assault boat. Having secured a foothold on the far side, pioneer companies set to work constructing a sixty-yard pontoon bridge. By evening tanks of the 14th Panzer Division were rattling across. The next morning, a bridge further upstream was seized before the Soviet troops guarding it could blow their charges. But this crossing was so narrow that, on the following day, traffic jams built up between minefields on both sides of the route, marked by white tape. A cloudburst turned the dirt road into a morass. Then two shells exploded, blasting fountains of mud and black smoke into the air. This panicked the horses of a baggage wagon. They reared, then bolted off the road, through the white tape. A mine exploded. One horse was blown to bits, the other fell to the ground bleeding. Their wagon caught fire. Flames then spread to another one close by, which was loaded with munitions. Small-arms ammunition and grenades started to explode in an instant battle.

The pattern of skirmishes, successes and relatively minor mishaps continued the next day. A major on the staff of a Swabian division was sitting next to his general on a railway embankment during a visit to a point unit. He was killed instantly by a shot from a Russian sniper concealed in a thicket. Their driver was also hit, in the left shoulder. The general, having ordered the infantry and a pair of self-propelled assault guns to exact revenge, had the corpse of his staff officer placed in his vehicle, and left 'the fateful place'. During dinner that evening in the headquarters mess tent, junior officers debated the advantages of a sudden death. Some regarded the major's unexpected end as desirable, almost a military ideal, others were depressed, seeing it as the robbery of a life, reducing the body of an officer to the level of shot game. The general remained angrily silent throughout, clearly unsettled by the death of a subordinate from a bullet intended for himself.

While the Sixth Army and the First Panzer Army secured the start-line for Operation Blue, due to start on 28 June, all the head-quarters concerned were thrown into confusion. On 19 June, Major Reichel, the operations officer of 23rd Panzer Division, flew in a Fieseler Storch light aircraft to visit a front-line unit. Contrary to all security procedures, he had taken with him a set of detailed orders for the whole operation. The Storch was shot down just beyond German lines. A patrol sent out to recover the bodies and the documents found that the Russians had got there first. Hitler, on hearing the news, became almost incoherent with rage. He demanded that Reichel's divisional commander and corps commander should face a court martial.

The great irony was that Stalin, when told of the captured papers, dismissed them out of hand as forgeries. Reverting to his obsessive obstinacy of the previous year, he refused to believe anything which contradicted his own view that Hitler would again strike at Moscow. South-Western Front headquarters sent Reichel's papers to the Kremlin by aircraft, but Stalin, during his meeting on 26 June with General Golikov, the commander of the threatened Bryansk Front, threw the papers aside angrily when he saw that Golikov believed them to be authentic. Golikov was sent straight back to his headquarters to prepare a quick pre-emptive attack to recapture Orel. He and his staff worked on a draft plan all the next day and through most of the night, but their labours were wasted. The German offensive began a few hours later.

On 28 June, the Second Army and the Fourth Panzer Army, which were deployed near Kursk, attacked due east towards Voronezh, not north towards Orel and Moscow, as Stalin expected. A forward air controller from the Luftwaffe, usually a lieutenant aided by a couple of NCOs with one of the latest radio sets, was attached to the headquarters of the leading panzer divisions, ready to call in air strikes. Once the initial breakthough was achieved, Hoth's panzer divisions advanced rapidly, with Richthofen's Stukas smashing strong-points or tank concentrations ahead.

The breakthrough of Hoth's Fourth Panzer Army caused great alarm in Moscow. Stalin agreed to Golikov's requests for more tanks, and transferred several brigades from the *Stavka* reserve and Timoshenko's South-Western Front. But because of bad communications, their deployment for a counter-strike took time. A Focke-Wulf 189 from a close reconnaissance squadron located their concentration areas and, on 4 July, Richthofen's VIII Air Corps struck again.

On 30 June, Paulus's Sixth Army crossed the start-line prepared on the eastern side of the river Donets. It had the Second Hungarian Army on its left and First Panzer Army on its right. The resistance encountered was stronger than expected, with T-34s and anti-tank guns both dug in and camouflaged from the Stukas as well as the panzers. This form of fighting, however, put the Russian tank troops at a disadvantage because the far more experienced German panzer troops outmanoeuvred them easily. Soviet crews either fought to the end without moving, or they made a run for it at the last moment. 'The Russian tanks come out of their emplacements like tortoises', wrote an observer, 'and try to escape by zigzagging. Some of them still wear their camouflage netting like green wigs.'

The German divisions advanced across immense fields of sunflowers or corn. One of the main dangers they faced was from Red Army soldiers, cut off by the rapid advance, attacking from behind or from the flank. On many occasions, when German soldiers fired back, the Red Army soldiers fell, feigning death, and lay there without moving. When the Germans approached to investigate, the Soviet soldiers waited until almost the last moment, then 'shot them at close range'.

In spite of their relentless advance, German staff officers remained uneasy after the capture of Major Reichel's plans. They had already been debating privately whether or not Kharkov had been a decisive victory: now, they feared a trick. They did not know if the enemy was preparing reserve armies for a surprise counter-attack, or planning to withdraw into the hinterland, extending their supply lines further across vast regions with poor communications. At this stage, however, their fears were greatly exaggerated. The chaos on the Soviet side was so great, owing to the breakdown in communications, that staff officers and commanders were having to fly around in biplanes, dodging the Messerschmitts, trying to locate their troops.

The Reichel affair cast a long shadow. This idea of the cunning Russian trap was perpetuated and enhanced after the battle of Stalingrad by many survivors and German historians of the Cold War period, who ignored the rather obvious fact that Stalin's greatest mistake since the invasion had been to refuse to let his forces retreat. The Red Army's starting to withdraw ahead of the Germans in July 1942 was not part of a devilish plan. Quite simply, Stalin had at last accepted the wisdom of allowing commanders to evade encirclement.

As a result, the German pincer attack west of the Don closed uselessly.

The *Stavka*, however, was agreed that Voronezh, a vital communications centre, should be defended to the last. They knew that if they did not hold on there, and prevent the Germans advancing across the upper Don, then the whole of Timoshenko's South-Western Front would be outflanked.

Voronezh was to be the first major battle for the recently mechanized 24th Panzer Division, which until the year before had been the Wehrmacht's only cavalry division. Flanked by the *Grossdeutschland* and 16th Motorized Divisions, 24th Panzer Division charged headlong at Voronezh. Its panzer grenadiers reached the Don on 3 July, and secured a bridgehead on the far side. The following evening, panzer grenadiers from the *Grossdeutschland* captured the bridge on the main road to Voronezh in an audacious *coup de main*, before the Russians realized what had happened.

Hitler flew once more to Poltava, on 3 July, with his retinue, to consult with Field Marshal von Bock. He was again in triumphant mood with the capture of Sevastopol, and had just made Manstein a field marshal. 'During the conversation', wrote Bock in his diary, 'the Führer took great pleasure in the idea that the English get rid of any general when things go wrong, and thus were burying any initiative in their army!' The German generals present were forced to join in the sycophantic laughter. Although the Führer was clearly in exuberant form, he was also anxious not to allow the Soviet armies to escape, especially those south-east of Voronezh within the Don bends. It looked as if the town would fall rapidly.

Hitler then made a disastrous compromise decision. He allowed Bock to continue the battle for Voronezh with the one panzer corps already engaged, while sending the rest of Hoth's army southwards. But the German forces left behind lacked the strength to achieve a rapid result. The Soviet defenders held out in ferocious street-fighting, where the Germans lost their main advantages.

More by happenstance than strategy, the fighting at Voronezh was part of a phase for the Red Army of concentrating defence on cities, not on arbitrary lines on the map. The new flexibility had allowed

Timoshenko's armies to pull back, avoiding encirclement, but they had already been so badly mauled that on 12 July a new army group command – the Stalingrad Front – was established by *Stavka* directive. Although nobody dared voice the defeatist suggestion that the Red Army might be forced back as far as the Volga, a suspicion began to grow that this was where the main battle would have to be fought. The most significant evidence was the prompt dispatch from Saratov of the 10th NKVD Rifle Division, whose five regiments came from the Urals and Siberia. Its divisional headquarters took over command of all local NKVD units and militia battalions, set up an armoured train detachment and two tank-training battalions, and took control of the river traffic across the Volga.

These seemed glorious days for German front-line regiments. 'As far as the eye can see', wrote an observer, 'armoured vehicles and half-tracks are rolling forward over the steppe. Pennants float in the shimmering afternoon air.' Commanders stood fearlessly erect in their tank turrets, one arm raised high, waving their companies forward. Their tracks stirred up dust and propelled it outwards like smoke clouds in their wake.

These days were especially intoxicating for young officers, racing to retake Rostov-on-Don. The recovery of their morale with the spring weather, the new equipment and the great success at Kharkov had laid to rest the nightmare of the previous winter. 'It was almost as if we had two parts to our head,' explained Count Clemens von Kageneck, a lieutenant in 3rd Panzer Division soon to win the Knight's Cross with Oak Leaves. 'We were charging ahead exultantly and yet we knew that the enemy would attack again in the winter.' They had also half-forgotten Russia's ability, with its huge distances, extreme weather and bad roads, to grind down their modern machinery and force them back to the tactics and conditions of the First World War.

In the early months of the campaign, the infantry calculated carefully how far they had marched since they crossed the frontier on the morning of Barbarossa. Now they did not bother any longer. They tramped ahead, their faces caked with sweat and dust, at the '10-Kilometer-Tempo' (six miles per hour) in an attempt to keep up with the motorized formations. Panzer commanders also seemed to forget that the artillery of most German divisions was still unmechanized, their plodding trace-horses coughing regularly in the dust-clouds, and gun crews swaying with fatigue on their backs. Yet technology and the flatness of the steppe brought one great advantage. Any wounded from the advance-to-contact engagements were rapidly evacuated by 'Sanitäts-Ju', a Junkers 52 converted into an air ambulance.

Struck by the limitless horizon and expanse of sky, and perhaps also influenced by the sight of vehicles swaying crazily in and out of potholes like ships in a heavy swell, the more imaginative saw the steppe as an uncharted sea. General Strecker described it in a letter as 'an ocean that might drown the invader'. Villages became the equivalent of islands. In the sun-baked steppe, they also offered the most likely source of water. But a panzer commander might spot an onion-domed church tower in the distance, then on arrival, find beside it the rest of the village destroyed, perhaps with timbers still smouldering. Only the brick chimneys remained standing. The carcasses of horses and livestock lay around, their bellies swollen in the heat forcing their legs grotesquely in the air. Often, the only sign of life would be the odd cat, miaowing in the ruins.

In a village unscathed by the fighting, an old peasant might appear hesitantly, then snatch off his cap as if for a *barin* before the revolution, and hurry to draw water for the visitors. Some of the village women might meanwhile be driving their geese off into a nearby gully or copse, to conceal them, but they soon found that German soldiers had as good a nose as any Communist Party requisition group.

Soldiers did not just take turnips and onions from the fields, they raided almost every allotment or kitchen garden that they passed. Chickens, ducks and geese were the favourite spoils of war because they were so portable and easy to prepare for the pot. Clemens Podewils, a war correspondent attached to the Sixth Army, described in his diary the arrival of a combat group in one village on 30 June following a sharp skirmish. 'Black figures jump down from tanks and half-tracks. Suddenly a great execution is carried out. The poultry, with bloody ruffs and beating their wings in a paroxysm, was carried back to the vehicles. The men jumped back on board, the tank tracks ground the soil, and the vehicles moved on again.' The one thing which they did not bother to take from the locals that summer was their sunflower seeds, which German soldiers jokingly called 'Russian chocolates'.

There is an unsettling disparity in many accounts, with no connection made between horrifying scenes and their own involvement. 'A really small boy stood in our way,' wrote a twenty-year-old theology student in a letter. 'He no longer begged, he just muttered: "*Pan*, bread". It was eerie how much sorrow, suffering and apathy could exist in a child's face.' Shortly afterwards, the same theology student turned soldier, just before his death, revealed the lyricism of an early nineteenth-century Romantic: 'Germany, I have not yet used this word, you country of big, strong hearts. You are my home. It is worth one's life becoming a seed for you.'

German allies looted with their own paradoxical notion of morality that it must be right to steal from Communists. 'Our lads have stolen three jugs of milk,' wrote a Hungarian corporal in his diary. 'The women had brought the milk down to the basement, when our lads appeared with grenades and pretended to throw them. The women were scared and ran away, and our lads took the milk. We pray to God to help us in future as well.'

That July, Hitler became increasingly impatient with delays that were essentially his own fault. Panzer divisions would streak ahead in sudden breakthroughs, but then came to a halt at a crucial moment when fuel ran out. This represented a doubly goading delay for the Führer, with his eyes constantly straying across the map to the oilfields of the Caucasus.

His feverish mood pushed him into the most disastrous change of plan, which in fact wasted more time and more precious fuel as formations were redirected. The central stage of Operation Blue had been a rapid advance by Sixth Army and Fourth Panzer Army towards Stalingrad to cut off Timoshenko's retreating troops, before the attack was launched against Rostov and across the lower Don into the Caucasus. But Hitler was so desperate to speed the attack into the

Caucasus, that he decided to run the two stages concurrently. This, of course, greatly reduced the concentration of force. Entirely against Halder's advice, he diverted Hoth's Fourth Panzer Army southwards and also deprived Sixth Army of XL Panzer Corps, thus slowing its advance down into a slow, frontal assault towards Stalingrad.

Field Marshal von Bock could not conceal his exasperation at the Führer's arbitrary decision to split Operation Blue from a coherent two-stage whole into two totally separate parts. Hitler also decided to divide Army Group South into two. Field Marshal List, a Bavarian, was to take Army Group A into the Caucasus, while Field Marshal Baron von Weichs was to command Army Group B, with the Sixth Army as its largest formation. The Führer, only too well aware of Bock's disapproval, dismissed him, blaming him for the delay at Voronezh. Hitler thus changed not only the organization, but also the timing and the sequence which formed the logic of Operation Blue. His next step, two weeks later, was to increase its scope considerably, while reducing the forces available still further.

The Führer's attention was focused firmly on the approaches to the Caucasus, as he waited impatiently for signs of a great battle of encirclement, trapping Timoshenko's forces on the steppe north of Rostov. But the only encirclement achieved was a comparatively small one by XL Panzer Corps at Millerovo on 17 July. The panzer divisions, wasting no time, left other troops to round them up. They wheeled south-eastwards, and their point units reached the town and railway station of Morozovsk on the following day. On the next day after that, they reached the lower Don, an advance of 125 miles in just over three days.

Once again, the fate awaiting Soviet prisoners was terrible. Stepan Ignatevich Odiniktsev, a clerk in 60th Cavalry Division, was one of those captured at Millerovo on 17 July. Along with thousands of other Russian prisoners, he was herded to a makeshift cage at Morozovsk, next to the main railway line which ran east to Stalingrad and westwards back through the Ukraine. Some prisoners were dispersed over the following weeks to other hastily erected camps, and Odiniktsev found himself in another open barbed-wire cage near the village of Golubaya. 'We were starved to death,' he recounted after being found over three months later by Red Army troops. 'On the best days we received a little rye in boiled water. Meat from a dead horse was a delicacy. We were constantly beaten with rifle butts, sometimes without any reason. Each day, dozens of people died from starvation or beating.' Although the NKVD was highly suspicious of any Red Army soldier taken by the Germans, Odiniktsev's interrogator believed his story. 'This man', he scribbled in pencil at the bottom of the typed report, 'looks like a skeleton covered with skin.'

So rapid was the German advance at this time that, on 19 July, Stalin personally ordered the Stalingrad Defence Committee to prepare the city for war immediately. The *Stavka* feared that Rostov would not hold out for long. The Seventeenth Army was poised to cross the Don on the Black Sea side, First Panzer Army was advancing on the city from the north, and part of Fourth Panzer Army was about to strike across the Don to the east of it. On 23 July, 13th and 22nd Panzer Divisions backed by panzer grenadiers from the SS *Wiking* Division, struck right into the heart of Rostov as far as the main Don bridge. Fighting in the city was fierce, especially the defence by NKVD troops of their headquarters, but by the end of the following day, the last main pockets of resistance were crushed in an operation of systematic clearance, building by building. The Führer was exultant. The retaking of Rostov obliterated his bad memories of the previous winter.

Hitler had arrived at his new advanced headquarters at the Ukrainian town of Vinnitsa on 16 July. As an alternative to the *Wolfsschanze* at Rastenburg, it was code-named *Werwolf*. (The word Wolf, the old German version of Adolf, clearly gave the Führer an atavistic thrill.) He was no doubt reassured to know that Vinnitsa was '*Judenrein*' – 'cleansed of Jews' – after mass executions by a police battalion the previous autumn. The town, it later transpired, had also been the site of Stalinist atrocities in 1938 when NKVD troops massacred over 10,000 Ukrainians, but the Germans did not discover the graves until 1943.

The *Werwolf* complex of large and comfortable log cabins had been built in a pine wood north of the town. The deceptively simple

'Führer house' was built round a private courtyard. Hitler, paranoid in enemy territory, also had a concrete bunker. His bodyguard, Rattenhuber, described the security precautions at Vinnitsa during his interrogation by SMERSH officers soon after the end of the war. Stalin, who was obsessed with every personal detail about Hitler, received a special report from Abakumov, the head of SMERSH.

The effort and attention to detail, when serving the Führer's needs and safety, were reminiscent of a Byzantine court. Before he arrived, Gestapo teams searched the walls for microphones and explosives. A large vegetable garden was organized by a German horticultural firm, Zeidenspiner, and dug by the Todt Organisation. Hitler's personal chef, Hauptsturmführer Fater, had to go out to select the vegetables himself. Any other vegetable destined for the Führer's plate had to be dug up under the eye of an appointed courier who then brought the produce direct to the kitchen. All the food was chemically analysed before cooking, and sampled by a taster before it reached his plate. Samples from the water supply also had to be checked several times a day. Mineral water was bottled in the presence of couriers, and brought in. Even the laundry was X-rayed to ensure that no explosive had been concealed. Oxygen tanks were stored outside the bunker ready to pump in air, because Hitler was afraid of noxious vapours from the ferroconcrete. The Gestapo supervised the filling of these tanks and tested them regularly.

The Führer's stay during the second part of July coincided with a period of great heat. The temperature was close to forty degrees. Hitler, sweating profusely, was most uncomfortable, especially in his state of feverish impatience during the advance on Rostov. Unable to bear the wait, he kept goading Halder to speed the operation. He had so convinced himself that the Red Army was in the final stages of collapse that on 23 July he rewrote Operation Blue, in Führer Directive No. 45. 'In a campaign which has lasted little more than three weeks, the deep objectives outlined by me for the south flank of the Eastern Front have been largely achieved. Only weak enemy forces have succeeded in escaping encirclement and reaching the far bank of the Don.'

Hitler, having already ignored the strategic rationale on which the whole plan had been based, now increased its objectives at a stroke. Sixth Army would take and occupy Stalingrad. He was no longer content with the original idea of just advancing to the Volga and destroying the arms factories. Paulus should then send motorized groups down the Volga to Astrakhan on the Caspian Sea. Army Group A under Field Marshal List was now ordered to seize the whole of the eastern seaboard of the Black Sea and most of the rest of the Caucasus.

List, on receiving this order two days later, stared in disbelief. He could only conclude that Hitler possessed intelligence confirming the collapse of the Red Army which had not been passed down. The army commanders also heard that Manstein's Eleventh Army, having now completed the conquest of the Crimea, was leaving for the Leningrad front, and that the *Grossdeutschland* and the SS *Leibstand-arte* panzer grenadier divisions were to be sent back to France. 'The constant underestimation of enemy potential', wrote Halder in his diary, 'is gradually taking on a grotesque form and becoming dangerous.'

Hitler tried to justify this high-risk gamble on the basis of reinforcements arriving from their allies. Although the Führer could be most persuasive in his full, uplifting, propaganda flow – what Rommel cynically called a 'sun-ray cure' – he convinced few generals on this particular subject. When he spoke in grandiose terms of the Third and Fourth Romanian Armies, the Second Hungarian Army and the Eighth Italian Army, they knew perfectly well that they could never be equated to a full German corps, let alone an army, mainly because of their lack of defence against tank attack. German generals also shared the opinion formed by Field Marshal von Rundstedt about this 'absolute League of Nations army', which included Romanians (whose officers and NCOs were in his view 'beyond description'), Italians ('terrible people') and Hungarians ('only wanted to get home quickly'). With a couple of exceptions, such as the Slovaks ('first rate, very unassuming') and Romanian mountain troops, he and other German commanders considered them ill-equipped, ill-armed, ill-trained, and completely unprepared for warfare on the *Ostfront*.

Although arrogantly expressed, many of Rundstedt's observations are confirmed from other sources. Diaries, letters and Soviet interrogation reports make the lot of allied soldiers and NCOs painfully, and sometimes pathetically, clear. Corporal István Balogh was part of the 1st Hungarian Motorized Brigade which left Budapest railway station on 18 June, 'amid silent people and sad sounds of bugles', destined for 'the blood-soaked land of Russia'. 'Mother of God guarding over Hungary,' he wrote in a minute diary, which was taken from his body on the bank of the river Don three months later and sent to Moscow, 'pray for us and defend us from all sins and disasters! Amen.' Moods were very mixed as they departed, with sadness, an ancient dread of the Russian steppe and moments of febrile optimism. In some of the troop trains 'songs were heard', another Hungarian recounted later when interrogated. 'Soldiers and officers drank wine and there was gaiety. Nobody knew what war was really like.'

Five days later, Balogh's train passed some of the battlegrounds of the previous year. 'Everywhere crushed Russian tanks can still be seen. We look at them and fear the idea of this Red hell moving against Hungary. Thanks be to God that this has been stopped. We are firmly confident that we shall smash the Red danger for Europe.' On 1 July at Ivanovka, they heard artillery fire for the first time. 'Everywhere the remains of burnt-out German vehicles can be seen. Aren't the Germans starting to lose their military luck? Believe in God so that good fortune will stay with us in spite of some defeats.'

The vast majority of all allied soldiers were conscripts, of whom at least half were illiterate. A lack of familiarity with technological advance made them liable to panic if attacked by tanks or aircraft. Their daily pay, as a Romanian cavalry lieutenant acknowledged when captured, was only 'enough to buy one litre of milk'. The medical services appeared to have changed little since the previous century.

Morale in Hungarian units was not improved by the way the officers treated their men. Field punishment in the allied armies could be arbitrary, if not chaotic. 'A man went to his comrade without the permission of his detachment commander,' Corporal Balogh recorded on 3 July. 'They wanted to hang him, but changed the punishment to eight hours' guard at night, but this was also postponed. Three other soldiers were hanged, however. To my regret, it is as if we were still living in the fourteenth century.' Romanian soldiers could still be condemned to flogging by their officers. Disciplinary measures had become even more necessary after the Romanian forces suffered 98,000 casualties in the siege of Odessa during the late summer of 1941. Few of them had understood the reason for continuing to advance east of the Dniester, once Bessarabia had been reoccupied.

The Balkan attitude to war remained primitive in other ways. A number of soldiers expressed their disappointment at the shortage of pickings in Russia after all that their officers had promised them. 'The habit of looting is in the blood of Germans and Hungarians alike,' one of them naively admitted to his NKVD interrogator after capture.

The true weakness of these allied armies was not put to the test until that autumn. By the time that Hitler came to recognize, but not to acknowledge, the mistake, it was too late to evade disaster. When one contemplates Hitler's almost compulsively over-optimistic ambitions at this stage, it is clear that he never read, or never digested, Leo Tolstoy's tale, 'How Much Land Does a Man Need?' written in 1886. In it a wealthy peasant named Pahom is told of the rich earth in the land of the Bashkirs beyond the Volga. They are simple folk and he will be able to get all the land he wants from them without much trouble. When Pahom reaches the land of the Bashkirs, they tell him that for a thousand roubles he can have as much land as he can walk round in a day. Pahom, despising them for their lack of sophistication, is exultant. He is certain that he can enclose a huge distance. Almost as soon as he starts out, however, he spots one attractive feature after another that he decides to include, a pond over there, or a stretch of land that would be good for flax. Then, he notices that the sun is starting to go down. Realizing that he risks losing everything, he runs faster and faster to make it back in time. 'I have grasped too much', he tells himself, 'and ruined the whole affair.' The effort kills him. He dies at the finishing post, and that is where he is buried. 'Six feet from his head to his heels was all he needed,' was Tolstoy's conclusion. The difference in the story less than sixty years later was that it was not a single man buried there in the steppe, but hundreds of thousands of proxies.

7

'Not One Step Backwards'

On 28 July 1942, while Hitler was still celebrating the capture of Rostov, Stalin sensed that the moment of crisis was at hand. Soviet forces retreating from Paulus's Sixth Army faced annihilation west of the Don. If the Germans then advanced across the Volga, forty miles further on, the country would be cut in two. Convoy PQ-17 had just been destroyed in the Barents Sea and the new Anglo-American supply line across Persia would soon be threatened. The Soviet Union faced strangulation.

That day, Stalin suddenly stopped pacing up and down his office in the Kremlin while listening to a report from General Vasilevsky. 'They've forgotten my *Stavka* Order!' he burst out. This order, issued the previous August, stated that 'anyone who removes his insignia during battle and surrenders should be regarded as a malicious deserter, whose family is to be arrested as the family of a breaker of the oath and betrayer of the Motherland. Such deserters are to be shot on the spot. Those falling into encirclement . . . and who prefer to surrender are to be destroyed by any means, while their families are to be deprived of all state allowance and assistance.'

'They've forgotten it!' Stalin said again. 'Write a new one on the same lines.'

'When do you want me to report with the new order?' Vasilevsky asked.

'Today. Come back as soon as it is ready.'

Vasilevsky returned that evening with the draft of Order No. 227, more commonly known as 'Not One Step Backwards'. Stalin made many changes, then signed it. The order was to be read to all troops in the Red Army. 'Panic-mongers and cowards must be destroyed on the spot. The retreat mentality must be decisively eliminated. Army commanders who have allowed the voluntary abandonment of positions must be removed and sent for immediate trial by military tribunal.' Anyone who surrendered was 'a traitor to the Motherland'. Each army had to organize 'three to five well-armed detachments (up to 200 men each)' to form a second line to shoot down any soldier who tried to run away. Zhukov implemented this order on the Western Front within ten days, using tanks manned by specially selected officers. They followed the first wave of an attack, ready 'to combat cowardice', by opening fire on any soldiers who wavered.

Three camps were set up for the interrogation of anyone who had escaped from German custody or encirclement. Commanders permitting retreat were to be stripped of their rank and sent to penal companies or battalions. The first on the Stalingrad Front came into being three weeks later on 22 August, the day before the Germans reached the Volga.

Penal companies – *shtrafroty* – were to perform semi-suicidal tasks such as mine clearance during an attack. Altogether some 422,700 Red Army men would 'atone with their blood for the crimes they have committed before the Motherland'. The idea so appealed to the Soviet authorities that civilian prisoners were transferred from the Gulag to *shtraf* units, some say almost a million, but this may well be an exaggeration. Promises of redemption through bravery usually proved to be false, mainly because of bureaucratic indifference. Men were left to die in their ranks. On the Stalingrad Front, the 51st Army was told to round up officers who had escaped from encirclement. The first group of fifty-eight officers heard that they would be sent in front of a commission to allocate them to new units, but nobody bothered to interrogate them. Instead, they found themselves, without trial or warning, in penal companies. By the time the mistake came to light nearly two months later, they were 'already wounded or killed'.

The system of NKVD Special Departments, re-established the year before to deal with 'traitors, deserters and cowards', was strengthened. The Special Department or OO (*Osobyi Otdel*) dated back to 1919, when Lenin and Felix Dzerzhinsky, the head of the Cheka, wanted complete control over the armed forces. In April 1943, less than two months after the battle of Stalingrad finished, the Special Departments, under their chief, Viktor Abakumov, became SMERSH, the acronym for *Smert Shpionam* – Death to Spies.

Rifle divisions had an NKVD Special Department staff of up to twenty officers, with one 'operational representative' per battalion, and a headquarters guard unit of twenty to thirty men, who held prisoners and executed 'cowards and traitors'. The Special Department officer recruited his own agents and informers. According to a former SMERSH informer, he tended to be 'pale because they usually worked during the night', and, on parade, he 'looked closely in our faces as if he knew something bad about each one of us'.

NKVD Special Departments took their work of rooting out spies and traitors with great seriousness. An officer, using the name Brunny, wrote to the author and journalist Ilya Ehrenburg complaining that the newspapers did not publish enough in praise of the Special Departments. 'It is very difficult to discover an experienced fascist spy. This requires great intelligence and a good eye. An NKVD soldier should be very keen and know the special rules of this game. The press publishes much about the terrible deeds of the Germans, which is necessary. But it is also important to make our soldiers hate traitors.'

The Wehrmacht tried to exploit the Stalinist approach to loyalty. One German instruction strongly recommended that Soviet prisoners should be warned 'of the treatment which awaits them at the hands of the NKVD' should they manage to escape 'from German captivity and return to the Red Army'.

Another department of the NKVD, set up by Beria in the autumn of 1939, dealt with enemy prisoners of war. Its first major task had been the liquidation of over 4,000 Polish officers in the forest at Katyn. In the summer of 1942, however, its officers were underemployed because so few Germans were captured during the Axis advance.

Every member of a small detachment from the 29th Motorized Division of Fourth Panzer Army was interrogated by Lieutenant Lepinskaya from the political department of South-Western Front headquarters. Her questions to gauge their morale provided little encouraging material. 'Most of the soldiers want to fight to the end,' she had to report. 'No cases of desertion or self-inflicted wounds. Officers strict but fair.'

Lepinskaya had more luck with Romanian prisoners. An officer admitted that his men hated Marshal Antonescu for having 'sold their motherland to Germany'. Romanian soldiers were even more forthcoming. They told her of 'fist-fights with Germans', even that a German officer had been killed after he shot two of their comrades. Their own officers were 'very rude' to them and often struck them. There had been numerous cases of self-inflicted wounds, despite lectures from officers that they were 'a sin against the Motherland and God'. Lepinskaya concluded that the Romanians were clearly in a 'low political moral state'. Her report was passed rapidly back to Moscow.

The advance across the Don steppe provided many mixed experiences for the Sixth Army after the winter snows. General Strecker, the commander of XI Corps, found it 'as hot as Africa, with huge dust clouds'. On 22 July, his chief of staff, Helmuth Groscurth, recorded a temperature of '53 degrees in the sun'.

Sudden rains, while temporarily turning tracks to mire, did little to solve the water shortage, which was the main preoccupation of the German *Landser* during that time. The Red Army polluted wells during the retreat, while collective farm buildings were destroyed, and tractors and cattle driven to the rear. Supplies which could not be moved in time were rendered unusable. 'The Russians have poured petrol over the grain supplies,' a corporal wrote home on 10 August. 'Soviet bombers drop phosphorus bombs at night to set the steppe on fire,' reported a panzer division. But many of the columns of black smoke on the horizon were started by cordite burns round artillery positions.

The German gunners in shorts, with their bronzed torsos muscled from the lifting of shells, looked like athletes from a Nazi propaganda film, but conditions were not as healthy as they might have appeared. Cases of dysentery, typhus and paratyphus began to increase. Around field ambulances, cookhouses and especially butchery sections, 'the plague of flies was horrible', reported one doctor. They were most dangerous for those with open wounds, such as the burns of tank crewmen. The continual movement forward made it very difficult to care for the sick and wounded. Evacuation by a 'Sanitäts-Ju' air ambulance was the best hope, but Hitler's insistence on speed meant that almost every transport aircraft had been diverted to deliver fuel to halted panzer divisions.

For soldiers of the Sixth Army, the summer of 1942 offered the last idylls of war. In Don Cossack country, the villages of whitewashed cottages with thatched roofs, surrounded by small cherry orchards, willows and horses in meadows provided an attractive contrast to the usual dilapidation of villages taken over by collective farms. Most of the civilians, who had stayed behind in defiance of Communist evacuation orders, were friendly. Many of the older men had fought the Bolsheviks in the Russian civil war. Only the previous spring, just a few weeks before the German invasion, Cossacks had risen in revolt at Shakhty, north of Rostov, declaring an independent republic. This had been stamped out by NKVD troops with a rapid and predictable brutality.

To the surprise of a company commander in the 384th Infantry Division, Cossacks remained friendly even after looting by his soldiers. They handed over eggs, milk, salted cucumber and even a whole ham as a gift. He then arranged to purchase geese for two Reichsmarks a bird. 'To be honest, people give everything they have if you treat them correctly,' he wrote in his diary. 'I've never eaten so much as here. We eat honey with spoons until we're sick, and in the evening we eat boiled ham.'

During the rapid German advances, Stalin sought to blame his generals. He kept changing commanders in the vain hope that a ruthless new leader could galvanize resistance and transform the situation. He even rang one army commander to dismiss him, then told him to call to the telephone one of his own corps commanders who was to be his replacement. A sense of failure and disaster spread, destroying the confidence partially rebuilt after the battle before Moscow. The Red Army, still suffering from Stalin's premature offensives early in the year, lacked trained troops and experienced NCOs and officers. Most of the conscripts hurled into battle had often received little more than a dozen days' training, some even less. Young peasants drafted in from collective farms were pitifully ignorant of modern warfare and weaponry. A cavalryman who found an aluminium tube on the ground thought he could use it as a handle for his horsebrush. It proved to be an incendiary bomb, which blew up in his hands.

The Germans never ceased to be astonished at the profligacy of Russian commanders with their men's lives. One of the worst examples came during the defensive battles west of the Don. Three battalions of trainee officers, without weapons or rations, were sent against the 16th Panzer Division. Their commandant, who surrendered after the massacre, told his captors that when he had protested 'about this senseless task', the army commander, who was clearly drunk, had bellowed at him to get on with it.

The Red Army still suffered from the old fear of initiative left from the purges. But out of the latest disasters in the south, which finally destroyed the reputations of Stalinist witch-hunters, a new breed of commander was starting to emerge – energetic, pitiless and much less afraid of commissars and the NKVD. Zhukov's achievements provided the light and the hope for many other rising officers, furious at the Red Army's humiliations.

General Vasily Chuikov, soon to become the army commander in Stalingrad, was one of the most ruthless of this new generation. His explosions of temper were compared to those of Zhukov. His strong, peasant face and thick hair were typically Russian. He also had a robust sense of humour and a bandit laugh which exposed gold-crowned teeth. Soviet propaganda later portrayed him as the ideal product of the October Revolution.

Chuikov had missed the first disastrous six months of war, having been in China as a military attaché accredited to Chiang Kai-shek.

After his recall to the Soviet Union, he became acting commander of a reserve army near Tula. Early in July, when still suffering from a spinal injury, he received orders to move his incomplete divisions, now designated the 64th Army, to hold the Germans west of the Don.

Chuikov, accompanied by his chief commissar, Konstantin Kirkovich Abramov, reached Stalingrad Front headquarters on 16 July. They heard that the enemy was advancing rapidly towards the Don, but nobody had any details. The 62nd Army was spread out on the upper part of the Don's eastern loop, and Chuikov had to bring his divisions in to cover the lower part, south of the river Chir. He was understandably worried about the morale of the army on his left, having intercepted a lorry full of officers with spare cans of fuel, escaping to the rear without permission.

Just to his right, above the river Chir, the Austrian 44th Infantry Division was heavily engaged against three divisions of 62nd Army. The fighting was particularly brutal. A captured corporal told his interrogator that an officer had ordered them to shoot two wounded Red Army soldiers they had found 'hiding in a ditch'. Further north, however, the Germans had broken through in strength, cutting off many regiments when they reached the Don at Kamensky.

German reconnaissance planes quickly pinpointed the weak points along the Don, and the deployment of Chuikov's forward divisions. On 25 July, the Germans attacked in force. This baptism of fire for the 64th Army was not made any simpler by dust storms, nor by the fact that essential detachments were still stuck behind in Tula. The next morning brought a German armoured attack, and although the panzers terrified the crews of the light T-60 tanks, who tried to hide in gullies, their shells could do little to the heavy KV tanks.

'They had a longer range,' explained a German panzer commander. 'We could not attack them across the open. So, like ships at sea, I pulled my tanks right back out of sight, made a wide detour, and attacked them from behind.' The Russian heavy tanks scattered, except for one which had lost a track; its traverse mechanism had jammed, so the turret could not turn. 'We lined up behind him, and started to shoot. We counted our hits on this tank, but none of them penetrated the armour. Then, I saw the hatch of the tank move. I guessed that they wanted to surrender, so over the radio I told my company to cease fire. The Russians then opened the hatch completely and climbed out.' The crew were totally confused, shaken and deafened, but not one of them was even wounded. 'It was depressing to realize how inferior our tank guns were.'

The German strike through the right flank of 62nd Army to the Don soon caused chaos. A rumour spread in the rear echelons of Chuikov's 64th Army on 26 July that German tanks were about to cut them off. A stampede to the pontoon bridge over the Don began. The panic then infected front-line troops. Chuikov sent staff officers to the river bank to restore order, but German aircraft had already spotted the opportunity. Waves of Richthofen's Stukas appeared and several of Chuikov's senior officers were among those killed.

The 62nd Army was in an even worse position. The 33rd Guards Rifle Division, commanded by Colonel Aleksandr Utvenko, found itself trapped on the west bank of the Don, attacked by two German divisions. 'They would have quickly finished us off if we had not dug ourselves in deeply,' Utvenko told the writer Konstantin Simonov shortly afterwards. His division, down to 3,000 strong, was having to send the wounded on carts and camels to the rear at night. The Germans were also sustaining heavy losses. On just one battalion sector, 513 German corpses were dragged into a *balka*, or gully. The Russians were so short of ammunition that they had to attack to capture enemy guns and ammunition. They had so little to eat that they boiled wheat from surrounding fields. On 11 August, the remains of the division split into small groups to fight through to the Don. 'I myself reloaded my pistol five times,' Utvenko recounted. 'Several commanders shot themselves. Up to 1,000 men were killed, but they sold their lives dearly. One man took a leaflet out of his pocket and started walking towards the Germans. Galya, a woman interpreter on our staff, shouted: "Look at him! The snake is going to surrender!", and she shot him with her pistol.'

The last pocket of resistance, having run out of anti-tank ammunition, was overrun by German panzers. Utvenko and his remaining companions jumped from a small cliff into a marsh, where he was wounded in the feet by shrapnel from a shellburst. Able only to crawl, Utvenko spent the next day hiding in a field of sunflowers with some twenty soldiers. That night, they collected more survivors, and swam across the Don. Eight of them drowned. Utvenko was pulled across by his adjutant, a former gynaecologist called Khudobkin, who had an epileptic fit just after they reached the far bank. Utvenko remarked afterwards that it was fortunate he had not had it in the river. 'If we don't die here,' Khudobkin replied, 'we'll survive the war.' Khudobkin had a particular reason for believing he would live. His mother had received notification of his death in the Crimea, where he had been badly wounded, and she had organized a church service. According to Russian superstition, if your memorial service took place when you were still alive, you would not go to an early grave. Simonov clearly sensed in that terrible summer of 1942 that this idea was symbolic for the whole country.

Despite the disasters and chaos from bad communications, Red Army units continued to fight back. They made the most of night raids, since an attack during daylight immediately brought a response from the Luftwaffe. The German company commander who kept a diary in the 384th Infantry Division recorded on 2 August: 'Russians resisting hard. These are fresh troops and young.' And again the next day: 'Russians resisting hard. They are getting reinforcements all the time. One of our sapper companies avoided battle. Very shameful.' His own soldiers then began to suffer badly from stomach-ache, perhaps due to contaminated water. 'It's terrible here,' he wrote a few days later. 'Such terrifying nights. Every single one of us is tense. One's nerves don't stand a chance.'

In an attempt to counter Luftwaffe air superiority, Red Army aviation regiments were transferred hurriedly from the central and northern fronts. A regiment of night-fighters landing for the first time at a new base to support the Stalingrad Front discovered that their aerodrome was no more than a large field planted with watermelons and surrounded by tomato plants, which the local peasants continued to harvest even while fighters landed and took off. The regiment's presence was soon spotted by a Focke-Wulf reconnaissance aircraft, and when strafing Messerschmitts came in just above ground level, the adjacent peasant market was caught in their fire. In an instant the rural scene became one of total chaos, with panic-stricken horses rearing in the shafts of wagons, children screaming, awnings ripped by machine-gun bullets and stallholders killed among their fruit and vegetables. Less damage was done to the night-fighter regiment, which found itself forced to maintain an exhausting schedule of sorties. Often there was no time to eat at the field kitchen by the side of the runway, so ground crew would bring plates out to the aircraft at dispersal and pilots ate in their cockpit. The rules of security drummed into the ground personnel by commissars were so absolute that they never counted the number of aeroplanes on the field, or even how many failed to return from a mission.

In the confused air skirmishes at this time, Major Kondrashov, the commander of the regiment, was shot down behind German lines. His left leg, which he later lost, was mangled in the crash, but a peasant woman who lived nearby managed to drag him clear of the wreckage and care for him in her house. The site had been marked by fellow pilots from his regiment, and soon after dawn, two of them landed by her house. They carried Kondrashov out and bundled him into the rear seat of one of the aircraft. The pilot then flew him to a military hospital.

Aerial dogfights over the Don during those last days of July and early August attracted the attention of the whole battlefield below. German infantrymen and panzer crews alike would shade their eyes with a hand against the sun, peering up at the blue sky and vapour trails. Russian aircraft generally attacked ground targets at midday. It was such a regular run that Messerschmitt 109s would often make sure that they were around, ready to jump them. There were cheers whenever an enemy machine was hit, and the stricken aircraft, pouring smoke, corkscrewed down and exploded on the ground. The reputation of star fighter pilots began to grow within the German Army as well as the Luftwaffe.

In this war of movement, the staffs of panzer and motorized divisions seldom bothered to have their headquarters camouflaged. Working in hastily pitched tents through the night on new sets of orders, or checking ammunition and casualty returns, they found that their spirit lamps attracted swarms of insects, not enemy bullets. They caught up on sleep during the day, their heads nodding and rolling around, as the headquarters vehicles moved to the next location.

The commander of the 16th Panzer Division, General Hans Hube, would take a nap in the middle of a battle in front of his staff, thus inspiring confidence in his unflappability. 'Papa Hube', as he was known to his troops, made an immediate impression with his powerful, solid face and black artificial hand, having lost an arm in the First World War. Hube was a creature of firm habit and organization. Battle or no battle, he made sure that he ate regularly every three hours, 'consuming so many calories and vitamins'. Although no intellectual he was 'a brilliant, clear-thinking man', according to more than one officer who knew him well. Hitler admired him greatly as a soldier, but because this 'old warhorse' was a realist who said what he felt, the Führer considered him 'too pessimistic' towards the end of the battle of Stalingrad.

A number of Hube's panzer commanders made dismissive remarks about the stupidity of the enemy, leaving tanks halted in the open, and thus presenting perfect targets for Stukas or the 88-mm anti-aircraft guns, deadly in a ground role. They knew that the T-34 was overall a much better armoured fighting vehicle than anything which Germany had yet produced. On the other hand its gunsight was not very good, few Russian commanders had decent binoculars, and even fewer had radios. The Red Army's greatest weakness, however, was its poverty of tactics. Their tank forces failed to use terrain properly and demonstrated little familiarity with the principles of fire and movement. And, as Chuikov readily acknowledged, they were incapable of coordinating attacks with Red Army aviation.

Complacency sometimes led the Germans into relaxing their guard. At first light on 30 July, a group of T-34s, having approached under cover of darkness, surprised Hube's headquarters in a village. Officers struggled into their clothes as shells exploded among the headquarters and rear-echelon vehicles. Podewils, the war correspondent then attached to the division, stuck his head outside. 'Not an encouraging sight', he noted in his diary. 'Vehicles of every sort chaotically trying to overtake each other as fast as they could to get away!' The Germans had also been surprised on the previous day by another unexpected skirmish, which Hube drily called a 'Hussar affair'.

The initial shock was soon over. A company from the 2nd Panzer Regiment arrived, and very soon six T-34s were ablaze in the open on some marshy low ground. One T-34, in a suicidal attack, charged at the divisional transport vehicles in the village, but suddenly encountered a German panzer which, 'with a direct hit at point-blank range, literally blasted its turret into the air'. Hube, after observing the early morning action, remarked to Podewils: 'You'd better go up to the front line. It's safer there.' Podewils and his companion left later in the morning. They drove forward over the corduroy road across the marsh. One of the blackened T-34s still smouldered. It gave off 'the smell of burnt flesh'.

At corps headquarters he heard that over the last eight days the Red Army had sent nearly a thousand tanks across the Don: just over half of them had been destroyed. These figures were greatly exaggerated. The Red Army commander had only 550 tanks allocated, and many of them never managed to cross the Don. Wildly over-optimistic reports from the front were largely to blame. One panzer crewman observed that 'whenever a Russian tank was hit, almost every panzer in the battle claimed it as a kill'. Yet the sight of so many destroyed Russian tanks impressed all who saw it. General von Seydlitz said that from afar the shot-out KVs looked like 'an enormous herd of elephants'. Whatever the exact figure destroyed, many Germans felt convinced that they must be close to total victory. The Russian hydra could not go on for ever growing more heads for them to chop off.

The Führer, again frustrated at the slow progress, reverted to the original plan of the Fourth Panzer Army assisting the Sixth Army to capture Stalingrad. The loss in time and the cost in fuel were not mentioned. Hoth's armoured divisions reacted quickly. Advancing north against very weak opposition, they soon threatened Kotelnikovo, just under a hundred miles south-west of Stalingrad. But the main question was whether they could make up for Hitler's changes of plan. General von Richthofen, on the basis of the air reconnaissance reports, noted in his diary on 2 August: 'The Russians are throwing forces from all directions towards Stalingrad.'

Paulus, in a confident mood according to Richthofen, launched pincer attacks led by 16th and 24th Panzer Divisions and supported by Richthofen's Stukas. After two days of fighting, they surrounded eight rifle divisions and all the artillery left west of the Don. The encirclement was finally accomplished at Kalach. From the top of a small precipice overlooking the 'quiet Don', the first panzer crews gazed across at the town of Kalach in the violet evening light. The setting sun behind their tanks threw long shadows in front of them towards the east. Beyond Kalach, the steppe stretched ahead to Stalingrad. Kalach itself consisted mainly of small workshops, a dilapidated railway station and '*höchst primitiv*' wooden shacks.

After their success, the panzer crews joked among themselves with relief and happiness, coming down from the tension of battle. Songs rang out from some of the tanks. But soon their commanders pulled them back into 'hedgehog' defensive position. After dusk had fallen, the thousands of Russian stragglers trapped on the west bank started to attack, and the night was continually broken with bursts of machine-gun fire, flares and crackling exchanges of rifle fire.

The next day, the Germans started to clear the woods systematically, a number of officers comparing it to a rather large deer shoot. The prisoners taken included a senior signals officer and his personnel, most of whom were women. That night, another battle broke out, this time by moonlight, around the German positions. The following morning, the Germans set fire to the dry brush to drive the remaining Russians out of the woods. Finally, the area was regarded as 'cleansed of enemy'. Few escaped. Of the 181st Rifle Division of 62nd Army, which had been 13,000 strong at the start of the fighting, only 105 men slipped back across the Don.

The fighting had indeed been hard. Many German soldiers did not share Paulus's confidence, nor Hitler's opinion that the enemy was finished. On the first day, the anti-tank battalion of the 371st Infantry

Division lost twenty-three men. More and more often, Sixth Army soldiers, like those in the 389th Infantry Division, were hearing the '*Urrah!*' of charging Soviet infantry. One soldier writing home was utterly dejected by 'the many, many crosses and graves, fresh from yesterday', and the implications for the future. Heavy losses in other divisions also seem to have dented morale. The 76th Infantry Division had to detail extra soldiers for burial parties. One of those men selected told his Russian interrogator, when captured a month later, that he and his two companions had had to deal with seventy-two corpses in a single day. An artillery corporal, on the other hand, who had worked for twenty-nine hours without a proper break, was in no doubt about a victorious outcome for the Wehrmacht. 'The Russians can shoot as much as they want, but we'll shoot more. It's a great pleasure when a couple of hundred Russians attack. One self-propelled assault gun is enough, and they all make a run for it.'

Some units were rewarded with extra rations of chocolate and cigarettes for their exertions, which they enjoyed during the relative cool of the evening. The fighting had been hard. 'The only conso-lation', a pioneer wrote home, 'is that we will be able to have peace and quiet in Stalingrad, where we'll move into winter quarters, and then, just think of it, there'll be a chance of leave.'

Nowhere was Stalin's 'Not one step back' order more applicable than in the threatened city that bore his name. The civil-war battle, which took place when the town was still called Tsaritsyn (in Tartar it meant the town on the Tsaritsa, or yellow river), was invoked along with the myth that Stalin's leadership there had turned the tide against the White armies and saved the Revolution. The regional military committee did not shrink from using every measure to turn the city into a fortress. The task was far from easy. Stalingrad curved for twenty miles along the high western bank of the Volga. The defenders would have a broad stretch of exposed water behind them, across which all supplies and reinforcements would have to come.

Throughout the region, the population was mobilized. All available men and women between sixteen and fifty-five – nearly 200,000 – were mobilized in 'workers' columns', organized by their district

Party committees. As in Moscow the year before, women in kerchiefs and older children were marched out and given long-handled shovels and baskets to dig anti-tank ditches over six feet deep in the sandy earth. While the women dug, army sappers laid heavy anti-tank mines on the western side.

Younger schoolchildren, meanwhile, were put to work building earth walls round the petroleum-storage tanks on the banks of the Volga. Supervised by teachers, they carried the earth on wooden stretchers. A German aircraft suddenly appeared. The girls did not know where to hide, and the explosion from a bomb buried two fourteen-year-old girls. When their classmates dug them out, they found that one of them, Nina Grebennikova, was paralysed with a broken back. Her shocked and weeping friends cleaned off the wooden stretcher, and carried her on it to a Stalingrad hospital, next to where the Tsaritsa gorge opens on to the Volga.

Anti-aircraft defences were a high priority, but many of the guns had not yet received shells. Most batteries were formed with young women, mainly Komsomol members, who had been recruited in April with the inescapably pointed question: 'Do you want to defend your Motherland?' Batteries were sited on both banks of the Volga to defend key installations, such as the power station at Beketovka just to the south, and the large factories in the northern sector of the town. There, the workers on arms-production lines, such as the Stalingrad tractor factory, which had converted to the production of T-34 tanks, received rudimentary military training.

The Stalingrad Defence Committee issued decree after decree. Collective farms were ordered to hand their grain reserves over to the Red Army. Tribunals were set up to try those who failed in their patriotic duty. Failure to denounce a member of the family who deserted or failed to enlist carried a ten-year sentence. The director of a high school ordered to take sixty-six of his seventeen-year-old pupils to enlist them at the district military commission, was put in front of a tribunal because thirty-one of them deserted en route.

Tribunals also dealt *in absentia* with civilian 'deserters', most of them denounced by retreating refugees. Those pronounced guilty were sentenced as a 'Traitor to the Party and to the Soviet State'. All too often guilt was a matter of timing. Y. S., who ran away when her village was bombed, was sentenced to six months' labour camp 'for deserting her place of work', while A. S., who refused to leave her home when the Germans were approaching, was condemned *in absentia* as a 'traitor to the Motherland'. A minimum of ten years in a Gulag labour camp awaited her.

For some time to come, the political department of the Stalingrad Front paid 'special attention to the investigation of male conscripts from regions of the Ukraine liberated by the Red Army in the winter 1941/2'. Those who had 'refused to evacuate' their towns and villages were, by definition, suspect of being 'systematically anti-Soviet' and of having collaborated with the Germans.

Declarations in Moscow about freedom of religion carried little weight in the Stalingrad region. The head of the agricultural bank in one district, who sent his brother, an officer in the Red Army, some prayers, 'advising him to recite them before battle', was condemned for 'Anti-Party action'. Civilians also had to be very careful about commenting on the speed of the German advance or the incompetence of the Russian defence. A. M., a worker in a Volga fish-factory, was accused of 'political and moral degeneracy' and 'counter-revolutionary propaganda' because he allegedly 'praised the Germans and blackened the leaders of the Party, the Government and the Red Army'.

Stalin, warned of the atmosphere of panic behind the front, resorted once again to changing commanders. Having dismissed Timoshenko on 21 July, to replace him with General V. N. Gordov, supervised by Vasilevsky, he then decided in early August to split the front into two commands, with the southern part extending from the Tsaritsa (see Map 6) in the centre of Stalingrad southwards into the Kalmyk steppe. Colonel-General Andrey Yeremenko, who had not yet entirely recovered from his leg wound, on hearing of his appointment to command the southern half, argued against splitting the front through the centre of Stalingrad, but this only irritated the supreme commander-in-chief.

Yeremenko flew down on 4 August in a Douglas transport aircraft and landed at the small airfield on the north-west edge of the city.

Khrushchev met him with a car and they drove to the headquarters. For Yeremenko, the lack of information about the enemy was depressing. Five days later, Stalin reorganized the front commands again and promoted Yeremenko to command both. But Stalin, still nervous, sent Zhukov down to investigate and report back.

The chief danger, as Yeremenko soon spotted, was a simultaneous attack from Paulus's Sixth Army attacking across the Don from the west and Hoth's Fourth Panzer Army attacking from the south-west. The whole of the lower Volga was in danger, and there was panic in Astrakhan after German bombing. The oil refineries by the estuary into the Caspian burned for a week, emitting filthy black clouds. Other raids caused chaos, for the ports were packed with refugees, and the quays piled with factory machinery, destined for evacuation eastwards. Now, apart from the desert, the only escape route was across the Caspian Sea.

Few forces were available to oppose Hoth's forces in the semi-barren Kalmyk steppe, which Russians from the north thought of as 'the end of the world'. Lev Lazarev, who commanded a detachment of marine infantry there, said of the area: 'It's not Russia, it's Asia. It was hard to understand the reason to fight for such territory, yet we all knew that we had to stand or die there.' With no soldiers available, the Soviet military authorities had turned to the navy. Brigades of sailors were transferred by rail across Siberia from the Far East fleet. Their officers were eighteen-year-old cadets originally from the naval academy in Leningrad, where they had fought in the early part of the siege. In August, while the sailors were en route from the Far East, the cadets received three weeks' field training on the Kalmyk steppe. These eighteen-year-olds awaited the tough sailors they were to command with trepidation. But they did not disgrace themselves in battle. The casualty rate for the young lieutenants would be terrible. Out of Lazarev's class of twenty-one cadets, only two remained alive the following year.

On the German side, meanwhile, a sense of unease began to grow in spite of their victories. 'After the Don we will advance to the Volga,' wrote the company commander who kept a diary in the 384th Infantry Division. But he recognized the danger. Germany simply did not have 'enough troops to push forward along the whole front'. He began to suspect that the war had developed a momentum of its own. It would not come to an end when they reached the great river that was supposed to mark their final destination.

8

'The Volga is Reached!'

On 21 August 1942, infantry companies from General von Seydlitz's LI Corps crossed the Don at dawn in inflatable assault boats. They rapidly established a bridgehead near the village of Luchinsky. More and more companies paddled furiously over the broad expanse of water. A few miles downstream at Vertyachy, a whole battalion crossed the Don in relays in less than seventy minutes.

Once bridgeheads were secured, pioneer battalions went to work building pontoon bridges to take the tanks and other vehicles of General von Wietersheim's XIV Panzer Corps. The German pioneers, intrigued by the mysterious contrasts of the 'quiet Don', referred to the river affectionately as 'the stream'. A number of soldiers and officers in the Sixth Army seem to have fallen for this stretch of Don Cossack country. Some dreamed of having a farm there once the war was won.

Soon after midday on 22 August, the bridge was ready, and General Hube's 16th Panzer Division, 'the battering ram of the corps', began to cross. The tanks, half-tracks, self-propelled assault guns, eight-wheeled reconnaissance vehicles and trucks rattled deafeningly over the pontoon bridge.

That night, as soon as the moon rose, Russian aircraft began their bombing runs. Vehicles were hit on both banks, and they burned brightly, illuminating the target area, but the bombs continued to miss the bridge itself. Hube's divisional headquarters received reports of skirmishes around the edges of the bridgehead. From time to time, the shrieking whoosh of *Katyusha* rockets from 'Stalin organs' could be heard. The sound was unsettling, but the enemy batteries were firing blind. Behind the infantry screen the laagered panzer troops made final checks on their vehicles, or caught up on a little sleep. At 04.30 hours, as the dawn rose ahead of them in the east, Count von Strachwitz's Abteilung of the 2nd Panzer Regiment, reinforced with panzer grenadier companies, moved forward towards the Volga. The tank crews, conscious of the historic event, found it 'a very exhilarating moment'.

The steppe between the Don and Volga, stone-hard in the summer drought, offered fast going. Tank commanders standing in their turrets, wearing goggles against the dust, had to keep an eye out ahead for a hidden *balka* or gully that might not be visible to the driver. For the first dozen miles, the panzer crews sighted few enemy. The slightly rolling terrain of dry, rough grass seemed eerily empty.

The sun had still not risen high in the sky when General Hube, after a flurry of radio transmissions, suddenly halted his headquarters. Engines were switched off to conserve fuel. They waited in the baking heat. Soon the droning of a small aeroplane could be heard. A Fieseler Storch liaison aircraft appeared. It circled, then came in to land alongside the armoured vehicles. The pilot climbed out and strode over. It was General von Richthofen. Richthofen, now commander-in-chief of the Fourth Air Fleet, hardly bothered to conceal his mood of impatience with the army. 'General Paulus is worried about his left flank,' he had noted in his diary only three days before. He was also displeased when told that the Luftwaffe's main priority was 'to shoot up tanks!' For fighter pilots, ground attack was regarded as menial and unnecessarily dangerous work. It had none of the skill of aerial combat and ran the risk of a lucky shot from the ground when Russian infantry lay flat on their backs and fired away with their rifles.

Richthofen, in shirtsleeves and with his uniform cap pushed back, exposing part of his shaved head, greeted Hube curtly. On orders from Führer headquarters, all of Fourth Air Fleet's resources were to be diverted to the Stalingrad Front, 'to cripple the Russians completely'. 'Make use of today!' he told Hube. 'You'll be supported by 1,200 aircraft. Tomorrow I can't promise you any more.'

In the afternoon, the panzer crews looked up, squinting against the sunlight, to see waves of Junkers 88 and Heinkel 111 bombers, as well as squadrons of Stukas 'in tightly packed groups', flying towards Stalingrad. A mass of shadows passed across the steppe. On their return, the Stuka pilots 'sounded their sirens' to greet the advancing troops. The panzer crews waved back exultantly. In the distance, they could already see the columns of smoke rising from the city, which Sixth Army headquarters, in an excess of propagandistic enthusiasm, described as 'Stalingrad, the city of Stalin, the starting-point of the Red revolution'.

For the citizens of Stalingrad, Sunday, 23 August, was 'a day which will never be forgotten'. The model city of which they were so proud, with its gardens along the high west bank of the Volga and the tall white apartment buildings which gave the place its modern, cubist look, became an inferno.

The loudspeakers in the streets attached to lamp-posts began to repeat: 'Comrades, an air-raid warning has been sounded in the city. Attention, comrades, an air-raid warning . . .' The population had heard so many false air-raid warnings, broadcast in the same monotonous voice, that few took this one seriously at first. Only after anti-aircraft batteries opened fire did people begin to run for cover. Those picnicking on the Mamaev Kurgan, the huge Tartar burial mound which dominated the centre of the city, were the most exposed. Down in the long broad streets which ran parallel to the Volga, the mass of refugees from outlying districts found little protection, apart from trenches in courtyards and gardens dug by block committees for those who could not reach a cellar in time.

Richthofen's aircraft began to carpet-bomb in relays, 'not just industrial targets, but everything', said one student present that day. The high-explosive bombs oscillated gently as they dropped in sticks from the Heinkels. Descriptions of scenes in the city make it hard to imagine anyone surviving outside a cellar. Incendiary bombs showered on the wooden houses down the south-western edge of the city. They burned to the ground, but in the smoking ash, their spindly brick chimneys remained standing in rows like a surrealist graveyard. Closer to the banks of the great river, the shells of the tall white apartment blocks remained standing, even when hit, but most of the floors inside collapsed. Many other buildings were smashed open, or set afire. Mothers cradled dead babies, and children tried to rouse mothers killed beside them. Hundreds of other families were buried alive in rubble.

One German pilot, after his aircraft was hit by one of the women's anti-aircraft batteries, managed to bale out, but when his parachute opened, he drifted straight down into a blaze. Those citizens of Stalingrad who saw his end were so shocked by the onslaught around that even the satisfaction of poetic justice was beyond them.

The huge petroleum-storage tanks on the Volga bank were also hit. A ball of flame rose about 1,500 feet into the sky, and over the following days, the column of black smoke could be seen from over two hundred miles away. Blazing oil spread across the Volga. Bombs destroyed the telephone exchange and waterworks, and the main Stalingrad hospital was straddled by a stick of bombs. Windows were blasted in and children hurled from their beds. They included Nina Grebennikova, the fourteen-year-old whose spine had been broken a week before by the bomb which fell near the petroleum-storage tanks. The attack on the hospital so terrorized members of the staff that they ran away, abandoning their patients, some of whom were left for five days without food or care.

One mother, caught in the open with a daughter whose legs froze in shell-shock, 'literally had to drag her home' through the bombing. No driver would attempt the journey. With virtually all the fathers away at the front, or now mobilized, women were left to cope with the appalling aftermath. Viktor Goncharov's wife, helped by her eleven-year-old son, Nikolay, buried her father's corpse in the yard of their apartment block, which had received a direct hit. 'Before filling in the grave,' the son remembered, 'we searched for his head, but could not find it.' Her mother-in-law, Goncharova, the wife of the Cossack veteran, was lost in the chaos. Somehow the old woman managed to live through the battle to come, surviving for just over five months in a bunker. They did not find each other again until the end of the war, nearly three years later.

The aerial assault on Stalingrad, the most concentrated on the *Ostfront*, represented the natural culmination of Richthofen's career since Guernica.* Fourth Air Fleet aircraft flew a total of 1,600 sorties that day and dropped 1,000 tons of bombs for the loss of only three machines. According to some estimates, there had been nearly 600,000 people in Stalingrad, and 40,000 were killed during the first week of bombardment.

The reason why so many citizens and refugees still remained on the west bank of the Volga was typical of the regime. The NKVD had commandeered almost all river craft, while allotting a very low priority to evacuating the civil population. Then Stalin, deciding that no panic must be allowed, refused to permit the inhabitants of Stalingrad to be evacuated across the Volga. This, he thought, would force the troops, especially the locally raised militia, to defend the city more desperately. 'No one bothered about human beings,' observed one of the boys trapped behind with their mothers. 'We too were just meat for the guns.'

While Richthofen's bombers pounded Stalingrad, the armoured spearhead of 16th Panzer Division had advanced virtually unopposed across the steppe for nearly twenty-five miles. 'Around Gumrak', the division recorded, 'enemy resistance became stronger and anti-aircraft guns began firing wildly at our armoured vehicles from the north-west corner of Stalingrad.'

This resistance came from the batteries operated by young women volunteers, barely out of high school. Few had fired the guns before, owing to the shortage of ammunition, and none of them had been trained to take on targets on the ground. They had switched targets from the bombers over the city on sighting the panzers, whose crews

* There were other echoes of the Spanish Civil War. Rubén Ruiz Ibarruri, the son of La Pasionaria, was killed commanding a machine-gun company of 35th Guards Rifle Division south of Kotluban. Four subsequent Marshals of the Soviet Union closely linked to the battle of Stalingrad – Voronov, Malinovsky, Rokossovsky and Rodimtsev – had been Soviet advisers in Spain, as had General Shumilov, the commander of 64th Army. Voronov had directed the Republican artillery during the siege of Madrid against Franco's Army of Africa.

'seemed to think they were on a Sunday promenade'. The young gun crews furiously wound the handles, depressing the barrels to zero elevation – the Soviet 37-mm anti-aircraft guns were fairly crude copies of the Bofors – and traversed on to the leading armoured vehicles.

The German panzer crews quickly overcame their initial surprise, and deployed to attack some of the batteries. Stukas soon arrived to deal with others. This unequal battle was watched in anguish by Captain Sarkisyan, the commander of a Soviet heavy-mortar battalion, who later related what he saw to the writer Vasily Grossman. Every time the anti-aircraft guns fell silent, Sarkisyan exclaimed: 'Oh, they're finished now! They've been wiped out!' But each time, after a pause, the guns started to fire again. 'This', declared Grossman, 'was the first page of the Stalingrad defence.'

The German spearhead pushed on for the last few miles. At about four in the afternoon, just as the August sunlight was softening, they reached Rynok, to the north of Stalingrad, and there 'the soldiers of the 16th Panzer Division gazed on the Volga, flowing past right before their eyes'. They could hardly believe it. 'We had started early in the morning on the Don,' recalled one of Strachwitz's company commanders, 'and then we were on the Volga'. Somebody in the battalion produced a camera and they took photographs of each other, standing on the backs of their vehicles, gazing through binoculars to the far shore. These were included in Sixth Army headquarters records with the caption: 'The Volga is reached!' The camera, turned southwards, took other souvenir pictures. One showed columns of smoke from the Luftwaffe raids and is recorded as 'view from the outskirts of Stalingrad on fire'.

Soon after their arrival, the fighter ace Kurt Ebener and a companion from the 'Udet' fighter wing wheeled over the Volga just north of Stalingrad. The pilots spotted the tanks and panzer grenadiers below, and 'a feeling of overwhelming joy and relief for their comrades on the ground below' inspired victory rolls and other aerobatics in celebration.

Like the other panzer commanders, Captain Freytag-Loringhoven stood on top of his tank to gaze through binoculars across the wide river. The view was excellent from the much higher western bank. 'We looked at the immense, immense steppe towards Asia, and I was overwhelmed,' he remembered. 'But I could not think about it for very long because we had to make an attack against another anti-aircraft battery that had started firing at us.'

The anti-aircraft battery crews were astonishingly resilient. According to Captain Sarkisyan, 'the girls refused to go down into the bunkers'. One of them, called Masha, is said to have 'stayed at her post for four days without being relieved', and was credited with nine hits. Even if that figure is an exaggeration, like many at the time, the 16th Panzer Division's report casts no doubts on their bravery. 'Right until the late afternoon', stated one account, 'we had to fight, shot for shot, against thirty-seven enemy anti-aircraft positions, manned by tenacious fighting women, until they were all destroyed.'

The panzer troops were horrified when they found that they had been firing at women.* The Russians still find this squeamishness curiously illogical, considering that Richthofen's bombers had killed many thousands of women and children in Stalingrad that very same afternoon. German officers in Stalingrad did not suffer chivalresque illusions much longer. 'It is completely wrong to describe Russian women as "soldiers in skirts",' wrote one of them later. 'The Russian woman has long been fully prepared for combat duties and to fill any post of which a woman might be capable. Russian soldiers treat such women with great wariness.'

The Soviet defenders of Stalingrad were in a dangerous position, partly because General Yeremenko had concentrated most of his available forces to slow Hoth's Fourth Panzer Army advancing on Stalingrad from the south-west. He had never imagined that Paulus's forces would break through so suddenly and so boldly on his right.

Nikita Khrushchev joined him at the underground headquarters

---

* Few members of the Sixth Army seem to have heard about the Sarmatae of the lower Volga – an interbreed of Scythians and Amazons, according to Herodotus – who allowed their women to take part in war.

tunnelled deep into the Tsaritsa gorge. The threat they faced was so urgent that when two engineer officers arrived to report that their men had just finished building a pontoon bridge across the Volga, they were told to destroy it immediately. The two sappers stared at their commander-in-chief in horrified disbelief. Protests were cut short. It is not hard to imagine the panic there would have been in Stalingrad, to say nothing of the reaction in Moscow, if the Germans were to have carried straight through in one swoop and seized a bridgehead on the east bank of the Volga – as Strachwitz had in fact wanted to do.

Stalin was furious when he heard that German troops had reached the Volga. He forbade the mining of factories, the evacuation of machinery or any other action which 'might be taken as a decision to surrender Stalingrad'. The city was to be defended to the very end. The Military Council had posters put up all over the city proclaiming a state of siege: 'We shall never surrender the city of our birth. Let us barricade every street. Let us transform each district, each block, each building into an impregnable fortress.' Many men panicked, including even the secretary of the Stalingrad Komsomol Committee, who 'deserted his post' and fled to the eastern bank without permission.

Those workers not directly involved in producing weapons for immediate use were mobilized in militia 'special brigades' under the commander of the 10th NKVD Division, Colonel Sarayev. Ammunition and rifles were distributed, but many men received a weapon only after a comrade was killed. In the northern industrial suburb of Spartakovka, badly armed worker militia battalions were sent into battle against the 16th Panzer Division with predictable results. Students from the technical university, digging trenches on the northern flank of the city, carried on although already under direct fire from 16th Panzer Division. Their faculty buildings near the Stalingrad tractor plant had been destroyed by bombs dropped in the first waves. The teaching staff helped form the nucleus of a local defence 'destroyer battalion'. One of the professors was a company commander. The battalion commissar was a young woman mechanic from the tractor plant, which had been converted to build T-34s. There, volunteers jumped into the tanks even before they had been painted. As soon as ammunition, stacked in the factory, had been loaded, they drove them off the production line and straight into battle. These tanks lacked gunsights, and could only be aimed at almost point-blank range by the loader peering down the barrel while the gunner traversed the turret.

Hube sent off his motorcycle battalion, probing the northern flank. 'Yesterday we reached the railway line', a corporal wrote home next day, 'and captured a train with weapons and supply vehicles, which had not even been unloaded. We also took many prisoners. Among them were many "soldiers in skirts", whose faces are so repulsive that one can scarcely bear to look at them. Hopefully this operation won't last much longer.' The booty of American Lend–Lease material proved very popular. The officers of 16th Panzer Division especially appreciated the American jeeps, fresh in their new Russian markings, which they considered a much better vehicle than their own equivalent – the Kübelwagen.

Red Army aviation regiments were also thrown into the battle on 24 August, but a Yak stood little chance against a Messerschmitt 109, and the Shturmovik fighter-bombers, although armoured underneath, were extremely vulnerable when tailed by a competent pilot. German soldiers cheered from below when Luftwaffe pilots dispatched their enemy '*mit Eleganz*', as if the air war was a sort of bullfight conducted for the pleasure of spectators on the ground.

German bombing raids on the city continued, with another 'major air attack' on the afternoon of 25 August. The power station at Beketovka was badly damaged, but soon repaired. Otherwise Luftwaffe squadrons continued pulverizing the length of the city. Many people lost all their possessions, but families spontaneously shared whatever they had left. They knew well that the next day they might find themselves in the same state; and nothing reduced the notion of private property more rapidly than such destruction from the sky.

Permission was at last given to allow Stalingrad women and children to cross to the east bank on the NKVD's commandeered craft. Only a few steamers were spared, however, because most were needed for

evacuating wounded and bringing back ammunition and reinforcements. The journey was certainly as hazardous as remaining on the
west bank, because the Luftwaffe continued to attack boats crossing
the Volga. The ferry jetty, upstream of the Tsaritsa gorge, was hit
again, and the Shanghai restaurant just above it, a favourite peacetime
meeting-place in a strip of park on top of the river bank, was burned
to a shell. The families crossing saw blackened bodies floating past
like charred logs, and patches of the river still burned with oil from
the storage tanks. The children from the hospital, including Nina
Grebennikova, tied to a stretcher, were moved across the Volga on
28 August, and taken to a field hospital on the east bank.

The guns of 16th Panzer Division had also been at work since that
first Sunday evening, announcing their presence on the Volga by
sinking a freight steamer and shelling a gunboat. They also shelled
the railway ferry, leaving a tangle of burnt and destroyed carriages,
and over the next few days sank seven river craft. The tank crews
claimed them as 'gunboats' and did not seem to realize that they
might be evacuating civilians.

On their third evening, German panzers sank a paddle-steamer
taking women and children from the city to the east bank. Hearing
screams and cries for help, soldiers asked their commander if they
could use some of the pioneers' inflatable boats to rescue them. But
the lieutenant refused. 'We know how the enemy fights this war,' he
replied. After night had fallen, the panzer crews pulled their blankets
up over their heads so that they did not hear the cries any more.
Some women managed to swim to the west bank, but most swam to
a sandbank where they stayed the whole of the next day. The Germans
did not fire when they were evacuated the next night, as proof that
they were different from the Russians. '*We* wouldn't hinder such a
thing!'

Behind the foremost German positions on the Volga bank was a
sort of semi-cultivated parkland, with oaks, walnut trees, sweet chest-
nut and oleanders, bordered by allotments with melons, tomatoes,
vines and fruit trees. There the advance units of 16th Panzer Division
dug in, using the vegetation for cover. The pioneer battalion's headquarters was hidden under a large pear tree. During lulls in the firing,

panzer crews and combat engineers picked ripe fruit, using caps and helmets as baskets. After the weeks of desiccated steppe, to gaze upon the broad Volga, 'like a calm lake', from leafy shade, somehow intensified the sensation of having reached the end of their journey to the frontier of Europe. It seemed such a pity that the Russians continued to resist. Soldiers, at the very first opportunity, wrote home from the Volga, proud to be among the first to stand at the new eastern extremity of the German Reich. A few who had served in the Balkan campaign the year before found that their first glimpse of white apartment buildings on the high western bank had reminded them of Athens. This curiously inapposite connection led some of them to refer to Stalingrad as the 'Akropolis'.

Units of Sixth Army still waiting to cross the Don were jealous of the glory seized by the vanguard. An anti-aircraft gunner wrote home: 'Soon we too will have the right to sing: "There stands a soldier on the Volga bank".' An artilleryman also wrote home about the *Wolgalied*, for which Franz Lehár wrote the music: 'The song will really be true in our case.'

Many were convinced that victory could not be far off. 'You can't imagine the speed of our dear motorized comrades,' a soldier in the 389th Infantry Division wrote home. 'And with it the rolling attacks of our Luftwaffe. What a feeling of security we get when our pilots are above us, because you never see any Russian aircraft. I would like to share with you a little glimmer of hope. Our division will have fulfilled its duty as soon as Stalingrad falls. We should then, God willing, see each other again this year. If Stalingrad falls, the Russian Army in the south is destroyed.'

The position of Hube's division, however, was far from secure. The threat to the Volga river traffic, to say nothing of furious telephone calls from the Kremlin, increased the urgency for Yeremenko to order counter-attacks from the northern flank to crush the Germans' narrow corridor. Russian artillery could fire into this strip, little more than four miles wide, from both sides, and the Germans were in no position to respond. Not only Hube's 16th Panzer Division, but the rest of Wietersheim's Corps was almost out of fuel.

On 25 August, Richthofen flew to join Paulus and General von Seydlitz at the headquarters of 76th Infantry Division. Paulus's nervous tic on the left side of his face became more pronounced when he was under strain, and he also suffered from recurrent dysentery – what the Germans called 'the Russian sickness' – which did not help him relax. The intolerant Richthofen noted that the commander-in-chief of the Sixth Army was 'very nervous' about the situation. That night, the Luftwaffe dropped supplies to Wietersheim's XIV Panzer Corps by parachute, but most fell into no man's land or into enemy hands. The following morning, German air reconnaissance reported Soviet armoured forces gathering to the north.

Richthofen, like Hitler, subscribed to the view that a rapid victory at Stalingrad would solve all the problems of an extended left flank at a stroke by bringing about the final collapse of the Red Army. To weaken now was the biggest danger, like teetering on a tightrope. Paulus was perfectly aware of such logic. He persevered, keeping his faith in Hitler's judgement that the Russian forces must be all but finished. When General von Wietersheim subsequently recommended the partial withdrawal of XIV Panzer Corps, Paulus dismissed him and promoted General Hube to take his place.

Much depended on the rapid advance of the Fourth Panzer Army from the south, but Hitler had obliged Hoth to leave a panzer corps behind in the Caucasus. He was thus reduced to XLVIII Panzer Corps and IV Corps. Also, as General Strecker observed at this time, 'the closer the German attack gets to the city, the smaller are the daily gains'. An even fiercer defence was being prepared behind the lines. The Stalingrad Defence Committee issued its orders: 'We will not abandon our city to the Germans! All of you, organize brigades, go to build barricades. Barricade every street . . . quickly in such a way so that the soldiers defending Stalingrad will destroy the enemy without mercy!'

On 27 August, the first rain for five weeks fell, but the real cause for delay to Hoth's right flank had come from the resistance put up by Soviet troops around lake Sarpa, and near Tundutovo in the hills south of the Volga bend below Stalingrad. That day, for example, the penal company attached to the 91st Rifle Division repulsed numerous attacks by superior enemy forces. The political department of Stalingrad Front later reported to Shcherbakov: 'Many men have compensated for their faults through bravery and should be rehabilitated and returned to their regiments.' But once again, most of them died long before anything was done.

The advance went better two days later when Hoth suddenly switched XLVIII Panzer Corps over to the left flank out in the Kalmyk steppe. The German Army's chief advantage lay in the close cooperation of the panzer division and the Luftwaffe. In the constantly changing battle, German infantrymen used the red flag with swastika as identification panels on the ground to ensure they were not bombed by their own aircraft. But the real danger of Stukas attacking their own ground forces by mistake came in fast-moving armoured operations.

Lieutenant Max Plakolb, the commander of a small Luftwaffe forward air control section, was attached to the headquarters of 24th Panzer Division. At this time, when 14th and 24th Panzer Divisions and 29th Motorized Infantry Division were starting to swing round the south-west of Stalingrad, Plakolb settled himself at the radio. The point units of 24th Panzer Division had advanced much faster than the neighbouring division, and Plakolb suddenly overheard on his radio a contact report: 'Concentration of enemy vehicles . . .' The pilot then proceeded to give 24th Panzer Division's position. With 'the greatest alarm', since the Stukas were approaching, Plakolb called up the squadron himself, using the code word 'Bonzo', and persuaded them to abort their attack just in time.

So rapid was the advance of XLVIII Panzer Corps from the south that by the evening of 31 August its point units had reached the Stalingrad–Morozovsk railway line. Suddenly, it looked as if an opportunity of cutting off the remnants of the Soviet 62nd and 64th Armies had appeared. Paulus's infantry divisions, slowly advancing eastwards from the Don, could never have got round the Russian rear. The only chance was to send XIV Panzer Corps down from the Rynok corridor to seal the trap, as Army Group headquarters strongly urged. This represented a considerable gamble, and Paulus decided against the plan. Hube would have had to turn his ill-supplied panzers round, break off the running battles and ignore the enemy armies then massing just to the north. Yeremenko, alerted to the danger, pulled his remaining forces back out of the trap.

In some cases the retreat was dictated by panic, rather than design. In 64th Army, the crews of Anti-Aircraft Battery 748 ran away, abandoning their guns. This incident rapidly became a case of conspiracy, in the ever-suspicious eyes of commissars, with the allegation that a member of the battery then 'led a battalion of German submachine-gunners' in an attack against the neighbouring 204th Rifle Division.

On Paulus's northern flank, XIV Panzer Corps had hardly been idle. The Russians continually mounted diversionary attacks on both sides of the corridor. General Hube's responses to these ill-coordinated lunges were sharp and successful. He moved his headquarters on 28 August into a tapering ravine which offered better protection against the nightly air attacks. He ensured himself an undisturbed night's rest by sleeping in a straw-lined pit under his tank.

Russian bombers began to attack by day as well as night, flying in low over the Volga. Black puffs from the German flak guns marked their approach in the morning sky. On one occasion, a German fighter roared in at ground level above Hube's ravine before climbing to attack the bombers in the clear sky. For those watching from the headquarters, this fighter seems to have offered the magical vision of an aerial Teutonic knight in shining armour. 'This silver streak', wrote one of those present in his diary with revealing emotion, 'veered to the east over the river into enemy territory, a crystal, a harbinger of the dawn.'

On 28 August, Russian fighters also attempted to attack the new Luftwaffe base near Kalach, but a Messerschmitt 109 fighter group chased them off. Proud of their victory, the suntanned young fighter pilots assembled for debriefing, but their austere commander – who was known as 'the Prince' because of his resemblance to a medieval statue in a cathedral – did not congratulate them. Instead he passed on the order which had so irritated Richthofen. 'Gentlemen, flying for fun and seeing who can shoot down the most enemy machines must stop. Every machine, every drop of fuel, every hour's flying is irreplaceable. The easy ground life we are leading is completely irresponsible: in the air it is even more so. Every shot must go to assist the infantry, if there is no target in the air.' Resentful murmurs greeted his words.

As is often the case at the end of August, the weather changed suddenly. On Saturday, 29 August, rain fell for almost a whole day and night. Soldiers were soaked, and trenches filled with water. 'This shitty Russia' was a common reaction in letters home at this time. They seemed so close to what they thought was their final objective after an advance of almost four months without respite.

The 16th Panzer Division at Rynok on the bank of the Volga no longer enjoyed its earlier mood of heady optimism. The allotments and orchards in which they had concealed their vehicles had been smashed by Soviet artillery fire, leaving shell craters and trees shattered by shrapnel. They were all concerned by the growing concentrations to the north. Hube would have come under strong pressure earlier if the Russian railhead at Frolovo had been closer to the front, and the Soviet infantry could have deployed more quickly. The 24th Army joined the 66th Army and the 1st Guards Army preparing for a counter-attack. Once formations had detrained, they marched off in different directions, but in the chaos, nobody seemed to know where they were. The 221st Rifle Division did not even know for sure to which army it belonged and its commander had no information on the positions or strength of the enemy.

On 1 September, he ordered the reconnaissance company to go off in groups of ten to find out where the Germans were. With soldiers mounted on local horses, they moved southwards across the Stalingrad–Saratov railway line. The division followed in a mass. Suddenly, German aircraft returning from a raid on the city sighted the advancing force. Some twin-engined Messerschmitt 110s peeled off to strafe them while the other aircraft returned to base to bomb up again. They came back at around midday, but by then the division had deployed and the tempting target was dispersed.

The reconnaissance groups returned having sighted some German units, but they were unable to draw a front line for their commander. It simply did not exist in a recognizable form. The Russian commanders were 'worried and angry'. Although their infantry greatly outnumbered the Germans facing them, none of their tanks, no artillery, and few of their anti-tank guns had arrived.

The situation proved even more disastrous for 64th Rifle Division, which was assembling to the rear. Morale collapsed under German air attacks, which also destroyed its field hospital killing many doctors and nurses. The wounded being taken to the rear recounted tales of horror which unnerved the inexperienced troops waiting in reserve to be marched forward. Individuals, then whole groups, began to desert. The divisional commander ordered the most fragile units to form up. He harangued and cursed them for such a cowardly failure to serve the Motherland. He then adopted the Roman punishment of decimation. With pistol drawn, he walked along the front rank counting in a loud voice. He shot every tenth man through the face at point-blank range until his magazine was empty.

Zhukov, having just been appointed Deputy Supreme Commander, second only to Stalin, had arrived in Stalingrad on 29 August to oversee operations. He soon discovered that the three armies earmarked for the operations were ill-armed, manned by older reservists, and short of ammunition, as well as artillery. On the scrambler line to Moscow, he persuaded Stalin that the attack must be delayed by a week. Stalin agreed, but the German advance to the western edge of the city, now that Seydlitz's corps had linked up with Fourth Panzer Army, alarmed him again on 3 September. He rang General Vasilevsky, the chief of staff, demanding to know the exact position. As soon as Vasilevsky admitted that German tanks had reached the suburbs, his exasperation with Zhukov and other generals exploded. 'What's the matter with them, don't they understand that if we surrender Stalingrad, the south of the country will be cut off from the centre and will probably not be able to defend it? Don't they realize that this is not only a catastrophe for Stalingrad? We would lose our main waterway and soon our oil, too!'

'We are putting everything that can fight into the places under threat,' Vasilevsky replied as calmly as possible. 'I think there's still a chance that we won't lose the city.'

A short time later Stalin rang back, then dictated a signal to be sent to Zhukov. He ordered that the attack must take place immediately, whether or not all the divisions were deployed or had received their artillery. 'Delay at this moment', he insisted, 'is equivalent to a crime.' Stalingrad might fall the very next day. After a long and argumentative telephone call, Zhukov finally persuaded him to wait two more days.

Whether or not Stalin had been right and Zhukov wrong is hard to tell. Paulus had time to reinforce XIV Panzer Corps, and the Luftwaffe took full advantage of its power against targets on the open steppe. The 1st Guards Army managed an advance of only a few miles, while 24th Army was forced right back to its start-line. But at least this unsuccessful offensive managed to deflect Paulus's reserves at the most critical moment, when the tattered remnants of 62nd and 64th Armies fell back to the edge of the city.

The Germans also suffered one of their heaviest casualty rates that summer. No fewer than six battalion commanders were killed in a single day, and a number of companies were reduced to only forty or fifty men each. (Total casualties on the *Ostfront* had now just exceeded one and a half million.) The interrogation of Soviet prisoners indicated the determination which they faced. 'Out of one company,' ran a report, 'only five men were left alive. They have received orders that Stalingrad will never be given up.'

Red Army soldiers felt that they had fought hard and well during the first ten days of the battle. 'Hello my dear ones!' wrote a soldier to his family. 'Since the 23rd of August, we have been constantly involved in hard battles with a cruel cunning enemy. The platoon commander and commissar were badly wounded. I had to take over command. About seventy tanks came towards us. We discussed the situation between comrades and decided to fight to the last drop of blood. When the tanks rolled over the trenches, we threw grenades and bottles filled with petrol.' In a very short space of time, most Russian soldiers became fiercely proud of fighting at Stalingrad. They knew that the thoughts of the whole country were with them. They had few illusions, however, about the desperate fighting which still lay ahead. Stalingrad at this moment had fewer than 40,000 defenders to hold off the Sixth Army and the Fourth Panzer Army. No commander forgot that 'the Volga was the last line of defence before the Urals'.

The Germans were full of confidence during that first week of September. The fighting had been hard, a soldier wrote home, 'but Stalingrad will fall in the next few days'. 'According to what our officers tell us', wrote a gunner in the 305th Infantry Division, 'Stalingrad will certainly fall'. And the sense of triumph at Sixth Army headquarters was undisguised when, on 3 September, a staff officer recorded the link-up between the southern flank of LI Army Corps and the left flank of Fourth Panzer Army: 'The ring round Stalingrad on the west bank of the Volga is closed!' From the crossing of the Don on 23 August up to 8 September the Sixth Army claimed to have taken '26,500 prisoners, and destroyed 350 guns and 830 tanks'.

Paulus received a letter from Colonel Wilhelm Adam, one of his staff officers, who was on sick leave in Germany and bitterly regretted his absence at such a historic moment. 'Here, everyone is awaiting the fall of Stalingrad,' he wrote to his commander-in-chief. 'One hopes it will be a turning point in the war.' Yet on the edge of Stalingrad, the nights suddenly became colder, to the point of finding frost on the ground in the morning and a skim of ice in the canvas buckets for the horses. The Russian winter would soon be upon them again.

Only a very few, however, foresaw the worst obstacle facing the Sixth Army. Richthofen's massive bombing raids had not only failed to destroy the enemy's will, their very force of destruction had turned the city into a perfect killing ground for the Russians to use against them.

Part Three

'THE FATEFUL CITY'

9

'Time is Blood': The September Battles

The first time the German people heard of the city of Stalingrad as a military objective was in a communiqué of 20 August. Just over two weeks later, Hitler, who had never wanted his troops to become involved in street-fighting in Moscow or Leningrad, became determined to sieze this city at any price.

Events on the Caucasus Front, supposedly his main priority, played a major part in his new obsession with Stalingrad. On 7 September, a day when Halder noted 'satisfying progress at Stalingrad', Hitler's exasperation at the failure to advance in the Caucasus came to a head. He refused to accept that Field Marshal List did not have enough troops for the task. General Alfred Jodl, having just returned from a visit to List's headquarters, observed at dinner that List had only followed the Führer's orders. 'That is a lie!' screamed Hitler, and stormed out. As if to prove that he had been misquoted, instructions were sent back to Germany by teleprinter, ordering Reichstag stenographers to be sent to Vinnitsa to take down every word at the daily situation conference.

After the triumphs in Poland, Scandinavia and France, Hitler was often ready to despise mundane requirements, such as fuel supplies and manpower shortages, as if he were above the normal material constraints of war. His explosion on this occasion appears to have brought him to a sort of psychological frontier. General Warlimont, who returned after a week's absence, was so shocked by Hitler's 'long stare of burning hate' that he thought: 'This man has lost face; he has realized that his fatal gamble is over, that Soviet Russia is not going to be beaten in this second attempt.' Nicolaus von Below, the Führer's Luftwaffe adjutant, also returned to find 'a completely new situation'. 'The whole of Hitler's entourage made a uniformly depressing impression. Hitler suddenly was completely withdrawn.'

Hitler probably did sense the truth – he had, after all, told his generals that a failure to take the Caucasus would mean having to end the war – but he still could not accept it. The Volga was cut and Stalingrad's war industries as good as destroyed – both of the objectives defined in Operation Blue – yet he now had to capture the city which bore Stalin's name, as though this in itself would achieve the subjugation of the enemy by other means. The dangerous dreamer had turned to symbolic victory for compensation.

One or two spectacular successes remained to sustain the illusion that Stalingrad would be the crucible in which to prove the superiority of German might. In continued fighting on the north front, Count von Strachwitz, the star commander of 16th Panzer Division, had shown that in a prolonged tank battle success depended on a cool head, straight aim and rapidity of fire. The Russians sent in wave after wave of T-34s and Lend-Lease American tanks. The American vehicles, with their higher profile and thinner protection, proved easy to knock out. Their Soviet crews did not like them. 'The tanks are no good,' a driver told his captors. 'The valves go to pieces, the engine overheats and the transmission is no use.'

'The Russians attacked over a hill,' recalled Freytag-Loringhoven, 'and we were on the reverse slope. Over two days they kept coming in exactly the same way, exposing themselves on the skyline.' More than a hundred were destroyed. 'As far as the eye could see,' a pioneer corporal wrote home, 'there were countless shot-up and burned-out tanks.' The forty-nine-year-old Strachwitz received the Oak Leaves to the Knight's Cross, and was posted back to Germany soon afterwards on account of his age. He handed over command to Freytag-Loringhoven.

The Russian attacks at this point may have been appallingly wasteful and incompetent, but there could be no doubt about the determination to defend Stalingrad at any cost. It was a resolve which more than matched the determination of the invader. 'The hour of courage has struck on the clock . . .', ran Anna Akhmatova's poem at that moment when the very existence of Russia appeared to be in mortal danger.

Since the fall of Rostov, any means of arousing resistance had become permissible. A picture in *Stalinskoe znamia*, the Stalingrad Front newspaper, on 8 September showed a frightened girl with her limbs bound. 'What if your beloved girl is tied up like this by fascists?' said the caption. 'First they'll rape her insolently, then throw her under a tank. Advance warrior. Shoot the enemy. Your duty is to prevent the violator from raping your girl.' Such propaganda – almost a repeat of the theme in Konstantin Simonov's poem 'Kill Him!' – was undoubtedly crude, yet its symbolism closely reflected the mood of the time. Alexey Surkov's poem 'I Hate' was equally ferocious. The German violation of the Motherland could only be wiped out with bloody revenge.* On 9 September, an advance unit from the Fourth Panzer Army came across copies of *Red Star* with Ilya Ehrenburg's appeal to Soviet soldiers, which ended: 'Do not count days; do not count miles. Count only the number of Germans you have killed. Kill the German – this is your mother's prayer. Kill the German – this is the cry of your Russian earth. Do not waver. Do not let up. Kill.'

For Yeremenko and Khrushchev, the main decision at this moment of crisis was to chose a successor to the commander of 62nd Army, who clearly did not believe that Stalingrad could be held. On 10 September, 62nd Army fought a retreat right back into the city. It was cut off from the 64th Army to the south when the 29th Motorized Infantry Division broke through to the Volga at Kuporosnoe at the southern tip of Stalingrad. On 11 September, Yeremenko's head-quarters in the Tsaritsa gorge had come under heavy fire. Konstantin Simonov arrived at this moment. He was struck by the 'sad smell of burnt iron' as he crossed the Volga to the still smouldering city. In the airless bunker Khrushchev, 'who was gloomy and replied

* There can be little doubt that the 'violation' propaganda in the late summer of 1942 contributed significantly to the mass rape committed by the Red Army on its advance into German territory in late 1944 and 1945.

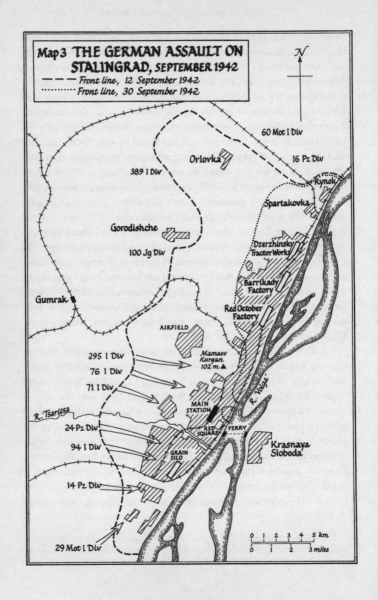

Map 3 THE GERMAN ASSAULT ON
STALINGRAD, SEPTEMBER 1942
--- Front line, 12 September 1942
.... Front line, 30 September 1942

N

60 Mot I Div

16 Pz Div

Orlovka

389 I Div

Rynok

Spartakovka

Gorodishche

Dzerzhinsky
Tractor Works

100 Jg Div

Barrikady
Factory

Red October
Factory

Gumrak

AIRFIELD

Mamaev
Kurgan
102 m ▲

295 I Div

76 I Div

71 I Div

MAIN
STATION

R. Volga

R. Tsaritsa

24 Pz Div

RED
SQUARE

FERRY

94 I Div

Krasnaya
Sloboda

GRAIN
SILO

14 Pz Div

29 Mot I Div

0 1 2 3 4 5 km
0 1 2 3 miles

monosyllabically . . . took out a packet of cigarettes and tried lighting one match after another, but the flame died at once because the ventilation in the tunnel was so bad'.

Simonov and his companion went to sleep on their overcoats in a corner of the tunnel system close to the Tsaritsa entrance. When they awoke next morning, the place was deserted. 'There were no staff officers, no typewriters, nobody.' Eventually they found a signalman rolling up the last of the wire. They discovered that Front headquarters had been evacuated across the Volga. The constant cutting of land lines during the bombardment had forced Yeremenko and Khrushchev to seek Stalin's permission to withdraw their command post to the other side of the river. The only major headquarters left on the west bank was that of the 62nd Army.

The following morning, General Chuikov received a summons to the new headquarters at Yamy of the joint military council for the Stalingrad and South-Western Fronts. It took him all day and most of the night to cross the Volga and find the spot. The glow from the blazing buildings in Stalingrad was so strong that, even on the east bank of the broad Volga, there was no need to switch on the headlights of his Lend-Lease jeep.

When Chuikov finally saw Khrushchev and Yeremenko the next morning, they stated the situation. The Germans were prepared to take the city at any price. There could be no surrender. There was nowhere to retreat to. Chuikov had been proposed as the new army commander in Stalingrad.

'Comrade Chuikov,' said Khrushchev. 'How do you interpret your task?'

'We will defend the city or die in the attempt,' he replied. Yeremenko and Khrushchev looked at him and said that he had understood his task correctly.

That evening, Chuikov crossed by a ferry boat from Krasnaya Sloboda, along with two T-34 tanks, to the central landing stage just above the Tsaritsa gorge. As the craft approached the bank, hundreds of people, mainly civilians hoping to escape, emerged silently from shell craters. Others prepared to carry the wounded on board. Chuikov and his companions set off to find his headquarters.

After many false directions, the commissar of a sapper unit took them to the Mamaev Kurgan, the huge Tartar burial mound, also known as Hill 102, from its height in metres. There, Chuikov found 62nd Army headquarters and met his chief of staff, General Nikolay Ivanovich Krylov. The harsh and blunt Chuikov was very different from Krylov, a precise man, with an analytical mind, yet the two understood each other and the situation. There was only one way to hold on. They had to pay in lives. 'Time is blood,' as Chuikov put it later, with brutal simplicity.

Supported by Krylov and Kuzma Akimovich Gurov, the sinister-looking army commissar, with a shaven head and thick eyebrows, Chuikov began to instil terror into any commander who even contemplated the idea of retreat. Some senior officers had started to slip back over the river, abandoning their men, most of whom, as Chuikov realized, also wanted 'to get across the Volga as quickly as possible, away from this hell'. He made sure that NKVD troops controlled every landing stage and jetty. Deserters, whatever their rank, faced summary execution.

There were many other alarming reports about the reliability of troops. Earlier that day, in 6th Guards Tank Brigade, a senior sergeant killed his company commander, then threatened the driver and radio operator with his pistol. As soon as they were out of the tank, he drove it off towards the lines of the German 76th Infantry Division. Because the sergeant had a white flag ready to stick out of the turret, the investigators concluded that this 'experienced traitor' had 'planned all the details of his disgusting plot' in advance. The two soldiers forced out of the tank at gun point were deemed to have 'displayed cowardice'. Both faced the military tribunal later and were probably shot.

At that stage, 62nd Army was reduced to some 20,000 men. It had fewer than sixty tanks left. Many were only good for immobile fire points. Chuikov, however, had over 700 mortars and guns, and he wanted all the heavier artillery to be withdrawn to the east bank. His main preoccupation was to reduce the effect of the Luftwaffe's overwhelming air superiority. He had already noticed the reluctance of German troops to engage in close-quarter combat, especially in the hours of darkness. To wear them down, 'every German must be made to feel that he was living under the muzzle of a Russian gun'.

His most immediate concern was to control a mixture of troops he did not know, in positions he had not reconnoitred, just when the Germans were about to launch their first major attack. Chuikov described the improvised defences he found as little more than barricades which could be pushed over with the front of a truck. Sixth Army headquarters, on the other hand, exaggerated in the other direction, with reports of 'strong positions with deep bunkers and concrete emplacements'. The real obstacle to the attackers, as they soon found, lay in the ruined cityscape.

That same day, 12 September, Paulus was at Hitler's *Werwolf* headquarters at Vinnitsa with General Halder and General von Weichs, the commander-in-chief of Army Group B. Accounts of the discussions vary. Paulus claims to have raised the question of the extended left flank along the Don all the way back to Voronezh, and the lack of 'corset' stiffening for the Italian, Hungarian and Romanian armies. According to Paulus, Hitler's plans were based on the assumption that the Russians were at the end of their resources, and that the Don flank would be strengthened with more allied formations. Hitler, who was interested only in Stalingrad, wanted to know how soon it would fall. Paulus presumably repeated the estimate he had given to Halder the day before: ten days of fighting, 'then fourteen days of regrouping'.

The first phase of the German onslaught began the next morning at 4.45 a.m. German time, 6.45 a.m. Russian time. (Hitler still insisted on the Wehrmacht in Russia operating on the same time as his *Wolfsschanze* headquarters in East Prussia.) On the left flank of LI Army Corps, the 295th Infantry Division headed for the Mamaev Kurgan and on the right, the 76th and the 71st Infantry Divisions attacked towards the main railway station and the central landing stage on the Volga. The officers of the 295th had fired their men with the idea that they would make it to the Volga in one rush.

The artillery and air assault on Soviet positions during the previous day had been intense. 'A mass of Stukas came over us,' wrote a corporal in the 389th Infantry Division, 'and after their attack, one could not believe that even a mouse was left alive.' The bombardment continued right through 13 September as well. From his command post on the Mamaev Kurgan, Chuikov watched it through periscope binoculars. A pall of dust from fragmented masonry turned the sky a pale brown. The ground vibrated continually from the explosions. Inside the bunker, fine soil, as if from an hourglass, trickled down between the logs which formed the low ceiling. Staff officers and signallers were coated in it. The shells and bombs also cut the field telephone cables. Linesmen sent out to discover a fault and make repairs stood little chance in the open. So frequent were the breaks that even the young women telephonists had to venture out. Chuikov managed to get through to Yeremenko on the rear link only once during the course of the day, and by the late afternoon he had completely lost contact with his divisions on the west bank. He was forced to resort to runners, whose life expectancy crossing the shell-torn city was even shorter than that of linesmen.

Although the Germans made progress into the western edge of the city, capturing the small airfield and barracks, their attempts to batter in the northern bulge proved unsuccessful. The fighting was much harder than expected. Many privately realized that they might well be spending the winter in Stalingrad.

Chuikov decided to move during that night to the former head-quarters tunnel, which ran in from the Tsaritsa gorge and had a rear exit up into Pushkinskaya Ulitsa, a street close to the Volga bank. The line of the Tsaritsa gorge had also been the obvious choice for Paulus and Hoth as the boundary between their two armies. While Seydlitz's divisions, to the north, pushed towards the Mamaev Kurgan and the main railway station, Hoth's 14th and 24th Panzer Divisions and the 94th Infantry Division, to the south, advanced ready to strike towards the rectangular concrete grain elevator which dominated the Stalingrad skyline.

News of the 71st Infantry Division's advance into the centre of Stalingrad just north of the Tsaritsa was greeted with fierce exultation at Führer headquarters. The same information reached the Kremlin that evening. Stalin was discussing the possibility of a great strategic counterstroke at Stalingrad with Zhukov and Vasilevsky, when Poskrebyshev, the chief of his secretariat, entered to say that Yeremenko was on the telephone. After speaking with him, Stalin told the two generals the news. 'Yeremenko says the enemy is bringing up tank forces near the city. He expects an attack tomorrow.' He turned to Vasilevsky. 'Issue orders immediately for Rodimtsev's 13th Guards Division to cross the Volga and see what else you can send over.' An hour later, Zhukov was on an aeroplane back to Stalingrad.

In the early hours of 14 September, Chuikov and his staff made their way southwards through the destroyed city to the Tsaritsa bunker in two vehicles. The rubble-strewn streets were only just passable, and their short journey was frequently delayed. Chuikov was impatient because he had ordered a counter-attack and needed to be ready in the new headquarters. His troops surprised the Germans in several places, but they were smashed back at sunrise as soon as the Luftwaffe Stuka squadrons became operational. The only encouraging news he received that morning was that the 13th Guards Rifle Division would cross the river that night. But the enemy advances that day were so strong and rapid, that many began to doubt whether Rodimtsev's troops would manage to land on the west bank.

The German 295th Infantry Division fought its way to the far slope of the Mamaev Kurgan, but the most immediate threat to Stalingrad's survival came just to their south. 'Both divisions [71st and 76th] managed to advance,' went Sixth Army's over-optimistic report, 'with an attacking wedge, to the central station at midday, and 3.15 p.m., with the waterworks captured, they reached the bank of the Volga!' The main station in fact changed hands three times in two hours in the morning, and was retaken by an NKVD rifle battalion in the afternoon.

General Aleksandr Rodimtsev's uniform was filthy by the time he reached Chuikov's headquarters early that afternoon. Ever since he had set foot on the west bank of the Volga, the constant air attacks had forced him to dive into craters for shelter. Humorous, yet with the intense air of a passionate student, Rodimtsev looked more like a Moscow intellectual than a Red Army general and Hero of the Soviet

Union. The prematurely grey hair, cut short at the sides and standing high on top, made his head appear elongated. The thirty-seven-year-old Rodimtsev belonged to that tiny minority of people who could be said genuinely to scorn danger. In the Spanish Civil War, serving under the cover name 'Pablito', he had been a key Soviet adviser at the Battle of Guadalajara in 1937, when the Spanish Republicans put Mussolini's expeditionary corps to flight. He was a hero to his troops, who claimed that their greatest fear if wounded was of a transfer to another formation when passed fit for duty.

Chuikov left Rodimtsev in no doubt about the danger of the position. He had just deployed his very last reserve, the nineteen tanks left from an armoured brigade. He advised Rodimtsev to leave all heavy equipment behind. His men needed just personal weapons, machine-guns and anti-tank rifles, and as many grenades as they could carry.

Chuikov summoned Colonel A. A. Sarayev, the commander of the 10th NKVD Rifle Division and also the garrison commander of Stalingrad. Sarayev, who had been in Stalingrad since July with five regiments of NKVD troops (just over 7,500 men), had greatly increased his empire. He had created a private army over 15,000 strong on both banks of the Volga. He also controlled the crossings and river traffic. Chuikov, who had little to lose at such a moment, threatened to ring Front headquarters at once if Sarayev did not accept his orders. Although Beria had threatened to 'break the back' of a commander in the Caucasus for even suggesting that NKVD troops should go under army command, Sarayev realized that in this case he would be wiser to obey. The wind from the Kremlin was starting to swing in the army's favour.

The militia battalions under his command were ordered to occupy key buildings and hold them to the last. A regular NKVD battalion was sent up on to the Mamaev Kurgan, while two rifle regiments were ordered to block the enemy's advance to the river. Rodimtsev's guardsmen must be allowed to land. The NKVD troops fought bravely, suffering heavy casualties, and the division later received the Order of Lenin and the title 'Stalingradsky'. Sarayev stayed in his post during the fighting, but soon lost his fiefdom. His successor as commander of NKVD forces, Major-General Rogatin, took over in the second week of October, with a new headquarters established on the east bank.

Another unpleasant encounter took place that evening. Across the Volga, Stalin's civilian delegate, Georgy Malenkov, had summoned the senior officers of the 8th Air Army to Front headquarters. They thought, as they came in, that they must have been called there to receive medals. Yeremenko and Zhukov stood in the background. Malenkov, who on the first day of the war had disbelieved Admiral Kuznetsov's report of the German air raid on Sevastopol, now turned his displeasure on the officers of Red Army aviation. He demanded to know which units had been in action on which days and then accused them of insufficient activity. He dictated court-martial sentences for the commanders. To make the point of his power, he called forward one officer, a short major with dark, brushed-back hair, and a face which was rather puffy from self-indulgence. 'Major Stalin,' he said to the son of Josef Vissarionovich.* 'The combat performance of your fliers is revolting. In the last battle not one of your twenty-four fighters shot down a single German. What is it? Did you forget how to fight? How are we to understand this?' Malenkov then humiliated General Khryukin, the commander of the 8th Air Army. Only the intervention of Zhukov brought the proceedings to a close. He reminded them that Rodimtsev's division was about to cross the Volga. The fighter regiment responsible for covering them had better make sure that not a single German bomb was allowed to fall. The aviation officers filed out, too shaken to speak.

The *Stavka* had ordered the 13th Guards Rifle Division forward to Stalingrad three days before. Although over 10,000 men strong, a tenth of them had no weapons. The division was dispersed away from the sight of German air reconnaissance under the elms, Ukrainian

---

* Two other sons of Soviet leaders, Vladimir Mikoyan and Leonid Khrushchev, served in Red Army aviation at Stalingrad. Vasily Stalin, who was much more of a playboy, soon escaped combat duties to make a propaganda film about the air force.

poplars, and willows of the east bank around Krasnaya Sloboda. They were given little time to prepare after the journey south from Kamyshin. Rodimtsev, knowing the urgency, had harried his commanders all the way. Truck radiators had boiled over, the pack camels had been nervous and the dust raised by vehicles had been so thick that 'the kites perched on the telegraph poles became grey'. On several occasions, the troops had scattered when yellow-nosed Messerschmitts screamed in at low level to strafe their columns.

As they had approached the Volga, the parched dusty steppe ended, with maple trees announcing the nearness of water. An arrowed sign, nailed to a tree, bore the single word 'Ferry'. Soldiers caught sight of the heavy black smoke ahead, and nudged their neighbours in the ranks. It had been the first indication of the battle which awaited them on the far side of the great river.

On the river bank, they were rapidly issued with ammunition, grenades and rations – bread, sausage and also sugar for their brew-ups. Rodimtsev, after his meeting with Chuikov, decided not to wait until darkness had completely fallen. The first wave of guardsmen were rushed forward in the twilight to a mixture of gunboats from the Volga flotilla and commandeered civilian craft – tugs, pinnaces, barges, fishing barques, even rowing boats. Those left to wait their turn on the eastern bank tried to calculate how long it would be before the boats returned for them.

The crossing was probably most eerie for those in the rowing boats, as the water gently slapped the bow, and the rowlocks creaked in unison. The distant crack of rifle shots and the thump of shell bursts sounded hollow over the expanse of river. Then, German artillery, mortars and any machine-guns close enough to the bank switched their aim. Columns of water were thrown up in midstream, drenching the occupants of the boats. The silver bellies of stunned fish soon glistened on the surface. One gunboat of the Volga flotilla received a direct hit, and twenty members of a detachment on board were killed. Some men stared at the water around them to avoid the sight of the far bank, rather like a climber refusing to look down. Others, however, kept glancing ahead to the blazing buildings on the western shore, their steel-helmeted heads instinctively withdrawn into the shoulders.

They were being sent into an image of hell. As darkness intensified, the huge flames silhouetted the shells of tall buildings on the bank high above them and cast grotesque shadows. Sparks flew up in the night air. The river bank ahead was 'a jumble of burned machines, and wrecked barges cast ashore'. As they approached the shore, they caught the smell of charred buildings and the sickly stench from decaying corpses under the rubble.

The first wave of Rodimtsev's guardsmen did not fix bayonets. They leaped over the sides of boats into the shallow water of the river's edge and charged straight up the steep, sandy bank. In one place, the Germans were little more than a hundred yards away. Nobody needed to tell the guardsmen that the longer they tarried, the more likely they were to die. Fortunately for them, the Germans had not had time to dig in or prepare positions. A battalion of the 42nd Guards Regiment on the left joined the NKVD troops, and pushed the Germans back around the main station. The 39th Guards Regiment on the right charged towards a large red-brick mill (kept, bullet-riddled, to this day as a memorial), which they cleared in pitiless close-quarter combat. When the second wave arrived, the reinforced regiment pushed forward to the rail track which ran past the base of the Mamaev Kurgan.

The 13th Guards Rifle Division suffered 30 per cent casualties in the first twenty-four hours, but the river bank had been saved. The few survivors (only 320 men out of the original 10,000 remained alive at the end of the battle of Stalingrad) swear that their determination 'flowed from Rodimtsev'. Following his example, they too made the promise: 'There is no land for us behind the Volga.'

The Germans at first saw Rodimtsev's counter-attack as little more than a temporary setback. They were convinced that their advance into the centre of the city was irreversible. 'Since yesterday the flag of the Third Reich flies over the city centre,' wrote a member of the 29th Motorized Infantry Division on the following day. 'The centre and the area of the [main] station are in German hands. You cannot imagine how we received the news.' But soldiers, shivering in the colder weather, 'dream already of underground winter quarters, glowing Hindenburg stoves, and lots of post from our beloved homes'.

German infantry companies had advanced down the Tsaritsa gorge. The entrance to 62nd Army headquarters came under direct fire, and the Tsaritsyn bunker filled with wounded. Soon, the warm moist air became unbreathable. Staff officers were fainting from lack of oxygen. Chuikov decided to change the site of his headquarters yet again, this time by crossing the river, driving north, and then crossing back to the west bank.

The struggle became intense for the Mamaev Kurgan. If the Germans took it, their guns could control the Volga. One of the NKVD rifle regiments managed to retain a small part of the hill until reinforced by the remainder of Rodimtsev's 42nd Guards Rifle Regiment and part of another division just before dawn on 16 September. The new arrivals attacked the summit and shoulders of the hill early that morning. The Mamaev Kurgan was now completely unrecognizable from the park where lovers had strolled a few weeks before. Not a blade of glass remained on the ground, now sown with shell, bomb and grenade fragments. The whole hillside had been churned and pocked with craters, which served as instant trenches in the bitter fighting of attack and counter-attack. Guardsman Kentya achieved fame by tearing down the German flag erected at the summit by soldiers of the 295th Infantry Division, and trampling on it. Much less was heard of unheroic episodes. A Russian battery commander on the Mamaev Kurgan was said to have deserted because 'he was afraid of being held responsible for his cowardice during the battle'. The gun crews had panicked and run away when a group of German infantry broke through and attacked the battery. Senior Lieutenant M. had displayed 'indecisiveness' and had failed to kill Germans, a capital offence at such a time.

At eleven o'clock on the night of 16 September, Lieutenant K., a platoon commander in the 112th Rifle Division, some five miles to the north, discovered the absence of four soldiers and their NCO. 'Instead of taking measures to find them and stop this act of treason, all he did was report the fact to his company commander.' At about 1 a.m., Commissar Kolabanov went to the platoon to investigate. As he approached its trenches, he heard a voice call in Russian from the German positions, addressing individual soldiers in the platoon by name, and urging them to cross over: 'You should all desert, they'll feed you well and treat you well. On the Russian side, you'll die whatever happens.' The commissar then noticed several figures crossing no man's land towards the German side. To his fury, other members of the platoon did not fire at them. He found that ten men, including the sergeant, had gone. The platoon commander was arrested and court-martialled. His sentence, presumably either execution or a *shtraf* company, is not recorded. In the same division, a captain apparently tried to persuade two other officers to desert with him, but one of them 'did not agree and executed the traitor', but one cannot be sure that this version of events was not camouflaging a personal argument.

The Germans counter-attacked again and again over the following days, but Rodimtsev's guardsmen and the remnants of the NKVD rifle regiment managed to hold on to the Mamaev Kurgan. The 295th Infantry Division was fought to a standstill. Their losses were so heavy that companies were merged. Officer casualties were particularly high, largely due to Russian snipers. After less than two weeks in the line, a company in Colonel Korfes's regiment of the 295th Infantry Division was on its third commander, a young lieutenant.

'Skirmishes to the death' continued on the Mamaev Kurgan and German heavy artillery continued to bombard Soviet positions for the next two months. The writer Vasily Grossman observed the shells throw the soil high into the air. 'These clouds of earth then passed through the sieve of gravity, the heavier lumps falling straight to the ground, the dust rising into the sky.' Corpses from the battle on its blackened slopes were disinterred and then buried again in the ceaseless, churning shellfire. Years after the war, a German soldier and a Russian soldier are said to have been uncovered during clearance work. The two corpses had apparently been buried by a shell burst just after they had bayoneted each other to death.

In Zhukov's deliberate understatement, these were 'very difficult days for Stalingrad'. In Moscow, US Embassy officials were certain that the city was finished, and the mood in the Kremlin was extremely nervous. On the evening of 16 September, just after dinner, Poskrebyshev came in silently and placed on Stalin's desk a transcription from the General Staff main intelligence department. It was the text of an intercepted radio message from Berlin. 'Stalingrad has been taken by brilliant German forces. Russia has been cut into two parts, north and south, and will soon collapse in her death throes.' Stalin read the message several times, then stood for a few moments at the window. He told Poskrebyshev to put him through to the *Stavka*. Over the telephone, he dictated a signal to Yeremenko and Khrushchev: 'Report some sense about what is happening in Stalingrad. Is it true Stalingrad has been captured by the Germans? Give a straight and truthful answer. I await your immediate reply.'

In fact the immediate crisis had already passed. Rodimtsev's division had arrived just in time. Already during that day, German commanders were conscious of the reinforcements brought across the river, such as Gorishny's 95th Rifle Division and a brigade of marine infantry detailed to reinforce the gravely weakened 35th Guards Rifle Division south of the Tsaritsa. The Luftwaffe also noticed an increase in the number of aircraft put up against them by the 8th Air Army, although Soviet fighter pilots still suffered from an instinctive fear of the enemy. 'Whenever an Me-109 appears,' complained a commissar's report, 'a merry-go-round starts, with everyone trying to protect their own tail.'

Luftwaffe personnel observed, above all, an intensification of anti-aircraft fire. 'As soon as Stuka squadrons appear,' noted the liaison officer with 24th Panzer Division, 'the sky was covered with countless black puffs from flak fire.' A fierce cheer rose from Russian positions below when one of the hated Stukas exploded in mid-air in a burst of smoke, and bits of flaming wreckage dropped away. Even the much faster fighters suffered from the increasingly heavy fire from across the Volga. On 16 September, a Luftwaffe NCO, Jürgen Kalb, was forced to bale out of his stricken Me-109 over the Volga. He parachuted into the river and swam to the river bank where Red Army soldiers awaited him.

Luftwaffe bomber crews were allowed little respite. Every aircraft was required for shuttle-bombing. On 19 September, one pilot calculated that in the last three months he had flown 228 missions: as many as during the previous three years over 'Poland, France, England, Yugoslavia and Russia combined'. He and his crew were in the air six hours a day.

Based mostly on improvised airfields out in the steppe, their life on the ground was a rush of hastily snatched meals, jangling field telephones, and an intensive study of maps and air reconnaissance photographs in the operations tent. Back in the air, identifying targets was not easy when below stretched 'an unbelievable chaos of ruins and fires', and huge widening columns of black oily smoke billowed from the blazing oil tanks, blotting out the sun up to an altitude of 10,000 feet.

Mission requests came constantly from the army: 'Attack target area A 11, north-west sector, the large block of houses, heavy enemy resistance there.' The Luftwaffe pilots, however, did not feel they were achieving much by continuing to pulverize a wasteland of 'torn apart, burnt-out factory sheds, in which not a wall was left standing'.

For the ground crews, 'mechanics – armament, bomb and radio specialists', preparing aircraft for take-off 'three, four, five times a day' there was no respite. For aircrews, their only moments of peace came at dusk and at dawn, but even then they did not linger long beside the airfield, gazing at the sky above this 'limitless country': already by the third week in September, the frosts were sharp. On 17 September, the temperature dropped suddenly. Men put on woollen garments under their jackets, which were in most cases disintegrating already. 'The soldiers' clothing', noted a doctor, 'was so worn out, that frequently they were obliged to wear items of Russian uniform.'

While the bitter struggle for the Mamaev Kurgan continued, an equally ferocious battle developed for the huge concrete grain silo down by the river. The rapid advance of Hoth's XLVIII Panzer Corps had virtually cut off this natural fortress. The defenders from the 35th Guards Division cheered and joked when reinforcements from a marine infantry platoon commanded by Lieutenant Andrey Khozyanov reached them during the night of 17 September. They had two old Maxim machine-guns and two of the long Russian anti-tank rifles, which they used to fire at a German tank when an officer and an interpreter appeared under a flag of truce to ask them to surrender. German artillery then ranged on to the vast structure preparing the ground for the Saxon 94th Infantry Division, whose insignia were the crossed swords of Meissen porcelain.

The fifty-odd defenders fought off ten assaults on 18 September. Knowing that they could not expect resupply, they conserved their ammunition, rations and water carefully. The conditions in which they continued to fight over the next two days were terrible. They were choked with dust and smoke, even the grain in the elevator had caught fire, and they soon had almost nothing left to drink. They were also short of water to fill the barrel jackets of the Maxim machine-guns. (Presumably the marines resorted to their own urine for the purpose, as was so often the practice in the First World War, but Soviet accounts avoid such details.)

All their grenades and anti-tank projectiles had been expended by the time more German tanks arrived to finish them off on 20 September. Both Maxims were put out of action. The defenders, unable to see inside the elevator for smoke and dust, communicated by shouting to each other through parched throats. When the Germans broke in, they fired at sounds, not at objects. That night, with only a handful of ammunition left, the survivors broke out. The wounded had to be left behind. Although a fierce fight, it was hardly an impressive victory for the Germans, yet Paulus chose the huge grain silo as the symbol of Stalingrad in the arm badge he was having designed at army headquarters to commemorate the victory.

Similarly stubborn defences of semi-fortified buildings in the centre of the town cost the Germans many men during those days. These 'garrisons' of Red Army soldiers from different divisions held out defiantly, also suffering terribly from thirst and hunger. There was a violent battle for possession of the Univermag department store on Red Square, which served as the headquarters of the 1st Battalion of the 42nd Guards Rifle Regiment. A small warehouse known as 'the nail factory' formed another redoubt. And in a three-storey building not far away, guardsmen fought on for five days, their noses and parched throats filled with brick dust from pulverized walls. Their wounded died in the cellars, untended once their young nurse succumbed to a chest wound. Six men, out of what had originally been close to half a battalion, escaped in the last moments when German tanks finally smashed in the walls.

Of the German gains in the centre of the city, the most serious for the Red Army was their advance to the central landing stage. This enabled them to strike at the main night-time crossing points with artillery, Nebelwerfer launchers and machine-guns, firing by the light of magnesium parachute flares. They were determined to stop reinforcements and supplies from reaching the defenders.

The main station, having changed hands fifteen times in five days, ended with the Germans as occupants of the ruins. Rodimtsev, in agreement with Chuikov's policy, ordered that the front line was always to be within fifty yards of the Germans, to make it hard for their artillery and aviation. The men of his division took a special pride in their marksmanship. 'Each Guards soldier shot like a sniper' and thus 'forced the Germans to crawl, not to walk'.

German soldiers, red-eyed with exhaustion from the hard fighting, and mourning more comrades than they ever imagined, had lost the triumphalist mood of just a week before. Everything seemed disturbingly different. They found artillery fire far more frightening in a city. The shellburst itself was not the only danger. Whenever a tall building was hit, shrapnel and masonry showered from above. The *Landser* had already started to lose track of time in this alien world, with its destroyed landscape of ruins and rubble. Even the midday light had a strange, ghostly quality from the constant haze of dust.

In such a concentrated area, a soldier had to become more conscious of war in three dimensions, with the danger of snipers in tall buildings. He also needed to watch the sky. When Luftwaffe strikes went in, a *Landser* hugged the ground in exactly the same way as a Russian. There was always the fear of Stukas failing to see the red, white and black swastika flags laid out to identify their positions. Often, they fired recognition flares to underline the point. Russian bombers also came in low, certainly low enough to reveal the red star on the tailplane. Much higher in the sky, fighters twinkled in the sun. One observer noticed that they twisted and turned more like fish in the sea than birds in the air.

Noise assailed their nerves constantly. 'The air is filled', wrote a panzer officer, 'with the infernal howling of diving Stukas, the thunder of flak and artillery, the roar of engines, the rattle of tank tracks, the shriek of the launcher and Stalin organ, the chatter of sub-machine-guns back and forth, and all the time one feels the heat of a city burning at every point.' The screams of the wounded affected men most. 'It's not a human sound,' one German wrote in his diary, 'just the dull cry of suffering of a wild animal.'

In such circumstances, the longing for home became acute. 'Home is so far away – Oh, beautiful home!' wrote one wistfully. 'Only now do we know quite how wonderful it is.' Russian defenders, on the other hand, clearly regarded homesickness as a luxury they could not afford. 'Hello, my dear Palina!' wrote an unknown soldier to his wife on 17 September. 'I am well and healthy. No one knows what's going to happen but we shall live and we shall see. The war is hard. You have the information about what is happening at the Front from the news. The mission of each soldier is simple: to destroy as many Fritzes as possible and then to push them back towards the west. I miss you very much but nothing can be done as several thousand kilometres separate us.' And on 23 September, a soldier called Sergey wrote to his wife Lyolya, with a simple message: 'The Germans won't withstand us.' There was no mention of home.

A renewed attempt by the three Soviet armies on the northern front to attack the Sixth Army's left flank failed on 18 September. The rapid redeployment of Luftwaffe squadrons against the threat, combined with counter-attacks from XIV Panzer Corps, proved far too effective on the open steppe. A second attempt failed the following day. All the three armies achieved, at great cost, was to spare the 62nd Army from Luftwaffe attack for less than two days.

Chuikov, knowing that there would be no let-up, started to bring Colonel Batyuk's 284th Rifle Division, mainly Siberians, across the Volga. He held them in reserve below the Mamaev Kurgan, in case the Germans established themselves solidly round the central landing stage, and then thrust north up the river bank in an attempt to cut his army off from behind. On the morning of 23 September, a few hours after the last of Batyuk's Siberians had reached the west bank of the Volga, the division was thrown into the attack in an attempt to clear the Germans from the central landing stage and link up with the Soviet troops isolated south of the Tsaritsa. But the German divisions, although suffering heavy losses, forced them back. On that day, which happened to be Paulus's fifty-second birthday, the Germans finally secured the broad corridor which cut off the left wing of the 62nd Army in its pocket south of the Tsaritsa gorge.

With predictable thoroughness, the Germans continued their attempts to crush resistance in this southern sector of Stalingrad. Two days later they achieved a breakthrough. This led to a panic in two militia brigades, which were already virtually out of food and ammunition. The collapse, however, started at the top, as Stalingrad Front headquarters reported to Shcherbakov in Moscow. The commander of 42nd Special Brigade, 'left the line of defence, pretending that he was off to consult with the staff of the army'. The same happened with the 92nd Special Brigade, despite its strengthening with marine infantry. On 26 September, the commander and commissar, followed by their staff, abandoned their men, also 'pretending that they were off to discuss the situation with higher command', but in fact they withdrew to safety on the large island of Golodny in the middle of the Volga. The following morning, 'when the soldiers learned that their commanders had deserted them, the majority rushed to the bank of the Volga and started preparing rafts for themselves'. Some of them tried paddling out to Golodny island on tree trunks and pieces of driftwood, some just swam. The enemy, spotting their desperate attempts to escape, opened fire with mortars and artillery, and killed many in the water.

'When Major Yakovlev, the commander of the machine-gun battalion, by then the highest-ranking officer of the brigade left on the west bank, learned that the brigade commander had deserted and sown panic among the troops, he took over command of the defence.' He soon found he had no communications, since the signallers were among those who had escaped to the island. Aided by Lieutenant

Solutsev, Yakovlev rallied the remaining troops, and established a defence line which, in spite of the shortage of men and ammunition, held against seven attacks over the next twenty-four hours. All this time, the brigade commander remained on the island. He did not even try to send more ammunition to the defenders left behind. In an attempt to hide what was happening, he sent fictitious reports on the fighting to 62nd Army headquarters. This did him little good. Chuikov's staff became suspicious. He was arrested and charged with 'Criminal disobedience of Order No. 227'. Although no details are given in the report to Moscow of the sentence pronounced by the NKVD tribunal, clemency is hard to imagine.

10

Rattenkrieg

Hitler's frustrations over the lack of success in the Caucasus and at Stalingrad came to a head on 24 September, when he dismissed General Halder, the chief of the Army General Staff. Both men had been suffering from a form of nervous exhaustion with each other. Halder had been exasperated with what he regarded as the erratic and obsessive meddling of an amateur, while the Führer saw any implied criticism of his leadership as the resentment of reactionary generals who did not share his will for victory. Hitler's main concern, Halder noted in his diary that night, was the 'necessity of indoctrinating the General Staff in a fanatical belief in the Idea'. This preoccupation with subjugating the general staff became a substitute struggle in itself. The consequences were not hard to imagine. A dangerous situation could easily turn into a disaster.

In the wake of the row with Jodl and List, Paulus heard that he would be appointed to replace Jodl as the chief of the Wehrmacht command staff. General von Seydlitz was strongly tipped as his successor to command Sixth Army. Hitler, however, decided to stick with faces he knew well. Jodl was reinstated and the sycophantic Field Marshal Keitel remained in place to reassure the Führer of his military genius and assist in the Nazification of the Army. Professional officers referred to him as 'Lakeitel' or 'the nodding donkey', but they held many other generals in contempt too for their moral cowardice. 'The general staff is heading directly towards its own destruction,' wrote

Groscurth to General Beck, later the head of the July Plot. 'It no longer contains a shred of honour.' Groscurth's only consolation was that his corps commander, General Strecker, and fellow staff officers at XI Corps headquarters felt the same way. 'It is a real pleasure to be together with such men.'

The dismissal of Halder, as well as marking the end of the general staff as an independent planning body, also removed Paulus's sole remaining protector at a critical moment. Paulus must have been secretly dejected to lose the chance of a new appointment. Hitler had said that with the Sixth Army he could storm the heavens, yet Stalingrad still did not fall. A team from the propaganda ministry awaited its capture, 'ready to film the raising of flags', and the press begged to be allowed to proclaim '*Stalingrad Gefallen!*', because Paulus's own headquarters had announced on 26 September that 'the battle flag of the Reich flies over the Stalingrad Party building!' Even Goebbels started to become concerned that the German press was depicting events 'in much too rosy a light'. Editors were instructed to emphasize the toughness and complexity of the fighting. A week later, however, he became certain that 'the fall of Stalingrad can be expected with certainty', then another three days later, his mood changed yet again, and he ordered that other subjects should be brought to the fore.

The pressure and criticism Paulus had received 'from morning to night' for not having taken Stalingrad made him 'highly nervous', according to Groscurth. The strain exacerbated his recurring dysentery. Staff officers noticed that the tic from which he suffered on the left side of his face became more pronounced. In Sixth Army headquarters at Golubinsky, a village on the west bank of the Don, he stared at the detailed, large-scale map of Stalingrad. Much of the city had already been taken, and his intelligence staff estimated that the Soviet casualty rate was running at roughly double the German. He could only hope that Hitler was right about the enemy running out of reserves at any moment. His own resources were dissipating rapidly, and the astonishing tenacity of the enemy dismayed them all.

Much of the criticism directed against him was based on the fact that the Sixth Army, with two corps from the Fourth Panzer Army, was the largest formation in the German Army, at nearly a third of a million men strong. Outsiders, with no experience of the fighting, could not understand the problem. One can certainly argue that Paulus could have used his troops better, but his critics appeared to forget that while around eight of his divisions were committed to the fighting in the city, another eleven divisions manned nearly 130 miles of front, stretching across the greater and lesser Don bends and then over the steppe to the Volga north of Rynok, as well as a strip south of Stalingrad opposite Beketovka. (See Map 4.) Only a single division remained in reserve.

On the northern flank, out in the increasingly bleak steppe, Strecker's XI Army Corps, General Walther Heitz's VIII Army Corps and Hube's XIV Panzer Corps faced constant attacks from four Soviet armies, attempting to relieve pressure on the city itself. On the right, General Jaenecke's IV Army Corps (opposite General Shumilov's 64th Army) linked up with the weak Romanian Fourth Army, an over-extended defence line which petered out in the northern Caucasus. In all, Yeremenko's command included Chuikov's 62nd Army, the 64th Army round Beketovka, the 57th Army down to beyond lake Sarpa, the 51st Army holding the line of the rest of the lakes and then the 28th Army stretching down into the emptiness of the Kalmyk steppe.

For the German, Romanian and Russian armies on the southern flank, the war in the steppe was essentially like the First World War, only with better weapons and the occasional appearance of modern aircraft. For the armoured formations out on both flanks, the sun-baked plains, over which they had charged like warships at full speed just weeks before, now struck them as deeply depressing. The lack of trees and mountains made southern Germans and Austrians homesick. The rains of the *rasputitsa* produced squalid conditions. Soldiers in dugouts, listening to the rain, and watching the level of water rise above their ankles, had little to do but think about trench foot and observe sodden rats chewing corpses in no man's land. Reconnaissance patrols, raids and probing attacks offered the only activity on both sides. Small groups crept forward to the enemy line, then hurled grenades forward into the trenches. The only change came on 25 September when 51st and 57th Armies attacked the Romanian divisions south of Stalingrad along the line of salt lakes and pushed them back, but it did not succeed in diverting German divisions from the city.

Fighting in Stalingrad itself could not have been more different. It represented a new form of warfare, concentrated in the ruins of civilian life. The detritus of war – burnt-out tanks, shell cases, signal wire and grenade boxes – was mixed with the wreckage of family homes – iron bedsteads, lamps and household utensils. Vasily Grossman wrote of the 'fighting in the brick-strewn, half-demolished rooms and corridors' of apartment blocks, where there might still be a vase of withered flowers, or a boy's homework open on the table. In an observation post, high in a ruined building, an artillery spotter with a periscope might watch for targets through a convenient shell-hole in the wall, seated on a kitchen chair.

German infantrymen loathed house-to-house fighting. They found such close-quarter combat, which broke conventional military boundaries and dimensions, psychologically disorientating. During the last phase of the September battles, both sides had struggled to take a large brick warehouse on the Volga bank, near the mouth of the Tsaritsa, which had four floors on the river side and three on the landward. At one point, it was 'like a layered cake' with Germans on the top floor, Russians below them, and more Germans underneath them. Often an enemy was unrecognizable, with every uniform impregnated by the same dun-coloured dust.

German generals do not seem to have imagined what awaited their divisions in the ruined city. They lost their great Blitzkrieg advantages and were in many ways thrown back to First World War techniques, even though their military theorists had argued that trench warfare had been 'an aberration in the art of war'. The Sixth Army, for example, found itself having to respond to Soviet tactics by reinventing the 'storm-wedges' introduced in January 1918: assault groups of ten men armed with a machine-gun, light mortar and flame-throwers for clearing bunkers, cellars and sewers.

In its way, the fighting in Stalingrad was even more terrifying than the impersonal slaughter at Verdun. The close-quarter combat in ruined buildings, bunkers, cellars and sewers was soon dubbed 'Rattenkrieg' by German soldiers. It possessed a savage intimacy which appalled their generals, who felt that they were rapidly losing control over events. 'The enemy is invisible,' wrote General Strecker to a friend. 'Ambushes out of basements, wall remnants, hidden bunkers and factory ruins produce heavy casualties among our troops.'

German commanders openly admitted the Russian expertise at camouflage, but few acknowledged that it was their aircraft which had produced the ideal conditions for the defenders. 'Not a house is left standing,' a lieutenant wrote home, 'there is only a burnt-out wasteland, a wilderness of rubble and ruins which is well-nigh impassable.' At the southern end of the city, the Luftwaffe liaison officer with 24th Panzer Division wrote: 'The defenders have concentrated and fortified themselves in the sections of the town facing our attacks. In parkland, there are tanks or just tank turrets dug-in, and anti-tank guns concealed in the cellars make it very hard going for our advancing tanks.'

Chuikov's plan was to funnel and fragment German mass assaults with 'breakwaters'. Strengthened buildings, manned by infantry with anti-tank rifles and machine-guns, would deflect the attackers into channels where camouflaged T-34 tanks and anti-tank guns waited, half-buried in the rubble behind. When German tanks attacked with infantry, the defenders' main priority was to separate them. The Russians used trench mortars, aiming to drop their bombs just behind the tanks to scare off the infantry while the anti-tank gunners went for the tanks themselves. The channelled approaches would also be mined in advance by sappers, whose casualty rate was the highest of any specialization. 'Make a mistake and no more dinners' was their unofficial motto. Wearing camouflage suits, once the snow came, they crawled out at night to lay anti-tank mines and conceal them. An experienced sapper could lay up to thirty a night. They were also renowned for running out from cover to drop a mine in front of a German tank as it advanced.

Much of the fighting consisted not of major attacks, but of relentless, lethal little conflicts. The battle was fought by assault squads, generally six or eight strong, from 'the Stalingrad Academy of Street Fighting'. They armed themselves with knives and sharpened spades for silent killing, as well as sub-machine-guns and grenades. (Spades were in such short supply, that men carved their names in the handle and slept with their head on the blade to make sure that nobody stole it.) The assault squads sent into the sewers were strengthened with flame-throwers and sappers bringing explosive charges. Six sappers from Rodimtsev's guards division even managed to find a shaft under a German stronghold and blew it up, using 300 pounds of explosive.

A more general tactic evolved, based on the realization that the German armies were short of reserves. Chuikov ordered an emphasis on night attacks, mainly for the practical reason that the Luftwaffe could not react to them, but also because he was convinced that the Germans were more frightened during the hours of darkness, and would become exhausted. The German *Landser* came to harbour a special fear of the Siberians from Colonel Batyuk's 284th Rifle Division, who were considered to be natural hunters of any sort of prey. 'If only you could understand what terror is,' a German soldier wrote in a letter captured by the Russians. 'At the slightest rustle, I pull the trigger and fire off tracer bullets in bursts from the machine-gun.' The compulsion to shoot at anything that moved at night, often setting off fusillades from equally nervous sentries down a whole sector, undoubtedly contributed to the German expenditure of over 25 million rounds during the month of September alone. The Russians also kept up the tension by firing flares into the night sky from time to time to give the impression of an imminent attack. Red Army aviation, partly to avoid the Messerschmitts by day, kept up a relentless series of raids every night on German positions. It also served as another part of the wearing-down process to exhaust the Germans and stretch their nerves.

The Russians used both their twin-engined night bombers, which attracted the fire of every German flak battery on the front, and large numbers of manoeuvrable little U-2 biplanes which dropped small bombs on night raids. 'The Russkies keep buzzing over us the whole night long,' a pioneer corporal wrote home. The worst part was the eerie change in sound. In the distance, the U-2 sounded like one of its many nicknames, the 'sewing machine'. Then, as the pilot approached his target, he would switch off the engine to glide in like a bird of prey. The only sound would be the swishing of air through its struts, until the bomb fell. Even though the bomb load was only 400 kilos, the aircraft's psychological effect was considerable. 'We lie exhausted in our holes waiting for them,' wrote another soldier. The U-2 attracted more nicknames than any other machine or weapon at Stalingrad. Others included 'the duty NCO', because of the way it crept up unannounced, the 'midnight bomber', the 'coffee-machine' and the 'railway crow'. Sixth Army requested Army Group headquarters to keep up Luftwaffe pressure on Russian airfields with round-the-clock attacks. 'The Russians' unchallenged air superiority at night has reached an unbearable level. The troops get no rest, and their strength will soon be completely dissipated.'

There is no overt reference in surviving files to cases of battle stress. German medical authorities tended to use the euphemism of 'exhaustion', like the British, but their prescription was closer to the brutal simplicity of the Red Army. The German Army had refused even to acknowledge its existence. In 1926, nearly seven years before Hitler took power, war neurosis was simply abolished as a condition along with the pension that had gone with it. Take away the disease, went the argument, and you take away the reason for leaving the front line. Breakdown was classified as cowardice, and therefore could be a capital offence. It is thus impossible to say what proportion of disciplinary offences on either side at Stalingrad, especially desertion, was caused by battle shock and general strain. All one can be certain about from studies of comparable situations is that the rate of battle-shock casualties must have started to rise sharply in September as soon as the war of movement turned into a war of virtually stationary annihilation. Psychological casualties would have started to soar – if one goes by British studies of battle-shock cases at Anzio and Normandy – as soon as troops were pinned down or surrounded.

Chuikov's main disagreement with senior officers at front headquarters concerned the positioning of divisional, army and front artillery regiments. Eventually, he won the argument that they should be based on the east bank of the Volga, because there was simply not enough room for them with his troops on the west bank. It would also have been increasingly difficult to transport sufficient supplies of artillery shells across the Volga, and 'in Stalingrad, a field-gun was worth nothing without shells'.

'One house taken by the Russians, one taken by the Germans,' scribbled Vasily Grossman in his notebook just after his arrival. 'How can heavy artillery be used in such a battle?' He soon discovered the answer. Soviet artillery massed on the far side of the Volga, as Chuikov had insisted, did not attempt to shell German front-line positions. Their purpose was to hammer enemy lines of communications and, above all, smash battalions forming up for an attack. To achieve this, scores of Soviet artillery observation officers concealed themselves like snipers at the top of ruined buildings. The Germans, well aware of the danger they represented, treated them as a high-priority target for their own snipers, or anti-tank guns.

Whenever a German troop concentration was spotted, and the target coordinates passed back to the batteries on the east bank by wireless or field telephone, the volume of fire was devastating. 'On the other side of the Volga', wrote Grossman, 'it seemed as if the whole universe shook with the mighty roaring of the heavy guns. The ground trembled.'

The only artillery batteries to remain on the west bank were *Katyusha* rocket launchers mounted on lorries. Hidden behind the high Volga bank, they would reverse out, almost to the water's edge, fire their sixteen rockets in rapid succession, then drive back in again. The Soviet multiple-rocket launcher was the most psychologically effective of the Red Army's longer-range weapons. Its sixteen 130-mm rockets, each nearly five feet long, were fired in rapid succession, with a heart-stopping noise. Many of those experiencing a salvo of *Katyushas* for the first time thought that they were under air attack. Red Army soldiers had coined the name *Katyusha* for the rocket after the crescendo in the tune of that name, the most popular Russian song of the whole war. In it, Katyusha promises her fiancé to keep their love alive in her heart while he defends the Motherland at the front.

Russian soldiers affected to despise the German counterpart, the six-barrelled mortar, known as the Nebelwerfer. They called it the 'footler', or the 'donkey' because it made a braying noise, or the 'Vanyusha' (meaning little Ivan, just as Katyusha was the diminutive of Katya). There was a joke in the 62nd Army about what would happen if 'Vanyusha tried to marry Katyusha'.*

Chuikov soon recognized that the key infantry weapons in Stalingrad would be the sub-machine-gun, the grenade and the sniper's rifle. After the Winter War, following the devastating attacks of Finnish ski troops, shooting on the move, the Red Army accepted the idea of sub-machine-gun squads of eight men, designed to be carried into battle if necessary on the back of a T-34. In Stalingrad street-fighting, this size of squad proved ideal for close-quarter fighting. During house- and bunker-clearing, the hand grenade proved essential. Red Army soldiers called it their 'pocket artillery'. It was also effective in defence. On Chuikov's orders, grenades were stocked ready to hand in recesses dug into the side of every trench. Not surprisingly, there were many accidents caused by untrained soldiers. The second-in-command of a company was killed and several men were badly wounded when a newly arrived recruit mishandled a grenade. Others were killed when soldiers, mainly from Central Asia, tried to fit captured German detonators in their own grenades. 'Further weapon training is needed,' the chief of the political department reported to the military council of Stalingrad Front.

Another weapon, often as dangerous to the user as to its intended victims, was the flame-thrower, which was effectively terrifying when clearing sewer tunnels, cellars and inaccessible hiding places. The operator knew that as soon as the enemy sighted him, he would be the first target for their bullets.

Red Army soldiers enjoyed inventing gadgets to kill Germans. New booby traps were dreamed up, each seemingly more ingenious and unpredictable in its results than the last. Angered at their inability to

---

* The list of nicknames and slang is almost endless. Bullets were 'sunflower seeds' and mines were 'gherkins'. A 'tongue' was an enemy sentry captured for interrogation purposes.

fight back against the Stuka attacks, Captain Ilgachkin, a battalion commander, decided with one of his soldiers, Private Repa, to construct their own form of anti-aircraft gun. They fastened an anti-tank rifle to the spokes of a cartwheel which in turn was mounted on a tall stake driven into the ground. Ilgachkin made complicated calculations on the basis of the gun's muzzle velocity, and the estimated speed of a diving aircraft, but whether 'the gaunt and melancholy' Repa paid much attention to these figures is another matter. In any case their contraption achieved a certain success, with Repa managing to bring down three Stukas.

The real anti-aircraft batteries also amended their tactics. The Stukas came over at an altitude of between 4,000 and 5,000 feet, then half-rolled to drop into a dive at an angle of about seventy degrees, their siren screaming. They came out of the dive at just under 2,000 feet. Anti-aircraft gunners learned to put up a curtain of fire to hit them either at the point of going into the dive, or at the point of coming out. Shooting at them on the way down was a waste of ammunition.

Another device was dreamed up by Vasily Ivanovich Zaitsev, who soon became the most famous sniper in the Stalingrad army. Zaitsev attached the telescopic sight from his sniper's rifle to an anti-tank gun to take on machine-gun nests, by slotting a shell right through their loophole. But he soon found that the charges in the mass-produced shells were not consistent enough for precision shooting. Fame could be achieved even with conventional weapons. Bezdiko, the ace mortarman in Batyuk's division, was renowned for having achieved six bombs in the air at the same time. These stories were exploited in an attempt to spread a cult of the expert to every soldier. The 62nd Army's slogan was: 'Look after your weapon as carefully as your eyes.'

The 'garrisons' holding the fortified buildings so central to Chuikov's strategy, who included young women medical orderlies or signallers, suffered great privations when cut off for days at a time. They had to endure dust, smoke, hunger and, worst of all, thirst. The city had been without fresh water since the pumping station was destroyed in the August raids. Knowing the consequences of drinking polluted water, desperate soldiers shot at drainpipes in the hope of extracting a few drops.

Supplying forward positions with food was a constant problem. An anti-tank detachment had a Kazan Tartar cook who filled a large army thermos with tea or soup, fastened it to his back and crawled up to the front-line positions under fire. If the thermos was hit by shrapnel or bullets, the hapless cook was soaked. Later, when the frosts became really hard, the soup or tea froze and he was 'covered in icicles by the time he got back'.

With ill-defined front lines, and a defence in depth of no more than a few hundred yards in places, command posts were almost as vulnerable as forward positions. 'Shells exploding on top of our command post were a common occurrence,' wrote Colonel Timofey Naumovich Vishnevsky, the commander of the 62nd Army's artillery division, to a friend from hospital. 'When I left the bunker, I could hear sub-machine-gun fire on all sides. Sometimes it seemed as if the Germans were all around us.' A German tank came right up to the entrance of his bunker and 'its hull blocked the only way out'. Vishnevsky and his officers had to dig for their lives to escape into the gully on the far side. The colonel was badly wounded. 'My face is completely disfigured,' he wrote, 'and consequently I will now be the lowest form of life in the eyes of women.'

German command bunkers ran little risk of being overrun during September and October, and the standard three feet of earth on top of the wooden beams served as sufficient protection only against *Katyushas*. The main danger was a direct hit from the heavy artillery across the Volga. Divisional and regimental commanders were concerned with personal comfort as well as efficiency. A wind-up gramophone often sat next to a crate of brandy or wine brought from France. Some officers took to wearing sports trousers, even tennis shorts, when down in the damp, heavy air of their bunkers, because their combat clothes were infested with lice.

It was much more of an upside-down world for their soldiers. Instead of saying 'good-night', they wished each other a 'quiet night' for the dangerous hours of darkness. In the frosty morning, they emerged stiff in every joint, seeking a patch of sunshine in the bottom of the trench like lizards to absorb the warm rays. Feeling braver in the daylight, the Germans shouted insults and threats from their front lines: 'Russkies! Your time has come!' or '*Hei, Rus, bul-bul, sdavaisa!*', their pidgin Russian for: 'Surrender or you'll be blowing bubbles!' The notion of pushing Soviet troops back into the Volga, where they would drown like a stampeding herd, became a constant refrain.

During lulls in the battle, Russian soldiers too sought patches of sun, out of enemy sniper fire. Trenches were sometimes like a 'tinker's factory', as shell cases were made into oil lamps, with a piece of rag for a wick, and cartridge cases into cigarette lighters. The ration of rough *makhorka* tobacco, or lack of it, was a constant preoccupation. Connoisseurs insisted that no fancy paper should be used when rolling *makhorka* into fat, shaggy cigarettes, only newspaper. The printer's ink was supposed to contribute to the taste. Russian soldiers smoked constantly in battle. 'It's permissible to smoke in action,' an anti-tank rifleman told Simonov, 'what's not permissible is to miss your target. Miss it just once and you'll never light up again.'

Even more important than tobacco was the vodka ration, theoretically 100 grams a day. Men fell silent when the vodka was produced, everyone eyeing the bottle. The strain of battle was so great that the ration was never considered enough, and soldiers were prepared to go to desperate lengths to meet their need. Surgical spirit was seldom used for its official purpose. Industrial alcohol and even anti-freeze were drunk after being passed through the activated carbon filter of a gas mask. Many soldiers had thrown their gas masks away during the retreats of the previous year, so those who had held on to them could bargain. The result could be much worse than just a bad headache. Most recovered because they were young and healthy and did not resort to it frequently, but those who tried too often went blind.

In the armies out in the steppe, soldiers often drank up to a litre of spirit a day in winter. The balance above the official ration was made up by failing to report casualties and sharing out their allocation, or through bartering uniform or bits of equipment with villagers behind the lines. Home-brews obtained this way out on the Kalmyk steppe included 'every imaginable sort of alcohol, even a spirit made from milk'. Such commerce proved more dangerous for civilians than soldiers. A 'military tribunal of NKVD Forces' sentenced two women to ten years each in the Gulag for trading alcohol and tobacco in exchange for parachute silk to make underclothes.

The medical services in the Red Army were seldom regarded as a high priority by commanders. A seriously wounded soldier was out of the battle, and senior officers were more concerned with replacing him. Yet this attitude did not deter the very bravest figures on the Stalingrad battlefield, who were the medical orderlies, mainly female students or high-school graduates with only the most basic first-aid training.

The commander of 62nd Army's hundred-strong sanitary company, Zinaida Georgevna Gavrielova, was an eighteen-year-old medical student, who had received the job on the basis of a strong recommendation from the cavalry regiment in which she had just served. Her medical orderlies, few of them much older than herself, had to conquer their terror and crawl forward, often under heavy fire, to reach the wounded. They then dragged them out of the way, until it was safe to carry them on their backs. They had to be both 'physically and spiritually strong', as their commander put it.

There was no question of medical personnel being non-combatant. The beautiful Gulya Koroleva, a twenty-year-old from a well-known Moscow literary family, had left her baby son in the capital and volunteered as a nurse. Serving with the 214th Rifle Division in the 24th Army on the northern flank, she was credited with having 'brought over a hundred wounded soldiers back from the front line and killed fifteen fascists herself'. She was posthumously awarded the Order of the Red Banner. Natalya Kachnevskaya, a nurse with a Guards Rifle Regiment, formerly a theatrical student in Moscow, brought back twenty wounded soldiers in a single day and 'threw grenades at the Germans'. Stalingrad Front headquarters also singled out (posthumously) the bravery of another female orderly, Kochnevskaya, who had volunteered for the front, and carried more than twenty soldiers out of the firing line. Although wounded twice, she carried on bandaging and carrying officers and soldiers.*

The sacrifices of these medical orderlies were often wasted through the subsequent treatment of their charges. The casualties they carried or dragged down to the edge of the Volga were left uncared for until, long after nightfall, they were loaded like sacks of potatoes on to the supply boats, empty for the return crossing. When the wounded were offloaded on the east bank, the conditions could be even worse, as an aircraftwoman discovered.

The survivors of a disbanded aviation regiment who spent the night asleep in woods east of the Volga awoke at dawn to strange sounds. Mystified, they crept through the trees towards the river bank to investigate. There, they saw 'thousands of wounded, as far as the eye could see', left on the sandy banks, having been ferried back across the Volga during the night. The casualties were calling for water, or 'screaming and crying, having lost arms or legs'. The ground-crew staff went to help as best they could. The former maternity nurse, Klavdia Sterman, vowed that as soon as they reached Moscow, she would apply to transfer to a front-line medical unit.

Survival was far from guaranteed even on reaching one of the score of field hospitals on the east bank of the Volga. Conditions in Red Army hospitals, despite the presence of some of the finest Russian doctors, made them seem more like a meat-processing factory. The field hospital at Balashchov, which specialized in arms and legs, some six miles from the city, was very meagrely equipped. Instead of normal hospital beds, it had three-tiered bunks. One young woman surgeon, newly arrived, was worried not only about the physical state of the wounded. 'They often closed in on themselves and wanted no contact with anybody else.' She at first presumed that the wounded soldiers

---

* Apart from one well-known member of a tank crew, Yekaterina Petlyuk, very few women served as combat soldiers in the city. In the air armies supporting Stalingrad Front, however, there was a women's bomber regiment led by the famous aviator, Marina Raskova. 'I had never seen her close to,' Simonov wrote in his diary after meeting her at the Kamyshin aerodrome, 'and I did not realize that she was so young and so beautiful. Maybe I remember it so well because soon afterwards I heard that she was killed.'

brought back across the Volga out of the 'hell' of Stalingrad would never want to return. 'On the contrary: it became apparent that soldiers and officers wanted to go back to the front.' Amputees certainly showed no sense of relief at missing the fighting. In fact, most of those incapacitated or permanently scarred, like the artillery colonel whose face had been sliced up by shrapnel, felt that they were no longer proper men.

Bad rations did not help either recovery or morale. Grossman, in an emotional state, clearly assumed that this was Russia's fate at that time. 'In hospital,' he jotted in his notebook, 'the wounded are given a very small piece of salted herring by nurses who cut them up with great care. This is poverty.' In those days, before his eyes were opened, he seemed unable to recognize the truth. Soviet logic mercilessly dictated that the best rations went to the fighting troops. The wounded, if they were lucky, received three helpings of *kasha*, or buckwheat porridge, a day, nothing more. The salted herring seen by Grossman was an unusual treat.

A more revealing hint of the state of mind controlling the Stalingrad Front medical services came from the results of 'socialist competition' in hospitals, reported to Shcherbakov in Moscow. The caterers came first, the surgeons came second, and the drivers came third. Any criteria on which this exercise was based utterly demeaned the genuine sacrifice of medical workers, who gave so much of their own blood for transfusion – sometimes twice in an evening – that they frequently collapsed. 'If they don't give blood', a report explained, 'soldiers will die'.

In the great battle of attrition, the shipments of wounded to the east bank had to be matched by fresh 'meat for the cannon' taken across the Volga into the city. The *Stavka* drip-fed the 62nd Army with reinforcement divisions as their predecessors were shot to pieces. The new battalions were marched forward at nightfall for embarkation under the eyes of the NKVD troops. They could only stare across at the city on the skyline opposite, lit by fires, and try to ignore the smell of burning. Patches of the river were still aflame with oil. There were also NKVD detachments on many of the ships, ready to shoot anyone who dived overboard in a final attempt to avoid their fate on the west bank. German shellbursts in the river ahead were enough to make many lose their head. If anybody panicked, a sergeant or officer would shoot the offender on the spot and roll his body over the side.

The boats on which they had embarked bore every sign of the crossing's dangers. One of the fire-fighting launches, refitted as a naval craft for the Volga flotilla, was said after one outward and return trip to have received 436 bullet and shell holes; only a single square yard of hull was untouched.

The easiest targets for German guns were the rafts used by engineer regiments to ferry heavy supplies, such as timber for bunkers, across to the city. When one of these rafts drifted on to the west bank, and soldiers there ran forward to help unload, they found a sapper lieutenant and three of his men so riddled by machine-gun fire that 'it seemed as though iron teeth had savagely torn the sodden logs of the raft and these human bodies'.

Sixth Army headquarters knew that, with winter approaching, there was no time to lose. Even before Red Square and the grain silos south of the Tsaritsa were seized, it started to prepare for a knock-out blow in the industrial, northern half of the city.

Chuikov had moved to his new headquarters on the Volga river bank half a mile north of the Red October metalworks early on the morning of 18 September. His staff officers, however, had chosen an unprotected site just below a huge oil-storage tank, which they assumed to be empty.

Great efforts were made to bring across more ammunition and supplies at night, as well as reinforcements, which landed on the bank behind the Red October and Barrikady plants. Unessential personnel who could be better used elsewhere were evacuated. Most of the anti-aircraft defences round Stalingrad power station had been knocked out and their ammunition dump destroyed, so the young women from the surviving gun crews were withdrawn across the Volga on 25 September, and reassigned to other batteries on the east bank.

At 6.00 (German time) on the morning of Sunday, 27 September, the offensive opened with concentrated Stuka bombing. As the Stukas peeled off, one by one, dropping into the attack with sirens screaming, their gull-winged shapes were black silhouettes against an autumnal dawn. On the ground, a total of two panzer divisions and five infantry divisions advanced to crush the main triangular salient which stuck out westwards from the Volga bank.

The 62nd Army pre-empted the main thrust of the German oper-ation, north of the Mamaev Kurgan, with several spoiling attacks on its southern side. These seemed to confirm the hyperactive suspicions of some German staff officers that Russian signallers had sneaked into their territory and tapped into German landlines. They could not accept that the preparations for their attack had been so obvious.

The main Soviet effort had been to prepare anti-tank obstacles and thick minefields in front of the main factories which extended northwards from the Mamaev Kurgan for five miles – the Lazur ('Azure') chemical plant, the Red October metalworks, the Barrikady weapons factory and the Stalingrad Tractor Factory.

The heavily laden *Landsers* started to move forwards to their start lines during the bombardment, down and up the sides of *balkas* turned into scree slopes with rubble. They were breathless from exertion as well as dry-mouthed from fearful anticipation of the battle ahead. On the left, part of the 389th Infantry Division prepared to advance towards the Barrikady workers' housing. One observer described them as 'white symmetrical blocks of buildings and little houses with their corrugated tin roofs sparkling'. The air bombardment soon set them ablaze. In the middle, the 24th Panzer Division pushed forward from the small airfield. The Austrian 100th Jäger Division attacked the Red October workers' settlements. Meanwhile, at the base of this flank, the top of the Mamaev Kurgan was retaken from Gorishny's 95th Rifle Division, which had been crushed by the air and artillery bombardment.

The Red Army again proved itself pitiless towards its own civilians. During the fighting for the Barrikady workers' settlements, a sergeant in the 389th Infantry Division (a former police sergeant from

Darmstadt) observed that 'Russian women who came out of the houses with their bundles and then tried to seek shelter from the firing on the German side, were cut down from behind by Russian machine-gun fire'.

The enemy's attack had been so strong that Chuikov said to himself: 'One more battle like that and we'll be in the Volga.' A little later, Khrushchev rang through from front headquarters to make sure that morale was holding. Chuikov replied, thinking no doubt of the fate of the 95th Rifle Division on the Mamaev Kurgan, that their main concern was German air power. Khrushchev also spoke to Gurov, the army commissar, urging him to greater efforts.

The next morning, Monday, 28 September, the Luftwaffe concentrated its attacks on the west bank and Volga shipping to destroy the 62nd Army's lifeline. The anti-aircraft guns of the Volga flotilla were in such constant use during this period that the rifling was rapidly worn smooth. Five supply boats out of six were seriously damaged. Chuikov begged for more support from the 8th Air Army, to keep off the Luftwaffe while he threw additional regiments into a counter-attack to retake the summit of the Mamaev Kurgan. They forced the Germans back, but the summit itself ended as a no man's land between the two sides. The vital task for Chuikov was to prevent the Germans establishing it as an artillery fire-base, from where they could control northern Stalingrad and the river crossings. That evening, Chuikov and his staff could feel some relief that the worst had been averted, but they knew that the loss of shipping was serious. Thousands of wounded lay on the river bank, unevacuated, and the front-line troops would soon run out of ammunition as well as rations.

On Tuesday, 29 September, the Germans began to crush the apex of the remaining triangle of Soviet territory. The village of Orlovka was attacked from the west by part of the 389th Infantry Division, and from the north-east by the 60th Motorized Infantry Division. The resistance of the outnumbered Soviet troops was so desperate that a corporal from the 389th wrote home: 'You can't imagine how they're defending Stalingrad – like dogs.'

The Soviet armies to the north again attacked XIV Panzer

Corps on 30 September. The 60th Motorized Infantry Division and the 16th Panzer Division between them claimed to have destroyed seventy-two tanks, in a 'major defensive success' against at least two Soviet rifle divisions and three tank brigades. The Don Front's costly attack did not deflect much pressure away from Orlovka or the industrial plants, but it helped slow the elimination of the Orlovka salient, a process which in the end took the Germans nearly ten days.

The 24th Panzer Division, most of the 389th Infantry Division and the 100th Jäger Division advanced towards the Red October metalworks and the Barrikady gun factory – 'the confusing tangle of a completely destroyed factory area', as one Jäger described the huge complex, in which almost every window and roof had been smashed by bombing, with rusted machinery twisted out of recognition. 'Already the first comrades were falling. The cries for medical orderlies increased. The fire intensified, but not just from in front, it was also now coming from both sides.' Russian artillery shells and mortar-bomb explosions also caused heavy casualties with stone fragments from the rubble as well as shrapnel.

Next day, to speed the attack on the Red October complex, Paulus ordered the 94th Infantry Division and 14th Panzer Division up from the southern sector of the city. On the Russian side, the hard-pressed 62nd Army also received some badly needed reinforcements when General Stepan Guriev's 39th Guards Rifle Division crossed the Volga. It was sent straight in to bolster the line on the right of the Red October works. Another fresh division, Colonel Gurtiev's 308th Rifle Division, a second formation made up mainly of Siberians, also started to cross the Volga, but these additions barely made up the losses already suffered.

Chuikov soon faced an unexpected danger. On 1 October, the 295th Infantry Division infiltrated down gullies on Rodimtsev's right flank. His guardsmen countered savagely, ambushing them at close quarters, with sub-machine-guns and grenades. But during the night, a large group of German infantry clambered through the main drain running down the Krutoy gully, and reached the Volga bank. They turned south and attacked the rear of Rodimtsev's division. This raid coincided with another breakthrough on the right. Rodimtsev reacted quickly, ordering every company he could spare into impromptu counter-attacks, and the situation was saved.

On 2 October, the Germans attacked the oil-storage tanks on the river bank just above Chuikov's headquarters. The tanks were not empty after all. Direct hits from German bombs or shells set them on fire. Burning oil poured down the hill, all around the headquarters and out into the river. Only the radio transmitter worked. 'Where are you?' Stalingrad Front headquarters signalled repeatedly. The reply eventually came back: 'We're where the most smoke and flames are.'

During the first week of October, Chuikov clearly had started to wonder whether they would be able to hold the rapidly narrowing strip of river bank. Everything depended on the Volga crossing. He knew that his badly mauled regiments had inflicted heavy casualties on the Germans, but the outcome of the battle depended on nerve as much as resources. They had no alternative but to stick with the 62nd Army's slogan: 'For the defenders of Stalingrad there is no ground on the other side of the Volga.' This really had become a sacred oath for many soldiers. One of the most famous acts of courage occurred at this time on the southern part of the factory district, when German tanks advanced on a position held in the ruins of a school by a detachment of marine infantry attached to 193rd Rifle Division. They had run out of anti-tank grenades, so Marine Mikhail Panikako seized two petrol bombs. As he was poised to throw the first one, a lucky German bullet shattered it in his hand, covering him in flames. He hurled himself forward over the last few yards, and flung himself against the side of the tank, smashing the other one in a ball of fire on the engine decks behind the turret.

German commanders were also alarmed. Their men were exhausted, and morale had suffered. Soldiers in the 389th Infantry Division, for example, did not disguise their hopes that they would have to be posted back to France because of the heavy casualties they had suffered. German war cemeteries behind the lines were growing every day. Those who heard Hitler's speech on 30 September from the Berliner Sportpalast were not encouraged when he boasted that the

Allied powers did not appreciate Germany's achievements, above all their advance from the Don to the Volga. Once again throwing down a gauntlet in the face of fate, Hitler insisted that 'no man will shift us from this spot'.

11

Traitors and Allies

'We Russians were ideologically prepared for the battle of Stalingrad,' said an officer veteran. 'Above all, we had no illusions about the cost, and were prepared to pay it.' The complete truth would have been to say that the Soviet state and perhaps a majority of the soldiers had few illusions. It is not an insult to their courage – if anything, it confirms it – to remember also the minority who would not, or could not, stand the appalling strain of the battle.

The Soviet authorities were pitiless. 'In the blazing city,' wrote Chuikov, 'we did not suffer cowards, we had no room for them.' Soldiers and civilians alike were warned with Stalin's quotation from Lenin: 'Those who do not assist the Red Army in every way, and do not support its order and discipline, are traitors and must be killed without pity.' All 'sentimentalism' was rejected. In total war, there were bound to be miscarriages of military justice, just as front-line troops risked being killed by their own artillery or aircraft.

Establishing a ferocious discipline was hard at first. Not until 8 October did the political department of the Stalingrad Front feel able to report to Moscow that 'the defeatist mood is almost eliminated, and the number of treasonous incidents is getting lower'. That the Soviet regime was almost as unforgiving towards its own soldiers as towards the enemy is demonstrated by the total figure of 13,500 executions, both summary and judicial, during the battle of Stalingrad. This included all crimes classed by the commissars as 'extraordinary

166

events', from retreating without orders to self-inflicted wounds, desertion, crossing over to the enemy, corruption and anti-Soviet activities.
Red Army soldiers were also deemed guilty if they failed to shoot
immediately at any comrades seen trying to desert or to surrender to
the enemy. On one occasion in late September, when a group of
Soviet soldiers surrendered, German tanks advanced rapidly to protect
them from fire directed at them from their own lines.

Chuikov's weakest units were the militia Special Brigades, made up
mainly of workers from factories in the northern part of Stalingrad.
Blocking groups of well-armed Komsomol volunteers or NKVD
detachments were placed behind them to prevent retreat. Their commissars in black leather jackets and armed with pistols reminded the
writer Konstantin Simonov of Red Guards in 1918. In the case of the
124th Special Brigade, facing the 16th Panzer Division up at Rynok,
the blocking groups behind the lines forced those who were cracking
under the strain to escape to the enemy. Dobronin reported to Khrushchev that, on 25 September, a group of ten deserters, including two
NCOs, crossed over to the Germans. The following night another five
men slipped away. According to the German report on the interrogation
of the first group of these very same deserters, their company strength
was down to fifty-five men. 'Since their last attack on 18 September, in
which they suffered heavy losses, they have been given no more tasks.
Behind the front line there is a second line of Party and Komsomol
members, armed with heavy machine-guns and machine pistols.'

A Soviet senior lieutenant from Smolensk deserted for a different
reason. He had been captured in the battle for the Don bend in
August, but managed to escape from German custody soon afterwards.
When he reported for duty again with the Red Army, 'he was arrested
according to an order of Stalin, treated as a deserter', and sent to a
penal company in 149th Special Brigade sector.

Others deserted for reasons which led the Germans into a false
optimism. 'Morale among the Russians is really bad,' an NCO from
the 79th Infantry Division wrote home. 'Most deserters are driven
over to us through hunger. It's possible that the Russians will suffer
from a famine this winter.'

*

Soviet records reveal a great deal about the mentality of the time. When three soldiers deserted from the 178th Reserve Rifle Regiment, a lieutenant was ordered to go off and grab three other men, either soldiers or civilians, to make up the loss. Many if not most deserters were from batches of civilian reinforcements drafted in to make up numbers. For example, a large proportion of the ninety-three deserters from 15th Guards Rifle Division had been 'citizens of Stalingrad evacuated to Krasnoarmeysk'. 'These men were completely untrained and some of them had no uniforms. In the haste of mobilization, their passports were not taken from many of them.' This, the report to Moscow acknowledged, was a serious mistake. 'Clad in civilian clothes and having passports, they easily managed to get back over the Volga. It is necessary and urgent to take passports from all soldiers.'

Commissars were incensed by rumours that the Germans allowed Russian and Ukrainian deserters to go home if they lived in the occupied territories. 'A shortage of political training is exploited by German agents, who carry out their work of corruption trying to persuade unstable soldiers to desert, especially those whose families are left in the territories temporarily occupied by the Germans.' These refugees from the German advance lacked any news on the fate of their families and homes.

Sometimes deserters were shot in front of an audience of a couple of hundred fellow soldiers from their division. More usually, however, the condemned man was led off by a squad from the guard detachment of the NKVD Special Department to a convenient spot behind the lines. There, he was told to strip so that his uniform and boots could be reused. Yet even such a straightforward task did not always go according to plan. After an execution in the 45th Rifle Division, a suspicious medical orderly found that the condemned man still had a pulse. He was about to shout for help, when an enemy artillery bombardment began. The executed soldier sat up, then climbed to his feet, and staggered off in the direction of the German lines. 'It was impossible to tell', ran the report to Moscow, 'whether [he] survived or not'.

The Special Department of the 45th Rifle Division must have contained unusually inaccurate marksmen; in fact one wonders whether they were encouraged in their work with an extra ration of vodka. On another occasion, they were ordered to execute a soldier, condemned for a self-inflicted wound. He was stripped of his uniform as usual, shot, and then thrown into a shell hole. Some earth was thrown over the body, and the firing party returned to divisional headquarters. Two hours later, the supposedly executed soldier, his underclothes caked in blood and mud, staggered back to his battalion. The same execution squad had to be called out to shoot him again.

In many cases, the authorities in the deserter's home neighbourhood were also informed. The family could then be persecuted under Order No. 270 as an extra punishment but, above all, as a warning. Commissars and the Special Department officers on the Stalingrad Front saw reprisals against close relatives as absolutely essential to deter others who might be tempted to run away.

NKVD Special Departments, when investigating cases of desertion, undoubtedly put heavy pressure on a suspect to denounce others. A newly arrived soldier in 302nd Rifle Division (51st Army) was accused by a comrade of having said: 'If I am sent to the front line, I will be the first to cross to the Germans.' 'Under interrogation', he is claimed to have confessed to persuading five others to go with him and 'revealed' their names, but he may have been pushed by the NKVD into inventing a conspiracy which had never existed.

Commissars blamed 'the carelessness and good-heartedness of officers' for desertion in a unit. But there were also countless cases of officers using their accepted right to shoot to kill as 'an extreme measure to be used only on active service when a Red Army man refuses to fulfil a military order or retreats from the field of battle'. On a rare occasion, however, the authorities considered that officers had been overharsh. 'During the night of 17/18 October, two soldiers disappeared from [204th Rifle Division in 64th Army]. The regimental commander and the commissar ordered the company commander to execute the platoon commander of the men who had deserted.' This nineteen-year-old junior lieutenant had joined the regiment only five days before, and scarcely knew the two deserters from his platoon. 'The company commander obeyed the order. He went to his trench and, in the presence of the commissar, shot him dead.'

*

Commissars, wanting to vaunt the all-embracing nature of the Soviet Union, could have pointed to the fact that nearly half the soldiers of the 62nd Army were not Russian. Propaganda sections, however, had good reasons to remain silent on the subject. Far too much was expected of the *levée en masse* from Central Asia. 'It is hard for them to understand things,' reported a Russian lieutenant sent in to command a machine-gun platoon, 'and it is very difficult to work with them.' The lack of familiarity with modern technology also meant that they were more likely to be confused and terrorized by air attack. Language difficulties and consequent misunderstandings naturally made things worse. One formation, 196th Rifle Division, which was mostly Kazakh, Uzbek and Tartar, 'received such severe losses that it had to be withdrawn from the front to be reconstituted'.

The commissars realized that things were badly wrong, but their only prescription was predictable: 'To indoctrinate soldiers and officers of non-Russian nationality in the highest noble aims of the peoples of the USSR, in the explanation of their military oath and the law for punishing any betrayal of the Motherland.' Their indoctrination cannot have been very successful, because many clearly had little idea what the war was about. A Tartar in 284th Rifle Division, unable to stand the fighting any more, decided to desert. He crawled forward in the dark from his position without being seen, but then lost his bearings in no man's land. Without realizing, he crossed back into the sector occupied by 685th Rifle Regiment. He found a command bunker and entered. Convinced that he had reached his destination, he presumed that the officers staring at him must be German officers wearing Russian uniform as a sort of disguise. 'He announced that he had come to surrender,' the report recorded. 'The traitor was executed.'

Commissars also faced a bureaucratic problem. 'It is very difficult to classify extraordinary events', the front political department explained to Shcherbakov in Moscow, 'because we cannot tell in many cases whether a soldier deserted or crossed over to the enemy.' 'In battle conditions', the department reported on another occasion, 'it is not always possible to determine for sure what happened to particular soldiers or groups of men. In 38th Rifle Division, a sergeant and a soldier who went off to collect their company's rations were never seen again. Nobody knew what had happened to them. They might have been buried by a large shell, or they might have deserted. Unless there are eyewitnesses, we can only suspect.'

The fact that officers often failed to count their soldiers properly did not help. Some absentees were listed as traitors, and then found to have been evacuated to a field hospital with serious wounds. Even a soldier who discharged himself from hospital to return to his unit to fight could find himself listed as a deserter and condemned. On occasions, the carelessness of officers was deliberate. The deaths of soldiers were sometimes not reported in order to obtain more rations, a practice as old as organized armies, but now defined as 'criminal disorder on the military roll'.

Dobronin's acknowledgement of the statistical difficulties should certainly be remembered when looking at the total of 446 desertions during September. No mention is made of the other category, 'crossing over to the enemy'. Yet even Stalingrad Front's own reports of group desertions indicate a serious problem. For example, after twenty-three men from a single battalion deserted over three nights, 'a protective zone' was 'set up in front of the front line', and officers formed 'a twenty-four-hour guard'.

Self-inflicted wounds were regarded as desertion by dishonesty. A soldier from Rodimtsev's 13th Guards Rifle Division, who was suspected of having shot himself in the hand, was escorted to the dressing station. He tried to escape in the dark when German artillery opened up, but was dragged back. A committee of doctors examined him and declared that the wound had been self-inflicted. The prisoner was then executed in front of an audience of soldiers drawn from his battalion. Even officers were charged with self-inflicted wounds. A nineteen-year-old lieutenant in 196th Rifle Division, having been accused of shooting himself through the left palm with a sub-machine-gun, was executed in front of an audience of officers from his formation. The report implies, with unconvincing logic, that his guilt was self-evident because he had 'tried to hide his crime by applying a bandage'.

Malingerers were seen to belong in the same category. 'Eleven soldiers in a field hospital pretended to be deaf and dumb,' Dobronin recorded, then added with grim satisfaction: 'but as soon as the medical commission decided that they were fit for military duty, and their papers were passed to the military tribunal, they started talking.'

The ultimate self-inflicted wound was suicide. Like the Wehrmacht, the Soviet authorities defined it as 'a sign of cowardice' or the product of 'unhealthy moods'. Even the definition of cowardice could take many forms. One pilot, who baled out of his burning plane, tore up his Communist Party candidate's card immediately after landing, because he thought he had come down behind German lines. On his return to base, the commissar accused him of cowardice under Stalin's Order No. 270, even though Soviet propaganda emphasized that the Germans executed Communists on the spot.

The NKVD and the political department of Stalingrad Front worked extremely closely on any hint of 'anti-Soviet' activity. For example, 'men found with German leaflets were handed over to the NKVD'. It was dangerous to pick one up, even for rolling a cigarette of *makhorka* tobacco. A soldier who lost his temper and told a superior officer what he thought of him and the Red Army, could face an accusation of 'counter-revolutionary propaganda' or 'non-belief in our victory'. Corporal K. in the 204th Rifle Division was executed for having 'discredited the leaders of the Red Army and uttered terroristic threats against his commanding officer'. Those who criticized the regime, like two soldiers in the 51st Army, were also handed over to the NKVD. One had 'spread fascist statements that collective farm workers were like slaves', and the other had said that 'Soviet propaganda lies to raise morale in the army'.

Cases of 'anti-Soviet activities', which were often treated as synonymous with the crime of 'treason to the Motherland', seem to have been comparatively rare in the front line. Officers generally followed the informal advice of the Russian Army in 1812: 'When soldiers mutter, officers should not listen.' Most recognized that in war, when men faced death, they needed to say what they thought. Among front-line comrades, soldiers did not shrink from criticizing the incompetence, corruption and bullying of Communist Party officials. The constant risk of being killed at any moment made them careless of commissars and Special Department informers. With their trenches so close to the Germans, there seemed little difference between an enemy bullet and that final ration from the Soviet state, the NKVD's 'nine grams of lead'.

Most of the reported cases of anti-Soviet activities took place behind the lines. Newly arrived recruits who grumbled were more likely to be denounced by fellow conscripts. A Stalingrad civilian in Training Battalion 178 who ventured to say that they would freeze and starve when winter came, was quickly arrested 'thanks to the political consciousness of Trainees K. and I.'. NKVD paranoia stretched back among the transport and engineer detachments of the Stalingrad Front on the east bank of the Volga. Twelve soldiers and five officers, including two senior officers, were arrested in October for 'anti-Soviet activities of a defeatist nature'. 'A majority of those arrested are from the occupied territories', the report added, claiming for good measure that they had a plan 'to betray the Motherland and join the enemy'.

The newspaper reports which claimed that *frontoviki* eagerly discussed the heroic leadership of Comrade Stalin in their trenches, and went into the attack with the battle-cry *'Za Stalina!'* ('For Stalin'), were pure propaganda. Yury Belash, a soldier poet, once wrote a verse:

> To be honest about it –
> in the trenches the last thing we thought about
> was Stalin.

However much the Soviet press played up stories of personal heroism, the authorities' total lack of respect for the individual was clearly confirmed by the propaganda at Stalingrad. Newspapers took up the slogan, apparently coined by Chuikov at a meeting of the military council: 'Every man must become one of the stones of the city.' One of Chuikov's officers added admiringly that the 62nd Army 'cemented the stones of the Stalin-inspired city like living concrete'. This theme reached its ultimate expression in the monstrous post-war memorial constructed on the Mamaev Kurgan, where the figures of soldiers among the ruins are deliberately portrayed in a bas-relief of brickwork. This monument to the Soviet Union, not to the soldiers themselves, virtually turns them into a terracotta army, like those of Chinese emperors.

Even day-to-day administrative policy confirmed the impression of soldiers as discardable items. New boots, uniforms and equipment were reserved for new armies being formed in the rear. For front-line soldiers at Stalingrad, replacement items did not come from the quartermaster's store, they came off the bodies of dead comrades. Nothing was wasted when it came to burial. Men were even sent forward at night into no man's land to strip corpses to their underclothes. The sight of fallen comrades, left semi-naked in the open, revolted many. When winter came in its full force, snow-camouflage suits became especially precious. A wounded soldier would try to take off the white coverall before it became bloodstained. It was a well-known occurrence for a soldier, too badly wounded to remove his snow-camouflage suit, to apologize for any marks to those taking it from him.

Grossman, a close observer of his fellow countrymen at Stalingrad, rejected the idea that they had been completely brutalized into indifference. 'Life is not easy for a Russian,' he wrote, 'but in his heart he does not feel that this is unavoidable. During the war at the front, I observed just two feelings towards events: either an incredible optimism or a complete gloom. No one can bear the thought that the war is going to last a long time, and anyone who says that only months and months of hard work will lead to victory is not believed.' The truth was that in such a terrible battle you could think only about surviving for the rest of that day or even hour. To look forward to any point beyond was dangerous dreaming.

Soldiers at least had some sort of purpose and fairly regular rations to keep them going. The civilians trapped in Stalingrad had virtually nothing. How over 10,000 of them, including 1,000 children, were still alive in the city's ruins after over five months of battle, remains the most astonishing part of the whole Stalingrad story.

Soviet sources claim that between 24 August, the day after the first air raids, when Stalingrad inhabitants were finally allowed to cross the Volga, and 10 September, 300,000 civilians were evacuated to the east bank. It was totally inadequate, considering the swollen population of the city. What was not admitted at the time was that well over 50,000 civilians were trapped on the west bank, partly due to the NKVD's control of river crossing.

1. (*Previous page*) Autumn 1941. Soviet prisoners of war being herded to the rear.
2. July 1942. German infantry marching towards Stalingrad.

3. A village destroyed in the advance.

4. German tanks on the Don steppe.

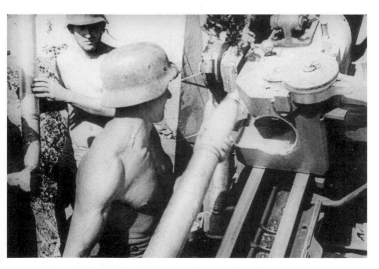

5. August 1942. German artillery outside Stalingrad.

6. Dr Alois Beck, chaplain of the 297th Infantry Division, writing letters for the wounded.

7. Paulus, Hitler, Keitel, Halder and Brauchitsch at the *Wolfsschanze*, near Rastenburg.

8. September 1942. Tanks of the 24th Panzer Division advancing into the outskirts of Stalingrad.

9. September 1942. Red Army tank troops listening to a speech from Khrushchev before going into battle.

10. The view which greeted Russian reinforcements about to cross the Volga into battle.

11. German officer and soldiers attacking factory buildings
in northern Stalingrad.

12. Russian infantry defending.

13. October 1942. Round-up of Stalingrad civilians.

14. 62nd Army HQ. Krylov, Chuikov, Gurov and Rodimtsev.
15. (*Overleaf*) Red Army assault squad in the
'Stalingrad Academy of street-fighting'.

The last official evacuation was chaotic and tragic. The crowd was huge. It included many families that had been refused permission to leave until the last moment, often without any good reason. The steamer became dangerously overloaded, so no more people were allowed on board. Those left behind on the jetty stood watching the ferry leave. They despaired for themselves, but then, 'only fifty yards out from the jetty, it was hit by a bomb' and sank, blazing, in front of their eyes.

Many civilians could not even get near the river's edge, having been trapped behind German lines by the Sixth Army's rapid advances. Hitler, on 2 September, had ordered Stalingrad to be cleared of civilians, yet the first exodus was more spontaneous than organized. A large column of refugees left the city heading west into German-occupied territory on 14 September, with their few remaining possessions piled on handcarts or carried in cardboard suitcases. A German correspondent saw civilians caught by shellfire turned into a bloody mess of torso and torn clothes, with a severed hand stuck in telegraph wires overhead. Yet those who escaped to safety in German territory had little hope of finding food. Detachments from the Sixth Army were already at work, requisitioning and harvesting any crops in the region for their own use. Even Cossack farmers, some of them former White Guards, who had welcomed the Germans as liberators with bread and salt, were robbed of all livestock and grain.

The sight of refugees could produce strange confusions of thinking, as a senior NCO from the 295th Infantry Division unintentionally revealed in a letter home. 'Today I saw many refugees coming from Stalingrad. A scene of indescribable misery. Children, women, old men – as old as grandpa – lie here by the road only lightly clothed and with no protection from the cold. Although they're our enemy, it was deeply shocking. For that reason we can't thank our Führer and the Good Lord enough, that our homeland has still been spared such terrible wretchedness. I have already seen much misery during this war, but Russia surpasses everything. Above all Stalingrad. You won't understand this – one has to have seen it.'

The many thousands of women and children left behind in the

city sought shelter in the cellars of ruins, in sewers and in caves dug into steep banks. There were apparently even civilians cowering in shell holes on the Mamaev Kurgan during the worst of the fighting. Many, of course, did not survive. Simonov, on his first visit, was astonished. 'We crossed a bridge over one of the gullies intersecting the city. I shall never forget the scene that opened out before me. This gully, which stretched to my left and right, swarmed with life, just like an anthill dotted with caves. Entire streets had been excavated on either side. The mouths of the caves were covered with charred boards and rags. The women had utilized everything that could be of service.'

He wrote of the 'almost incredible' suffering of all those in Stalingrad, whether soldier or civilian, but then quickly dismissed any notion of sentimentality – 'these things cannot be helped: the struggle being waged is for life or death'. He then went on to describe the body of a drowned woman washed up on the Volga shore holding on to a charred log 'with scorched and distorted fingers. Her face is disfigured: the suffering she underwent before death released her must have been unbearable. The Germans did this, did it in front of our eyes. And let them not ask for quarter from those who witnessed it. After Stalingrad we shall give no quarter.'

Although shelter was the first priority, civilians faced the virtual impossibility of finding food and water. Each time there was a lull in the bombardments, women and children appeared out of holes in the ground to cut slabs of meat off dead horses before homeless dogs and rats stripped the carcass. The chief foragers were children. Younger, smaller and more agile, they presented less of a target. They sneaked down at night to the badly burned grain elevator south of the Tsaritsa, which the Germans had finally captured. There, they often managed to fill bags or satchels with scorched wheat and scamper away, but German sentries, protecting the silos for their own army's use, shot a number of them. Those who attempted to steal German Army ration tins were also shot on the spot, both in Stalingrad itself, and in the rear areas.

German soldiers made use of Stalingrad orphans themselves. Daily tasks, such as filling water-bottles, were dangerous when Russian snipers lay in wait for any movement. So, for the promise of a crust of bread, they would get Russian boys and girls to take their water-bottles down to the Volga's edge to fill them. When the Soviet side realized what was happening, Red Army soldiers shot children on such missions. A precedent for such ruthlessness had been set during the early stages of the siege of Leningrad, when civilians had been used by German troops as a shield. Stalin had immediately issued an order that Red Army troops were to kill any civilians obeying German orders, even if they were acting under duress. This instruction was implemented in Stalingrad. 'The enemy', reported the 37th Guards Rifle Division, 'forced civilians forward to drag back dead German soldiers and officers. Our soldiers opened fire no matter who tried to carry away the fascist corpses.' Other children were much luckier. They attached themselves to Soviet regiments and head-quarters. Many were used as runners, scouts or spies, but the smaller orphans, some as young as four or five, were just mascots.

Sixth Army headquarters established one *Kommandantur* for the centre and north of the city, and another for south of the Tsaritsa. Each had a company of Feldgendarmerie responsible, among other things, for guarding against sabotage and registering and evacuating civilians. Instructions were issued that anyone who failed to register would be shot. Jews were ordered to wear a yellow star on their sleeve. The Feldgendarmerie worked closely with the Secret Field Police under Kommissar Wilhelm Möritz. One *Kommandantur* officer, cap-tured after the battle, admitted during interrogation that their tasks had also included the selection of 'suitable' civilians for forced labour in Germany and the handing over of Communist activists and Jews to the SD. Soviet sources claim that the Germans executed over 3,000 civilians during the fighting, and that more than 60,000 civilians from Stalingrad were transported back to the Reich, on Hitler's order, as slave labour. The number of Jews and Communists arrested by the Sixth Army's Feldgendarmerie and handed over to the SS is not given. Sonderkommando 4a, following the Sixth Army's advance, had reached Nizhne-Chirskaya in the wake of XXIV Panzer Corps on 25 August, and promptly massacred two truck-loads of children, 'the majority aged between six and twelve'. They had also executed a number of Communist officials and NKVD informers denounced by Cossacks, whose 'Kulak' families had suffered greatly at the regime's hands. The Sonderkommando remained in the Stalingrad area until the fourth week of September.

A major evacuation of civilians took place on 5 October, and the last at the beginning of November. Batches of civilians were selected for loading on to cattle trucks at railheads to the rear. The misery of refugees was all too evident. The wise took every blanket they could carry to barter for food in the weeks ahead. These Stalingrad civilians were marched first to an improvised camp near the village of Voroponovo (now Gorkovsky), then on to other camps at Marinovka, Kalach and Nizhne-Chirskaya.

The treatment they received was still not quite as bad as that suffered by captured Russian soldiers. In the cage near Gumrak there were, by 11 September, over 2,000 prisoners of war, many of them from worker militia battalions. Soviet officers were left to keep order, if necessary with their fists, when the food was thrown in over the wire. No medical facilities were provided. A Soviet doctor did what he could for the wounded, but 'in hopeless cases, he could only put them out of their misery'.

Subsequent round-ups were more brutal. Finally, 'a huge black crowd' was forced out into the first snows. This last and largest group of Stalingrad civilians was marched to Karpovka and other camps. Conditions were appalling. Even the name 'camp' was optimistic, since they were just a large encirclement of barbed wire on the open steppe. There were no huts. The prisoners tried to dig holes in the ground with their bare hands to escape the biting winds, then huddle together. On the night of 7 November, the anniversary of the revolution, the Russian prisoners celebrated, singing quietly among themselves, but that evening it began to rain heavily. Towards morning, the temperature fell rapidly, bringing a hard frost and they shivered uncontrollably in their sodden clothes. Many died. In one hole, the mother next to Valentina Nefyodova sat clasping an infant son and an infant daughter on her knees: the girl survived, but the boy died in her arms. Nefyodova's teenage cousin also froze to death that night.

The guards in these camps were mostly Ukrainians in German uniform.* Many were *bulbovitsi*, extreme right-wing nationalists named after Taras Bulba, who treated their victims terribly. Not all the guards, however, were cruel. Some allowed their charges to escape, in exchange for a bribe. But escapers were soon hunted down in the open steppe by Feldgendarmerie. In the Morozovsk camp, however, the Goncharov family, mother, grandmother and two children, were saved by the kindness of a German doctor, who arranged for them to be moved to a nearby farmstead because the eleven-year-old Nikolay was suffering from such bad frostbite.

Of the thousands who still managed to avoid the round-ups in the city, leading a troglodyte existence under the rubble – 'no one knows how' – virtually all fell sick from food poisoning or polluted water. On the outskirts of the town, children crept out, like wild animals at night, to search for roots and wild berries. Many survived for three or four days on a piece of stale bread given to them by either a German or a Russian soldier, depending on the front line. Women were often forced to offer their emaciated bodies to survive or to feed an infant. There are even reports of improvised brothels in the ruins. In several instances, love of a sort grew in the unpromising circumstances between Russian women and German soldiers. It was almost invariably a fatal liaison. A Stalingrad woman accused of 'signalling to the enemy with a white handkerchief', was found to have 'hidden three fascists' in her cellar. She was handed over to the NKVD. The three German soldiers were shot on the spot.

On the sectors away from the city itself, fewer German prisoners seem to have been killed on capture, once Soviet military intelligence started to become more sophisticated. Their need for accurate information from prisoners grew rapidly in October, while Zhukov and his staff were planning the great counterstroke.

---

* Some 270,000 Ukrainians had already been recruited from prison camps by 31 January 1942. Others were civilian volunteers. The *Stadtkommandantur* in Stalingrad, according to one NKVD report, had 800 armed and uniformed Ukrainian youths for sentry and escort duty.

The Soviet interrogation of German prisoners of war, which usually took place on the day after capture, followed a fairly set pattern. The chief objective was to identify their formation and assess its current strength, supply situation and morale. German prisoners were also asked such questions as: Had they been a member of the Hitler Youth? What did they know of preparations for chemical warfare? What partisan actions had they heard about or witnessed? How effective were Soviet propaganda leaflets? What did their officers tell them about Communists? What had been their division's route of advance since June 1941? (This was to see whether they could be linked to war crimes reported in any areas through which they had passed.) If the prisoner had come from a farming family, did they have Russian prisoners of war working for them at home? What were their names? Letters from home were confiscated to see if they gave any indication of civilian morale back in Germany. During the late summer and autumn of 1942, after the RAF's 'thousand-bomber raids', NKVD interrogators were particularly interested in their effect on civilian morale and also on soldiers at the front. Later, when the NKVD was shaken to discover that so many Soviet citizens, mainly former Red Army soldiers, were attached to the German Army, interrogators tried to discover from prisoners how many had been with each company.

Out of an instinct of self-preservation, prisoners often said what they expected the Russians to want to hear. In some cases it also happened to be the truth. 'Older soldiers', said another corporal, 'do not believe the propaganda stuffed into our heads by Goebbels. We remember the unforgettable lessons of 1918.' By mid-September, captured Germans soldiers were openly admitting to their Russian interrogators that they and their comrades were 'afraid of the approaching winter'.

Many of the prisoner interviews were carried out by Captain N. D. Dyatlenko of the NKVD, a German speaker transferred to the 7th Department of Stalingrad Front. Lieutenant-Colonel Kaplan, the 62nd Army's deputy chief of intelligence, on the other hand, had to interrogate prisoners through his interpreter Derkachev. Kaplan clearly wasted little time when he got to work. After a badly wounded corporal revealed that 24th Panzer Division was reduced to sixteen tanks, Kaplan noted at the bottom of the page: 'The interrogation was not completed because the man soon died of his wounds.'

Already aware of the tensions between the German and Romanian armies, Kaplan was also interested in strained relations within the Wehrmacht. Austrian prisoners, perhaps in the hope of better treatment, complained of the behaviour of German officers who discriminated against them. A thirty-two-year-old Czech in the 24th Panzer Division, who was captured on 28 September, even volunteered to fight for the Soviet Union. Red Army intelligence's main priority at this time, however, was to form an accurate assessment of the Germans' dependence on allied divisions along the Don Front and in the Kalmyk steppe.

A number of German regimental commanders at this time were horrified at the replacements they were being sent. One in the 14th Panzer Division wrote that 'very energetic measures' were needed to correct the 'absence of strength of will and bravery'.

The greatest weakness, however, remained the allied troops, represented as full armies on Hitler's situation map. The morale of Italians, Romanians and Hungarians alike had been shaken by isolated partisan raids on their trains to the front. It soon began to suffer badly from Russian air attack, even when few casualties were inflicted. And when they faced a Russian ground attack with *Katyusha* rockets from a 'Stalin organ', their troops began to wonder what they were doing there.

Soviet aircraft dropped leaflets written in Hungarian, Italian and Romanian, telling allied soldiers not to die uselessly for the Germans. This propaganda worked best on national minorities. Serbs and Ruthenians drafted into the Hungarian forces were the most likely to desert. 'How can we possibly trust those who are not Hungarians?' wrote Corporal Balogh in his diary. Red Army intelligence reported to Moscow that a number of small groups formed plans to desert together even before they reached the front. When the Russians attacked they hid in their trenches and waited to surrender.

A Ruthenian deserter from another regiment interviewed by the

NKVD reported that most of his comrades were praying 'God keep me alive' for 'whole days as they sat in their trenches. The majority of soldiers don't want to fight, but they are afraid to desert because they believe the officers' stories that the Russians will torture and shoot them.'

One of the greatest problems with allied armies was confusion. Front-line units were continually being shelled or bombed by their own allies. 'God help us and make this battle short,' wrote Corporal Balogh. 'Everyone is bombing and shelling us.' Less than a week later, he wrote: 'Oh God, stop this terrible war. If we are to take part in it for much longer our nerve will break . . . Will we ever again have a nice pleasant Sunday at home? Will we have the chance to lean on our gates again? Will they remember us at home?' Morale became so low that the Hungarian military authorities forbade soldiers to write home in case it led to severe unrest back in Budapest. Even bribery failed to work. Before the next attack, the soldiers were encouraged 'with the best meal possible – chocolate slabs, preserves, lard, sugar and goulash', but most of them suffered badly from stomach-ache afterwards, because 'a man here isn't accustomed to such a meal'.

'The Russians have remarkable marksmen,' wrote Balogh on 15 September. 'God, don't let me be their target. We are facing the best Russian units,' added the ill-informed corporal, 'Siberian riflemen under the command of Timoshenko. We are cold, but it is not winter yet. What would happen in winter if we are left to stay here? Help us, Blessed Virgin, to return home.' The next day's entry – another plea to 'God and the Blessed Virgin' – was the very last. Balogh's diary, retrieved from his body near the bank of the Don, was translated into Russian a few days later at the headquarters of General Vatutin's South-West Front and sent to Moscow.

The Italian 8th Army, which held the Don flank between the Hungarians and the 3rd Romanian Army, had caused concern to the Germans ever since late August. Führer headquarters was forced to agree that XXIX Army Corps should be used to strengthen the Italian defence. Its staff issued the following advice to liaison officers: 'You should treat them politely, and a political and psychological understanding is necessary . . . The climate and environment in Italy makes an Italian soldier different from a German soldier. Italians tire more easily on one hand, and on the other they are more exuberant. You should not be superior towards our Italian allies who came here fearlessly into hard and unfamiliar conditions to help us. Don't call them rude names, and don't be sharp with them.' Understanding did little to change the Italians' manifest lack of enthusiasm for the war. A sergeant, when asked by a Soviet interpreter why his whole battalion surrendered without firing a shot, replied with sound civilian logic: 'We did not fire back because we thought it would be a mistake.'

The Sixth Army, in a show of Anti-Comintern unity, even had an allied unit in the form of the 369th Croatian Regiment attached to the Austrian 100th Jäger Division. On 24 September, the Poglavnik of Croatia, Dr Ante Pavelić, arrived by air to inspect his troops and present medals. He was greeted by General Paulus and a guard of honour provided by Luftwaffe ground troops.

Strategically, the most important allied formations were the two Romanian armies on either flank of Paulus's Sixth Army. Not only were they ill-equipped, they were not even up to strength. The Romanian regime, under pressure from Hitler to provide more troops, had drafted more than 2,000 civilian convicts sentenced for rape, looting and murder. Half of them were sent to 991 Special Straf-battalion, but so many deserted on its first encounter with the enemy that the unit was disbanded, and the remainder transferred to the 5th Infantry Division on the Don Front opposite Serafimovich.

Romanian officers appear to have been unusually paranoid about the enemy infiltration of their rear. Outbreaks of dysentery were regarded with more than suspicion. 'Russian agents', declared a warning circular from 1st Romanian Infantry Division, 'have been carrying out mass poisonings in the rear to cause casualties among our troops. They use arsenic, one gram of which is enough to kill ten people.' The poison was supposedly concealed in matchboxes, and the 'agents' were identified as 'women, cooks and helpers connected with the provision of food'.

Germans of all ranks who came in contact with their allies were often dismayed at the way in which Romanian officers treated their men. They had an attitude of 'lords and vassals'. An Austrian count, Lieutenant Graf Stolberg, reported: 'Above all the officers were no good . . . they did not take any interest in their men.' A pioneer corporal from 305th Infantry Division noticed that the Romanian field kitchens prepared three sets of meals – 'one for officers, one for NCOs and one for the men, who got only a little to eat'.

Relations between the two allies were expressed in frequent brawls. 'To avoid in future lamentable incidents and misunderstandings between Romanian and German soldiers, whose friendship is sealed with blood shed in the common cause on the field of battle,' the commander-in-chief of the Third Romanian Army recommended the organization of 'visits, dinners, parties, small feasts and so on, so that Romanian and German units should establish a closer spiritual link'.

During the early autumn of 1942, Red Army intelligence officers had only an inkling of the Wehrmacht's dependence on 'Hiwis' – short for 'Hilfswillige' or volunteer helper. While some were genuine volunteers, most were Soviet prisoners of war, drafted from camps to make up shortages in manpower, primarily as labourers, but increasingly even in combat duties.

Colonel Groscurth, the chief of staff of XI Corps in the greater Don bend, observed in a letter to General Beck: 'It is disturbing that we are forced to strengthen our fighting troops with Russian prisoners of war, who already are being turned into gunners. It's an odd state of affairs that the "Beasts" we have been fighting against are now living with us in the closest harmony.' Sixth Army had over 50,000 Russian auxiliaries attached to its front-line divisions, representing over a quarter of their strength. The 71st and the 76th Infantry Divisions had over 8,000 Hiwis each, roughly the same number of men, by mid-November, as their total German strength. (There is no figure for the number of Hiwis attached to the rest of the Sixth Army and other ancillary formations, which, according to some estimates, would bring the total to over 70,000.)

'Russians in the German Army can be divided into three categories,' a captured Hiwi told his NKVD interrogator. 'Firstly, soldiers mobilized by German troops, so-called Cossack sections, which are attached to German divisions. Secondly, Hilfswillige made up of local people or Russian prisoners who volunteer, or those Red Army soldiers who desert to join the Germans. This category wears full German uniform, with their own ranks and badges. They eat like German soldiers and are attached to German regiments. Thirdly, there are Russian prisoners who do the dirty jobs, kitchens, stables and so on. These three categories are treated in different ways, with the best treatment naturally reserved for the volunteers. The ordinary soldiers treated us well, but the worst treatment came from officers and NCOs in an Austrian division.'

This particular Hiwi had been one of eleven Russian prisoners taken from the camp at Novo–Aleksandrovsk, at the end of November 1941, to work for the German Army. Eight were shot when they collapsed on the march from starvation. This survivor was attached to a field kitchen with an infantry regiment, where he peeled potatoes. Then he was transferred to looking after horses. Many of the so-called Cossack units formed for anti–partisan and rear-area repression, which he mentioned, contained a high proportion of Ukrainians and Russians. Hitler loathed the idea of *Untermensch* Slavs in German uniforms, so they had to be redefined as Cossacks, who were considered racially acceptable. This reflected the fundamental disagreement between the Nazi hierarchy, obsessed with the total subjugation of the Slav, and professional army officers who believed that their only hope was to act as the liberators of Russia from Communism. As early as the autumn of 1941, German Army intelligence had come to the conclusion that the Wehrmacht could not possibly win in Russia unless it turned the invasion into another civil war.

Hiwis who were induced, through promises, to volunteer from prison camp, were soon disabused. The Ruthenian deserter, during his interrogation, described some Hiwis he had encountered when looking for water in a village. They were Ukrainians who had deserted to the Germans in the hope of getting home to their families. 'We believed the leaflets,' they told him, 'and wanted to get back to our wives.' Instead, they found themselves in German uniform being trained by German officers. Discipline was ruthless. They could be shot 'for the smallest fault', such as falling behind on route marches.

Soon they would be sent to the front. 'Does this mean you will kill your own people?' asked the Ruthenian. 'What can we do?' they answered. 'If we run back to the Russians, we would be treated as traitors. And if we refuse to fight, we'll be shot by the Germans.'

Most front-line German units seem to have treated their Hiwis well, albeit with a measure of affectionate contempt. An anti-tank gun detachment in 22nd Panzer Division west of the Don used to give their Hiwi, whom they of course called 'Ivan', a greatcoat and a rifle to guard their anti-tank gun when they went down to the local village for a drink, but on one occasion they had to run back to rescue him because a group of Romanian soldiers, having discovered his identity, wanted to shoot him on the spot.

To the Soviet authorities, the idea of former Red Army soldiers serving with the Wehrmacht was distinctly disturbing. They jumped to the conclusion that the purges and the work of the Special Departments had not been nearly thorough enough. The Stalingrad Front political department and the NKVD were obsessed with the use of Hiwis to infiltrate and attack their lines. 'On some parts of the front', Shcherbakov was informed, 'there have been cases of former Russians who put on Red Army uniform and penetrate our positions for the purpose of reconnaissance and seizing officer and soldier prisoners for interrogation.' On 38th Rifle Division's sector (64th Army) on the night of 22 September, a Soviet reconnaissance patrol had bumped into a German patrol. The Red Army soldiers reported on their return that there had been at least one 'former Russian' with the Germans.

The phrase 'former Russian' was to serve as a death sentence for hundreds of thousands of men in the course of the next three years, as SMERSH concentrated on the question of treason, which lay so close to Stalin's heart. By summarily stripping opponents and defectors of their national identity, the Soviet Union attempted to suppress any hint of disaffection in the Great Patriotic War.

12

Fortresses of Rubble and Iron

'Will Stalingrad turn into a second Verdun?' wrote Colonel Groscurth on 4 October. 'That's what one's asking here with great concern.' After Hitler's speech at the Berlin Sportpalast four days before, claiming that nobody would ever shift them from their position on the Volga, Groscurth and others sensed that the Sixth Army would not be allowed to break off this battle, whatever the consequences. 'It has even become a matter of prestige between Hitler and Stalin.'

The great German assault against the factory district in northern Stalingrad had started well on 27 September, but by the end of the second day, German divisions knew that they were in for their hardest fight yet. The Red October complex and the Barrikady gun factory had been turned into fortresses as lethal as those of Verdun. If anything, they were more dangerous because the Soviet regiments were so well hidden.

Officers from Gurtiev's 308th Rifle Division of Siberians, on reaching the Barrikady factory and its railway sidings, took in 'the dark towering bulk of the repair shops, the wet glistening rails already touched in spots with rust, the chaos of shattered freight cars, the piles of steel girders scattered in confusion over a yard as large as a city square, the heaps of coals and reddish slag, the mighty smoke-stacks pierced in many places by German shells'.

Gurtiev designated two regiments to defend the plant, and the third to hold the flank including the deep ravine running through to the Volga from the workers' housing estate, which was already in flames. It soon became known as the 'Gully of Death'. The Siberians wasted no time. 'In grim silence they dug into the stony earth with their picks, cut embrasures in the walls of the workshops, fashioned dugouts, bunkers and communications trenches.' One command post was set up in a long concrete-sided bay which ran under the huge sheds. Gurtiev was well known as a tough trainer of troops. When waiting in reserve east of the Volga, he had made them dig trenches, then brought in tanks to roll over them. 'Ironing' like this was the best way to teach them to dig deep.

Fortunately for the Siberians, their trenches were ready by the time the Stukas arrived. The 'screechers' or the 'musicians', as the Russians called the dive-bombers with their wailing sirens, caused fewer casualties than usual. The Siberians had kept their trenches narrow, to reduce their exposure to bomb fragments, but the continual shock waves from bomb explosions made the earth vibrate as if from an earthquake and caused a sick pain in the stomach. The heavy percussion left everyone temporarily deaf. Sometimes, the shock waves were so intense that they shattered glass and threw radio sets out of tune.

These aerial softening-up attacks, known as 'house-warmings', lasted most of the day. Next morning, the Barrikady yards were carpet-bombed by Heinkel 111 squadrons, and shelled by artillery and mortars again. Suddenly the German guns ceased firing. Even before the shouted warning, 'Get ready!', the Siberians prepared themselves, knowing full well what the uneasy lull heralded. Moments later they heard the grinding and metallic screech of tank tracks on rubble.

The German infantry discovered over the next few days that Gurtiev's Siberian division did not sit waiting for them. 'The Russians made attacks every day at first and last light,' an NCO from the 100th Jäger Division reported. Chuikov's appallingly wasteful policy of repeated counter-attacks astonished German generals, although they were forced to acknowledge that it wore down their troops. The most successful defensive measures, however, were the heavy guns on the east bank of the Volga, once their fire plans were coordinated.

In the Red October plant, detachments from the 414th Anti-Tank Division had concealed their 45-mm and 96-mm guns in the rubble, using lumps of discarded metal as camouflage and protection. They were sited for firing from ranges as short as 150 yards or less. By dawn on 28 September, two regiments of the 193rd Rifle Division had also crossed the Volga, and rapidly prepared positions. Their 'house-warming' was carried out by massed Stuka attacks the following day. The German advance made further reinforcements an urgent need. The 39th Guards Rifle Division was sent across even though it was only a third of its proper strength.

The German attacks grew heavier into October, especially when reinforced with the 94th Infantry and the 14th Panzer Division as well as five combat engineer battalions flown in specially. On the Soviet side, units were completely fragmented, and often all communications broke down, but individuals and groups fought on without orders. On the Barrikady sector, Sapper Kossichenko and an unnamed tank driver, each with one arm shattered, pulled the pins from grenades with their teeth. At night, sappers continually ran forward carrying more anti-tank mines, two at a time, 'holding them under their armpits like loaves of bread', to bury them in the rubble of the approaches. The German attacks, wrote Grossman, were eventually blunted by 'dogged, rugged, Siberian obstinacy'. One German pioneer battalion in a single attack at this time sustained forty per cent casualties. The commander returned from visiting his men, stony-faced and silent.

Chuikov's divisions were badly mauled, exhausted and very short of ammunition. Yet on 5 October, General Golikov, Yeremenko's deputy commander, crossed the river to pass on Stalin's order that the city be held and the parts occupied by the Germans recaptured. Chuikov disregarded such an impossible instruction. He knew that his only chance of holding on depended on massive artillery bombardments from across the river. The Germans soon made Yeremenko's urgings irrelevant. After a relatively quiet day on 6 October, they launched a heavy assault on the Stalingrad tractor plant with the 14th Panzer Division attacking from the south-west and the 60th Motorized from the west. One of the 60th's battalions was virtually destroyed by salvoes of *Katyushas* fired at maximum range. The extra elevation was achieved by backing the launcher trucks so that their rear wheels hung over the steep Volga bank. Meanwhile, part of the 16th Panzer Division attacked the northern industrial suburb of Spartakovka, pushing back the remains of the 112th Rifle Division and the 124th Special Brigade. Chuikov's army, now down to a drastically reduced area along the west bank, felt that it was being relentlessly pushed back into the river.

The Volga crossings became increasingly vulnerable with the 62nd Army's perimeter so drastically reduced. German batteries and even machine-guns on direct fire ranged in on the landing points. A narrow pontoon bridge from Zaitsevsky island to the west bank had been built by a battalion of Volga watermen from Yaroslavl. This enabled a constant ant-like stream of bearers to cross during darkness, carrying rations and ammunition. Its small size reduced the target, but for those treading the constantly moving planks, the shells exploding in the river either side made each journey terrifying. Cargo boats were still needed for larger and heavier items, as well as evacuating the wounded. Replacement tanks were taken across by barge. 'As soon as dusk falls', wrote Grossman, 'the men responsible for the river crossing come out of their dugouts, bunkers, trenches and hidden shelters.'

Close to the landing points on the east bank there were field bakeries in bunkers, underground kitchens providing hot food in thermos containers, even bathhouses. Despite such comparative comforts, the regime on the east bank was virtually as harsh as in the city itself. The cargo boats and their crews, drafted into the 71st Special Service Company, came directly under the new NKVD commander, Major-General Rogatin, who also commanded the military office of the River District.

Casualty rates among the riverboat crews ranked with those of front-line battalions. For example, the steamer *Lastochka* ('the Swallow'), while evacuating wounded, received ten direct hits on a single crossing. The surviving members of the crew repaired the holes during the day, and were ready to sail again the following night.

Losses could also be heavy from accidents under pressure. On 6 October, an overloaded boat capsized and sixteen men out of twenty-one were drowned. Shortly afterwards, another craft landed in the dark at the wrong place and thirty-four people were killed in a minefield. Although slightly late in the day, the incident prompted the authorities to 'encircle minefields with barbed wire'.

The strain of the work often led to an alcoholic binge if the opportunity arose. On 12 October, when NKVD troops searching for deserters carried out a spot check on houses in the riverside village of Tumak, they found a 'disgraceful scene'. A captain, a commissar, a stores sergeant, a corporal from the Volga flotilla and the local secretary of the Communist Party had 'drunk themselves out of consciousness', as the report put it, and were lying on the floor 'in a sleeping state with women'. Still in their hopelessly inebriated condition, they were dragged in front of 'the chief of NKVD troops in Stalingrad, Major-General Rogatin'.

There were the odd scandals on land as well. On 11 October, in the thick of the fighting for the Stalingrad tractor plant, T-34s from the 84th Tank Brigade, with soldiers from the 37th Guards Rifle Division clinging on to turrets and engine decks, counter-attacked the 14th Panzer Division on the south-west side of the works. Both of these Soviet formations were newcomers to the west bank. One tank driver, failing to spot a shell hole through his hatch visor, drove into it. According to the report 'the infantry company commander, who was drunk', flew into a rage at the jolt they received and jumped down. 'He ran round to the front of the tank, opened the hatch and fired two shots, killing the driver.'

In that second week of October, a lull occurred in the fighting. Chuikov rightly suspected that the Germans were preparing an even bigger attack, probably with reinforcements.

Paulus was under as much pressure from Hitler as Chuikov was from Stalin. On 8 October, Army Group B, on orders from Führer headquarters, had instructed the Sixth Army to prepare another major offensive against northern Stalingrad to start at the latest by 14 October. Paulus and his headquarters staff were dismayed by their losses. One of his officers noted in the war diary that 94th Infantry Division was reduced to 535 front-line troops, 'which signifies an average fighting strength per infantry battalion of three officers, eleven NCOs and sixty-two men!' He also described 76th Infantry Division as 'fought out'. Only the 305th Infantry Division, recruited from the northern shores of Lake Constance, could be spared within the Sixth Army to strengthen the formations already committed.

The Germans, with shouted taunts and leaflets, made no secret of their preparations. The only question was the precise objective. Reconnaissance companies from Soviet divisions were out every night to seize as many 'tongues' as possible. Hapless sentries or ration-carriers were dragged back for intensive interrogation, and the prisoner, usually out of sheer terror after all the Nazi propaganda about Bolshevik methods, was only too eager to talk. The intelligence section at 62nd Army headquarters soon concluded from a combination of sources that the main thrust would again be directed against the tractor plant. The remaining workers there and at the Barrikady, who had been repairing tanks and anti-tank guns right through the fighting, were either drafted into front-line battalions or, in the case of specialists, evacuated across the Volga.

Fortunately for the 62nd Army, their intelligence analysis proved correct. The German objectives were to clear the tractor factory and the brickworks on its southern side, then push on to the Volga bank. Chuikov's risky decision to bring regiments from the Mamaev Kurgan to the northern sectors paid off. He was, however, horrified to hear that the *Stavka* had reduced the Stalingrad Front's allocation of artillery ammunition. This was the first hint that a major counter-attack was in preparation. Stalingrad, he suddenly realized with mixed emotions, now represented the bait in an enormous trap.

On Monday, 14 October, at 6 a.m. German time, the Sixth Army's offensive began on a narrow front, using every available Stuka in General von Richthofen's Fourth Air Fleet. 'The whole sky was full of aircraft,' wrote a soldier in 389th Infantry Division, waiting to go into the attack, 'every flak gun firing, bombs roaring down, aircraft crashing, an enormous piece of theatre which we followed with very mixed feelings from our trenches.' German artillery and mortar fire smashed in dugouts, and phosphorus shells ignited any remaining combustible material.

'The fighting assumed monstrous proportions beyond all possibility of measurement,' wrote one of Chuikov's officers. 'The men in the communication trenches stumbled and fell as if on a ship's deck during a storm.' Commissars clearly felt an urge to become poetic. 'Those of us who have seen the dark sky of Stalingrad in these days', Dobronin wrote to Shcherbakov in Moscow, 'will never forget it. It is threatening and severe, with purple flames licking the sky.'

The battle began with the main attack on the tractor plant from the south-west. At midday, part of XIV Panzer Corps recommenced its push from the north. Chuikov did not hesitate. He committed his main armoured force, the 84th Tank Brigade, against the major assault of three infantry divisions spearheaded by the 14th Panzer Division. 'Our support from heavy weapons was unusually strong', wrote an NCO in the 305th Infantry Division. 'Several batteries of Nebel-werfer, Stukas shuttle-bombing and self-propelled assault guns in quantities never seen before bombarded the Russians, who in their fanaticism put up a tremendous resistance.'

'It was a terrible, exhausting battle', wrote an officer in 14th Panzer Division, 'on and below the ground, in ruins, cellars, and factory sewers. Tanks climbed mounds of rubble and scrap, and crept screech-ing through chaotically destroyed workshops and fired at point-blank range in narrow yards. Many of the tanks shook or exploded from the force of an exploding enemy mine.' Shells striking solid iron installations in the factory workshops produced showers of sparks visible through the dust and smoke.

The stamina of Soviet soldiers was indeed incredible, but they simply could not withstand the force at the central point of the attack. During the first morning, the German panzers broke through, cutting off Zholudev's 37th Guards and the 112th Rifle Division. General Zholudev was buried alive in his bunker by an explosion, a common fate during that terrible day. Soldiers dug him out and carried him to army headquarters. Others seized the weapons of the dead and fought on. The dust-covered German panzers smashed right into the huge sheds of the tractor plant, like prehistoric monsters, spraying machine-gun fire all around, and crunching the shards of glass from the shattered skylights under their tracks. During the close-quarter fighting which followed, there were no clear front lines. Bypassed groups of Zholudev's guardsmen would suddenly attack as if from nowhere. In such conditions, a wise German medical officer set up his forward dressing station inside a smelting furnace.

By the second day of the offensive, 15 October, Sixth Army headquarters felt able to record: 'The major part of the tractor works is in our hands. There are only some pockets of resistance left behind our front.' The 305th Infantry Division also forced the Russians back across the railway lines at the brickworks. That night, after 14th Panzer Division's breakthrough into the tractor works, its 103rd Panzer Grenadier Regiment boldly cut through to the Volga bank by the oil tanks, harried by Soviet infantry attacking out of gullies. Fortunately for 62nd Army, Chuikov had been persuaded to move his headquarters, because communications were so bad. The fighting had hardly slackened. The 84th Tank Brigade claimed to have destroyed 'more than thirty medium and heavy fascist tanks' for the loss of eighteen of their own. The brigade's human losses were 'still being calculated' when the report went in two days later. Although the figure for German tanks was almost certainly optimistic, the brigade's junior commanders demonstrated inspiring courage that day.

The commissar of a light-artillery regiment, Babachenko, was made a Hero of the Soviet Union for his bravery when a battery was cut off. The defenders' farewell radio message received at headquarters read: 'Guns destroyed. Battery surrounded. We fight on and will not surrender. Best regards to everyone.' Yet, using grenades, rifles and sub-machine-guns, the gunners broke the enemy encirclement and made a fresh stand, helping to restore the sector's line of defence.

There were countless cases of unsung bravery by ordinary soldiers – 'real mass heroism', as the commissars put it. There were also trumpeted incidents of individual bravery, such as a company commander of 37th Guards Rifle Division, Lieutenant Gonychar, who with a captured machine-gun and just four men, managed to disperse an attacking German force at a critical moment. Nobody knew how many Red Army soldiers died that day, but 3,500 wounded were taken back across the Volga that night. The overworked medical orderlies suffered so many casualties that many of the wounded crawled to the river bank alone.

German commanders out in the steppe demanded constant news of progress in the city. 'Factory walls, assembly lines, the whole superstructure collapses under the storm of bombs,' wrote General Strecker to a friend, 'but the enemy simply reappears and utilizes these newly created ruins to fortify his defensive positions.' Some German battalions were down to fifty men. They sent back the corpses of their comrades at night for burial. Inevitably, a certain cynicism arose in German ranks about their leadership. 'Our General,' a soldier of 389th Infantry Division wrote home, 'Jeneke [Jaenecke] he's called, received the Knight's Cross the day before yesterday. Now he's achieved his objective.'

During the six days of fighting from 14 October, the Luftwaffe maintained relays of aircraft attacking river crossings and troops. There was hardly a moment when German aircraft were not overhead. 'The help of our fighter force is needed,' noted the political department of Stalingrad Front in a coded criticism of Red Army aviation passed on to Moscow. In fact, the 8th Air Army was down to fewer than 200 machines of all types, of which only two dozen were fighters. Yet even Luftwaffe pilots shared the growing suspicion of ground troops that the Russian defenders of Stalingrad might prove invincible. 'I cannot understand', one wrote home, 'how men can survive such a hell, yet the Russians sit tight in the ruins, and holes and cellars, and a chaos of steel skeletons which used to be factories.' These pilots also knew that their effectiveness would soon decrease rapidly as daylight hours shortened and the weather deteriorated.

The successful German thrust to the Volga just below the Stalingrad tractor plant entirely cut off the remains of the 112th Rifle Division and the militia brigades which had been facing XIV Panzer Corps to the north and west. While encircled fragments of Zholudev's 37th

Guards Rifle Division continued to fight on in the tractor plant, the remnants of the other formations were squeezed southwards. The great threat to the 62nd Army's survival was a German thrust down the river bank, cutting off Gorishny's division from the rear.

Chuikov's new headquarters were in constant danger. Its close-defence group was frequently thrown into the fighting. Since the 62nd Army lost communications so often, Chuikov asked permission for a rear headquarters group to cross to the left bank, while a forward group, including the whole military council, remained on the east bank. Yeremenko and Khrushchev, only too aware of Stalin's reaction, refused point-blank.

Also on 16 October, the Germans pushed down from the tractor works towards the Barrikady plant, but the combination of Russian tanks buried in the rubble and screaming salvoes of *Katyusha* rockets from the river bank broke up their attacks. That night, the rest of Lyudnikov's 138th Rifle Division was brought across the Volga. As they marched forward from disembarkation, they had to step over 'hundreds of wounded crawling towards the landing stage'. The fresh troops were thrown into an oblique line of defence just north of the Barrikady works.

General Yeremenko also crossed the river that night to assess the situation for himself. Leaning heavily on a walking stick after his wounds the previous year, he limped up the bank to the overcrowded bunkers of 62nd Army headquarters. The craters and smashed timbers of dugouts which had received direct hits left little to the imagination. Objects and individuals alike were covered in dust and ash. General Zholudev broke down in tears, recounting the destruction of his division in the tractor works. Yet next day, after Yeremenko's return, Front headquarters had to warn Chuikov that even less ammunition would be available.

After the Germans had cut off the Soviet forces north of the Stalingrad tractor plant on the night of 15 October, Chuikov received little encouraging news from them, only 'many requests' from the head-quarters of 112th Rifle Division and 115th Special Brigade for per-mission to withdraw across the Volga. Both headquarters apparently provided 'false information', claiming that their regiments had been virtually wiped out. This request to withdraw, tantamount to treason after Stalin's order, was rejected. During a lull in the fighting several days later, Chuikov sent Colonel Kamynin to the enclave to check the state of their regiments. He found that 112th Rifle Division still had 598 men left, while 115th Special Brigade had 890. The senior commissar, according to the report, 'instead of organizing an active defence . . . did not emerge from his bunker and tried in a panic-stricken way to persuade his commander to withdraw across the Volga'. For 'their betrayal of Stalingrad's defence' and 'exceptional cowardice', the accused senior officers and commissars were later court-martialled by the Military Council of 62nd Army. Their fate is not recorded, but they can have expected little mercy from Chuikov.

Diversionary offensives were mounted on 19 October by the Don Front to the north-west, and by 64th Army to the south. These efforts took the pressure off the 62nd Army for only a few days, but the breathing-space enabled shattered regiments to be pulled back across the Volga to re-form with reinforcements. Spiritual help came in a strange form. Rumours spread that Comrade Stalin himself had been seen in the city. An old Bolshevik who had fought in the siege of Tsaritsyn even claimed that the Great Leader had appeared in his former headquarters. This visitation, reminiscent of St James's miraculous appearance to the Spanish Army when fighting the Moors, had absolutely no foundation in truth.

One prominent civilian, however, was particularly keen to visit the west bank at this time. This was Dmitry Manuilsky, the Comintern veteran responsible for German affairs, who had made a doomed attempt with Karl Radek to launch a second German revolution in October 1923 before Lenin finally expired. He had later been the Ukrainian largely responsible for Stalin's devastation of the Ukraine in 1933. Manuilsky had a special interest which was to manifest itself later, but Chuikov firmly refused his requests to visit the west bank.

Back in Berlin, Goebbels's moods vacillated again between a conviction that the fall of Stalingrad was imminent – he gave orders on 19 October that all recipients of the Knight's Cross should be brought back for press interviews – and moments of caution. Concerned that the German people might be disappointed at the slow progress, he felt that they should be reminded of how far the German armies had advanced in just sixteen months. He gave orders that signs should be put up in German cities showing the distance to Stalingrad. Three days later he ordered that names such as Red October and Red Barricade should be avoided at all costs when reporting the tough fighting, in case it encouraged 'Communist-infected circles'.

During the huge battles for the northern industrial sector of the city, house-fighting, with local attacks and counter-attacks, had continued in the central districts. One of the most famous episodes of the Stalingrad battle was the defence of 'Pavlov's house', which lasted for fifty-eight days.

At the end of September, a platoon from the 42nd Guards Regiment had seized a four-storey building overlooking a square, some 300 yards in from the top of the river bank. Their commander, Lieutenant Afanasev, was blinded early in the fighting, so Sergeant Jakob Pavlov took over command. They discovered several civilians in the basement who stayed on throughout the fighting. One of them, Mariya Ulyanova, took an active part in the defence. Pavlov's men smashed through cellar walls, to improve their communications, and cut holes in the walls, to make better firing points for their machine-guns and long-barrelled anti-tank rifles. Whenever panzers approached, Pavlov's men scattered, either to the cellar or to the top floor, from where they were able to engage them at close range. The panzer crews could not elevate their main armament sufficiently to fire back. Chuikov later liked to make the point that Pavlov's men killed more enemy soldiers than the Germans lost in the capture of Paris. (Jakob Pavlov, made a Hero of the Soviet Union, later became the Archimandrite Kyrill in the monastery at Sergievo – formerly Zagorsk – where he attracted a huge following of the faithful that had nothing to do with his fame from Stalingrad. He is now very frail.)

Another story, more of a vignette gleaned from letters, concerned Lieutenant Charnosov, an artillery observer from the 384th Artillery Regiment. His observation post was at the top of a shell-wrecked building from where he called down artillery fire. His last letter to his wife read: 'Hello, Shura! I send kisses to our two little birds, Slavik and Lydusia. I am in good health. I have been wounded twice but these are just scratches and so I still manage to direct my battery all right. The time of hard fighting has come to the city of our beloved leader, to the city of Stalin. During these days of hard fighting I am avenging my beloved birthplace of Smolensk, but at night I go down to the basement where two fair-haired children sit on my lap. They remind me of Slavik and Lyda.' On his body was found his wife's previous letter. 'I am very happy that you are fighting so well,' she had written, 'and that you have been awarded a medal. Fight to the last drop of your blood, and don't let them capture you, because prison camp is worse than death.'

This exchange of letters was seen as exemplary, and also as typical of the moment. They may well be genuine, but like many others, they revealed only a partial truth. When soldiers sat down in the corner of a trench or ill-lit cellar to write home, they often had trouble expressing themselves. The single sheet, which would later be folded into a triangle, like a paper boat, because there were no envelopes, seemed both too large and too small for their purposes. The resultant letter stuck, as a result, to three main themes: enquiries after the family at home, reassurance ('I'm getting along all right – still alive'), and preoccupation with the battle ('we are constantly destroying their manpower and equipment. Day or night, we won't leave them in peace'). Red Army soldiers in Stalingrad were well aware that the whole nation's eyes were on them, but many must have tailored part of their letters because they knew that the Special Departments censored mail carefully.

Even when they wanted to escape when writing to their wife or sweetheart, the battle stayed with them always, partly because a man's worth was defined by the opinion of his comrades and commander. 'Mariya,' wrote a certain Kolya, 'I think you will remember our last evening together. Because now, this minute, it is exactly a year since we were parted. And it was very difficult for me to say goodbye to you. It's very sad, but we had to part because it was the order of the Motherland. We are carrying out this order as well as we can. The Motherland requires those of us who are defending this town to resist to the end. And we are going to carry out that order.'

The majority of Russian soldiers seem to have subsumed their personal feelings within the cause of the Great Patriotic War. They may have been more afraid of the censor than their German counterparts; they may have been more effectively brainwashed by the Stalinist regime, and yet the concept of self-sacrifice comes across as much more than an ideological slogan. It appears almost atavistic, a moral compulsion in the face of the invader. 'People might reproach me', wrote a Red Army lieutenant in Stalingrad to his bride of a few weeks, 'if they read this letter about the reason why I am fighting for you. But I can't distinguish where you end, and where the Motherland begins. You and it are the same for me.'

A comparative study of letters home written by officers and soldiers on both sides is most instructive. In many of the letters from Germans in Stalingrad at this time, there is often a hurt, disabused, even disbelieving note at what was happening, as if this was no longer the same war on which they had embarked. 'I often ask myself', wrote a German lieutenant to his wife, 'what all this suffering is for. Has mankind gone crazy? This terrible time will mark many of us for ever.' And despite the optimistic propaganda of imminent victory at home, many wives sensed the truth: 'I can't stop worrying. I know that you are fighting constantly. I will always be your faithful wife. My life belongs to you and to our world.'

There was also a surprising number of dissatisfied Russian soldiers who either forgot that their letters were censored, or were so downcast that they no longer cared. Many complained about their rations. 'Aunt Lyuba,' wrote one young soldier, 'please send me some food. I am ashamed to ask you, but hunger makes me do it.' Many admitted that they were reduced to scavenging, and others told their families that soldiers were falling ill 'because of bad food and insanitary conditions'. One soldier suffering from dysentery wrote: 'If it goes on like this, it won't be possible to avoid an epidemic. We also have lice, which are the first source of disease.' The soldier's prediction soon proved correct. In Hospital 4169, soldiers with typhus were rapidly isolated. The doctors thought that 'the wounded caught typhus from local people on the way to the hospital and that it spread from there'.

As well as complaints about bad food and conditions, strong traces of defeatism still surfaced. The commissars, always ready to jump at their own shadows in the Stalinist night, were clearly unsettled by the results of NKVD postal censorship. 'In 62nd Army alone, in the first half of October, military secrets were divulged in 12,747 letters,' the political department reported to Moscow. 'Some letters contain clear anti-Soviet statements, praising the fascist army and failing to believe in the victory of the Red Army.' A few examples were quoted. 'Hundreds and thousands of people die every day,' wrote a soldier to his wife. 'Now it is all so hard that I do not see a way out. We can consider Stalingrad as good as surrendered.' At a time when most Russian civilians had been living off little more than soups made from nettles and other weeds, a soldier in the 245th Rifle Regiment wrote to his family: 'In the rear they must be shouting that everything should be for the front, but at the front we have nothing. The food is bad and there is little of it. The things they say are not true.' Almost any form of honesty in a letter home was fatal. A lieutenant who wrote that 'German aircraft are very good . . . Our anti-aircraft people shoot down only very few of them' was also identified as a traitor.

The danger did not lie only with the censors. A very naive eighteen-year-old Ukrainian, drafted as a reinforcement into Rodimtsev's division, told fellow soldiers that they should not believe all that they were told about the enemy: 'In the occupied territory, I have a father and a sister and the Germans there don't kill or rob from anyone. They treat people well. My sister has been working for Germans.' His comrades arrested him on the spot. 'The investigation is under way,' the report to Moscow concluded.

One form of political repression within the Red Army was in fact easing at this time. Stalin, in a deliberate policy to boost morale, had already announced the introduction of awards with a decidedly reactionary flavour, such as the Orders of Kutuzov and Suvorov. But his most overt reform, announced on 9 October, was Decree 307, which re-established the single command. Commissars were downgraded to an advisory and 'educational' role.

Commissars were appalled to discover quite how much Red Army officers loathed and despised them. Officers in aviation regiments were said to have been particularly insulting. The political department of Stalingrad Front deplored the 'absolutely incorrect attitude' which had emerged. One regimental commander said to his commissar: 'Without my permission, you have no right to enter and speak to me.' Other commissars found their 'living standards decrease', since they were 'forced to eat with the soldiers'. Even junior lieutenants dared to remark that they did not see why commissars should receive officers' pay any more, 'because now that they are no longer responsible for anything, they will read a newspaper and go to bed'. Political departments were now considered an 'unnecessary appendix'. To say that commissars were finished, Dobronin wrote to Shcherbakov in a clear attempt to seek support, was 'a counter-revolutionary statement'. Dobronin had already revealed his own feelings when, earlier in October, he reported, without criticism, that a soldier had said: 'They've invented the Orders of Kutuzov and Suvorov. Now they should also have medals of St Nicholas and St George, and that'll be the end of the Soviet Union.'

The principal Communist awards – Hero of the Soviet Union, Order of the Red Banner, Order of the Red Star – were still, of course, taken very seriously by the political authorities, even if the Red Star had become something of a Stakhanovite ration issued to every man who destroyed a German tank. When, on the night of 26 October, the chief of the manpower department of 64th Army lost a suitcase containing forty Orders of the Red Banner, while waiting for a ferry to cross the Volga, a terrible consternation ensued. One might almost have thought that the defence plans for the whole of the Stalingrad Front had been lost. The suitcase was finally rediscovered two miles away on the following day. Only a single medal was missing. It may well have been taken by a soldier who decided, perhaps warming to the idea after a few drinks, that his efforts at the front had been insufficiently recognized. The chief of the manpower department was put in front of a military tribunal, charged with 'criminal carelessness'.

Soldiers, on the other hand, had a much more robust attitude toward these symbols of bravery. When one of them received an award, his comrades dropped it in a mug of vodka, which he then had to drink, catching the medal in his teeth as he drained the last drops.

The real Stakhanovite stars of the 62nd Army were not in fact the destroyers of tanks, but snipers. A new cult of 'sniperism' was launched, and as the twenty-fifth anniversary of the October Revolution approached, the propaganda surrounding this black art became frenzied, with 'a new wave of socialistic competition for the largest numbers of Fritzes killed'. A sniper on reaching forty kills would receive the 'For Bravery' medal, and the title of 'noble sniper'.

The most famous sniper of them all, although not the highest scorer, was Zaitsev in Batyuk's division, who, during the October Revolution celebrations, raised his tally of kills to 149 Germans. (He had promised to achieve 150, but was one short.) The highest scorer, identified only as 'Zikan', killed 224 Germans by 20 November. For the 62nd Army, the taciturn Zaitsev, a shepherd from the foothills of the Urals, represented much more than any sporting hero. News of further additions to his score passed from mouth to mouth along the front.

Zaitsev, whose name means hare in Russian, was put in charge of training young snipers, and his pupils became known as *zaichata*, or 'leverets'. This was the start of the 'sniper movement' in the 62nd Army. Conferences were arranged to spread the doctrine of 'sniperism', and exchange ideas on technique. The Don and South-West Fronts took up the 'sniper movement', and produced their star shots, such as Sergeant Passar of 21st Army. Especially proud of his head shots, he was credited with 103 kills.

Non-Russian snipers were singled out for praise: Kucherenko, a Ukrainian, who killed nineteen Germans, and an Uzbek from 169th Rifle Division who killed five in three days. In 64th Army, Sniper Kovbasa (the Ukrainian word for sausage) worked from a network of at least three trenches, one for sleeping and two fire trenches, all connected. In addition, he dug fake positions out to the side in front of neighbouring platoons. In these he installed white flags attached to levers, which he could agitate from a distance with cords. Kovbasa proudly claimed that as soon as a German saw one of his little white flags waving, he could not help raising himself in his trench to take a better look, and shout '*Rus, komm, komm!*' Kovbasa then got him from an angle. Danielov in 161st Rifle Regiment also dug a false trench, and fashioned scarecrow figures with bits of Red Army equipment. He then waited for inexperienced German soldiers to shoot at them. Four of them fell victim. In 13th Guards Rifle Division Senior Sergeant Dolymin, installed in an attic, picked off the crews of an enemy machine-gun, and a field gun. The most prized targets, however, remained German artillery spotters. 'For two days [Corporal Studentov] tracked an observation officer and killed him with the first shot.' Studentov vowed to raise his score to 170 Germans from 124 by the anniversary of the Revolution.

All the star snipers had their own techniques and favourite hiding places. 'Noble sniper' Ilin, who was credited with '185 Fritzes', sometimes used an old barrel, or pipe, as a hide. Ilin, a commissar from a Guards rifle regiment, operated on the Red October sector. 'Fascists should know the strength of weapons in the hands of Soviet supermen,' he proclaimed, promising to train ten other snipers.

Some Soviet sources claim that the Germans brought in the chief of their sniper school to hunt down Zaitsev, but that Zaitsev outwitted him. Zaitsev, after a hunt of several days, apparently spotted his hide under a sheet of corrugated iron, and shot him dead. The telescopic sight off his prey's rifle, allegedly Zaitsev's most treasured trophy, is still exhibited in the Moscow armed forces museum, but this dramatic story remains essentially unconvincing. It is worth noting that there is absolutely no mention of it in any of the reports to Shcherbakov, even though almost every aspect of 'sniperism' was reported with relish.

Grossman was fascinated by the character and life of snipers. He got to know Zaitsev well, and several others, including Anatoly Chekov. Chekov had followed his father, a drunkard, to work in a chemical plant. He had 'learned the dark sides of life' since childhood, but also discovered a love of geography, and now dreamed of different parts of the world during the long days in hides, waiting for a victim to appear. Chekov turned out to be one of those naturally gifted killers which wars bring out. He had excelled at sniper school and as a twenty-year-old in Stalingrad, he seemed to experience no fear – 'just as the eagle is never afraid of heights'. He possessed a rare skill for camouflage in hides at the top of tall buildings. To prevent the muzzle flash from giving away his position, he improvised a flash concealer for the end of his barrel and never fired in bad light. As a further precaution to reduce the visibility of the flash, he tried to position himself in front of a white wall.

One day, he took Grossman with him. The easiest, and most regular, targets were the soldiers who brought forward food containers to the front-line positions. It was not long before an infantryman on ration detail appeared. Using the telescopic sight, Chekov aimed two inches above the tip of the nose. The German soldier fell backwards, dropping the food container. Chekov quivered with excitement. A second soldier appeared. Chekov shot him. Then a third German crawled forward. Chekov killed him too. 'Three,' Chekov murmured to himself. The full score would be noted down later. His best was seventeen kills in two days. Shooting a man carrying water-bottles was a bonus, Chekov remarked, since it forced others to drink polluted water. Grossman posed the question whether this boy, who dreamed of foreign parts and 'who wouldn't hurt a fly', was not 'a saint of the Patriotic War'.*

The sniper cult produced imitators with different weapons. Manenkov of 95th Rifle Division became renowned with the long and unwieldy PTR (anti-tank) rifle. He became a Hero of the Soviet Union after destroying six tanks in the fighting round the Barrikady gun factory. A Lieutenant Vinogradov in 149th Artillery Division became famous as the best grenade thrower. When he and twenty-six men were cut off without food for three days, the first message Vinogradov passed back was a request for grenades, not rations. Even when wounded and deaf, Vinogradov was 'still the best Fritz-hunter'.

---

* Grossman seems to have been going through a period of spiritual idealization, seeing the Red Army soldier in quasi-Tolstoyan terms. 'In war,' he wrote in another notebook, 'the Russian man puts a white shirt on his soul. He lives sinfully, but he dies like a saint. At the front, the thoughts and souls of many men are pure and there is even a monk-like modesty.'

He once managed to stalk and kill a German company commander and take his papers from the corpse.

As the German divisions pushed southwards from the tractor works towards the line of defence at the Barrikady factory, Chuikov, on the night of 17 October, changed his headquarters yet again. He ended up on the river bank, level with the Mamaev Kurgan. A strong force of Germans broke through to the Volga the next day, but were forced back in a counter-attack.

The only reassuring news was from Colonel Kamynin, sent to the pocket of resistance left north of the tractor works in Rynok and Spartakovka. The situation had been restored, and the troops were in general fighting bravely. There were still problems, however, with the militia brigades. On the night of 25 October, a whole section of 124th Special Brigade, 'formerly workers at Stalingrad tractor works', set out to cross over to the Germans. Only a single sentry had been against the idea, but he had agreed to join them when threatened. Out in no man's land, the sentry pretended that he had a problem with a foot cloth, and stopped. He took the opportunity to escape from the others, and ran back to the Russian lines. The deserters fired after him, but without success. The sentry, Soldier D., reached his regiment safely, but was then arrested and court-martialled 'for not taking decisive measures to inform his commanders of the forthcoming crime and preventing the traitors from deserting'.

The battle of attrition continued around the Barrikady factory and Red October, with attack and counter-attack. A battalion command post of the 305th Infantry Division, according to one officer, was 'so close to the enemy that the regimental commander could hear the Russian "*Urrah!*" at the other end of the telephone'. A Russian regimental commander, however, was in the midst of the fighting. When his headquarters was overrun, he radioed for a *Katyusha* strike right on to his own position.

German soldiers had to admit that 'the dogs fight like lions'. Their own casualties mounted rapidly. The cries of '*Sani! Hilfe!*' from the wounded became almost as much part of the scene as the explosions, and the sounds of ricochets off the rubble. Yet the 62nd Army was reduced to several bridgeheads on the west bank, none more than a few hundred yards deep. Streets were taken, Soviet positions pushed back even closer to the Volga, the Barrikady gun factory partially overrun. The 62nd Army's last crossing point was under direct machine-gun fire, and all reinforcements had to be thrown into that sector to save it. Soviet divisions were reduced to a few hundred men each, but they still fought back at night. 'We felt at home in the dark,' wrote Chuikov.

'Father,' a German corporal wrote home, 'you kept telling me: "Be faithful to your standard and you'll win." You will not forget these words because the time has come for every sensible man in Germany to curse the madness of this war. It's impossible to describe what is happening here. Everyone in Stalingrad who still possesses a head and hands, women as well as men, carries on fighting.' Another German soldier also wrote home in bitter mood: 'Don't worry, don't be upset, because the sooner I am under the ground, the less I will suffer. We often think that Russia should capitulate, but these uneducated people are too stupid to realize it.' A third soldier surveyed the ruins around him. 'Here a saying from the Gospel often passes through my thoughts: No stone will be left standing one upon another. Here it is the truth.'

13

Paulus's Final Assault

Out in the steppe, the routine of German divisions was a world apart from the fighting in the city. There were defence lines to be held and probing attacks to be repulsed, but life offered a much more conventional existence, especially back from the front. On Sunday, 25 October, the officers of a regiment in the Bavarian 376th Infantry Division invited General Edler von Daniels, their divisional commander, to a Munich *Oktoberfest* shooting contest.

The main preoccupation at that time was the preparation of good winter quarters. 'It's not an enticing picture out here,' a soldier in the 113th Infantry Division wrote home. 'For far and wide there are no villages, no woodland, neither tree nor shrub, and not a drop of water.' Russian prisoners and Hiwis were put to work digging bunkers and trenches. 'We really need to make good use of these men because we're so short-handed,' wrote a senior NCO. Out in the treeless steppe, infantry divisions were forced to send trucks and working parties into Stalingrad to fetch beams from the rubble of destroyed houses for the roofs of their bunkers. South of Stalingrad, the 297th Infantry Division excavated man-made caves in the sides of *balkas* to form stables, stores and eventually an entire field hospital, for which all the equipment arrived by rail from Germany. During the Indian summer of early and mid-October, Germans were keen to get their '*Haus*' ready. Even the youngest soldiers recognized the implications of digging in: they would now be there for the whole winter.

Hitler issued his own instructions for the winter. He expected 'a highly *active* defence' and a 'proud sense of victory'. Tanks were to be protected from the cold and bombardment in specially built concrete bunkers, but the necessary materials never arrived, so vehicles stayed in the open. Sixth Army headquarters also drew up elaborate plans for the winter. Even a Finnish training film, *How to Construct a Sauna in the Field*, was ordered, but none of these preparations carried much conviction. 'The Führer has ordered us to defend our positions to the last man,' Groscurth wrote home to Germany, 'something we would do of our own accord, since the loss of a position would hardly improve our situation. We know what it would be like to be stranded without shelter in the open steppe.'

Führer headquarters also decided that the majority of Sixth Army's draught animals should be sent over a hundred miles to the rear. This would save on the supply trains required to bring forward the huge quantities of fodder. Altogether some 150,000 horses, as well as a number of oxen and even camels, had accumulated between the Don and the Volga. Motor transport and repair units were also moved back. The reasons behind such a move were understandable from a purely logistic point of view, but it would prove a serious mistake in a crisis. The Sixth Army, especially the vast majority of its artillery and medical units, depended almost entirely on horses for their mobility.

Morale, according to a sergeant-major in the 371st Infantry Division, 'rises and falls with the quantity of incoming post'. Almost everyone seemed to be suffering from acute homesickness. 'Here one must become a completely different person', wrote a senior NCO of the 60th Motorized Infantry Division, 'and that is not so easy. It's exactly as if we were living in another world. When the post arrives, everybody rushes out of their "little houses" – and they just can't be stopped. For the time being, I must stand by and watch with an indulgent smile.'

Thoughts were already turning to Christmas: the 'most beautiful festival of the whole year'. Soldiers began to discuss presents with wives. On 3 November, one division put in its 'requirements for musical instruments, party games, Christmas tree decorations and candles'.

Leave rosters were planned, a subject which excited more hopes and disappointments than any other. Paulus insisted that priority was given to soldiers 'who have been in the eastern theatre without a break since June 1941'. For the lucky ones who set out on the long journey, time slipped past in a sense of unreality. Home now seemed to have the dreamlike quality of a former existence. Back among their families, men found it impossible to talk about their experiences. Many were dismayed to find how few civilians had any grasp of what was happening. Worst of all, it seemed pointlessly cruel to enlighten them, if it meant that wives would agonize all the more. The only reality now seemed to be the nightmare existence they could not escape. It was human to be tempted by ideas of desertion, but few took them seriously. The most vivid memory of their leave was saying goodbye. For many, it was the last time. They knew they were re-entering hell when they passed the sign on the main route into Stalingrad: 'Entry to the city forbidden. Onlookers put their own lives and those of comrades in danger.' Many found it hard to decide whether this was a joke or not.

New winter outfits started to be issued at the end of October. 'It's a typically German affair,' noted one officer, 'with reversible trousers and jacket, field-grey and white.' But soldiers out in the waterless steppe were increasingly infested with lice. 'For the time being there is no point in even thinking of washing. Today I killed my first batch of eight lice.' Jokes about 'the little partisans' soon wore off. Some of the Russian Hiwis told their German companions of a folk remedy for getting rid of them. This consisted of burying each article of clothing under the ground with just one corner left above the soil. The lice moved there and could be burned off.

Regimental doctors began to be increasingly concerned about the general health of troops at this time. When the medical obituary of the Sixth Army was debated in Berlin by consultants late the next January, they charted a vertiginous rate of increase in the death rate from infectious diseases, dysentery, typhus, and paratyphus.* This

---

* Jaundice was recorded separately. 'Jaundice especially predominates here,' wrote one officer. 'And since jaundice means a ticket home, everybody is longing to get it.' There do not appear to be any recorded examples of soldiers eating picric acid from shells, to make them turn yellow, as in the First World War.

'*Fieberkurve*' had started to mount rapidly from as early as July. Although the total number of sick was roughly the same as the previous year, the Berlin specialists were astounded to establish that five times as many soldiers were succumbing.

The Russians themselves had noticed the number of ill Germans with surprise and spoken of a 'German sickness'. The doctors in Berlin could only speculate that 'the troops' reduced resistance' had been due to cumulative stress, and short rations. The most vulnerable appear to have been the youngest soldiers, those aged between seventeen and twenty-two. They alone accounted for 55 per cent of these deaths. Whatever the exact causes, there can be no doubt that the health of the Sixth Army was already a matter of serious concern in early November, when the worst prospect appeared to be no more than yet another winter in bunkers under the snow.

While the Soviet 64th Army launched attacks to bring troops down from Stalingrad, the 57th Army seized a dominant hill between the Romanian 20th and 2nd Infantry Divisions. Further out, down in the Kalmyk steppe, the 51st Army carried out raids deep into the Romanian positions. One night, Senior Lieutenant Aleksandr Nevsky and his company of sub-machine-gunners infiltrated through the defence line to raid the headquarters of the 1st Romanian Infantry Division in a village to the rear, where they caused chaos. Nevsky was badly wounded twice during the action. The Stalingrad Front political department, following the new Party line of invoking Russian history, decided that Nevsky must belong to the bloodline of his glorious namesake. This 'fearless commander, the full inheritor of his ancestor's glory', was awarded the Order of the Red Banner.

In the city, the great German offensive had petered out at the very end of October through exhaustion and a lack of ammunition. The last attack by 79th Infantry Division against the Red October factory collapsed on 1 November under heavy artillery fire from across the Volga. 'The effect of massed enemy artillery has decisively weakened the division's attacking strength,' noted Sixth Army headquarters. The 94th Infantry Division attacking the northern pocket at Spartakovka was also ground down.

'In the last two days', noted a report to Moscow of 6 November, 'the enemy has been changing his tactics. Probably because of big losses over the last three weeks, they have stopped using large formations.' Along the Red October sector, the Germans had switched to 'reconnaissance in force to probe for weak points between our regiments'. But these new 'sudden attacks' were achieving no more success than the old ones preceded by heavy bombardments.

Also during the first week of November, the Germans started 'to install wire netting over windows and shell holes' of their fortified houses so that hand grenades would bounce off. To break the netting, 62nd Army needed small-calibre artillery, of which it was short, yet it was increasingly difficult to ship anything across the Volga. Red Army soldiers started to improvise hooks on their grenades to catch on to the netting.

Soviet forces hit back in any way they could during early November. Gunboats of the Volga flotilla, some with spare T-34 tank turrets mounted on the forward deck, bombarded 16th Panzer Division at Rynok. And the 'heavy enemy night bombing attacks', continued to wear down the resilience of German soldiers.

'Along the whole of the eastern front', wrote Groscurth to his brother on 7 November, 'we are expecting today a general offensive in honour of the anniversary of the October Revolution.' But observance of the twenty-fifth anniversary was restricted on a local level to Soviet soldiers 'exceeding their socialist promises to destroy Fritzes which they made in socialist competition'. Komsomol members especially were expected to keep an accurate tally of their score. In 57th Army, the chief political officer reported, 'out of 1,697 Komsomol members, 678 have not yet killed any Germans'. These underachievers were presumably taken in hand.

Some celebrations of the October Revolution did not attract the approval of the authorities. A battalion commander and his second-in-command bringing forward reinforcements for 45th Rifle Division 'got drunk' and were 'missing for thirteen hours'. The battalion was left wandering around aimlessly on the east bank of the Volga. A number of Stalingrad Front divisions had little with which to celebrate, either because the special vodka ration was not delivered, or because it arrived too late. Several units did not even receive their food ration that day.

Many soldiers, deprived of vodka, resorted to desperate substitutes. In the worst case, the effects were not immediately apparent. The night after the anniversary celebration, twenty-eight soldiers from 248th Rifle Division died on an approach march out in the Kalmyk steppe. No medical assistance was sought and nobody admitted to knowing what the matter was. Officers pretended to think that they had died from cold and exertion on the march. The NKVD Special Department was suspicious, however, and autopsies were performed on twenty-four of the bodies. Death was determined to have been caused by excessive consumption of 'anti-chemical liquids'. The soldiers had drunk large amounts of a solution designed to be taken in minute quantities in the case of a gas attack. This noxious liquid apparently contained some alcohol. One of the survivors was interviewed in hospital. He admitted that someone had claimed it was 'a sort of wine'. The NKVD refused to accept that this might be a straightforward case of theft of army material and drunkenness. The case was deemed to be 'an act of sabotage to poison soldiers'.

On 8 November, the day after the anniversary of the Revolution, Hitler made a long speech to the Nazi 'Old Combatants' in the Bürgerbraukeller in Munich. The broadcast was heard by many in the Sixth Army. 'I wanted to reach the Volga', he declared with heavy irony, 'to be precise at a particular spot, at a particular city. By chance it bore the name of Stalin himself. But don't think that I marched there just for that reason, it was because it occupies a very important position . . . I wanted to capture it and, you should know, we are quite content, we have as good as got it! There are only a couple of small bits left. Some say: "Why aren't they fighting faster?" That's because I don't want a second Verdun, and prefer instead to do the job with small assault groups. Time is of no importance. No more ships are coming up the Volga. And that is the decisive point!'

His speech ranked among the greatest examples of hubris in history. Rommel's Afrika Korps was already retreating from Alamein into Libya and Anglo-American forces had just landed along the North African coast in Operation Torch. Ribbentrop took the opportunity to suggest an approach to Stalin through the Soviet embassy in Stockholm. 'Hitler refused outright,' noted his Luftwaffe adjutant. 'He said that a moment of weakness is not the right time for dealing with an enemy.' The fatuous boasts about Stalingrad, which followed this refusal, were not merely hostages to fortune: they were to trap him into a course for disaster. The political demagogue had manacled the warlord. Ribbentrop's worst fears on the eve of Barbarossa were soon to be confirmed.

In Stalingrad, real winter weather arrived the next day, with the temperature dropping to minus eighteen degrees centigrade. The Volga, which because of its size was one of the last rivers in Russia to freeze over, started to become unnavigable. 'The ice floes collide, crumble and grind against each other,' noted Grossman, 'and the swishing sound, like that of shifting sands, can be heard quite a distance from the bank.' It was an eerie sound for soldiers in the city.

This was the period which General Chuikov had been dreading, what he called war on two fronts: the hostile Volga behind, and the enemy attacking their narrow strips of remaining territory from in front. Sixth Army headquarters, knowing the problems that the Russians faced, concentrated their fire again on the Volga crossing. One steamer of the Volga flotilla, bringing guns and ammunition across, was hit and settled in shallow water on a sandbank. Another boat came alongside, and all the cargo was transferred under heavy fire. The sailors working in the freezing water were as likely to die as the French *pontonniers* building the bridge across the Berezina more than a century before.

'The blunt, broad bows of the barges slowly crush the white beneath them, and behind them the black stretches of water are soon covered with a film of ice.' Boats creaked under the pressure of the ice and hawsers snapped under the strain. Crossing the river became 'like a Polar expedition'.

During the first ten days of November, German pressure was kept up with constant, small-scale attacks, sometimes with tanks. The fighting may have been in smaller groups, but it was still just as fierce. A company of the 347th Rifle Regiment, dug in only 200 yards forward of the Volga, was down to nine men when overrun on 6 November, but its commander, Lieutenant Andreev, rallied his survivors and they counter-attacked with sub-machine-guns. A group of reinforcements, arriving just in time, cut off the Germans, and saved the 62nd Army's northern crossing point. The Russians carefully watched the German system of signalling with flares, and turned it to their own advantage by adapting their colour combinations using captured cartridges. One platoon commander was credited with having tricked German artillery into switching their fire at a critical moment on to their own troops.

With such narrow strips of no man's land, desertion remained an escape of last resort, but now there were cases of German soldiers attempting to cross the lines. In the centre of the sector of 13th Guards Rifle Division, a German soldier slipped forward from one of their defended houses towards a Russian-held building. His action was clearly supported by some of his comrades, because they called out: '*Rus!* Don't shoot!' But when the man was halfway across no man's land, a newly arrived Russian soldier fired from a second-floor window and hit him. The wounded German crawled on, also screaming out: '*Rus!* Don't shoot!' The Russian fired again, and this time killed him. His body lay there for the rest of the day. That night, a Russian patrol crawled forward, but found that the Germans had already sent their own party forward to retrieve his weapon and documents. The Soviet authorities decided that 'more explanatory work' was needed 'to explain to soldiers that they should not shoot deserters straight away'. Troops were reminded of Order No. 55, which dealt with encouraging enemy deserters through good treatment. On the same sector, 'it was noticed that German soldiers raised their hands above the trench in order to be wounded'. The political department was immediately instructed to step up propaganda activities with broadcasting and leaflets.

*

On 11 November, just before dawn, the final German assault began. Newly organized battle groups from the 71st, 79th, 100th, 295th, 305th and 389th Infantry Divisions, reinforced with four fresh pioneer battalions, attacked the remaining pockets of resistance. Even though most of the divisions were severely depleted by the recent fighting, it was still a massive concentration.

Once again, VIII Air Corps Stukas prepared the way, but General von Richthofen had lost almost all patience with what he regarded as 'army conventionality'. At the beginning of the month, in a meeting with Paulus and Seydlitz, he had complained that 'the artillery isn't firing and the infantry isn't making any use of our bombing attacks'. The Luftwaffe's most spectacular achievement, on 11 November, was to bring down the factory chimneys, but once again they failed to crush the 62nd Army in its trenches and bunkers and cellars.

Batyuk's Siberians fought desperately to retain their foothold on the Mamaev Kurgan, but the main point of the enemy thrust was half a mile further north, towards the Lazur chemical factory and the so-called 'tennis racket', a loop of railway track and sidings resembling that shape. The main force for this attack was the 305th Infantry Division and most of the pioneer battalions flown in to reinforce the offensive. Key buildings were captured but then retaken by the Russians in bitter fighting. The following day, this attack came to a halt.

Further north, the men of Lyudnikov's 138th Rifle Division, cut off behind the Barrikady factory with their backs to the Volga, resisted fiercely. They were down to an average of thirty rounds for each rifle and sub-machine-gun, and a daily ration of less than fifty grams of dried bread. At night, U-2 biplanes tried to drop sacks of ammunition and food, but the impact often damaged the rounds, which then jammed weapons.

On the night of 11 November, 62nd Army launched attacks, including 95th Rifle Division, south-east of the Barrikady plant. The intention, according to the report sent to Shcherbakov on 15 November, was to prevent the Germans from withdrawing troops to protect their flanks. This appears to contradict Chuikov's account in his memoirs, where he asserts that he and his staff had no knowledge of the great counter-offensive launched on 19 November, until informed the evening before by Stalingrad Front headquarters.

The Soviet attackers, however, were halted almost immediately by the weight of German shelling, and forced to take cover. From 5 a.m. on 12 November, there was a 'hurricane of fire' lasting for an hour and a half. Then a strong force of German infantry attacked, managing to act as a wedge between two of the Russian rifle regiments. At 9.50 a.m. the Germans sent in more troops, part of them advancing towards the petrol tanks on the bank of the Volga. One of the Soviet rifle regiments managed to hold off the main attack, while other assault groups surrounded and cut down German sub-machine-gunners who had broken through. Three German tanks were also set on fire in the desperate fighting. The regiment's first battalion was reduced to fifteen men. They somehow managed to hold a line seventy yards forward of the Volga bank until another battalion arrived.

Only one man survived from the marine infantry guarding the regimental command post. His right hand was smashed and he could no longer fire. He went down into the bunker, and on hearing that there were no reserves left, filled his cap with grenades. 'I can throw these with my left hand,' he explained. Close by, a platoon from another regiment fought until only four were left alive and their ammunition ran out. A wounded man was sent back with the message: 'Begin shelling our position. In front of us is a large group of fascists. Farewell comrades, we did not retreat.'

The 62nd Army's supply position became even more desperate because of the ice floes coming down the Volga. Icebreakers were needed at the banks where the river froze first. On 14 November, the steamer *Spartakovets* took 400 soldiers and 40 tons of supplies to the right bank just behind Red October, and on its return it brought back 350 wounded under fire, but few other craft got through. Rescue teams were on standby throughout the night to help any boat which became ice-bound, and thus an easy target for the German guns. 'If they can't finish the business,' Richthofen noted caustically, 'when the Volga's icing up and the Russians in Stalingrad are suffering severe shortages, then they'll never succeed. In addition, the days are constantly getting shorter, and the weather's getting worse.'

Paulus was under heavy strain. His doctor warned him that he was heading for a breakdown if he continued without a rest. 'Hitler was obsessed with the symbolism of Stalingrad,' explained one of Paulus's staff officers. 'To clean up the last few points of resistance in November, he ordered that even tank drivers should be assembled as infantry for a last push.' Panzer commanders were horrified at such a mad waste, but they could not get Paulus to cancel the order. In the end, they tried to scrape together enough reserve drivers, cooks, medical orderlies and signals staff – in fact anybody rather than their experienced tank crewmen – in order to keep their divisions operational. The very heavy losses in panzer regiments were to prove serious, if not disastrous, within a matter of days.

General von Seydlitz was deeply concerned. By the middle of November, Sixth Army headquarters judged that '42 per cent of his battalions must be considered "fought out".' Most infantry companies were down to under fifty men and had to be amalgamated. Seydlitz was also concerned about the 14th and 24th Panzer Divisions, which needed to refit, ready for the inevitable Soviet winter offensive. In his view, the fighting had been continued far too late into the year. Hitler himself had admitted to him during lunch at Rastenburg that German troops should start to prepare for 'all the trials of a Russian winter' at the beginning of October. The troops in Stalingrad had been specifically excluded from the instructions to prepare winter defences, and yet Hitler in Munich had boasted that time was of no importance.

The worst casualties were in experienced officers and NCOs. Only a small minority of the original combatants remained on both sides. 'These were different Germans from those we had fought in August,' remarked one Soviet veteran. 'And we also were different.' Front-line soldiers on both sides seemed to feel that the best and the bravest were always the first to die.

German staff officers were also worried about the next spring. Simple calculations showed that Germany could not sustain such casualties for much longer. Any notion of a heroic adventure had turned bitter. A strong sense of foreboding set in. As a symbol of determination for revenge, the new Red Army practice in Stalingrad, when saluting the death of a well-regarded commander, was to fire a volley or salvo 'not in the air, but at the Germans'.

14

'All For the Front!'

The plan for Operation Uranus, the great Soviet counterstroke against the Sixth Army, had an unusually long gestation when one considers Stalin's disastrous impatience the previous winter. But this time his desire for revenge helped control his impetuousness.

The original idea dated back to Saturday, 12 September, the day that Paulus met Hitler at Vinnitsa, and that Zhukov was summoned to the Kremlin after the failed attacks against Paulus's northern flank. Vasilevsky, the Chief of the General Staff, was also present. There, in Stalin's office, overlooked by recently installed portraits of Aleksandr Suvorov, the scourge of the Turks in the eighteenth century, and of Mikhail Kutuzov, Napoleon's dogged adversary, Zhukov was made to explain again what had gone wrong. He concentrated on the fact that the three understrength armies sent into the attack had lacked artillery and tanks.

Stalin demanded to know what was needed. Zhukov replied that they should have another full-strength army, supported by a tank corps, three armoured brigades and at least 400 howitzers, all backed by an aviation army. Vasilevsky agreed. Stalin said nothing. He picked up the map marked with the *Stavka* reserves and began to study it alone. Zhukov and Vasilevsky moved away to a corner of the room. They murmured together, discussing the problem. They agreed that another solution would have to be found.

Stalin possessed sharper hearing than they had realized. 'And what', he called across, 'does "another" solution mean?' The two generals were taken aback. 'Go over to the General Staff,' he told them, 'and think over very carefully indeed what must be done in the Stalingrad area.'

Zhukov and Vasilevsky returned the following evening. Stalin did not waste time. He greeted the two generals with businesslike handshakes, to their surprise.

'Well, what did you come up with?' he asked. 'Who's making the report?'

'Either of us,' Vasilevsky replied. 'We are of the same opinion.'

The two generals had spent the day at the *Stavka*, studying the possibilities and the projected creation of new armies and armoured corps over the next two months. The more they had looked at the map of the German salient, with the two vulnerable flanks, the more they were convinced that the only solution worth considering was one which would 'shift the strategic situation in the south decisively'. The city of Stalingrad, Zhukov argued, should be held in a battle of attrition, with just enough troops to keep the defence alive. No formations should be wasted on minor counter-attacks, unless absolutely necessary to divert the enemy from seizing the whole of the west bank of the Volga. Then, while the Germans focused entirely on capturing the city, the *Stavka* would secretly assemble fresh armies behind the lines for a major encirclement, using deep thrusts far behind the point of the apex.

Stalin at first showed little enthusiasm. He feared that they might lose Stalingrad and suffer a further humiliating blow, unless something was done immediately. He suggested a compromise, bringing the points of attack in much closer to the city, but Zhukov answered that the bulk of the Sixth Army would also be much closer, and could be redeployed against their attacking forces. Eventually, Stalin saw the advantage of the much more ambitious operation.

Stalin's great advantage over Hitler was his lack of ideological shame. After the disasters of 1941, he was not in the slightest bit squeamish about reviving the disgraced military thinking of the 1920s and early 1930s. The theory of 'deep operations' with mechanized 'shock armies' to annihilate the enemy no longer had to remain underground like a heretical cult. On that night of 13 September, Stalin gave this plan for deep operations his full backing. He instructed the two men to introduce 'a regime of the strictest secrecy'. 'No one, beyond the three of us, is to know about it for the time being.' The offensive was to be called Operation Uranus.

Zhukov was not just a good planner, he was the best implementer of plans. Even Stalin was impressed by his ruthlessness in the pursuit of an objective. Zhukov did not want to repeat the mistakes of early September with the attacks north of Stalingrad, using untrained and badly equipped troops. The task of training was huge. Zhukov and Vasilevsky sent reserve-army divisions, as soon as they were formed, to relatively quiet parts of the front for training under fire. This also had the unintended advantage of confusing German military intelligence. Colonel Reinhard Gehlen, the highly energetic but over-rated head of Fremde Heere Ost, began to suspect that the Red Army was planning a large diversionary offensive against Army Group Centre.

Reconnaissance reports and prisoner interrogations confirmed the original hunch that Operation Uranus should aim for the Romanian sectors on each flank of the Sixth Army. In the third week of September, Zhukov made a tour of the northern flank of the German salient in the greatest secrecy. Aleksandr Glichov, a lieutenant from 221st Rifle Division's reconnaissance company, was ordered to report to divisional headquarters one night. There he saw two Willys staff cars. A colonel interviewed him, then told him to hand over his sub-machine-gun and get in the front of one of the staff cars. His task was to guide a senior officer along the front.

Glichov had to wait until midnight, when a burly figure, not very tall and almost dwarfed by bodyguards, appeared out of the headquarters bunker. The senior officer climbed into the back of the car without a word. Glichov, following instructions, guided the driver from one unit command post to the next along the front. When they returned shortly before dawn, he was given back his sub-machine-gun and told to return to his division with the message that his task had been completed. Many years after the war, he learned from his former commanding officer that Zhukov was the senior officer he had escorted that night, sometimes within two hundred yards of the German lines. It may not have been necessary for the deputy supreme commander to interview each unit commander himself about the ground and the forces opposite, 'but Zhukov was Zhukov'.

While Zhukov made his secret inspection along the northern flank, Vasilevsky had visited the 64th, 57th and 51st Armies south of Stalingrad. Vasilevsky urged an advance to just beyond the line of the salt lakes in the steppe. He did not give the real reason, which was to establish a well-protected forming-up area for Operation Uranus.

Secrecy and deception plans were vital to camouflage their preparations, yet the Red Army had two even more effective advantages in its favour. The first was that Hitler refused to believe that the Soviet Union had any reserve armies, let alone the large tank formations necessary for deep operations. The second German misconception was even more helpful, although Zhukov never acknowledged this. All the ineffective attacks mounted against XIV Panzer Corps on the northern flank near Stalingrad had made the Red Army appear incapable of mounting a dangerous offensive in the region, least of all a swift and massive encirclement of the whole Sixth Army.

During the summer, when Germany was producing approximately 500 tanks a month, General Halder had told Hitler that the Soviet Union was producing 1,200 a month. The Führer had slammed the table and said that it was simply not possible. Yet even this figure was far too low. In 1942, Soviet tank production was rising from 11,000 during the first six months to 13,600 during the second half of the year, an average of over 2,200 a month. Aircraft production was also increasing from 9,600 during the first six months of the year, to 15,800 for the second.

The very suggestion that the Soviet Union, deprived of major industrial regions, could outproduce the Reich, filled Hitler with angry disbelief. Nazi leaders had always refused to acknowledge the strength of Russian patriotic feeling. They also underestimated the ruthless programme of evacuation of industry to the Urals and the militarization of the workforce. Over 1,500 factories had been evacuated from the western regions of the Soviet Union to behind the Volga, particularly the Urals, and reassembled by armies of technicians slaving through the winter. Few factories had any heating. Many had no windows at first, or proper roofing. Once the production lines started, they never stopped, unless halted by breakdowns, power failures, or shortages of particular parts. Manpower posed less of a problem. The Soviet authorities simply drafted in new populations of workers. Soviet bureaucracy wasted the time and talents of its civilian people, and squandered their lives in industrial accidents, with as much indifference for the individual as military planners showed towards their soldiers, yet the collective sacrifice – both forced and willing at the same time – represented a terrifyingly impressive achievement.

At a time when Hitler still refused to countenance the idea of German women in factories, Soviet production depended on the mass mobilization of mothers and daughters. Tens of thousands of dungareed women – 'fighters in overalls' – swinging tank turrets on hoists down production lines, or bent over lathes, believed passionately in what they were doing to help the men. Posters never ceased to remind them of their role: 'What was Your Help to the Front?'

Chelyabinsk, the great centre of war industries in the Urals, became known as Tankograd. Soon, tank-training schools were established near the factories. The Party organized links between workers and regiments, while factories made collections to pay for more tanks. A tank gunner called Minakov composed a rhyme which seized the imagination of the Ural production lines:

> For the death of enemies
> For the joy of friends
> There is no better machine
> Than the T-34!

Somebody later suggested that production-line workers should form the First Ural volunteer tank regiment. The organizers claimed to have received, within thirty-six hours of putting up the first poster, '4,363 applications to join the tank regiment, of which 1,253 were from women'.

Even the slave-labour camps devoted to munitions production achieved a far higher output than their equivalents in Germany. There were also far fewer cases of sabotage. Gulag prisoners still believed in defeating the invader.

Allied aid is seldom mentioned in Soviet accounts, for reasons of propaganda, but its contribution towards keeping the Red Army fighting in the autumn of 1942 should not be overlooked. Stalin complained to Zhukov about the quality of the Hurricane fighters offered by Churchill, and the British and American tanks provided did not compare to the T-34. Consignments of British ammunition boots and greatcoats were just as unpopular with Soviet soldiers, because of their uselessness for winter warfare. But American vehicles – especially Ford, Willys and Studebaker trucks and jeeps – and food, whether the millions of tons of wheat in white sacks stamped with the American eagle and cans of Spam or corned beef from Chicago, made a huge, yet unacknowledged, difference to the Soviet Union's ability to resist.

Zhukov knew the importance of having the right commanders for mechanized warfare. At the end of September, he persuaded Stalin to appoint General Konstantin Rokossovsky, a former victim of Beria's NKVD, commander of the Don Front, which stretched from the northern tip of Stalingrad westwards to Kletskaya, just beyond the great Don bend. At the same time Lieutenant-General Nikolay Vatutin was put in charge of the new South-Western Front on Rokossovsky's right flank, which faced the Third Romanian Army.

On 17 October, Don Front headquarters gave the order that all civilians 'within fifteen miles of the front line' must be evacuated by 29 October. Apart from security considerations, the military authorities wanted to be able to hide troops in villages by day, during their approach marches. It was a considerable operation, since the evacuees would be taking 'their own cattle, sheep, pigs and hens and food for a month'. The cows were to act as draught animals, and all collective-farm tractors, combine harvesters and other valuable machinery were to be withdrawn. Several thousand civilians were drafted into a construction corps over 100,000 strong, repairing roads and bridges along the Saratov–Kamyshin–Stalingrad route and all others leading to the front.

From the newly laid Saratov–Astrakhan railroad, lines diverted to railheads in the steppe where the *Stavka* reserves would detrain, well to the rear, before proceeding to concentration areas behind the front. The strain on the Soviet railways system, moving 1,300 wagons a day to the three fronts, was immense. Confusion was inevitable. One division was left packed in troop trains for nearly two and a half months on sidings in Uzbekistan.

The plan for Operation Uranus was simple, yet daringly ambitious in its scope. The main assault, over a hundred miles west of Stalingrad, would be launched south-eastwards from the Serafimovich bridge-head, a forty-mile-long stretch south of the Don which the Romanian Third Army had not had the strength to occupy. This point of attack was so far to the rear of the Sixth Army that German mechanized forces in and around Stalingrad would not be able to get back in time to make a difference. Meanwhile, an inner strike would cut down from another bridgehead south of the Don at Kletskaya, then attack the rear of Strecker's XI Army Corps stretched across the greater and the lesser Don bends. Finally, from south of Stalingrad, another armoured thrust would attack north-westwards to meet up with the main assault around Kalach. This would mark the encirclement of Paulus's Sixth Army and part of Hoth's Fourth Panzer Army. Altogether some 60 per cent of the whole tank strength of the Red Army was allocated to Operation Uranus.

Soviet security proved better than one might have expected, con-sidering the number of Red Army prisoners and deserters passing through Wehrmacht hands. German intelligence had failed during the summer of 1942 to identify the creation of five new tank armies (each roughly the equivalent of a panzer corps) and fifteen tank corps (each the equivalent of a strong panzer division). As the moment of retribution approached, the Red Army paid great attention to *maskirovka*, a term covering deception, camouflage and operational security, by greatly reducing the quantity of radio traffic. Orders were given in person and not written down. Active deception measures

included stepping up activity around Moscow. The Germans identified the Rzhev salient as the most likely area for a Soviet offensive in
November. Meanwhile in the south, front-line divisions along the
sectors vital for Operation Uranus were ordered to construct defence
lines, purely for the benefit of German air reconnaissance, while the
Voronezh Front, which was not involved, received orders to prepare
bridging equipment and boats, as if for an offensive.

Troop activity in other sectors was concealed by the construction
of defences, which gave the opposite impression to plans for an
offensive. The approach marches of formations for Operation Uranus
were made at night, with troops hiding up during the day, a difficult
task on the bare steppe, but Red Army camouflage techniques were
remarkably effective. No fewer than seventeen false bridges were
constructed over the Don to attract the Luftwaffe's attention away
from the five real ones, over which crossed the 5th Tank Army, the
4th Tank Corps, two cavalry corps and numerous rifle divisions.

South of Stalingrad, the 13th Mechanized Corps, the 4th Mechanized Corps, the 4th Cavalry Corps and supporting formations –
altogether over 160,000 men, 430 tanks, 550 guns, 14,000 vehicles
and over 10,000 horses – were brought across the lower Volga in
batches at night, a difficult and dangerous operation, with the ice floes
coming down the river. They had to be camouflaged by dawn. The
Red Army could not of course hope to conceal the forthcoming
operation entirely, but, as one historian put it, their 'greatest feat was
in masking the scale of the offensive'.

In the early autumn of 1942, most German generals, although they
did not share Hitler's conviction that the Red Army was finished,
certainly considered it close to exhaustion. Staff officers, on the other
hand, tended to take a more sceptical view. When Captain Winrich
Behr, a highly decorated officer from the Afrika Korps, joined Sixth
Army headquarters, Lieutenant-Colonel Niemeyer, the chief of intelligence, welcomed him with a much more sombre assessment than
he had expected. 'My dear friend,' he said, 'come and see the situation
map. Look at all the red markings. The Russians are starting to
concentrate in the north here, and in the south here.' Niemeyer felt

that senior officers, although concerned by a threat to their lines of communication, did not take the danger of encirclement seriously.

Paulus and Schmidt, who saw all of Niemeyer's reports, thought his concern exaggerated. Both generals expected quite heavy attacks with artillery and tanks, but not a major offensive deep into their rear, using the German's own *Schwerpunkt* tactics. (After the event, Paulus seems to have fallen into that very human mistake of convincing himself that he had seen the true danger all along. Schmidt, however, was quite frank in his admission that they had gravely underestimated the enemy.) General Hoth, on the other hand, appears to have had a much clearer view of the threat posed by an attack from south of Stalingrad.

Most generals back in Germany were convinced that the Soviet Union was incapable of two offensives, and Colonel Gehlen's assessments, although deliberately delphic to cover any eventuality, continued to point to an attack against Army Group Centre as the most likely area for the main winter offensive. His organization had failed to identify the presence of the 5th Tank Army on the Don Front opposite the Romanians. Only a signals intercept shortly before the offensive pointed to its involvement.

The most striking aspect of this period was the apparent assumption by Paulus and Schmidt that, once Sixth Army staff had passed back their reports, nothing more could be done since the threatened sectors were outside their area of responsibility. This passivity was entirely contrary to the Prussian tradition, which regarded inactivity, waiting for orders and failing to think for yourself as unforgivable in a commander. Hitler, of course, had set out to crush such independence in his generals, and Paulus, who was by nature more of a staff officer than a field commander, had acceded.

Paulus has often been blamed for not disobeying Hitler later, once the scale of the disaster was clear, but his real failure as a commander was his failure to prepare to face the threat. It was his own army which was threatened. All he needed to do was to withdraw most of his tanks from the wasteful battle in the city to prepare a strong mechanized force ready to react rapidly. Supply and ammunition dumps should have been reorganized to ensure that their vehicles were kept ready to move at short notice. This comparatively small degree of preparation – and disobedience to Führer headquarters – would have left the Sixth Army in a position to defend itself effectively at the crucial moment.

Hitler had decreed in a Führer instruction of 30 June that formations should not liaise with their neighbours. General Schmidt was nevertheless persuaded by members of the headquarters staff to ignore this order. An officer with a wireless set from Sixth Army was attached to the Romanians to the north-west. This was Lieutenant Gerhard Stöck, who had won a gold medal for javelin-throwing in the 1936 Berlin Olympics. General Strecker also made arrangements to send a liaison officer from XI Corps.

The first warnings of a build-up on the Don flank had come in late October. General Dumitrescu, the commander-in-chief of the Third Romanian Army, had long argued that his sector could only be defended if they held the whole bank, using the river Don itself as their major anti-tank obstacle. Dumitrescu had recommended seizing the rest of the southern bank at the end of September, but Army Group B, while accepting his argument, explained that all spare troops had to be concentrated on Stalingrad, whose capture was still assumed to be imminent.

Once the Romanians began to notice the enemy build-up, they became increasingly anxious. Each of their divisions, only seven battalions strong, had to cover a front of twelve miles. Their greatest defect was a lack of effective anti-tank weapons. They had only some horse-drawn 37-mm Pak anti-tank guns, which the Russians had nicknamed the 'door-knocker' because its shells could not penetrate the armour of the T-34. Romanian artillery batteries were also severely short of ammunition, because priority had been given to the Sixth Army.

Dumitrescu's staff reported their concerns to Army Group headquarters on 29 October, and Marshal Antonescu also drew Hitler's attention to the dangerous situation which his troops faced, but Hitler, while still expecting news of the final conquest of Stalingrad almost any day, was also distracted by other momentous events. Rommel's retreat from the battle of El Alamein was soon followed by warnings of the Anglo-American invasion fleet heading for North Africa. The landings of Operation Torch also focused his attention on France. The entry of German forces into the unoccupied zone on 11 November took place on the day that Paulus launched his final assault in Stalingrad.

By then the warnings of a Soviet offensive against the salient had started to accumulate rapidly. The liaison officer reported on 7 November that 'the Third Romanian Army is expecting a strong enemy attack with tanks on 8 November in the Kletskaya–Raspopinskaya sector'. The only trouble was that the Romanians continually expected the Russian offensive to begin in the next twenty-four hours, and when nothing happened, especially after the uneventful twenty-fifth anniversary of the Revolution, this began to have the effect of the boy crying wolf.

General von Richthofen, on the other hand, was increasingly convinced by the evidence of his air reconnaissance squadrons. Even during Paulus's assault on 11 November, he diverted part of VIII Air Corps to attack Russian concentrations opposite the Third Romanian Army. The following day he wrote in his diary: 'On the Don, the Russians are resolutely carrying on with their preparations for an offensive against the Romanians. VIII Air Corps, the whole of Fourth Air Fleet and the Romanian air force are keeping up continuous attacks on them. Their reserves have now been concentrated. When, I wonder, will the attack come!'

On 14 November, he recorded: 'Weather getting steadily worse, with mists that cause wing icing and freezing-cold rain storms. On Stalingrad front all quiet. Our bombers have carried out successful raids on the railways east of Stalingrad, dislocating the flow of reinforcements and supplies. Fighters and fighter-bombers have been concentrating on smashing up the Russian approach march to the Don.'

German air sweeps over the Soviet rear areas caught part of the 5th Tank Army crossing the Don and nearly produced two important casualties. German aircraft surprised Khrushchev and Yeremenko at Svetly-Yar, where they were receiving a delegation from Uzbekistan bringing thirty-seven railway wagons of presents to the defenders of

Stalingrad, including wine, cigarettes, dried melon, rice, apples, pears and meat.

The reaction to the threat by the various levels of command – Führer headquarters, Army Group B and Sixth Army headquarters – was not just a question of too little, too late. Hitler's infectious illusions also played their part. He covered himself by issuing orders for the reinforcement of the Romanians with German troops and minefields, but he refused to accept that there were neither the resources nor sufficient formations available.

All that could be spared to strengthen the threatened northern flank was the XXXXVIII Panzer Corps, commanded by Lieutenant-General Ferdinand Heim, Paulus's former chief of staff. On paper, this formation appeared powerful, with 14th Panzer Division, 22nd Panzer Division and the 1st Romanian Panzer Division as well as an anti-tank battalion and a motorized artillery battalion, but on closer examination it proved much less impressive. The whole panzer corps had fewer than a hundred serviceable modern tanks between three divisions.

The 14th Panzer Division, which had been ground down in the Stalingrad fighting, had not been given a chance to refit. The Romanian contingent was equipped with Škoda light tanks from Czechoslovakia, which did not stand a chance against the Russian T-34. The 22nd Panzer Division, as a reserve formation, had been starved of fuel, and during its long period of immobility, mice had sought shelter from the weather inside the hulls. They had gnawed through the insulation of electric cables and no replacements were immediately available. Meanwhile, other regiments in the division were continually split up, and sent hither and thither in answer to cries for help from Romanian units. To keep the Romanians calm, detachments as small as a couple of tanks and a pair of anti-tank guns were sent 'on a wild-goose chase' from one sector to another like an increasingly unconvincing stage army. The Führer's Luftwaffe adjutant, Nicolaus von Below, claimed that 'Hitler was misinformed about the quality of this panzer corps', but even if that were true, he was the one who had created the atmosphere in which his headquarters staff avoided uncomfortable truths.

South of Stalingrad, the only reserve formation behind the Romanian VI Corps was the 29th Motorized Infantry Division, but on 10 November it was told that 'on receiving the codeword "Hubertusjagd", it was to set off within the shortest time possible towards Perelazovsky in the Third Romanian Army area.' Perelazovsky was the focal point of XXXXVIII Panzer Corps. Despite all of General Hoth's warnings, the threat to the southern flank was not taken seriously.

The weather in the first half of November made the approach march for Soviet formations difficult. Freezing rain was followed by sudden, hard frosts. Many units, in the rush to prepare for Operation Uranus, had not received winter uniforms. There was a shortage not just of gloves and hats, but even of basic items such as standard Red Army foot cloths, worn instead of socks.

On 7 November, when 81st Cavalry Division in 4th Cavalry Corps crossed the Kalmyk steppe to the southern flank, fourteen men, mainly Uzbeks and Turkomans who had not been given winter uniforms, died of frostbite 'due to the irresponsible attitude of commanders'. Officers rode on ahead, unaware of what was happening behind. Frozen soldiers fell from their horses, unable to hold on, and NCOs, not knowing what to do, just threw them on to carts where they froze to death. In one squadron alone they lost thirty-five horses. Some soldiers tried to shirk the battle ahead. In 93rd Rifle Division, during the approach march, there were seven cases of self-inflicted wounds, and two deserters were captured. 'In the next few days', Stalingrad Front reported to Shcherbakov, 'other traitors will be tried too, among them a member of the Communist Party, who when on sentry, shot himself in the left hand.'

The atmosphere in the Kremlin had become increasingly nervous ever since Zhukov had the unenviable task of warning Stalin that the launch of Operation Uranus would have to be postponed by ten days to 19 November. Transport difficulties, mainly the shortage of lorries, meant that the attacking formations had not yet received their allocations of fuel and ammunition. Stalin, though afraid that the enemy would get wind of what was afoot and escape the trap, had no option but to agree. He badgered the *Stavka* for information on any change in the Sixth Army's dispositions. Then, on 11 November, Stalin became anxious that they did not have enough aircraft to hold off the Luftwaffe. But the scale and detail of Zhukov's plans eventually reassured him. This time, he felt, they would at last get their revenge.

Zhukov and Vasilevsky flew back to Moscow to brief him on 13 November. 'We could tell he was pleased', wrote Zhukov, 'because he puffed unhurriedly on his pipe, smoothed his moustache and listened to us without interrupting.'

Red Army intelligence, for the first time, had made a determined attempt to coordinate its various sources. It was its first real opportunity to prove itself since all the earlier disasters, which were largely due to Stalin's obsessive preconceptions, totally discounting any accurate material produced.* Most intelligence came from 'tongues' seized by reconnaissance patrols, probing attacks and air reconnaissance. Signals intelligence from radio units also helped confirm the identity of a number of German formations. Artillery reconnaissance worked fairly well, with General Voronov supervising the concentrations of regiments on the key sectors. The sappers, meanwhile, were mapping out friendly and enemy minefields in advance. The main problem was the freezing fog, about which General von Richthofen also complained bitterly.

On 12 November, the first heavy fall of snow coincided with a series of reconnaissance missions. White camouflage suits were issued, and groups sent out to capture prisoners were told to check whether new formations had been moved into the sectors targeted for breakthrough. The reconnaissance company of 173rd Rifle Division for the first time discovered Germans preparing concrete bunkers. Other prisoners taken by raiding parties up and down the front soon confirmed that although concrete bunkers had been ordered, no new formations had arrived. On the Third Romanian Army's front, they

---

* Intelligence could be a dangerous branch in which to serve. On 22 November, three days after the great offensive began, the head of intelligence of 62nd Army was charged with 'defeatism and counter-revolutionary ideas' and accused of giving false information about the enemy. It is impossible to know whether the officer in question was being held responsible for political crimes or incompetence, either his own or as a scapegoat for a superior.

discovered that senior officers had commandeered all the supplies to concrete their headquarters in the rear first, and none were available for first-line positions. Russian troops manning these sectors where the offensive was about to take place 'knew something was going to happen, but they did not know exactly what'.

The major preoccupation in Moscow at this time was the lack of reliable information on the state of Sixth Army morale. So far during the fighting round Stalingrad not even a full regimental headquarters had been overrun, so apart from odd letters and orders taken at a junior level they had little to go on. At last, on 9 November, Major-General Ratov of Red Army intelligence was passed a captured document from the 384th Infantry Division opposite the lesser Don bend, a mixture of Saxon and Austrian regiments. He immediately saw that here at last was the evidence they had been waiting for. Translated copies were sent immediately to Stalin, Beria, Molotov, Malenkov, Voroshilov, Vasilevsky, Zhukov, and Aleksandrov, Chief of the Division of Propaganda and Agitation. General Ratov could no doubt imagine the glee which its contents would excite in the Great Leader's heart. They were doubly encouraging since this formation from Dresden had not been involved in the street fighting in Stalingrad.

'I am well aware of the state of the division,' wrote General Baron von Gablenz to all commanders in the 384th Infantry Division. 'I know that it has no strength left. It is not surprising, and I shall make every effort to improve the division's state, but the fighting is cruel and it becomes crueller every day. It is impossible to change the situation. The lethargy of the majority of soldiers must be corrected by more active leadership. Commanders must be more severe. In my order of 3 September 1942, No. 187–42, I stipulated that those who desert their post would be court-martialled . . . I will act with all the severity that the law requires. Those who fall asleep at their posts in the front line must be punished with death. There should be no doubt about this. In the same category is disobedience . . . expressed in the following ways: lack of care of weapons, body, clothing, horses and mechanized equipment.' Officers must warn their soldiers that 'they should count on staying in Russia for the whole of the winter'.

*

Soviet mechanized formations, which had been camouflaged well behind the lines, moved forward to their start-line positions. Smoke-screens were laid to cover them crossing the Don into the bridgeheads, and just behind the front line, loudspeakers from propaganda companies blasted out music and political messages to cover the sound of engines.

On the three 'Stalingrad axis' fronts, just over one million men were now assembled. General Smirnov, chief of medical services, had 119 field hospitals with 62,000 beds ready for casualties. Orders were given three hours before the attack. Red Army units were told that they were to make a deep raid on the enemy's rear. Encirclement was not mentioned. The troops were fiercely excited at the thought that the Germans did not know what was going to hit them. This was the start of the fight back. Vehicles were checked and checked again. They had huge distances to cover in front of them. Their engines were listened to 'as a physician would a heart'. The time for writing letters, shaving, washing foot bandages, and playing chess or dominoes was over. 'Men and commanders had been ordered to rest, but they were too keyed up. Everybody was turning over in his mind whether everything had really been done.'

On that eve of battle, the Germans did not sense that the next day would be any different. The Sixth Army's daily report was brief: 'Along the whole front, no major changes. Drift-ice on the Volga weaker than on the day before.' That night, a soldier longing for leave, wrote home, reflecting on the fact that he was '2,053 miles from the German frontier'.

Part Four

ZHUKOV'S TRAP

15

Operation Uranus

Soon after five in the morning, on Thursday, 19 November, the telephone rang in Sixth Army headquarters. The operations staff were housed in Golubinsky, a large Cossack village on the right bank of the Don. Outside, it had started to snow, which, combined with freezing fog, prevented sentries from seeing more than a few yards.

The call was from Lieutenant Gerhard Stöck, the javelin gold-medallist with the Romanian IV Army Corps on the Kletskaya sector. His message was logged in the war diary: 'According to the statement of a Russian officer captured in the area of the 1st Romanian Cavalry Division, the expected attack should start today at five o'clock.' Since there was still no other sign of the offensive starting, and it was after five, the duty officer did not wake the army chief of staff. General Schmidt was furious if disturbed by a false alarm, and there had been a good deal of those recently from the Romanian divisions to their north-west.

In fact, all through the night, Soviet sappers in white camouflage suits had been crawling forward in the snow, lifting anti-tank mines. The massed Russian artillery and mortar batteries loaded at 7.20 a.m. Russian time, 5.20 a.m. German time, on receipt of the code-word 'Siren'. One Soviet general said that the freezing white mist was 'as thick as milk'. Front headquarters considered a further postponement, due to the bad visibility, but decided against it. Ten minutes later, the guns, howitzers and *Katyusha* regiments received the order to prepare to fire. The signal was relayed by trumpets, which were clearly heard by the Romanian troops opposite.

At Sixth Army headquarters, the telephone rang again. Wasting few words, Stöck told Captain Behr, who answered it, that trumpet calls had signalled the start of a massive bombardment. 'I have the impression that the Romanians will not be able to resist, but I will keep you informed.' Behr did not hesitate to wake General Schmidt this time.

On the two main sectors chosen for the offensive from the north, some 3,500 guns and heavy mortars had been concentrated to blast a route for a dozen infantry divisions, three tank corps and two cavalry corps. The first salvos sounded like sudden thunderclaps in the still air. Shooting into a haze which was impenetrable to their forward observation officers, the artillery and *Katyusha* batteries were unable to make any corrections, but having ranged in a few days earlier, their fire remained accurate.

The ground began shaking as if from a low-intensity earthquake. The ice in puddles cracked like old mirrors. The bombardment was so intense that thirty miles to the south, medical officers in the 22nd Panzer Division were woken from a heavy sleep, 'because the ground trembled'. They did not wait for orders. 'The situation was clear.' They loaded up their vehicles ready to head for the front.

Russian soldiers on the Don and Stalingrad Fronts also heard the distant rumble of artillery and asked their officers what was happening. Commanders had to reply: 'I don't know.' The obsession with secrecy was so great that no announcement was made until the outcome of the battle was well and truly decided. Most, of course, guessed, and could hardly contain their excitement. Stalin, in his speech twelve days before on the twenty-fifth anniversary of the Revolution, had made a broad hint about a great counter-attack, with the words, 'there will be a holiday in our street too'.

After one hour, Soviet rifle divisions, unsupported by tanks, advanced. The guns and *Katyusha* batteries, still shooting blind, increased their range to take on the Romanian second line and artillery. The ill-equipped Romanian infantry, although shaken by the heavy bombardment, straightened up in their trenches, and fought back bravely. 'The attack was repulsed,' reported a German officer with the 13th Romanian Infantry Division. A second assault, this time supported by tanks, was also beaten off. Eventually, after another round of shelling, the Soviet guns abruptly ceased shooting. The mist seemed to make the silence deeper. Then, the Romanians heard the sound of tank engines.

The massive artillery preparation, which had churned up the snow and mud of no man's land, did not improve the going for the T-34s. It had also concealed the routes through the minefields. The sappers carried on the back of the second or third tank, ready in case the lead vehicle hit a mine, soon had to respond to the order 'Sappers, jump off!' Under fire from the Romanian infantry, they ran forward to clear a fresh route.

The Romanian soldiers stood up bravely to several more waves of Soviet infantry, and managed to knock out a number of tanks, but without enough anti-tank weapons, they were doomed. Several groups of tanks broke through, then attacked sideways. Unable to waste further time with infantry attacks, the Soviet generals sent their armoured formations straight at the Romanian lines en masse, and the main breakthroughs came around midday. The 4th Tank Corps and the 3rd Guards Cavalry Corps smashed through the Romanian IV Corps on the Kletskaya sector, and headed south. The Soviet cavalrymen, with sub-machine-guns slung across their backs, cantered on their shaggy little cossack ponies over the snow-covered landscape almost as fast as the tanks. The T-34s, with their turrets hunched forward on their hulls, looked equally impatient to be at the enemy.

Half an hour later, some thirty miles to the west, General Romanenko's 5th Tank Army shattered the defences of the Romanian II Corps. The broad tracks of the T-34s crushed the barbed wire, and collapsed the trenches. The 8th Cavalry Corps soon followed. Its mission was to protect their right flank and widen the encirclement westwards.

Wind had dispersed the fog a little in the middle of the morning, so some aircraft from the Soviet 2nd, 16th and 17th Air Armies went into the attack. The Luftwaffe bases seem to have suffered from poorer visibility, or else their air controllers would not take the same

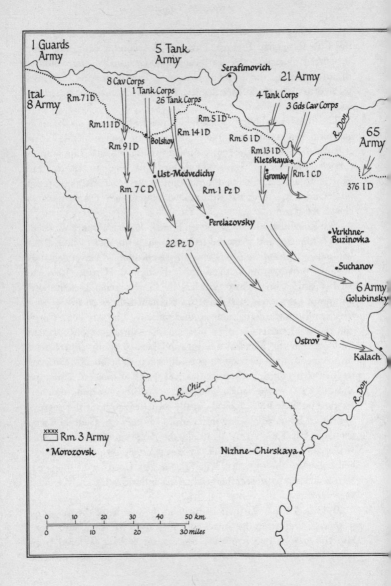

1 Guards Army

5 Tank Army

Serafimovich

21 Army

Ital 8 Army

Rm 7 I D

8 Cav Corps

1 Tank Corps

26 Tank Corps

4 Tank Corps

3 Gds Cav Corps

R. Don

65 Army

Rm 11 I D

Rm 5 I D

Rm 6 I D

Rm 9 I D

Bolshoy

Rm 14 I D

Rm 13 I D

Kletskaya

Rm 1 C D

376 I D

Ust-Medvedichy

Gromky

Rm 7 C D

Rm 1 Pz D

Perelazovsky

Verkhne-Buzinovka

22 Pz D

Suchanov

6 Army

Golubinsky

Ostrov

Kalach

R. Chir

R. Don

Rm 3 Army

Morozovsk

Nizhne-Chirskaya

0   10   20   30   40   50 km

0   10   20   30 miles

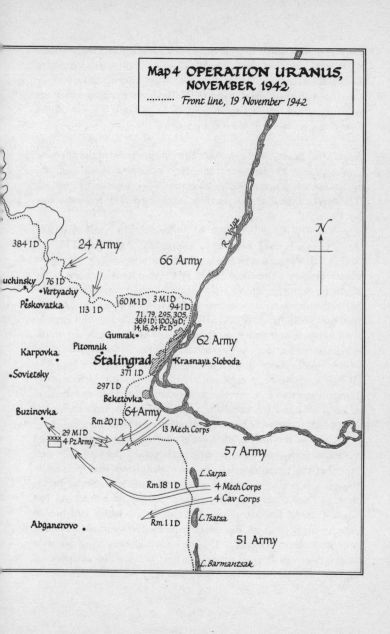

Map 4 OPERATION URANUS, NOVEMBER 1942
.... *Front line, 19 November 1942*

R. Volga

N

384 ID

24 Army

66 Army

uchinsky 76 ID
•Vertyachy
Peskovatka 113 ID 60 MID 3 MID
94 ID
71, 79, 295, 305,
389 ID; 100 JgD;
14, 16, 24 Pz D

Gumrak•

Karpovka Pitomnik
•Stalingrad
62 Army

•Krasnaya Sloboda

•Sovietsky 371 ID

297 ID
Beketovka

Buzinovka 64 Army
• Rm.20 ID
29 MID 13 Mech Corps
xxxx
4 Pz Army
57 Army

L.Sarpa
Rm.18 ID 4 Mech Corps
4 Cav Corps

Abganerovo • Rm.1 ID L.Tsatsa

51 Army

L.Barmantsak

risks as their Russian counterparts. 'Once again, the Russians have made masterly use of the bad weather,' wrote Richthofen, with more feeling than accuracy, in his diary that night. 'Rains, snow and icy mists have put a stop to all flying. VIII Air Corps managed with great difficulty to get one or two aircraft off the ground. To seal off the Don crossings by bombing is not possible.'

Sixth Army headquarters were not officially informed of the offensive until 9.45 a.m. The reaction at this stage indicates that, although the threat was taken seriously, it was certainly not regarded as mortal. The attacks in Stalingrad, even those involving panzer divisions, were not halted.

At five past eleven, General von Sodenstern, the chief of staff of Army Group B, rang Schmidt to inform him that General Heim's XXXXVIII Panzer Corps had been sent north to Bolshoy to support the Romanians. (The corps had in fact been advancing towards the Kletskaya sector, when, to Heim's fury, orders relayed from Hitler in Bavaria had dictated the change of direction.) Sodenstern suggested that the Sixth Army should tell General Strecker's XI Corps to send troops to strengthen the defences east of Kletskaya, where the Romanian 1st Cavalry Division was holding on. So far they had heard of only twenty enemy tanks sighted – 'up to now only a weak attack'. At half past eleven, a regiment from the Austrian 44th Infantry Division was told to move westwards that night. This was the start of a process which was to tie down part of the Sixth Army within the Don bend, and gravely hinder its freedom of action.

In spite of the liaison officers and new telephone lines that had been laid, little detailed information was getting through. The first hint that the situation might be more dangerous than previously thought did not arrive until over two hours after the Soviet break-through. News came of 'an enemy armoured spearhead' (in fact Major-General Kravchenko's 4th Tank Corps) which had broken right through the 13th Romanian Infantry Division and advanced over six miles to Gromky. This news had already sown panic in several Romanian formation headquarters: 'boxes of files and personal luggage' were thrown on to trucks, and their personnel departed in a rush. There was even more uncertainty about the progress of the larger attack by Romanenko's 5th Tank Army, further to the west.

The reassuring idea of sending the so-called XXXXVIII Panzer Corps north to counter-attack demonstrated how much senior German officers had allowed themselves to be corrupted by Hitler's own delusions. A panzer corps should have been more than a match for a Soviet tank army, but in serviceable battle tanks this one did not even amount to a full division. The 22nd Panzer Division had little more than thirty serviceable tanks and was so short of fuel that it needed to borrow the Romanians' reserves. Jokes about the sabotage by mice had run round the army, but few laughed once the implications became apparent.

Changes of orders only made things worse. Instead of deploying Heim's panzer corps en bloc as planned, the 1st Romanian Panzer Division was diverted when already on the move. This separation led to further disasters. A surprise Soviet attack on its headquarters destroyed the German liaison officer's radio set, the only means of communication with General Heim's headquarters, and all contact was lost for the next few days.

The most astonishing aspect of this day's events was the lack of reaction from General Paulus. Having failed to organize a mechanized strike force before the enemy offensive, he continued to do nothing. The 16th and 24th Panzer Divisions were left with many of their key units bogged down in street-fighting in Stalingrad. Nothing was done to bring up fuel and ammunition ready to resupply their vehicles.

During the afternoon of 19 November, the Soviet tanks advanced southwards in columns through the freezing mist. Because there were so few landmarks in this snowbound waste, local civilians had been attached as guides to the point units, but this was not enough. The visibility was so bad that the commanders had to steer by compass.

The advance was doubly dangerous. Drifting snow concealed deep gullies. In places tall steppe grass, covered in hoar frost, stuck up above the snow, while further on drifts extended in deceptively soft curves. Tank crews were thrown about so much that only their padded leather helmets saved them from being knocked senseless. Many limbs, mainly arms, were broken inside hulls and turrets, but the tank columns did not halt for any casualty. Behind they could see flashes and explosions as their infantry finished clearing the first and second lines of trenches.

Commanders with the 4th Tank Corps, advancing south beyond Kletskaya, anxiously watched their left flank, waiting for a counter-attack from the Germans. They knew the Romanians were incapable of it. As the blizzard intensified, snow blocked gunsights, and filled the slits of the coaxially mounted machine-gun beside the main armament. When night began to fall at about half past three in the afternoon, commanders gave the order to turn on headlights. There was no alternative if they wished to keep going.

On the western breakthrough, General Rodin's 26th Tank Corps sighted large fires ahead. They were part of a collective farm which the Germans had rapidly abandoned after setting the buildings ablaze. Clearly, the enemy were aware of their presence. The tank drivers turned off their headlights when German artillery opened fire.

It was Butkov's 1st Tank Corps to the right which finally encountered the gravely weakened XXXXVIII Panzer Corps. The German tanks still suffered from electrical problems, and their narrow tracks slid around on the black ice. The fighting in the gathering dark was chaotic. The usual German advantages of tactical skill and coordination were entirely lost.

The order from Army Group headquarters to block the broken dam near Kletskaya with part of XI Corps and 14th Panzer Division was already hopelessly late when it was issued. Headquarters Army Group B and Sixth Army were blinded by the absence of clear information. 'It is not even possible to get an overview of the situation through air reconnaissance,' wrote General von Richthofen in his diary. The Russians had also managed to confuse the picture, by launching attacks along almost all of Sixth Army's sectors.

At 5 p.m., by which time Kravchenko's 4th Tank Corps had advanced over twenty miles, General Strecker's XI Corps was ordered to form a new line of defence running southwards to protect Sixth Army's rear. But German commanders, including Richthofen, still did not guess the Red Army's objective. 'Hopefully', he wrote, 'the Russians will not reach the railway line, the main artery for our supplies.' They still could not imagine that the Russians were attempting a complete encirclement of the Sixth Army.

At 6 p.m., General von Seydlitz's headquarters received instructions that the parts of the 24th Panzer Division which had not been engaged in the fighting in Stalingrad were to leave for the area of Peskovatka and Vertyachy near the Don crossings. Yet it was not until ten o'clock that night – seventeen hours after the start of the offensive – that Sixth Army received a firm order from Colonel-General von Weichs to break off fighting in Stalingrad. 'Change of situation in area of Third Romanian Army compels radical measures with the objective of moving forces as rapidly as possible to cover the rear flank of Sixth Army and secure lines of communication.' All offensive activities in Stalingrad were 'to be halted with immediate effect'. Panzer and motorized units were to be sent westwards as quickly as possible. Due to the total lack of preparation for such an eventuality, this would not prove at all rapid. Chuikov's 62nd Army, as might have been expected, also launched strong attacks to prevent the Germans disengaging.

The 16th Panzer Division, 'in whose ranks many Russian Hiwis had been drafted to fill large gaps', was also ordered westwards to the Don. Like the 24th Panzer Division, it would have to replenish from reserve depots on the way, since there was not enough fuel in the immediate vicinity of Stalingrad. But first of all, the division had to extricate itself from the fighting round Rynok. This meant that although part of the division moved westwards the next evening, some of the tanks of the 2nd Panzer Regiment did not finally receive the order 'move out' until three in the morning on 21 November, forty-six hours after the opening of the Soviet attack.

Since the Soviet attacks were taking place to Sixth Army's rear, and outside its area of responsibility, Paulus had waited for orders from above. Army Group B, meanwhile, was having to react to orders relayed from the Führer in Berchtesgaden. Hitler's determination to control events had produced a disastrous immobilism when the greatest rapidity was needed. Nobody appears to have sat down to reassess enemy intentions. By sending the bulk of Sixth Army's panzer regiments back across the Don to defend its left rear flank, all flexibility was lost. Worst of all, it left the southern flank open.

On the Fourth Panzer Army's front to the south of Stalingrad, German regiments heard the artillery barrages on the morning of 19 November well over sixty miles to their north-west. They guessed that the big attack had started, but nobody told them what was happening. In the 297th Infantry Division, whose right flank adjoined the Romanian Fourth Army, Major Bruno Gebele, the commander of an infantry battalion, suffered 'no particular anxieties'. Their sector stayed quiet the whole day.

The earth was frozen hard, the steppe looked exceptionally bleak as the wind from the south whipped up the fine, dry snow like white dust. Their neighbouring division to the left, the 371st Infantry Division, could hear the ice floes on the Volga grating against each other. That night their divisional headquarters heard that all Sixth Army attacks in Stalingrad had been stopped.

Next morning, the freezing mist was again dense. Yeremenko, the commander of the Stalingrad Front, decided to postpone the opening bombardment despite nervous telephone calls from Moscow. Finally, at 10 a.m., the artillery and *Katyusha* regiments opened fire. Three-quarters of an hour later, the ground forces moved forward into the channels through minefields cleared by sappers during the night. South of Beketovka, the 64th and 57th Armies supported the thrust by the 13th Mechanized Corps. Twenty-five miles further south, by lake Sarpa and lake Tsatsa, the 4th Mechanized and the 4th Cavalry Corps led the 51st Army into the attack.

The German neighbours of the 20th Romanian Infantry Division watched 'masses of Soviet tanks and waves of infantry, in quantities never seen before, advancing against the Romanians'. Gebele had been in touch with the commander of the adjoining Romanian regiment, Colonel Gross, who had served in the Austro-Hungarian Army, and so spoke good German. Gross's men had only a single 3.7-cm horse-drawn Pak for the whole of their sector, but the Romanian peasant soldiers fought bravely, considering that they had been left on their own. Their officers and senior NCOs 'were never to be seen at the front, and spent their time instead in various buildings in the rear with music and alcohol'. Soviet reports credited the Romanian defences with much better armament than was the case. The first tank from the 13th Tank Brigade to break through was said to have crushed no fewer than four anti-tank guns under its tracks and destroyed three fire points.

Gebele watched the attack from an observation post on his sector. 'The Romanians fought bravely, but against the waves of Soviet attack, they had no chance of resisting for long.' The Soviet attack appeared to proceed 'as if on a training ground: fire – move – fire – move'. Yet newsreel images of T-34 tanks racing forwards, spewing snow from their tracks, each vehicle carrying an eight-man assault group in white camouflage suits, tend to hide often terrible deficiencies. The attack formations south of Stalingrad were desperately short of supplies, owing to the difficulty of ferrying them across the nearly icebound Volga. Divisions started to run out of food on the second day of the offensive. By the third day, the 157th Rifle Division had neither meat nor bread. To resolve the problem, all vehicles in 64th Army, including those which served as ambulances, were switched to reprovisioning the advance. The wounded were simply left behind in the snow.

The enthusiasm of most of the attacking troops was clearly evident. It was seen as a historic moment. Fomkin, a linesman with the 157th Rifle Division, volunteered to walk ahead of the attacking tanks to lead them through the minefield. One cannot even doubt the report of the political department of the Stalingrad Front about the happiness of troops 'that the long-awaited hour had come when the defenders of Stalingrad would make the enemy's blood flow for the blood of our wives, children, soldiers and officers'. For those who took part, it was the 'happiest day of the whole war', including even the final German surrender in Berlin.

The violated Motherland was at last being avenged, yet it was Romanian, not German, divisions which bore the brunt. Their infantry, in the opinion of General Hoth's chief of staff, suffered from 'panzer-fright'. According to Soviet reports, many of them promptly threw down their weapons, raised their hands and shouted: '*Antonescu kaputt!*' Red Army soldiers apparently also found that many had shot themselves through the left hand, then bandaged the wound with bread to prevent infection. The Romanian prisoners were rounded up into columns, but before they were marched off to camps, many – perhaps even hundreds – were shot down by Red Army soldiers on their own account. There were reports of bodies of Soviet officers found mutilated at a Romanian headquarters, but this was probably not what triggered the spontaneous killings.

Although the breakthroughs in the south-east were achieved rapidly, the attack did not go according to plan. There were 'cases of chaos in the leading units' due to 'contradictory orders'. This seems to be a euphemism for Major-General Volsky's caution and lack of control over his columns from the 4th Mechanized Corps, which became mixed up as they advanced westwards from the line of lakes.*

To Volsky's north, Colonel Tanashchishin's initial problem with the 13th Mechanized Corps was the shortage of lorries to keep his infantry advancing at the same rate as the tanks. But then he came up against much harder opposition than the Romanians. The only German reserve on that part of the front, General Leyser's 29th Motorized Infantry Division, advanced to intercept Tanashchishin's corps some ten miles south of Beketovka. Even though Leyser's division managed to inflict a sharp reverse on the Soviet columns, General Hoth received orders to withdraw it to protect the Sixth Army's southern flank. The Romanian VI Army Corps had virtually collapsed, there was little chance of re-establishing a fresh line of defence, and even Hoth's own headquarters were threatened. The 6th Romanian Cavalry Regiment was all that was left between the southern armoured thrust and the river Don.

---

* Volsky was already in almost everybody's bad books. Just before the attack, he had written a personal letter to Stalin, 'as an honest Communist', warning that the offensive would fail. Both Zhukov and Vasilevsky had had to fly back to Moscow on 17 November. After hearing their arguments, Stalin telephoned Volsky from the Kremlin. He retracted his letter. Stalin was curiously unruffled. The possibility cannot be ruled out that this was a precautionary ploy to be used by Stalin against Zhukov and Vasilevsky in case Operation Uranus failed.

The success of Leyser's attack suggests that if Paulus had established a strong mobile reserve before the offensive, he could have struck south with it, a distance of little more than fifteen miles, and quite easily smashed the lower arm of the encirclement. On the following day, he could then have sent it north-westwards in the direction of Kalach to meet the main threat from the northern offensive. But this presupposed a clear appreciation of the true danger, which both Paulus and Schmidt lacked.

On that morning of Friday, 20 November, at about the time the bombardments commenced south of Stalingrad, Kravchenko's 4th Tank Corps, nearly twenty-five miles deep into the rear beyond Strecker's XI Corps, switched its advance south-eastwards. The 3rd Guards Cavalry Corps was meanwhile turning in to attack XI Corps from behind. Strecker was trying to establish a defence line south from the greater Don bend to protect this open gap behind the whole army. The bulk of his corps meanwhile faced the Soviet 65th Army to the north which kept up the pressure, with constant attacks, to hinder any redeployment.

With the Romanians 'fleeing wildly, most of them leaving behind their weapons', the 376th Infantry Division had to pull round to face westwards, while trying to make contact with part of 14th Panzer Division to its south. The Austrian 44th Infantry Division also had to redeploy, but 'much material was lost because it could not be moved owing to the shortage of fuel'.

To their south, the panzer regiment of 14th Panzer Division still had no clear idea of the enemy's direction of approach. Having advanced westwards for a dozen miles, it then withdrew in the afternoon back to Verkhne-Buzinovka. On the way, it ran into a flanking regiment of the 3rd Guards Cavalry Corps which it virtually annihilated. Over the first two days, the panzer regiment destroyed thirty-five Soviet tanks. On the other hand, an unprotected flak detachment, using its 'eighty-eights' as anti-tank guns, was overrun by a Russian attack.

'The catastrophic fuel situation' continued to hamper the other panzer and motorized divisions, starting to move westwards from Stalingrad to reinforce this new front. They were also suffering from a shortage of tank crewmen after Hitler's order to send every available man into Stalingrad as infantry. The other decision bitterly regretted was the withdrawal of Sixth Army's horses to the west. The new war of movement suddenly imposed by the Russians forced German infantry divisions to abandon their artillery.

The Romanian collapse accelerated as the Soviet spearheads went deeper. Few of their rear support troops had been trained to fight and staff officers fled their headquarters. In the wake of the advancing tanks, wrote one Soviet journalist, 'the road is strewn with enemy corpses; abandoned guns face the wrong way. Horses roam the *balkas* in search of food, the broken traces dragging on the ground after them; grey wisps of smoke curl up from the trucks destroyed by shellfire; steel helmets, hand grenades and rifle cartridges litter the road.' Isolated groups of Romanians had continued to resist on sectors of the former front line, but the Soviet rifle divisions from the 5th Tank Army and 21st Army soon crushed them. Perelazovsky had contained a Romanian corps headquarters which, according to General Rodin, was so hurriedly abandoned that his 26th Tank Corps found 'staff papers scattered on the floor and officers' fur-lined greatcoats hanging on racks' – their owners having fled into the freezing night. More important for the Soviet mechanized column, they captured the fuel dump intact.

Meanwhile, the 22nd Panzer Division, unable to resist the T-34s of 1st Tank Corps, had retreated. It made an attempt to attack north-eastwards the following day, but was soon surrounded. Reduced to little more than the equivalent of a company of tanks, it later fought its way out and retreated south-westwards, harried by the Soviet 8th Cavalry Corps.

In the meantime, Rodin's 26th Tank Corps, having smashed part of the 1st Romanian Panzer Division which got in its way, also started its advance across the open steppe to the south-east. The Soviet columns had been told to forget the enemy left behind and concentrate on the objective. If Luftwaffe air reconnaissance had been able to identify the roughly parallel courses of the three tank corps during the afternoon of 20 November, then alarm bells at Sixth Army headquarters might have rung earlier.

The main Romanian formation still fighting effectively at this time was the 'Lascar Group'. This consisted of remnants from the V Army Corps, gathered together by the intrepid Lieutenant-General Mihail Lascar, when cut off between the two great Soviet armoured thrusts. Lascar, who had been awarded the Knight's Cross at Sevastopol, was one of the few senior Romanian officers the Germans really respected. He held out on the assumption that XXXXVIII Panzer Corps was coming to his relief.

Sixth Army headquarters, twelve miles north of Kalach at Golubinsky, seems to have started the morning of Saturday, 21 November, in a relatively optimistic mood. At 7.40 a.m., 'a not unfavourable description of the situation' was dispatched to Army Group B. Paulus and Schmidt, who still perceived the attacks on Strecker's left flank by the 3rd Guards Cavalry Corps as the main threat, clearly thought that their forces brought westwards from Stalingrad would transform the situation.

During the course of that morning, however, Paulus and Schmidt received a series of nasty shocks. Different signals all pointed to the same conclusion. Army Group B warned them that Sixth Army's southern flank was now threatened from both sides. A report came in that a large armoured column (in fact part of Kravchenko's 4th Tanks Corps) was less than twenty miles to their west. It was heading for the Don High Road, the showpiece of German military engineering on the west bank which linked most of the bridges on that vital stretch of the river. Sixth Army had no troops in the area capable of meeting the threat. To make matters worse, many of Sixth Army's repair bases and supply depots lay exposed. Paulus and Schmidt at last recognized that the enemy was aiming for a full encirclement. The diagonal Soviet thrusts, from both the north-west and south-east, were almost certainly aiming for Kalach and its bridge.

The disastrous German reactions to Operation Uranus had lain not just in Hitler's belief that the Russians had no reserves, but in the arrogant assumptions of most generals as well. 'Paulus and Schmidt had expected an attack,' explained an officer with Sixth Army headquarters, 'but not such an attack. It was the first time that the Russians used tanks as we did.' Even Richthofen implicitly admitted this when he wrote of the enemy offensive as 'for him an astonishingly successful breakthrough'. Field Marshal von Manstein, on the other hand, felt (perhaps with the benefit of hindsight) that Sixth Army headquarters had been far too slow to react and extremely negligent in its failure to foresee the threat to Kalach – the obvious Don crossing between the two breakthroughs.

Soon after midday, most of Paulus's headquarters staff were sent eastwards to the railway junction of Gumrak, some eight miles from Stalingrad, so as to be close to the bulk of the Sixth Army. Meanwhile, Paulus and Schmidt flew in two Fieseler Storch light aeroplanes to Nizhne-Chirskaya, where they were joined by General Hoth on the following day for a conference. At Golubinsky, they left behind columns of smoke rising into the freezing air from burning files and stores, as well as several unserviceable reconnaissance aircraft on the adjacent airstrip which had been set on fire. In their hurried departure, they also missed a 'Führer decision' relayed on by Army Group B at 3.25 p.m. It began: 'Sixth Army stand firm in spite of danger of temporary encirclement.'

There was little hope of holding positions on that afternoon of 21 November. The accumulation of delays to the panzer regiment of 16th Panzer Division had left a hole below Strecker's XI Army Corps and the other assorted groups attempting to form a new defence line. This was rapidly exploited by the Soviet 3rd Guards Cavalry Corps and 4th Mechanized Corps. Strecker's divisions, increasingly threatened from the north and north-east as well, had no option but to start withdrawing towards the Don. The ill-considered plan of sending the Sixth Army's panzer regiments westwards was now revealed to have been a dangerous diversion of effort.

Kalach, the principal objective for three Soviet tank corps, was one of the most vulnerable points of all. There was no organized defence, only an ill-assorted collection of sub-units, mainly supply and maintenance troops, a small detachment of Feldgendarmerie and a Luftwaffe anti-aircraft battery.

The transport company and workshops of the 16th Panzer Division had already established themselves in Kalach for the winter. 'The first news of any change in the situation' did not reach them until 10 a.m. on 21 November. They subsequently heard that the Russian tank columns which had broken through the Romanians to the north-west were now advancing towards their sector of the Don. At around 5 p.m. they heard for the first time of the breakthrough south of Stalingrad. They had no idea that Volsky's mechanized corps, despite all the hesitations which had enraged Yeremenko, was approaching Fourth Panzer Army's former headquarters, only thirty miles to their south-east.

The defences at Kalach were not only thoroughly inadequate for the task, they were also badly managed. On the west bank, on the heights above the Don, there were four Luftwaffe flak emplacements, and another two anti-aircraft guns on the east bank. Only a group of twenty-five men from the Organisation Todt were assigned to the immediate security of the bridge, while the scratch battalion of rear troops remained in the town on the east bank.

Major-General Rodin, the commander of 26th Tank Corps, gave the task of capturing the bridge at Kalach to Lieutenant-Colonel G. N. Filippov, the commander of the 19th Tank Brigade. Leaving Ostrov at midnight, Filippov's column advanced eastwards to Kalach during the early hours of 22 November. At 6.15 a.m., two captured German tanks and a reconnaissance vehicle, with their lights switched on to disarm suspicion, drove on to the temporary bridge across the Don and opened fire on the guards. Another sixteen Soviet tanks had meanwhile plunged into thick scrub on the heights above the river to cover them. It was the point from which German panzers had gazed down upon the town on 2 August.

Several Soviet tanks were set on fire, but Filippov's boldness had paid off. The detachment guarding the bridge was driven off, and enough T-34s crossed to fight off belated attempts to blow the bridge. Russian motorized infantry appeared on the Don heights, then another group of tanks appeared. Two more attacks followed, supported by artillery and mortars from the Don heights across the river. By mid-morning, Soviet infantry broke into the town. There was chaos in the streets, packed with Romanian stragglers separated from their units. It was not long before the few heavy weapons manned by the scratch battalion were out of ammunition or out of action, even though the drivers and mechanics had sustained few casualties. Having blown up their workshops, they withdrew from the town, climbed into trucks and drove back to find their division in Stalingrad. The way was open for the link-up the next day between the 4th and 26th Tank Corps, coming from the northern flank, and Volsky's 4th Mechanized Corps, coming from south of Stalingrad.

Guided towards each other by green recognition flares fired at intervals into the sky, the Russian spearheads met in the open steppe near Sovietsky with bear-hug embraces, a scene which was re-enacted at a later date for Soviet propaganda before newsreel cameras. The celebratory exchanges of vodka and sausage between tank crews at the time were unfilmed, but far more genuine.

News spread rapidly on the German side, with the phrase, 'We're surrounded!' That Sunday, 22 November, was for Protestants the day of remembrance of the dead. 'A sombre Totensonntag 1942,' wrote Kurt Reuber, a priest serving as a doctor with 16th Panzer Division, 'worry, fear and horror.' Many, however, were not too concerned on first hearing the news. Encirclements had happened the winter before, and been broken, but better-informed officers, on further reflection, began to realize that this time there were no reserves to rescue them quickly. 'We became very much aware of what danger we were in', remembered Freytag-Loringhoven, 'to be cut off so deep into Russia on the edge of Asia.'

Forty miles to the west, the last pocket of Romanian resistance was coming to an end, even though in the early hours of that day, General Lascar had rejected the Red Army's demand for surrender. 'We will continue to fight without thought of surrender', he declared, but his troops, although resisting bravely, were without supplies and short of ammunition.

The Soviet crossing at Kalach immediately put the XI Army Corps, to the north, in grave danger. It had already been fighting a defensive battle on almost three sides amid uncertainty and chaos, compounded by rumours. This confusion was revealed in the fragments of a diary taken from the body of a German artillery officer:

20.11. . . . is the offensive coming to a halt??!! Change of position northwards. We have only one gun left. All the others are out of action.

Saturday, 21.11. Enemy tanks early . . . Change of position to the rear. Russians already extremely near. Own infantry (motor-cyclists and pioneers) called in for close protection. Today still more Romanians passed by without stopping. We're pulling out. Already under pressure from Russians on two sides. New fire position. Only stayed a short time, then another change of position rearwards. Build a bunker.

Sunday, 22.11. Alarm at 3.30 a.m. Ordered out as infantry! Russians approaching. Romanians retreating. We can't hold this position on our own. We're anxiously waiting for another order to change position.

During this retreat, German infantry divisions found themselves in the open fighting off cavalry attacks 'as if it were 1870', as one officer put it. Their greatest problem was transport, mainly because of the shortage of horses. In some cases the solution adopted was brutally simple. An NCO would grab three-quarter-starved Russians from one of the prisoner-of-war cages to serve as draught animals. 'When the retreat started on 20 November,' reported one Russian prisoner of war, 'we were put instead of horses to drag the carts loaded with ammunition and food. Those prisoners who could not drag the carts as quickly as the Feldwebel wanted were shot on the spot. In this way we were forced to pull the carts for four days, almost without any rest. At the Vertyachy prison camp, an encirclement of barbed wire without any shelter, the Germans selected the least unhealthy prisoners and took them with them.' The remainder, the sickest prisoners, were left behind to starve and freeze in the snow. 'Only two out of ninety-eight were still alive', when they were discovered by an advance unit of the 65th Army. Photographers were summoned to record the horrific scene. Pictures were printed in the press and the Soviet government formally accused the German command of a war crime.

The 376th Infantry Division was the most exposed to the Russian attack, which was 'extraordinarily rapid', according to its commander, General Edler von Daniels. The division, reduced to 4,200 men, when trapped on the west bank of the Don as part of XI Army Corps, pulled back in a south-eastwards direction on 22 November. Two days later, in the early morning, the division crossed the Don by the bridge at Vertyachy.

The tank regiment of 16th Panzer Division had meanwhile been advancing, having finally crossed the Don on the night of 22 November to support XI Corps. On the way, it had managed to pass by its armoured workshops at Peskovatka, where some new and freshly repaired tanks were collected. From its position on the southern side of the German bridgehead in the Don loop, the panzer regiment attempted a counter-attack in the direction of Suchanov on 23 November in heavy mist, but was ambushed by Soviet infantry, in white camouflage suits, armed with anti-tank rifles. In the face of enemy strength, and owing to the acute shortage of fuel, the 16th Panzer Division was pulled back. It took up positions ready to cover the retreat, but communications were so bad that almost all orders had to go via dispatch rider.

The German retreat eastwards across the Don, back towards Stalingrad and away from the rest of the Wehrmacht, was in many ways worse than the retreat from before Moscow, the previous December. Fine snow, hard and dry, drove across the steppe, lashing their faces, however much they turned their collars up against the wind. Despite the bitter lessons of the previous year, many soldiers had still not yet received winter uniform. The lines of retreat were littered with discarded weapons, helmets and equipment. Most Romanian soldiers had little more than their brown uniforms. They had thrown away their steel helmets in the retreat. The luckier ones, mainly officers, wore Balkan sheepskin caps. Shot-up and burnt-out vehicles had been pushed to the side of the road or down the embankment. At one point there was an anti-aircraft gun whose barrel had exploded, curling out and back like an exotic flower. Closer to the bridges over the Don, there were solid traffic jams of trucks, staff cars, dispatch riders desperately trying to get through, farm carts and the odd field gun towed by exhausted and undernourished horses. From time to time there would be waves of panic, with cries of 'Russian tanks!' The Soviet 16th Tank Corps was attacking down through the 76th Infantry Division towards Vertyachy, threatening to cut off German units left west of the Don.

Some of the ugliest scenes developed at the approaches to the bridge at Akimovsky, with soldiers shouting, jostling and even fighting to get across to the eastern bank. The weak and the wounded were trampled underfoot. Sometimes, officers threatened each other for not letting their men pass first. Even the Feldgendarmerie detachment armed with sub-machine-guns was unable to restore a semblance of order. A considerable number of soldiers, to avoid the chaos and congestion, tried to cross the frozen Don on foot. The ice was thick and strong near the banks, but in the centre there were weak spots. Those who fell through the ice were doomed. Nobody even thought of going to their aid. Comparisons to the Berezina were uppermost in most people's minds.

Occasionally, on these lines of retreat, an officer as unshaven as the men around him decided that it was his duty to halt the disintegration. He drew his pistol to round up a few stragglers, then, using them as a core, press-ganged others until their force snowballed. Heavy weapons and gun crews would also be commandeered to form an improvised combat group. The scratch force, with varying degrees of compulsion, then took up positions and waited for Soviet tanks or cavalry to appear out of the icy mist.

Across the Don, on the east bank, every village was packed with German soldiers who had lost their divisions, all seeking food and shelter from the terrible cold. The exhausted and half-starved Romanians, who had been retreating for over a week already, received little sympathy from their allies. 'The numerous Romanians', observed one officer, 'were forced to bivouac outside.' The lines of retreat took in the supply depots, but this only added to the chaos. A panzer officer later reported on the chaos in Peskovatka, 'especially the frantic and nervous behaviour of a Luftwaffe flak unit', blowing up, burning and destroying stores and transport 'in a wild fashion'. Passing soldiers plundered any supply dump they found. From the mountains of cans, they filled rucksacks and pockets until they bulged. Nobody ever seemed to have an opener, so they used bayonets, in their impatience, often not knowing what the tin contained. If they discovered one with coffee beans, they poured them into a steel helmet and pummelled them with the hilt of the bayonet like a crude pestle and mortar. When soldiers who had not received any winter clothing saw supply troops throwing new outfits on to fires, they rushed over to seize them from the flames for themselves. Meanwhile the Feldpostamt was burning letters and parcels, many of which contained food sent from home.

Far more terrible scenes were to be found in field hospitals. 'Here everything's overflowing,' reported an NCO from a repair depot in Peskovatka suffering badly from jaundice. 'The lightly wounded and sick must find accommodation for themselves.' He had to spend the night in the snow. Others suffered much more. There were trucks parked on the frozen mud of the yard outside, still full of wounded, with bandaged heads and stumps. The drivers had disappeared and corpses were not removed from their midst. Nobody had offered the living any food or drink. The orderlies and doctors inside were too busy, and passing soldiers tended to ignore their cries for help. Malingerers or walking wounded who tried to gain entry to the field hospital found themselves referred to an NCO charged with rounding up stragglers to reform them as scratch companies. Frostbite casualties, unless very severe cases, were given ointment and bandages, then also marched off for duty.

Inside, patients dozed apathetically. There was little oxygen left in the heavy, damp air, but at least it was warm. Orderlies removed field bandages, many already crawling with grey lice, cleaned wounds, gave tetanus injections and rebandaged them. A man's chances of survival depended essentially on the type and place of injury. The missile – whether shell splinter, grenade fragment or bullet – mattered less than the point of entry. The triage was straightforward. Those with serious head wounds and stomach wounds were placed to one side and left to die, because such operations took a full surgical team between ninety minutes and two hours to complete, and only about one patient in two survived. A priority was given to walking wounded.

They could be sent back into the battle. Stretchers took up too much room and too much manpower. Shattered limbs were also dealt with quickly. Surgeons with rubber aprons and scalpels and saws, working in pairs, performed rapid amputations on limbs held down by a couple of orderlies. The ration of ether was reduced to make it stretch further. Severed matter was dropped into pails. The floor around the operating table became slippery with blood, despite the occasional hurried swab with a mop. A blend of sickly smells overcame all traces of the usual field-hospital carbolic. The surgical production line seemed endless.

Troops still left on the western bank of the Don wondered if they would escape. 'Right on towards the Don,' continued the diary entries of the artillery officer. 'Will it go off all right? Will we get through to the big pocket? Is the bridge still standing? Hours of suspense and anxiety. Defence sections to right and left of the route. Often the road is itself the front line. At last the Don! Bridge intact. A stone drops from our hearts! On the far side take up a fire position. Russians pushing forwards already. Cavalry crossed the Don to our south.'

'A number of tanks had to be blown up,' a corporal reported later, 'because we did not get fuel in time.' The 14th Panzer Division was left with only twenty-four tanks which could be repaired, so its spare crews were reorganized as an infantry company armed with carbines and machine pistols. Senior officers were close to despair. Early on the morning of 25 November, Prince zu Dohna-Schlobitten, the intelligence officer of XIV Panzer Corps, overheard a conversation between General Hube and his chief of staff, Colonel Thunert, in which they used phrases such as 'last resort' and 'a bullet through the head'.

The temperature dropped drastically. The hardness of the ground meant a much higher casualty rate from mortar fire, but it was not so much the frozen earth as the frozen water which affected the retreat. The dramatic frost meant that the Don would soon be easily passable for the enemy. During the following night, Soviet infantry were able to cross the Don near Peskovatka. Early the next morning, the patients in the field hospital woke to the sound of mortar and machine-gun fire. 'Everyone was running around like headless chickens', reported the NCO with jaundice from the repair depot, who had survived the night outside after finding there was no room for him. 'On the road there were queues of vehicles, one behind the other, while mortar bombs fell all around. Here and there one of them was hit and burned out. The badly wounded could not be transported, because of a lack of trucks. A hastily assembled company of soldiers from a variety of units managed to repulse the Russians just before they reached the field hospital.'

That evening, staff at XIV Panzer Corps headquarters received the order to destroy 'all items of equipment, files and vehicles that were not absolutely necessary'. They were to pull back across the Don towards Stalingrad. By the following day, 26 November, 16th Panzer Division and part of the 44th Infantry Division were among the last troops of Sixth Army left west of the Don. That night they crossed the bridge at Luchinsky to the Stalingrad side of the river. For the 16th Panzer Division, this was 'the very same bridge that we had crossed twelve weeks before in our first attack on the city on the Volga'.

A company of panzer grenadiers from its 64th Panzer Grenadier Regiment covered the withdrawal under the command of Lieutenant von Mutius. Their task was to defend the bridge, allowing through stragglers until half past three in the morning, when the three-hundred-yard-long bridge across the Don was to be blown. At ten past three, the eager young Mutius admitted to his company sergeant-major, Oberfeldwebel Wallrawe, that he was 'very proud' to be 'the last officer of the German Wehrmacht to cross this bridge'. Wallrawe made no comment. Twenty minutes later, with the panzer grenadiers back across to the east bank of the Don, the engineers blew the bridge. The Sixth Army was now sealed off between Don and Volga.

Triumph did not mellow the attitude of Red Army men towards their enemy. 'I feel much better because we have started to destroy Germans,' wrote one soldier to his wife on 26 November. 'This was the moment when we began to beat the snakes. We are capturing plenty. We hardly have time to pass them on back to prison camps. Now they are starting to pay for our blood, and for the tears of our people, for insults and for robbery. I received winter uniform so don't worry about me. Things go well here. Soon I will be home after the victory. Sending 500 roubles.' Those still in hospital, recuperating from wounds received earlier, bitterly regretted missing the fighting. 'The battles are strong and good now,' wrote one Russian soldier to his wife, 'and I am lying here missing all this.'

There were numerous Soviet claims of German atrocities that are hard to assess. Some, no doubt, were exaggerations or inventions for propaganda purposes, others were basically true. Advancing Soviet troops encountered women, children and old men evicted from their homes by the German Army, with their possessions on small sledges. Many had been robbed of their winter clothing. Vasily Grossman reported similar stories from the southern axis of advance. He wrote that Red Army soldiers searching their prisoners were angry to find on many the pathetic loot from peasant homes – 'old women's kerchiefs and earrings, linen and skirts, babies' napkins and brightly coloured girls' blouses. One soldier had twenty-two pairs of woollen stockings in his possession.' Gaunt civilians came forward to tell of their suffering under German occupation. Every cow, every hen, and every sack of grain that could be found had been seized. Old men were flogged until they revealed where they had concealed their grain. Homesteads had been burned, with many civilians marched off for slave labour and the rest left to starve or freeze. Revenge was often exacted by small groups of Russian troops, especially when drunk, on Germans who fell into their hands. Meanwhile NKVD squads descended on liberated villages. They arrested 450 collaborators. The biggest round-up would come just over a month later in Nizhne-Chirskaya where Cossacks had denounced NKVD agents to the German Secret Field Police. Some 400 camp guards were also executed, of whom 300 were Ukrainians.

Grossman watched the German prisoners of war being escorted back. Many had ragged blankets over their shoulders instead of greatcoats. String or wire served in the place of belts. 'On this vast, flat, bleak steppe, one can see them from a long way off. They pass us in columns of two to three hundred men, and in smaller groups of from twenty to fifty. One column, several miles long, slowly wends its way, faithfully reproducing every bend and turn in the road. Some of the Germans speak some Russian. "We don't want war," they call out. "We want to go home. To hell with Hitler!" Their guards observe sarcastically: "Now when our tanks have cut them off, they are ready to shout about not wanting war; but before that the thought never entered their heads."' The prisoners were shipped across the Volga in barges towed by tugs. 'They stand packed together on deck, wearing tattered field-grey greatcoats, stamping their feet and blowing on their frozen fingers.' A sailor watching them observed with grim satisfaction: 'Now they're getting a sight of the Volga.'

In Abganerovo, Soviet infantry found the railway junction was congested with abandoned freight cars, which to judge from their markings, had been taken from several countries in occupied Europe. French-, Belgian- and Polish-manufactured motor cars stood there, each branded with the black eagle and swastika of the Third Reich. For the Russians, the wagons full of supplies were like an unexpected Christmas. The sense of depriving the mighty German Army of its ill-gotten chattels was doubly pleasurable, but the old problems of semi-chronic alcoholism still arose. The commander, second-in-command and eighteen soldiers of a company on the southern flank became casualties from drinking a captured supply of German anti-freeze. Three died, while the remaining seventeen were 'in a serious condition in a field hospital'. On the northern flank, a captured Russian officer told Prince Dohna that when his battalion, half-starved from ration shortages, captured a Romanian supply dump, 150 men died 'owing to excessive consumption'.

Meanwhile in Stalingrad itself, the 62nd Army found itself in a strange position. Although forming part of the new encirclement of the Sixth Army, it remained cut off from the east bank of the Volga, short of supplies and its wounded unevacuated. Every time a boat hazarded a crossing through the dangerous ice floes, German artillery opened fire. Yet the atmosphere had changed now that the attackers had become the besieged. The men of the 62nd Army were still not quite able to believe that the turning point had come. Russian soldiers, with no prospect of any more tobacco supplies until the Volga froze solid, sang to divert their thoughts from their craving for nicotine. The Germans listened from their bunkers. They did not shout insults any more.

16

Hitler's Obsession

The task of informing the Führer about the great Soviet breakthrough on 19 November fell to the Army Chief of Staff, General Zeitzler, who had remained behind in East Prussia. Hitler was at the Berghof above Berchtesgaden, which was where he had received news of Stalin's agreement to the Nazi–Soviet pact in August 1939. On that occasion, he had banged the dinner table in triumph, to the surprise of the ladies of his court. 'I've got them!' he had shouted, leaping to his feet. 'I've got them!' This time, his reaction appears to have been one of nervous anger.

The Wehrmacht Supreme Command war diary referred, with revealing disingenuousness, to 'alarming news of the Russian offensive which has been long expected by the Führer'. Hitler's reaction to the unsuccessful counter-attack of the XXXXVIII Panzer Corps that day was even more indicative. After his clumsy interference had failed to stop the Romanian collapse, he wanted a scapegoat, and ordered General Heim's arrest.

Hitler recognized, although he did not admit it, that the whole of the German position in southern Russia was now at risk. On the second day of the offensive, he ordered Field Marshal von Manstein to return to the south from Vitebsk to form a new Army Group Don. Manstein was the most admired strategist in the German Army and had worked successfully with Romanian forces in the Crimea.

In the physical absence of the Führer, the Supreme Command of the Wehrmacht was paralysed. During 21 November, the day that Paulus and Schmidt abandoned their headquarters at Golubinsky when threatened by a column of Soviet tanks, Hitler's chief adjutant, General Schmundt, was preoccupied with 'alterations to the uniforms of officers and Wehrmacht officials'.

The Führer's order to the Sixth Army to stand firm despite the threat of 'temporary encirclement' eventually caught up with Paulus when he reached Nizhne-Chirskaya. Paulus was also told to take under command all of Hoth's troops south of Stalingrad and the remains of the Romanian VI Army Corps. The key part was: 'Keep open rail lines as long as possible. Orders to follow on subject of resupply by air.' Paulus, whose instinct was to consider withdrawal from the Volga to join up with the rest of Army Group B, was extremely reluctant to react to this abrupt decree until he felt that he had a better understanding of the overall situation.

He had flown to Nizhne-Chirskaya because the headquarters prepared there for the winter possessed secure communications with Army Group B and the *Wolfsschanze* near Rastenburg. But Hitler, on hearing of his arrival, suspected that he wanted to escape the Russians. He ordered him to fly back at once to join the rest of his staff at Gumrak within the encirclement. When General Hoth arrived early next morning, 22 November, he found Paulus angered and upset by Hitler's insinuation that he had abandoned his men. Paulus's chief of staff, General Schmidt, was on the telephone to General Martin Fiebig, the commander of VIII Air Corps. Schmidt re-emphasized that the Sixth Army urgently needed fuel and ammunition to break out, and Fiebig repeated what he had said the previous afternoon: 'It's impossible to resupply a whole army by air. The Luftwaffe hasn't got enough transport aircraft.'

The three generals spent most of the morning assessing Sixth Army's predicament. Schmidt did much of the talking. It was he who had spoken to General von Sodenstern at Army Group B the previous evening and heard details of the Soviet advance south-eastwards from Perelazovsky. Sodenstern had told him bluntly: 'We have nothing to stop them with. You've got to help yourselves.'

During the discussion, Major-General Wolfgang Pickert, the

commander of the Luftwaffe 9th Flak Division, entered the room. Schmidt, a classmate from staff college, called across with the favourite phrase of their instructor: 'Decision with reasons, please!' Pickert replied without hesitation that he intended to pull his division out at once.

'We also want to get out,' Schmidt replied, 'but first of all we must form an all-round defence to form a defence line on the southern side where the Russians are attacking.' He went on to say that they could not abandon the divisions on the west bank of the Don, and that Sixth Army would be in no position to break out for another five to six days. For the operation to have any chance of success, 'we must have fuel and ammunition delivered by the Luftwaffe'. General Hube had already radioed that his tanks were about to come to a halt.

'That makes no difference,' Pickert retorted. He did not intend to lose a whole flak division with all its weapons. 'The Sixth Army can never be supplied by air if we stay put.' Schmidt did not disagree, but pointed out that they had little idea of the overall situation, nor did they know what reserves were available to higher command. He emphasized that the lack of fuel and horses meant that 'more than 10,000 wounded and the bulk of heavy weapons and vehicles would have to be left behind. That would be a Napoleonic ending.'

Paulus, after his study of the 1812 campaign, was evidently haunted by the vision of his army's disintegration, cut to pieces as it struggled to escape across the snow-covered steppe. He did not want to go down in history as the general responsible for the greatest military disaster of all time. There must also have been a natural temptation for Paulus, never renowned for an independence of thought, to defer decisions that were politically and strategically dangerous, now that he knew that Field Marshal von Manstein was about to take over. But Manstein, unable to fly down from the north because of the weather, was stuck in his headquarters train, delayed by partisan action.

Paulus had the instincts of a staff officer, not those of a battle-group leader reacting to danger. He could not countenance a breakout unless it was properly prepared and supplied, and formed part of an overall plan approved by higher command. Neither he nor Schmidt seems to have appreciated that speed was the decisive factor. They had failed utterly to prepare the heavy mobile force which offered their only hope of smashing the encirclement before it was in place. Now they failed to appreciate that once the Red Army consolidated its position, almost every factor, but especially the weather, would turn increasingly against them.

Much time had already been lost by sending tank regiments to the rear across the Don. With confirmation that morning of the loss of Kalach, they had to tell Strecker's XI Army Corps and Hube's XIV Panzer Corps to prepare to pull back to the east bank to join up with the rest of Sixth Army. At the end of the morning, Schmidt communicated the relevant orders to General Hube and to Colonel Groscurth, Strecker's chief of staff.

At 2.00 p.m. that afternoon, Paulus and Schmidt flew back to the new headquarters at Gumrak inside the *Kessel*, or encircled area. Paulus brought along a supply of good red wine and Veuve-Cliquot champagne – a curious choice for someone supposedly planning to get out quickly. Once he reached the new Sixth Army headquarters by Gumrak railway station, he started to contact his corps commanders. He wanted their views on the Führer's order, renewed that evening, to take up a 'hedgehog' defence and await further orders. 'They all shared our view,' wrote Schmidt later, 'that a breakout to the south was necessary.' The most outspoken was General von Seydlitz, whose headquarters were only a hundred yards away.

Paulus's signal at 7.00 p.m. set out to paint a stark picture. 'Army surrounded' were his first words, even though the ring had not yet been sealed. It was a weak and badly structured signal, which did not follow the correct format. Most crucially of all, Paulus failed to propose a firm course of action. He asked for 'freedom of action if it proves impossible to achieve all-round defence on the southern flank'.

At a quarter past ten that night, Paulus received a radio message from the Führer. 'The Sixth Army is temporarily surrounded by Russian forces. I know the Sixth Army and your commander-in-chief and have no doubt that in this difficult situation it will hold on bravely. The Sixth Army must know that I am doing everything to relieve them. I will issue my instructions in good time. Adolf Hitler.' Paulus and Schmidt, convinced despite this message that Hitler would soon see reason, began to prepare plans for a breakout to the south-west.

Hitler, on that evening of 22 November, was setting out with Keitel and Jodl in his special train from Berchtesgaden for Leipzig, from where an aeroplane would take him to Rastenburg. During the journey north, he halted the train every few hours to speak to Zeitzler. He wanted to check that Paulus would not be given permission to withdraw. During one of these conversations, the Führer told Zeitzler: 'We've found another way out.' He did not say that he had been talking on the special train again to General Hans Jeschonnek, the Luftwaffe chief of staff, who had already indicated, despite warnings from Richthofen, that an air-bridge to supply the Sixth Army might be possible on a temporary basis.

Reichsmarschall Goering, on hearing what the Führer wanted, immediately summoned a meeting of his transport officers. He told them that 500 tons a day was needed. (The Sixth Army's estimate of 700 tons was ignored.) They replied that 350 tons would be the maximum, and then only for a short period. Goering, with breath-taking irresponsibility, promptly assured Hitler that the Luftwaffe could maintain the Sixth Army in its present position by air. Even on the lower figure, no allowance was made for bad weather, unserviceable aircraft or enemy action.

Early next morning, 24 November, the hopes of all the generals involved in the fate of the Sixth Army were firmly dashed. Another Führer decision reached Paulus's headquarters at 8.30 a.m. In it, the boundaries of what Hitler now termed 'Fortress Stalingrad' were clearly laid down. The front on the Volga was to be held 'whatever the circumstances'.

Zeitzler had been confident the evening before that Hitler was coming to his senses. Now, the Führer demonstrated indubitably that the opinion of all the generals responsible for the Stalingrad operation counted for nothing. Their feelings were summed up by Richthofen in his diary, when he wrote that they had become little more than 'highly paid NCOs'. Hitler's notion of the power of the will had completely parted company with military logic. He was fixated with the idea that if the Sixth Army withdrew from Stalingrad, the Wehrmacht would never return. He had sensed that this was the high-water mark of the Third Reich. Also, rather pertinently in the case of such an egomaniac, his personal pride was at stake after his boasts about Stalin's city during the Munich Bierkeller speech less than two weeks before.

Such a combination of circumstances was perhaps bound to produce moments of bitter irony. Just before the Führer decision was issued, General von Seydlitz, the commander of LI Corps in Stalingrad, had decided to jump the gun. He considered it 'completely unthinkable' that an army with twenty-two divisions 'should go into all-round defence and thus deprive itself of all freedom of movement'. He prepared a long memorandum on the subject for headquarters Sixth Army. 'Already the minor defensive battles over the last few days have used up our ammunition reserves.' The supply situation was decisive. It was their duty to ignore the catastrophic order to stay put.

On that evening of 23 November, Seydlitz ordered 60th Motorized Infantry Division and the 94th Infantry Division to burn their stores, and blow up their positions, then withdraw from their positions on the north side of Stalingrad. 'In thousands of rapidly lit fires,' wrote the quartermaster of the 94th Infantry Division, 'we burned overcoats, uniforms, boots, documents, maps, typewriters as well as food supplies. The general burned all his own equipment himself.' The Red Army, alerted by the explosions and flames, caught the already weakened division in the open as it withdrew from Spartakovka, and inflicted nearly 1,000 casualties. The neighbouring formation, the 389th Infantry Division in the Stalingrad tractor plant also suffered in the confusion.

Hitler, furious to hear of this withdrawal, blamed Paulus. To prevent any further disobedience to his orders, he made the extraordinary decision to split the command in the *Kessel*. General von Seydlitz, whom he believed to be a fanatic of resistance, was made commander-in-chief of the north-eastern part of the *Kessel*, including Stalingrad itself. The signal arrived at 6 a.m. on 25 November. A little later in the morning, Paulus took Captain Behr with him on a visit to Seydlitz's headquarters nearby. Paulus handed over the signal relayed from Army Group Don. 'Now that you have your own command,' he said pointedly, 'you can break out.' Seydlitz could not hide his embarrassment. Manstein, who was appalled by the idea of splitting a command, managed to have it redefined in a less nonsensical fashion.

Paulus's encounter with General von Seydlitz was not the only difficult interview in the wake of the Stalingrad encirclement. At the *Wolfsschanze*, Marshal Antonescu was subjected to a tirade in which the Führer blamed the Romanian armies for the disaster. Antonescu, the most loyal of Hitler's allies, replied with feeling. Both dictators, however, calmed down, not daring to cast aside an alliance which neither of them could repudiate. But their peacemaking was not reflected further down.

Romanian officers were furious that the German high command had ignored all their warnings, especially about the lack of anti-tank defences. Meanwhile German troops, unaware of Romanian losses, accused their allies of having caused the disaster by running away. Many unpleasant incidents developed between groups of soldiers on both sides. After his ill-tempered meeting with Antonescu, even Hitler was forced to acknowledge that some attempt must be made to restore relations between the allies. 'According to a Führer decree,' Sixth Army headquarters informed corps commanders, 'criticisms of the failings of Romanian officers and troops are to cease.' The tension between the allies was not hard to imagine for the Soviet authorities, who promptly organized the airdrop of 150,000 propaganda leaflets in Romanian.

Hitler remained merciless in his desire for retribution against General Heim, the commander of XXXXVIII Panzer Corps. 'The Führer ordered General Heim to be relieved of his command immediately,' noted General Schmundt in his diary just after Hitler's return to the *Wolfsschanze*. 'The Führer himself will decide on all further measures of military discipline in this matter.'

Many senior officers suspected that Hitler wanted not just Heim as the scapegoat for the disaster, but the whole officer corps. Groscurth had written scathingly of 'the grateful army of the victorious Party', not long after Hitler's radio broadcast in which he had claimed victory over the caste of general staff officers in their broad-striped breeches. Like that other anti-Nazi, Henning von Tresckow, Groscurth also believed that the general staff was no longer worthy of the name, because of its craven submission to Hitler. Yet the officer corps still remained the only group capable of opposing a totalitarian state.

Tresckow believed that a dramatic disaster could provoke change provided that the army had a widely respected commander in a key position who was prepared to stand up to Hitler. Field Marshal von Manstein certainly commanded the necessary respect, so Tresckow, when the opportunity arose, arranged for his young cousin, Alexander Stahlberg, to become Manstein's new aide. The timing appeared opportune. Stahlberg reported for duty on 18 November, two days before Hitler chose Manstein as the commander-in-chief of the new Army Group Don.

Manstein's military qualities and intelligence were undeniable, but his political instincts were much less predictable, despite encouraging appearances. Manstein despised Goering and loathed Himmler. To his most trusted colleagues, he admitted to Jewish antecedents. He could also be scathing about Hitler. As a joke, his dachshund Knirps had been trained to raise his paw in salute on the command '*Heil Hitler!*' On the other hand, his wife was a great admirer of Hitler, and more important, Manstein, as already mentioned, had even issued that order to his troops mentioning 'the necessity of hard measures against Jewry'.

Manstein's luxurious headquarters train of *wagons-lits* – the drawing room on wheels had belonged to the Queen of Yugoslavia – halted on its circuitous way south in Smolensk. There, the commander-in-chief of Army Group Centre, Field Marshal Hans Günther von Kluge, boarded the train to brief Manstein informally on the situation in southern Russia. Kluge, influenced by Tresckow, was one of the few active field marshals ready to join a plot. He told Manstein that Hitler had placed the Sixth Army in an untenable position. The situation map unfolded in the carriage clearly demonstrated the danger.

Kluge tried to impress on Manstein one piece of advice. The Führer's attempts to control movements down to battalion level must be stopped from the start. 'And be warned,' Kluge added in emphasis. 'The Führer ascribes the survival of the Ostheer during the great crisis of last winter, not to the morale of our soldiers and all our hard work, but exclusively to his own skill.' Very soon after this meeting, the Red Army launched an offensive against Army Group Centre to prevent the German command from bringing troops down to break the Stalingrad encirclement.

The heated train continued through the Russian landscape covered by the first snows of winter. Manstein and his staff officers discussed music and mutual friends and relations, played chess and bridge, and skirted round politics. Lieutenant Stahlberg, hearing that Manstein was related to the late President von Hindenburg, wondered which of the field marshals in this war might become 'the saviour of the Fatherland' in the event of total defeat. 'Certainly not me,' Manstein replied swiftly.

The field marshal's birthday, his fifty-fifth, fell on 24 November, the day of their arrival at the headquarters of Army Group B. General von Weichs, showing Manstein the updated operations map, did not conceal the gravity of the situation. The signal from Führer headquarters had just arrived, ordering the Sixth Army to maintain Fortress Stalingrad and await resupply by air. Manstein, according to his aide, appeared surprisingly optimistic. Even the 150-mile gap between the German troops on the southern side of the Stalingrad *Kessel* and Army Group A down in the Caucasus did not deter Manstein from selecting the old Don Cossack capital of Novocherkassk for his headquarters. He had Don Cossacks in sheepskin hats and Wehrmacht uniform as the guards on the main entrance. 'When we entered or left the house,' his aide-de-camp reported, 'they stuck out their chests and stood to attention as if for His Imperial Majesty the Tsar himself.'

Hitler gave strict instructions that the news of the encirclement at Stalingrad was to be kept from the German people. On 22 November, the communiqué had admitted that there had been an attack on the north front. The next day, just after the complete encirclement of the Sixth Army, only counter-attacks and enemy casualties were mentioned. A subsequent announcement made it sound as if the

Soviet attacks had been beaten back with heavy losses. Finally, on 8 December, three weeks after the event, it was acknowledged that there had also been an attack south of Stalingrad, but there was still no hint that the Sixth Army had been cut off. The fiction was maintained into January through the vague formula 'the troops in the area of Stalingrad'.

The Nazi authorities could not, of course, prevent the rapid spread of rumour, especially within the army. 'The whole Sixth Army is surrounded,' a soldier in a field hospital heard almost immediately from the chaplain. 'That's the beginning of the end.' Attempts to silence soldiers and officers with disciplinary measures backfired, and the lack of frankness only increased the sense of unease in Germany. Within a few days of the encirclement, civilians were writing to the front asking if the rumours were true. 'Yesterday and today', wrote a paymaster from Bernburg, 'people have been saying that there has been a breakthrough in your area?!'

The Nazi authorities believed that they could suppress everything until a relief force was ready to break through to Stalingrad. Paulus, meanwhile, may have been deeply sceptical of Goering's guarantee to supply Sixth Army by air, but he felt unable to dismiss the arguments of his own chief-of-staff that they could at least hold on until early December, when Hitler promised a breakthrough to relieve them.

Paulus faced what Strecker called 'the most difficult question of conscience for every soldier: whether to disobey his superior's orders in order to handle the situation as he deems best'. Officers who disliked the regime and despised the GRÖFAZ ('Greatest Commander of All Time'), as they privately referred to the Führer, hoped that Paulus would oppose this madness and trigger a reaction throughout the army.* They thought of General Hans Yorck von Wartenburg's revolt at Tauroggen in December 1812, when he refused to fight any longer

---

* Hitler, they thought, could be persuaded to step down as commander-in-chief by senior officers. A change of regime might then be accomplished without the disastrous chaos and mutiny of November 1918. This was an astonishingly naive reading of Hitler's character. The slightest opposition was more likely to trigger a fearful bloodbath. It was the younger ones, such as Tresckow and Stauffenberg, who recognized that Hitler could be removed only by assassination.

under Napoleon, an event which triggered a wave of patriotic feeling in Germany. Many believed in the comparison. General von Seydlitz apparently invoked it in conversation with Paulus, when trying to persuade him to break out; so did Colonel Selle, the Sixth Army's Engineer-in-Chief. Schmidt, on the other hand, considered that: 'Such an action against orders would become a mutiny with political undertones.'

Paulus's answer to Selle sounded fatalistic indeed: 'I know that the history of war has already pronounced judgement on me.' Yet he was right to reject the Tauroggen comparison. Yorck, without any communications, could claim to act in the name of the King of Prussia without being deprived of his command. But in an age when every headquarters was in constant touch by radio, courier and teleprinter, the order for a commander's arrest would be communicated immediately. The only actor in this drama capable of playing the part of Yorck was Manstein, as Tresckow and Stauffenberg had recognized, but Manstein, they would discover, had no intention of accepting such a dangerous role. 'Prussian field marshals do not mutiny,' he said the following year, emphatically contradicting the Yorck tradition when approached by a representative of Army Group Centre.

Many historians have also given the impression that almost every officer in the Sixth Army believed that an attempt should be made immediately to break out of the Russian encirclement. This is misleading. Corps commanders, divisional commanders and staff officers were firmly in favour of a breakout, but in the infantry especially, regimental and battalion commanders were much less convinced. Their troops, especially those who were already dug in with bunkers, did not want to abandon their positions and heavy weapons to 'march out into the snow', where they would be exposed to Russian attack in the open. Soldiers were also reluctant to move because they believed the promises of a strong counter-attack coming to rescue them. The slogan in support of this at the end of Paulus's order of the day on 27 November – 'Hold on! The Führer will get us out!' – had proved very effective. (Schmidt later tried to deny that this phrase had emanated from Sixth Army headquarters, and even suggested that it was invented by a subordinate commander.)

Within the *Kessel*, soldiers tended to believe the 'Hold on!' slogan as a firm promise. So did many officers, but others instinctively guessed the reality. One remembered how a fellow lieutenant of panzer grenadiers, on receipt of the news, signalled with his eyes for him to come to his vehicle so that they could discuss the situation in private.

'We're never going to get out of this one,' he said. 'This is a unique opportunity which the Russians aren't going to let slip by.'

'You're a real pessimist,' the other replied. 'I believe in Hitler. What he's said he'll do, he'll stick to.'

17

'The Fortress Without a Roof'

During the first week of December, the Russians made determined attacks to split the Sixth Army. In heavy defensive fighting, its panzer divisions lost almost half of their remaining 140 tanks. They were badly handicapped by the shortage of fuel and ammunition. On 6 December, a battle group from the 16th Panzer Division was sent into a counter-attack on foot because they had no fuel for their half-tracks. Lieutenant von Mutius, the young officer who had been so proud to be the last member of the Wehrmacht to withdraw across the Don, was the second-in-command.

Their objective was a hill north of Baburkin which they managed to seize, but suddenly Russian tanks appeared out of a *balka* supported by infantry. The battle-group commander gave the order to pull back. 'A systematic withdrawal was impossible,' reported a sergeant-major later. 'Each man ran for his life. The enemy fired after us with all their weapons. Half of the battle group was wiped out. Lieutenant von Mutius was badly wounded. In order to prevent worse casualties, he kept shouting "Spread out!"' The sergeant-major was convinced he had saved many lives, as he lay there helplessly waiting for the Russians. The survivors thought him 'a real hero'.

After numerous attacks, Soviet commanders realized that the besieged were far from beaten. The 57th Army of the crucial south-western sector had suffered heavy casualties. Explanations for Soviet failure were interesting. One report – 'artillery and infantry did not interact very well when storming the enemy defence line' – sounds like a circumlocution for heavy casualties from friendly fire. 'Soldiers are not well enough instructed on the need to dig trenches,' was another unhelpful observation. Their failure to do so led to 'irreparable losses from German tanks and aeroplanes'. No mention was made of the fact that the ground was frozen hard, and that entrenching tools were in very short supply.

Behind the lines, NKVD officers and interpreters worked late into the night interrogating German prisoners, including the first deserters, as well as 'tongues' captured by reconnaissance companies. 'The bolsheviks often seized prisoners from us,' reported a lieutenant from the Austrian 44th Hoch- und Deutschmeister Infantry Division. Don Front intelligence was trying to identify demoralized divisions, on which attacks should be concentrated. It soon observed that the 44th and the 376th Infantry Divisions, both of which had retreated from across the Don, had not been able to dig proper bunkers. Most of their men, during this period when the weather changed from hard frost to rain and back to hard frost again, were existing in holes in the ground covered by tarpaulins. The NKVD was particularly interested in any signs of national resentment. 'It is said of Austrian soldiers that they don't fight well,' replied a Lieutenant Heinrich Boberg, when interrogated by Captain Dyatlenko on 10 December. 'There is an element of truth in this, but I would not say it is true of the 44th Infantry Division. Austrians have historical reasons for not being as rigid as Prussians. And because Austrians are used to getting on with other nationalities, they don't have the same sort of national pride as Prussians do.' The Nazi designation of 'Ostmark' for Austria seemed to disappear remarkably quickly from an Austrian's vocabulary when captured.

Once the major attacks of early December ceased, Don Front continued to maintain pressure on the 44th Infantry Division with raids, using Shturmovik ground-attack aircraft. Yet Sixth Army morale remained, on the whole, remarkably robust. Another senior lieutenant from the 16th Panzer Division later reported that, at that stage, 'doubts about a positive outcome to the battle simply did not arise'. *Landsers*, especially those out in the snow-covered steppe, joked about 'the fortress without a roof'. Most of the younger ones, educated under a totalitarian system, did not expect to be told the reasons for their plight. The Führer's assurance was, for them, a promise that would never be broken.

Rations were soon reduced drastically, but officers and NCOs assured them that this situation would not last. The Luftwaffe would bring in what they needed, and then a great relief force, led by Field Marshal von Manstein, would advance from the south-west to break the encirclement. Many soldiers convinced themselves, or perhaps were told by less imaginative officers, that they would be out by Christmas. 'Since the 22nd of November we've been surrounded,' a soldier in the 376th Infantry Division wrote home. 'The worst is past. We all hope that we'll be out of the *Kessel* before Christmas . . . Once this battle of encirclement is over, then the war in Russia will be finished.' Some were persuaded that they would immediately be given leave, and actually spend Christmas at home with their families.

Those responsible for administering the air-supply operation were far less optimistic. The Sixth Army's chief quartermaster signalled on 7 December: 'Rations cut to between a third and a half so that the army can hold out until 18 December. The lack of fodder means that the bulk of the horses will have to be slaughtered by the middle of January.'

The Luftwaffe officers in charge of Pitomnik airfield, drawn from the 9th Flak Division, had no illusions. They knew that a minimum of 300 flights a day would be needed to restore the Sixth Army's fighting capacity, and that was out of the question. In any case, the greatly strengthened and bolder Red Army aviation, as well as anti-aircraft fire round the edge of the *Kessel*, represented a formidable challenge to the lumbering Junkers 52 trimotors. Jeschonnek and Goering did not consider that the airfields might lie within range of Soviet heavy artillery. Worst of all, they made no allowance for the weather, even after the experiences of the previous winter. There would be many days with zero visibility, and many when the temperature would be so low that it would be almost impossible to start aircraft engines, even with fires lit underneath them. Apart from Richthofen, however, Luftwaffe officers, either within the *Kessel* or outside, did not dare speak out. 'It was defeatism if you voiced doubts,' said one of them.

As well as bringing in fuel, ammunition and food – in theory two tons per Junkers 52, and rather less for a Heinkel 111 – the aircraft would fly out the wounded from the general field hospital next to Pitomnik airfield. Perhaps the best indication of officer pessimism was the secret decision to send out all German nurses, even before most of the wounded, to ensure that they never fell into Russian hands. Although great efforts were made to keep this secret, officers from the 369th Croat Infantry Regiment heard and lobbied the Luftwaffe to fly out their mistresses, disguised as nurses. The lieutenant whom they approached rather admired the Croats as soldiers and promised to help. His colonel, however, took a high moral line. 'But surely it doesn't matter', the lieutenant replied, 'whether they're Croat whores, nursing sisters or whatever. They must be got out to save them from the Russians.' The colonel still refused. The lieutenant later suspected that the Croats managed to smuggle their women on to planes.

Encampments, bunkers and tents spread to the side of the airfield. There were numerous headquarters and signals detachments with radio masts and vehicles, as well as the general field hospital. Pitomnik rapidly became the main focus for Soviet fighter and bomber regiments. During the course of 10, 11 and 12 December, Soviet aircraft carried out forty-two air raids.

The Russians, despite all their air activity over the *Kessel*, still did not realize how large a force they had surrounded. Colonel Vinogradov, the chief of Red Army intelligence at Don Front headquarters, estimated that Operation Uranus had trapped around 86,000 men. The probable figure, including allies and Hiwis, was nearly three and a half times greater: close to 290,000 men. The allies included the remnants of two Romanian divisions, the Croat regiment with 100th Jäger Division and a motor-transport column of Italians who had picked a bad moment to come to find wood in the ruins of Stalingrad.*

---

* The figures given at the time and in recent accounts range widely, sometimes without defining the nationalities involved. The most significant discrepancy is between the 51,700 Hiwis reported with divisions in mid-November, and the 20,300 listed in Sixth Army ration returns on 6 December. It is hard to know whether this was due to heavy casualties, Hiwis taking the opportunity to escape during the retreats of late November, or Russians being covertly incorporated into divisional fighting strengths. See Appendix B for more detail.

In the fighting west of the Don and on the northern flank, Strecker's XI Corps had suffered most. The Austrian 44th Infantry Division lost nearly 2,000 men, the 376th 1,600, and the 384th over 900. Officers throughout the Sixth Army sat down at makeshift tables in earth bunkers under the snow to write by candlelight to next of kin: 'I have the sad duty to have to inform you that . . .'

With the Sixth Army reduced to conditions very similar to those in the First World War, older soldiers found themselves remembering the existence of the Western Front and its gallows humour. After the cold of mid-November, a wet period of thaw had set in, with 'General Mud' reappearing briefly before 'General Winter'. Some returned to the old practices of trench life, such as resorting to the only certain source of warm liquid, when relieving themselves, to rinse the caked mud from their hands.

The construction of trenches and bunkers varied according to the circumstances of each division. Those who had been forced to withdraw or take up new positions faced heavy labour, although much of the work was given to Hiwis and other Russian prisoners. The Germans had learned from the street fighting in Stalingrad. They dug bunkers under knocked-out tanks and made better use of existing features. But in the first days after the encirclement, the ground had still been frozen, and even fires did little to soften the earth before digging. Out in the steppe, the greatest shortage was wood both for fires and for beams to cover the earth bunkers. Peasant houses close to the front line did not last long. Any inhabitants who had already packed straw round their houses, then a layer of planks and logs outside to insulate them for winter, were soon evicted. If they had stayed, they would have seen their home rapidly dismantled, as German soldiers took planks, beams, doors and even windows to improve their dugouts.

Soldiers, having demolished the houses of civilians, revealed an instinctive desire to turn their own dugout into a new home. The revetted communications trenches and the earthworks round the entrances to bunkers gave no impression of what one might find within. They fashioned frames for picture postcards or cherished snapshots. Some things were always respected. No man would touch or insult the photograph of a comrade's wife or children. Officers made sure that they had bunks, benches and a table. General Edler von Daniels, the commander of 376th Infantry Division, had a bunker complex designed by one of his staff with impeccable architectural plans after they moved to their new position on the south-west flank. The commanding officer of Dr Kurt Reuber, the priest serving as a doctor with 16th Panzer Division, had a particularly large bunker dug so that he could fit a piano inside, which had been abandoned by another division. And there, underground, unheard above and muffled by the earth walls, he played Bach, Handel, Mozart and Beethoven's Pathétique Sonata. His interpretation was beautiful, but also, it seems, obsessive. 'The commanding officer played on, even when the walls trembled from bombardments and soil trickled down.' He even continued to play when officers came in to report on the fighting outside.

Some units were fortunate enough to retain their old positions. The 297th Infantry Division, south of Stalingrad, had finished its elaborate underground sanatorium before the Russian offensive. They feared that they might lose it together with all the hospital equipment, beds, crockery and cutlery brought by train from Germany. But when the front line of the *Kessel* was established, their precious hospital, to their relief, was still just a few miles behind the new front line.

Many soldiers had still not received proper winter clothing before the encirclement, so they resorted to improvisation with varying degrees of success. Under their uniforms, more and more of them wore articles of Soviet uniform – buttonless tunic shirts and baggy quilted trousers and the highly prized quilted jackets. In hard frosts, a steel helmet became like a freezer compartment, so they wore puttees, scarves and even Russian foot bandages wrapped round their heads as insulation. Their desperation for fur gloves led them to kill stray dogs and skin them. Some even tried to make tunics out of amateurishly cured horse hide from the knacker, but most of these articles were uncomfortably crude, unless a former saddler or cobbler could be bribed to help.

The most insanitary conditions tended to occur in those units which had been forced by the Soviet attacks to take up new positions in the open steppe at the western end of the newly formed *Kessel*. 'Miserably frozen at night,' the artillery officer who had withdrawn across the Don wrote in his diary. 'How long are we expected to sleep in the open? The body won't stand it much more. On top of that the filth and the lice!!!' In such conditions, troops had not yet had a chance to dig communications trenches and latrines. Soldiers were sleeping, packed together like sardines, in holes in the ground covered by a tarpaulin. Infections spread rapidly. Dysentery soon had a debilitating and demoralizing effect, as weakened soldiers squatted over shovels in their trenches, then threw the contents out over the parapet.

Letter writers generally spared their relatives the full squalor of their lives. 'We squat together', wrote Kurt Reuber, 'in a hole dug out of the side of a gully in the steppe. The most meagre and badly equipped dugout. Dirt and clay. Nothing can be made of it. Scarcely any wood for bunkers. We're surrounded by a sad landscape, monotonous and melancholic. Winter weather of varying degrees of cold. Snow, heavy rain, frost then sudden thaw. At night you get mice running over your face.'

The progressive infestation of clothes really started during the chaotic days of the encirclement, with constant movement. 'The plague of lice was frightful,' wrote a corporal in a panzer regiment, 'because we had no opportunity to wash, change clothes or hunt them down. In my helmet, I found about 200 of these faithful little beasts.' An unknown soldier was prompted to write a new version of a favourite song:

> Underneath the lantern
>> in a little house
> I sit every evening
>> searching for a louse . . .

During the long nights of the Russian winter, there was ample opportunity for conversations about home and how much better life had been before coming to Russia. In the 376th Infantry Division, they bemoaned their departure from Angoulême for the

Ostfront, leaving behind cafés, cheap wine, and French girls. Other thoughts went further back, to the triumphant welcome home in the summer of 1940. The waving crowds, the kisses and the adulation had been largely inspired by the idea that the fighting was as good as over. The vast majority of the country had cheered Hitler for having brought them through a short victorious war with so few casualties.

Often, when thoughts turned to home, harmonicas played sentimental tunes in the bunker. After such a dramatic reversal of fortune, men grasped at rumours more than ever before, with constant questions and ill-informed speculation. Even their officers had little idea of the true situation. Another subject, linked to the chances of getting out, was the perfect wound which would not cripple, or be too painful, yet would still qualify its recipient for evacuation by air. Comrades who had gone on leave just before the encirclement were viewed with admiring envy, while those who had returned just before faced good-natured, but no doubt deeply provoking, jokes. One person who never complained of his bad luck was Kurt Reuber. He had returned to his unit just two days before the *Kessel* was closed. It would soon be hard to tell whose services would be more needed, those of the doctor or those of the priest.

Besieged Germans imagined that the Red Army soldiers opposite them lacked for little, in either rations or warm clothing, but this image was often inaccurate. 'Because of bad communications, food is not brought forward in time for soldiers at the front,' ran one Don Front report. 'The failure of officers and commissars to use bunkers to warm up soldiers', said another, 'has led to many men having to be sent to hospital with frostbite, mostly in the feet.'

The best-equipped Soviet soldiers were the snipers. Little was denied them. Out in the snowfields of the steppe in their white camouflage suits, they operated in pairs, one with a telescope and the other with the long-range rifle. They crawled forward at night into no man's land, where they dug snow-holes and hides from which to watch and shoot. Their casualty rates were much higher than in the city, because they had fewer choices for concealment and lines of escape. But the 'sniper movement' still attracted more volunteers than it could train or use.

Any lingering problems with morale usually reflected the Soviet authorities' indifference to the individual soldier. The obsession with secrecy meant that men not directly involved in Operation Uranus had not been told about it until up to five days *after* the start. At first sight, the most surprising aspect of this time of triumph is the number of deserters from the Red Army who continued to cross the lines to the surrounded German Army, thus entering a trap, but this paradox seems to be explicable mainly through a mixture of ignorance and mistrust. Colonel Tulpanov, the sophisticated NKVD officer in charge of recruiting German officers, admitted quite openly to one of his star prisoners, the fighter pilot Count Heinrich von Einsiedl, that: 'These Russians were most astonished to hear from the Germans the same story that had been put out by their own propaganda. They had not believed that the Germans were encircled.'

Zhukov was characteristically to the point when he described the encirclement of the Sixth Army as 'a tremendous education for victory for our troops'. Grossman was also right when he wrote: 'The morale of the soldiers has never been so high.' (Interestingly, neither of these observations exactly confirmed the official Soviet propaganda line that 'the morale of an army depends on the socially just and progressive order of the society it defends'.)

Red Army soldiers now took a predictable pleasure in taunting the enemy who had so recently taunted them. Some companies sent out a patrol at night with a scarecrow dressed up as Hitler. They then erected it in no man's land, and hung a placard inviting *Landsers* to shoot at it. The scarecrow would be booby-trapped with a couple of grenades, in case a German officer sent out a patrol to remove it the next night. On a more organized basis, NKVD propaganda companies set up their loudspeakers. For hours on end, the loudspeakers blasted out tango music, which was judged to convey a suitably sinister mood, interspersed by messages prepared on gramophone records to remind the beleaguered troops of their hopeless position. At first, these activities had little influence, but later, when German hopes began to fade, the effect became cumulative.

The Red Army, realizing that the Germans had to economize on artillery shells, because they were so heavy to fly in, went in for probing attacks, trying to provoke a reply. The most overworked troops at this time were the divisional reconnaissance companies that acted as pathfinders for these raids. 'We were like gypsies, here today gone tomorrow,' remembered an officer who was one of five survivors from the original company of 114 men. Patrols, usually of five or six men, would penetrate the *Kessel* and hide up near roads in white snowsuits to observe traffic and troop movements. On their return, they would seize a 'tongue' for interrogation.

Patrolling activity was particularly intense on the south-western flanks of the *Kessel*. Soviet commanders were certain that the Germans would make an attempt to break out, and they wanted to be forewarned. The flat, snow-covered steppe was dangerous for reconnaissance patrols, with the machine-gun posts enjoying good fields of fire. On one occasion, early in December, however, a reconnaissance party, backed by a raiding group, slipped up to the trenches opposite only to find them empty. The Germans had pulled back to warmer bunkers behind. After the first Russian infantrymen had explored the trenches and fire bunkers undisturbed, the commander of the reconnaissance party inspected the booty, including a long sheepskin coat. Then, next to the field telephone, he spotted 'a white mug with a rose' on it. It seemed incomparably beautiful because he had not seen a completely civilian object for so long. But his company commander then arrived, and decided, rather over-ambitiously for such a small force, to try to seize more ground. Once they advanced, everything quickly went wrong. The Germans countered with tanks, and their own artillery refused to fire in support because they had not received an order through the proper chain of command. A very messy fight ensued, and while the reconnaissance party was pulling back, the young commander received a serious wound in the leg from a shell burst. As he lay in the snow looking at the blood on his white camouflage suit, he thought of the mug with the rose.

Sometimes when Russian and German recce groups passed each other at night in no man's land, they pretended not to see each other.

Each had specific orders not to be deflected from their task by a firefight. If, however, small groups met head on, then the struggle was often conducted in deadly silence with knives or sharpened bayonets. 'When I killed a German with a knife for the first time,' a Russian recce platoon commander from the marine infantry remembered, 'I saw him in my dreams for three weeks afterwards.' One of the biggest dangers, however, was returning to your own lines away from where you were expected.

Fortunately for the Russian troops, the deficiencies in winter clothing, which had been serious, were made up after the successful completion of Operation Uranus. Almost all soldiers received rabbit-fur gloves, quilted jackets, sheepskin jerkins and a grey fur *ushanka* to which they transferred the red star from their summer cap.

A constant trickle of new arrivals brought divisions up to strength. For the *ingénu*, to join a platoon of battle-hardened soldiers was always daunting, but profiting from their experience offered a better chance of survival than joining an untested formation. Once the new soldier had accepted that survival was relative rather than absolute, and he learned to live minute by minute, the strain eased.

For a young Soviet citizen, the most shocking experience was not soldierly coarseness, but the frank speaking of *frontoviki* on political subjects. Many expressed themselves in a way that prompted new arrivals to glance over their shoulders in alarm. They declared that life after the war should be different. The terrible existence for those who worked on collective farms and in factories must be improved, and the privileges of the *nomenklatura* restricted.

At this stage of the war, the risk of being denounced at the front was really quite small. As one veteran put it: 'A soldier felt that, having paid with his blood, he had the right to free speech.' He had to be far more careful if evacuated to a field hospital, where informants and political officers were vigilant for any criticism of the regime. (Danger returned at the front towards the end of the war during the advance into Germany. The army's task was almost over, and the NKVD Special Departments, by then SMERSH, wasted no time in reimposing the Stalinist terror.)

Soldiers tantalized themselves with talk of food at home, as well as daydreaming. Some platoons were fortunate enough to have a gifted storyteller inventing modern fairy tales. They played cards (although it was officially forbidden) and chess. Now that they were in fixed positions for a little time, it was worth carving proper pieces and fashioning a board. Most of all they reminisced. Muscovites talked constantly of their home city, not so much to impress comrades from the provinces, but out of a genuine homesickness in the emptiness of the steppe.

Writing home was 'very difficult', confessed the lieutenant of marine infantry. It was 'impossible' to tell the truth. 'Soldiers at the front never sent bad news home.' His parents kept all his letters, and when he reread them after the war, he found that they contained no information whatsoever. In general, a letter home usually started as an exercise in reassuring mothers – 'I am alive and healthy, and we eat well' – but the effect was rather dissipated by subsequent remarks to the effect that they were all ready to sacrifice their lives for the Motherland.

Within platoons, there were anecdotes and jokes and teasing, but this, apparently, was seldom cruel among those of equal rank. There was also a surprising lack of crudeness. They talked of girls 'only when in a special mood', which usually meant when sentimentality was stimulated by the vodka ration or certain songs. Each company was supposed to have at least one concertina for purposes of morale. The Red Army's favourite song around Stalingrad in those last few weeks of 1942 was *Zemlyanka* ('The Dugout'), a Russian counterpart to *Lili Marlene*, with a similar lilting melody. This haunting song by Aleksey Surkov, written the previous winter – sometimes also known from its most famous line as 'The Four Steps to Death' – was initially condemned as ideologically unsound because of its mood of 'excessive pessimism'. But *Zemlyanka* proved so popular with front-line troops that commissars had to look the other way.

> The fire is flickering in the narrow stove
> Resin oozes from the log like a tear
> And the concertina in the bunker
> Sings to me of your smile and eyes.

The bushes whispered to me about you
In a snow-white field near Moscow
I want you above all to hear
How sad my living voice is.

You are now very far away
Expanses of snow lie between us
It is so hard for me to come to you,
And here there are four steps to death.

Sing concertina, in defiance of the snowstorm
Call out to that happiness which has lost its way
I'm warm in the cold bunker
Because of your inextinguishable love.

Within the *Kessel*, Sixth Army discipline was maintained rigidly. Hitler, meanwhile, in a typical attempt to secure loyalty, started to become generous with promotions and medals. Paulus was raised to Colonel-General.

For soldiers, the main source of consolation was the Führer's promise that he would do everything to secure their release. In fact, General Strecker was convinced that soldiers complained remarkably little about the drastic reduction in their rations because they were convinced that they would soon be saved. During one of his visits to the front line, a sentry held up a hand on hearing artillery fire in the distance. 'Listen, Herr General,' he said. 'Those must be our rescuers approaching.' Strecker was deeply affected. 'This faith of an ordinary German soldier is heart-warming,' he noted.

Even anti-Nazi officers could not believe that Hitler would dare to abandon the Sixth Army. The blow to the regime and morale at home in Germany would be far too great, they reasoned. Also the approach of Christmas and the New Year stimulated the notion that things were bound to change for the better. Even the sceptical Groscurth was more optimistic. 'Things seem to be slightly less bleak', he wrote, 'and one can now hope that we'll be got off the hook.' But he still referred to Stalingrad as the '*Schicksalsstadt*' – 'the city of fate'.

18

'Der Manstein Kommt!'

Snow began to fall heavily at the end of the first week of December. Drifts filled *balkas*, forcing those who lived in caves excavated from their sides to dig their way out. There was little fuel for any vehicles, and the horses pulling ration carts were so starved that their strength had to be spared on the smallest hills. Chaplain Altmann of the 113th Infantry Division, after hitching a ride on one, recorded: 'I can't remain seated, because the horse is so ill-nourished that he cannot stand the slightest strain.'

Altmann was above all struck by the pathetic youth of soldiers in the regiment he was visiting. Their first question was utterly predictable: 'When are we going to get more to eat?' He also noted that although it was only the second week of December, 'already their wretched bunkers in the middle of this treeless steppe have Christmas decorations'. At battalion headquarters, he received a telephone call warning him of an unChristmas-like duty. 'Tomorrow morning at dawn, execution of a German soldier (nineteen-year-old, self-inflicted wound).'

Although all soldiers suffered badly from hunger, most still had no idea of the size of the supply problem facing the Sixth Army. Hitler, when ordering Paulus to stay in place, had promised that more than one hundred Junkers 52 transport aircraft would be delivering supplies, yet during the air-bridge's first week of operations from 23 November the airlift did not even average thirty flights a day.

Twenty-two transport planes were lost through enemy action and crashes on 24 November, and another nine were shot down the following day. Heinkel 111s had to be taken off bombing missions in a desperate attempt to make up the losses. Richthofen rang Jeschonnek three times in an attempt to convince him that they lacked the aircraft to supply the Sixth Army by air. Goering could not be contacted. He had left for Paris.

The airlift did not provide anything like the bare minimum of 300 tons a day promised. Just 350 tons arrived during the course of the whole week. Out of this 350 tons, there were only 14 tons of food for a ration strength by then reduced to 275,000. Three-quarters of the total load consisted of fuel, of which part was for the Luftwaffe's own aircraft based at Pitomnik to protect the transport aircraft from Russian fighters. The Pitomnik-based Messerschmitts, however, were now facing fearsome odds as well as often appalling flying conditions. One captured pilot told his NKVD interrogator how, flying out of Pitomnik as escort, his Me-109 had been cut off and attacked by six Russian fighters.

In the second week up to 6 December, 512 tons (still less than a quarter of the minimum) arrived, delivered by an average of 44 transport aircraft a day. Only 24 tons were food supplies. More and more draught animals had to be slaughtered to make up the shortage. Soldiers saw their rations diminishing rapidly, but they convinced themselves that the situation would not last. They admired the bravery of the Luftwaffe crews and developed a great affection for 'Tante Ju' – the Junkers trimotors flying out wounded comrades and taking their letters home to Germany. 'I'm well and healthy,' they wrote in December, reassuring their families at home. 'Nothing worse can happen,' was another constant refrain. 'Don't be worried for me, I'll soon be home safe and sound.' They still hoped for a Christmas miracle.

Stalin, meanwhile, had been hoping for a second decisive blow, almost immediately after the encirclement of the Sixth Army. Operation Uranus had been seen at the *Stavka* as the first part of a master strategy. The second, and most ambitious phase, would be Operation

Saturn. This called for a sudden offensive by the armies of South-West and Voronezh Fronts, smashing through the Italian Eighth Army to advance south to Rostov. The idea was to cut off the rest of Army Group Don and trap the First Panzer and the Seventeenth Armies in the Caucasus.

Even before Sixth Army started to dig in on the steppe between the Don and the Volga, Vasilevsky had been discussing the next stage with the commanders of the South-West and Voronezh Fronts. He submitted his initial project to Stalin on the night of 26 November. The estimated start date for Saturn, allowing for redeployment and reinforcement, was 10 December. Stalin agreed, and told him to proceed. A more immediate preoccupation, however, had to be addressed first. This was the question of how Manstein would react to save the Sixth Army.

Stalin began to suffer from a characteristic bout of impatience. He wanted everything to happen at once – both Operation Saturn and the rapid destruction of the Sixth Army. He had already given orders for the 2nd Guards Army, the most powerful force in the Red Army, to deploy west of Stalingrad, ready for the attack on Rostov. But as Vasilevsky discovered in the first week of December, even with seven Soviet armies deployed against them, Paulus's divisions were going to be much more difficult to destroy than they had imagined.

On 28 November, Stalin asked Zhukov for an assessment of enemy intentions. Zhukov sent his report the next day. 'The trapped German forces are not likely to try to break out without help from a relief force from the direction of Nizhne-Chirskaya and Kotelnikovo,' he wrote. His predictions proved accurate, but a close study of the situation showed that this was the only practicable choice. After sending his answer to Stalin, Zhukov discussed the situation with Vasilevsky, who had now been told by Stalin to focus his attention entirely on the reduction of the Sixth Army. The two generals privately agreed that they would probably have to postpone Operation Saturn and instead consider an Operation Little Saturn. The plan would be to crash into the rear and left flank of Manstein's Army Group Don. This would bring any drive to relieve Stalingrad to an abrupt halt.

*

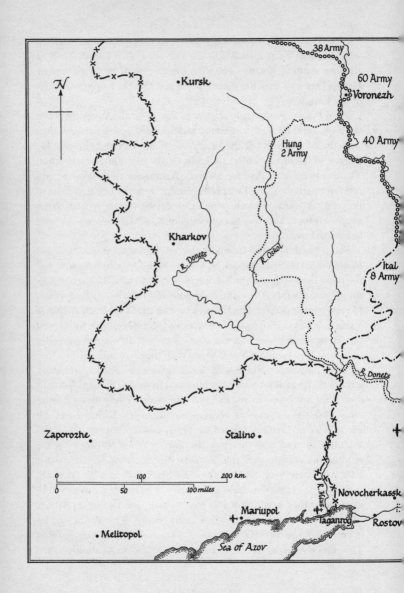

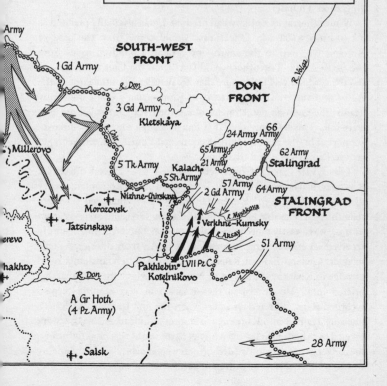

Map 5 OPERATION WINTER STORM AND
OPERATION LITTLE SATURN

ooooooo	Front line, 12 December 1942
➤	German Operation Winter Storm, 12–23 December 1942
⇦	Soviet Operation Little Saturn, 16–30 December 1942
⇦	Soviet counter-attack on A Gr Hoth, 24–30 December 1942
—·—·	Front line, 30 December 1942
········	Front line, 24 January 1943
—x—	Front line, 18 February 1943

5 Sh Army = 5 Shock Army   5 Tk Army = 5 Tank Army
2 Gd Army = 2 Guards Army   LVII Pz C = LVII Panzer Corps

VORONEZH FRONT

SOUTH-WEST FRONT

DON FRONT

R. Volga

Army

1 Gd Army

R. Don

3 Gd Army
Kletskaya

24 Army   66 Army

Millerovo

R. Chir

65 Army

62 Army
Stalingrad

5 Tk Army

Kalach
5 Sh Army

21 Army

57 Army

64 Army

Nizhne-Chirskaya

2 Gd Army

STALINGRAD FRONT

Morozovsk

Tatsinskaya

Verkhne-Kumsky
R. Myshkova
R. Aksay

51 Army

erevo

Pakhlebin
Kotelnikovo

LVII Pz C

shakhty

R. Don

A Gr Hoth
(4 Pz Army)

28 Army

Salsk

Manstein's plan to rescue the Sixth Army – Operation Winter Storm – was developed in full consultation with Führer headquarters. (See Map 5.) It aimed to break through to the Sixth Army and establish a corridor to keep it supplied and reinforced, so that, according to Hitler's order, it could maintain its 'cornerstone' position on the Volga, 'with regard to operations in 1943'. Manstein, however, who knew that Sixth Army could not survive the winter there, instructed his headquarters to draw up a further plan in the event of Hitler's seeing sense. This would include the subsequent breakout of Sixth Army, in the event of a successful first phase, and its physical reincorporation in Army Group Don. This second plan was given the name Operation Thunderclap.

Winter Storm, as Zhukov had predicted, was originally planned as a two-pronged attack. One thrust would come from the area of Kotelnikovo, well to the south, and around a hundred miles from the Sixth Army. The other would start from the Chir front west of the Don, which was little more than forty miles from the edge of the *Kessel*, but the continuing attacks of Romanenko's 5th Tank Army against the German detachments along the river Chir ruled out that start-line. This left only the LVII Panzer Corps round Kotelnikovo, supported by the rest of Hoth's very mixed Fourth Panzer Army, to relieve Paulus's trapped divisions.

The LVII Panzer Corps, commanded by General Friedrich Kirchner, had been weak at first. It consisted of two Romanian cavalry divisions and the 23rd Panzer Division, which mustered no more than thirty serviceable tanks. The 6th Panzer Division, arriving from France, was a vastly more powerful formation, but its members hardly received an encouraging impression. The Austrian divisional commander, General Erhard Raus, was summoned to Manstein's royal carriage in Kharkov station on 24 November, where the field marshal briefed him. 'He described the situation in very sombre terms,' recorded Raus. Three days later, when the first trainload of Raus's division steamed into Kotelnikovo station to unload, his troops were greeted by 'a hail of shells' from Soviet batteries. 'As quick as lightning, the panzer grenadiers jumped from their wagons. But already the enemy was attacking the station with their battle-cries of "*Urrah!*"'

Hoth was indeed glad to see the 6th Panzer Division. It had been refitted in Brittany, and was fully up to strength, with 160 long-barrelled Panzer Mark IVs and forty assault guns. The division soon had a chance to try out its new equipment. On 3 December, it became involved in a wild battle with the Soviet 4th Cavalry Corps near the village of Pakhlebin, seven miles north-west of Kotelnikovo. The panzer crews, exhilarated as their tank tracks crunched through the crust of ice in their outflanking armoured charge, cut off the 81st Cavalry Division, inflicting heavy losses. General Raus, pleased with the result, referred to the engagement as 'the Cannae of Pakhlebin'. The arrival of Raus's division confirmed Yeremenko's suspicions that the Germans were about to strike north-eastwards from Kotelnikovo, yet Stalin still refused to transfer reserves to the threatened sector.

Also on 3 December, Hoth produced his proposal for 'Winter Storm', which began: 'Intention: Fourth Panzer Army relieves Sixth Army', but valuable time was lost. The 17th Panzer Division, which was to complete his strike force, had been held back, on the orders of Führer headquarters, as a reserve behind the Italian Eighth Army. In the end it did not join Hoth's force until four days after the operation had begun. Hitler nevertheless insisted that no more time should be wasted. He was also impatient to discover how the new Tiger tank, with its 88-mm gun, would perform. The very first battalion to be formed had been rushed to the *Ostfront* and added to Kirchner's force. On the evening of 10 December, the commanders received the 'Order for the Relief Attack to Stalingrad'.

On 12 December, after a brief artillery bombardment, Hoth's panzers struck north. The German soldiers inside the *Kessel* listened eagerly to the distant sound of fighting. Confidence seemed boundless. Excited rumours ran round the Sixth Army. 'Manstein is coming!' soldiers said to each other, almost like the Easter greeting of the Orthodox Church. For Hitler loyalists, the distant guns were proof once more that the Führer always kept his word.

Hitler, however, had not the slightest intention of allowing the Sixth Army to break out. In his midday conference at the *Wolfsschanze*, he told Zeitzler that it was impossible to retreat from Stalingrad because this would involve sacrificing 'the whole meaning of the campaign' and argued that too much blood had been shed. As Kluge had warned Manstein, he was still obsessed with the events of the previous winter and his order to Army Group Centre to hold fast. 'Once a unit has started to flee,' he lectured the army chief of staff, 'the bonds of law and order quickly disappear in the course of flight.'

The Soviet commanders did not expect Manstein's offensive quite so soon. Yeremenko immediately feared for the 57th Army, which held the south-west corner of the *Kessel*. Vasilevsky was at 51st Army headquarters with Khrushchev on 12 December when the news of the German attack was received in a radio signal. He tried to ring Stalin in Moscow, but could not get through. Not wanting to waste a moment, he contacted General Rokossovsky, the commander of the Don Front, and told him that he wanted to transfer General Rodion Malinovsky's 2nd Guards Army to the command of the Stalingrad Front to block Manstein's offensive. Rokossovsky protested strongly, and to Vasilevsky's dismay when he finally got through to the Kremlin on the telephone that evening, Stalin was angry at what he thought was an attempt to force him into a decision. He refused to give an answer and forced Vasilevsky to spend a very anxious night.

In the meantime, Yeremenko had ordered the 4th Mechanized Corps and the 13th Tank Corps to block the headlong advance of the German armour. The 6th Panzer Division moved forward some thirty miles in the first twenty-four hours, crossing the river Aksay. Finally, after discussions in the Kremlin which lasted into the early hours of the next morning, and more telephone calls with Vasilevsky, Stalin agreed to the transfer of the 2nd Guards Army two days hence.

On the second day of the offensive, 6th Panzer Division reached Verkhne-Kumsky. Rain poured down in what was to prove a brief thaw. On the high ground round this village began what General Raus described as 'a gigantic wrestling-match'. This furious three-day 'revolving battle' became costly. It proved a success locally – Hoth's divisions and the Tiger tanks advanced to the line of the Myshkova, once 17th Panzer Division arrived and Richthofen threw in maximum air support – but events there soon proved irrelevant to the fortunes of the Sixth Army. They were being decided some 125 miles to the north-west.

Stalin quickly realized that Zhukov and Vasilevsky had been right. The most effective way to smash the whole attempt to relieve Paulus's army was by blocking Hoth's advance on the Myshkova, while delivering the decisive blow elsewhere. He agreed to the idea of adapting Operation Saturn. Orders were prepared on the first day of the fighting at Verkhne-Kumsky, instructing the commanders of the Voronezh and South-West Fronts to prepare to launch an amended version, known as Little Saturn. The plan was to smash through the Italian 8th Army into the rear of Army Group Don, rather than strike at Rostov. Their armies were to be ready to attack in three days' time.

Yeremenko was still nervous. With Hoth's Panzer Corps on the line of the Myshkova river, the 6th Panzer Division was less than forty miles from the edge of the *Kessel*, and the 2nd Guards Army, delayed by renewed blizzards, would not be fully in position to counter-attack before 19 December. He expected the Sixth Army's panzer forces to break out from the south-west of the *Kessel* at any moment, but he did not know that Hitler still refused his permission, and that Paulus's seventy remaining tanks had only enough fuel to advance a dozen miles.

Field Marshal von Manstein sent Major Eismann, his intelligence officer, into the *Kessel* by air on 19 December. His mission, Manstein claimed later, was to brief Paulus and Schmidt to prepare the Sixth Army for Operation Thunderclap. Different versions and different interpretations of what was said at this meeting will never be resolved. It is, however, clear that Manstein still avoided taking the responsibility for disobeying Hitler. He would not give Paulus a clear lead, and refused – no doubt, for sound reasons of security – to fly into the *Kessel* to discuss the matter with him face to face. Yet Manstein must have known from the start that Paulus, a firm believer in the chain of command, would never have broken out without a formal order from higher command. Manstein's efforts in his memoirs to absolve himself from any blame for the fate of Sixth Army are curiously exaggerated, as well as unfair on Paulus. It would appear that he suffered from an uneasy conscience, and yet nobody blamed him.

*

On 16 December, just four days into Hoth's offensive, the 1st and 3rd Guards Armies, as well as the Soviet 6th Army further up the Don, attacked south. Slowed by thick, freezing mist, with their tank formations blundering into minefields, the Soviet operation did not get off to a good start. Within two days, however, the Italian Eighth Army had crumbled after some acts of fierce resistance. There was no reserve ready to counter-attack, now that the 17th Panzer Division had joined Hoth's operation east of the Don, so the Soviet tank columns broke out southwards into open, snow-covered steppe. The great freeze in the region which began on 16 December did little to slow the brigades of T-34s rampaging in Army Group Don's rear. Railway junctions and stations were captured just after wagons full of equipment had been set ablaze by German support troops before they fled.

The gravest threat to the Germans was the 150-mile advance of Major-General Vasily Mikhailovich Badanov's 24th Tank Corps. On the afternoon of 23 December, it overran Skassirskaya, just to the north of Tatsinskaya, the main Junkers 52 base for Stalingrad. General Fiebig had received an order from Führer headquarters that his aircraft were not to abandon the airfield until it came under artillery fire. Nobody in Hitler's entourage seems to have considered the possibility that an armoured column might arrive at the edge of the field and then open fire.

Fiebig and his officers were furious. One could always recapture an airfield, but if the transport aircraft were lost, then so was the Sixth Army. They had no ground troops to defend 'Tazi', as the Luftwaffe called it. All they could do was to divert seven flak guns to cover the road, and prepare all serviceable aircraft for take-off in the early hours of the morning. There were so many that this did not prove easy. 'Around the runway it looked like chaos,' noted Richthofen's chief of staff, who was present. 'With engines running, one could hardly understand a single word.' To make matters worse, there was a fairly thick mist, cloud was down to 150 feet and light snow was falling.

At 5.20 a.m., the first shells exploded. The bulk of the Soviet tanks had come across country, not up the road. Many pilots, because of the noise and chaos on the airfield, did not at first realize what was happening, even when two Junkers 52s caught fire. Fiebig himself gave the order over the radio, 'Off you go, head for Novocherkassk!' The pilots did not waste time. 'The flight from Tatsinskaya' had started. Considering the earlier confusion, there was impressively little panic. The aircraft took off in a steady stream, despite a mounting rate of casualties. For the Russian T-34s, it was like a shooting range at a fairground. Some of the Soviet tanks fired wildly as they advanced across the snow. One even rammed a Junkers trimotor taxiing into position for take-off. The explosion and fireball consumed them both. Numerous other aircraft crashed into one another on the runway or were destroyed by gunfire. Visibility was becoming worse by the minute, and the remaining aircraft had to negotiate burning wrecks to escape. Finally at 6.15 a.m., General Fiebig's machine, one of the last to take off, was airborne. Altogether 108 Ju-52 trimotors and 16 Ju-86 trainers were saved, but the loss of 72 aircraft represented roughly 10 per cent of the Luftwaffe's total transport fleet.

Badanov, after this bold raid, found himself cut off for five days, badly mauled and out of ammunition. Stalin was unstinting in his appreciation. The formation was retitled the 2nd Guards Tank Corps, and Badanov was the first to receive the new Order of Suvorov. Red Army propaganda claimed that his tanks had destroyed 431 aircraft in all, but this was a typically wild exaggeration. The important result, however, was that Tatsinskaya was never used for transport missions again. The Luftwaffe had to move even further out to a completely makeshift airfield.

The outcome of Hoth's rescue mission had already been decided. The threat to the left flank of Army Group Don, and the possibility of a breakthrough towards Rostov (apparently confirmed by the interrogation of the chief of staff of the 3rd Guards Army, who was captured on 20 December), forced Manstein to reconsider his whole position. The panzer divisions on the Myshkova were also receiving a heavy battering, with 6th Panzer Division losing 1,100 men in a single day. On the evening of 23 December, Hoth's panzer corps received the order to pull back, without any explanation. 'Right down to the most junior soldier it was absolutely clear', wrote General Raus, 'that this signified defeat at Stalingrad. Although nobody yet knew the reasons behind the order, officers and men had a strong inkling that something ugly must have happened.'

That same night, Paulus and Manstein discussed the position in a conference conducted via teleprinter. Manstein warned that the 4th Panzer Army had met heavy resistance and that the Italian troops on the northern flank had collapsed. Paulus asked whether he had finally received permission for the Sixth Army to break out. Manstein replied that he still had not obtained agreement from supreme headquarters. He was sparing with the details. If Paulus had been given sufficient information to update his operations map, he would have seen that the Sixth Army was beyond help.

On 16 December, a hard and bitter wind had begun to blow from the north-east. Everything was rimed in frost: telegraph lines, stunted trees, the debris of war. The ground froze so hard that footsteps began to have the ring of walking on metal. As night fell, following a vivid red sunset, the white landscape briefly turned an arctic blue. The Russian defenders of Stalingrad welcomed the cold as natural and healthy. 'Yesterday and today winter really started here,' a soldier wrote to his wife. 'Good frosts. I live very well, but no letters from you.'

Nobody was happier than the members of Chuikov's 62nd Army in Stalingrad itself, after five weeks of listening to the terrible grinding of the ice floes on the virtually unnavigable Volga, and subsisting off the emergency reserve of twelve tons of chocolate and tiny supply drops by U-2 biplanes. The river finally froze solid on the night of 16 December, when a mass of ice floes crushed and stuck firm. First a footway over the ice was made with planks. Then motor highways were constructed using branches and water poured over them, which froze and bound the surface. In the course of the next seven weeks, tracked vehicles, 18,000 lorries and 17,000 other vehicles crossed over. Any wounded could now be driven straight across the ice to the field hospital. Guns were later trundled across to the west bank, including a 122-mm howitzer which was needed to break the deadlock

16. (*Previous page*) One of Chuikov's divisional commanders during the battle, with a young woman signaller.

17. October 1942. German infantry occupying a destroyed workshop in the factory district.

18. 'Noble Sniper' Zaitsev (*left*) from the Siberian 284th Rifle Division explains the doctrine of 'sniperism'.

19 and 20.
November 1942.
Operation Uranus:
the encirclement of
the Sixth Army.

21. Junkers 52 transport taking off.

22. December 1942. German artillery from Hoth's Fourth Panzer Army after the failure of Operation Winter Storm to relieve the Sixth Army.

23. Trapped Sixth Army soldiers retrieve parachute canisters.

24. 10 January 1943. General Rokossovsky awaits the opening barrage for Operation Ring to crush the *Kessel*.

25. 11 January 1943. German infantry retreating through a blizzard.

26. 28 January 1943. General Edler von Daniels marches into captivity past the body of one of his soldiers.

27. 30 January 1943. Goering on the tenth anniversary of Hitler's assumption of power, having just broadcast 'the funeral oration' of the Sixth Army.

28. 31 January 1943. Field Marshal Paulus and General Schmidt at 64th Army HQ after surrendering.

29. A German soldier booted and prodded out of a bunker.

30. Remnants of the Sixth Army marched off to captivity.

31. German and Romanian prisoners.

in the Red October works. On minimum elevation, it was used at short range to blast the main office building, which the Germans had turned into a fortress.

Most fortunate of all for the 62nd Army, the shortage of shells for the German artillery meant that the constant shelling of Volga crossing points was no longer possible. The bank itself often offered a peaceful scene. It resembled an early frontier mining settlement, with makeshift huts and tarpaulin shelters over holes in the bank. As men split logs, or sawed wood, a regimental postman walked past in the frozen sunshine to headquarters with his leather mailbag, hoping for a mug of hot tea from the copper samovar. Others went by bearing thermos containers with hot food for the troops in forward positions. Soldiers could now walk back in batches over the ice to steam baths set up on the east side of the river, to return clean and deloused the next night.

On 19 December General Chuikov crossed to the east bank of the Volga for the first time since changing his headquarters in October. He crossed the ice on foot, and when he reached the far side, he apparently turned to gaze at the ruins which his army had held. Chuikov had come over for a party given by the commander of NKVD troops, Major-General Rogatin, in honour of the twenty-fourth anniversary of the founding of the Special Department of the Cheka. Chuikov on his return, when very drunk, fell through a hole in the ice, and had to be fished out of the freezing water. The commander of the 62nd Army nearly met an ignominious and anti-climactic end.

While the Russians welcomed the low temperatures, the doctors in Paulus's army dreaded them, for several reasons. The resilience of their patients, both the sick and the wounded, declined. Frost in an open wound could rapidly prove lethal. The hardness of the ground when shells, *Katyusha* rockets and mortar bombs exploded, seemed to be the only explanation for the great increase in stomach wounds with which they were faced. And from the middle of December there was 'a steadily increasing number of serious frostbite cases'. The feet were not just swollen and purple – a degree treated with ointment, a bandage and return to duty – but black and potentially gangrenous, often requiring rapid amputation.

As early as the second week of December, doctors had started to notice a more disturbing phenomenon. An increasing number of soldiers died suddenly 'without having received a wound or suffering from a diagnosable sickness'. Rations were indeed severely reduced, but for doctors, it still appeared to be far too early for cases of death by starvation. 'The suspected causes', wrote the pathologist entrusted with the inquiry, 'included exposure, "exhaustion" [none of the approximately 600 doctors in the *Kessel* ventured to mention starvation] and above all a hitherto unidentified disease.'

On 15 December, Dr Girgensohn, the Sixth Army pathologist then working in the hospital next to Tatsinskaya airfield, received the order to fly into the *Kessel* next day. 'Unfortunately we don't have a spare parachute for you,' the pilot told him when he reported next morning at dawn, but they were forced to turn back. Finally, on 17 December, they reached the *Kessel*. The pilot told him they were over Pitomnik, and Girgensohn, peering through the small window, saw 'in the white blanket of snow a brown cratered landscape'.

Girgensohn found General Doctor Renoldi, the chief medical officer, in a railway carriage dug into the ground on the edge of the airfield. Renoldi pretended to know nothing about Girgensohn's mission, because Dr Seggel, a specialist in internal medicine at Leipzig University, had requested his presence, and Renoldi, at that stage, considered the issue exaggerated.* From Pitomnik, Girgensohn was taken to the army field hospital next to Gumrak station and also close to Paulus's headquarters. His base was a wood-lined bunker, dug into the steep side of a *balka*. This accommodation was indeed 'luxurious', since it contained an iron stove and two double bunk beds with, to his astonishment, clean sheets. It was a great contrast to the nearby accommodation for the wounded, which largely consisted of unheated tents in temperatures down to minus twenty.

---

* General Doctor Renoldi took more interest later. From his railway carriage, he rather chillingly described the collapse of soldiers' health in the *Kessel* as 'a large-scale experiment into the effects of hunger'.

Girgensohn had preliminary discussions with divisional medical officers, then travelled round the *Kessel*, carrying out post-mortems on the corpses of soldiers who had died from no obvious causes. (Such was the shortage of wood in this treeless waste that a fork or crossroads along the snowbound route was marked by the leg from a slaughtered horse stuck upright in a mound of snow. The relevant tactical sign and directional arrow were attached to the top of this gruesome signpost.) The autopsies had to be carried out in a variety of inconvenient places: tents, earth bunkers, peasant huts, even in railway wagons. The extreme cold had maintained the cadavers in good condition, but most were frozen solid. Thawing them out proved very difficult with the shortage of available fuel. An orderly had to spend the night turning the corpses stacked around a small cast-iron oven. On one occasion, he fell asleep, and the result was 'a corpse frozen on one side and seared on the other'.

The cold was so bad that it was both difficult and painful for Girgensohn to pull on his rubber gloves. Each evening, he typed up the results by candlelight. In spite of such difficulties, which included Soviet air attacks and artillery bombardments, Girgensohn managed to perform fifty autopsies by the end of the month. In exactly half of this sample, he found clear signs of death by starvation: atrophy of the heart and liver, a complete absence of fatty tissue, a severe shrinkage of muscle.

In an attempt to compensate for the low-calorie diet of bread and '*Wasserzuppe*' with a few tiny bits of horsemeat, Army Group Don flew in small tins of meat paste with a high fat content, but this proved counter-productive. Quite often, when a sergeant was making his rounds of the sentry positions and a soldier said, 'I'm fine, I'll now have something to eat,' and then consumed some of the high-fat meat paste, the man was dead by the time the sergeant made his next round. Death from starvation, Girgensohn observed, was '*undramatisch*'.

The highest proportion of cases of death by starvation occurred in the 113th Infantry Division. Here at least, Girgensohn discovered a clear explanation. The quartermaster of the division had cut rations before the encirclement to hoard them as a precaution against insufficient supplies during the autumn rains. As a result, the men were already undernourished by the second half of November. Then, after several divisions had lost all their supplies during the retreat, Sixth Army headquarters centralized all remaining supplies to share them out equally. Thus the quartermaster's prudence backfired badly against his division.

Girgensohn, who spent seven years in Russian labour camps after the surrender, never lost his interest in the subject. He has always vigorously disputed any suggestion of 'stress illness', both as a condition in itself, and as an explanation for many of the unexplained deaths, even though recent research, which has shown that rats deprived of sleep for three weeks will die, suggests that humans deprived of sleep burn out rapidly. The pattern of Russian night attacks and constant activity to allow no rest undoubtedly had a contributory effect, as he acknowledges. But his explanation, after all these years, is more complex. He became convinced that the combination of exhaustion, stress and cold gravely upset the metabolism of most soldiers. This meant that even if they received the equivalent of, say, 500 calories a day, their bodies absorbed only a fraction. Thus, one could say that Soviet tactics, combined with the weather conditions and food shortages, produced, or at least contributed to, an accelerated process of starvation.

Severe malnutrition also reduced a patient's ability to survive infectious diseases, such as hepatitis and dysentery in the earlier period of the encirclement, and more serious diseases right at the end, particularly typhoid and typhus. Out in the steppe there was no water for washing bodies, let alone clothes, simply because there was not enough fuel to melt snow and ice. 'There's little new here,' wrote a panzer grenadier lieutenant in the 29th Motorized Infantry Division. 'Top of the list is the fact that every day we become more infested with lice. Lice are like the Russians. You kill one, ten new ones appear in its place.' Lice would be the carriers for the epidemics which decimated the survivors of Stalingrad.

The immediate concerns of medical staff, however, still focused on weakness from lack of food. 'Slowly, our brave fighters are starting to become decrepit,' wrote an assistant doctor. He went on to describe an amputation at the thigh which he performed by torchlight in a dugout without any form of anaesthetic. 'One is apathetic towards everything and can only think about food.'

The need of German soldiers for hope was mixed with a hatred for the Bolshevik enemy and a longing for revenge. In a state of what was called 'Kesselfever', they dreamed of an SS Panzer Corps smashing through the encircling Russian armies to rescue them, thus turning the tables in a great, unexpected victory. They tended to be the ones who still listened to Goebbels's speeches. Many kept up their spirits by singing the Sixth Army's song, *Das Wolgalied*, to the tune by Franz Lehár: 'There stands a soldier on the Volga shore, keeping watch there for his Fatherland'.

The operational propaganda department at Don Front head-quarters, using its German Communist assistants, decided to exploit the *Landser*'s fondness for songs. They broadcast from their loud-speaker vans an old favourite, which in present circumstances had a cruel twist: 'In the homeland, in the homeland, there awaits a warm reunion!' The German Communists under NKVD supervision con-sisted of Walter Ulbricht (later the East German president), the poet Erich Weinert, the writer Willi Bredel and a handful of German prisoners – four officers and a soldier – who had been recruited to the anti-Nazi cause. They taught 'criers', who were Red Army men chosen to crawl forward to dead ground in front of German lines and shout slogans and items of news through megaphones. Few of them knew any German, and most were killed.

The main activity of the propaganda detachment was to prepare 20- to 30-minute programmes on a gramophone record, with music, poems, songs and propaganda (especially the news of the breakthrough on the Italian Army's front). The programme was then played on a wind-up gramophone, and broadcast by the loudspeakers, either mounted on the van, or sometimes pushed forwards on sledges with a wire running back. Most propaganda broadcasts of this sort immediately attracted German mortar fire, on the order of officers afraid that their men might listen. But during December, the response became weaker owing to the shortage of munitions.

Different sound tricks were adopted, such as 'the monotonous ticking of a clock' followed by the claim that one German died every seven seconds on the Eastern Front. The 'crackling sound of the propaganda voice' then intoned: 'Stalingrad, mass grave of Hitler's army!' and the deathly tango dance music would start up again across the empty frozen steppe. As an extra sonic twist, the heart-stopping shriek of a real *Katyusha* rocket would sometimes follow from a 'Stalin organ' launcher.

Russian leaflets had greatly improved, now that they were written by Germans. Prisoner interrogations by the 7th Department confirmed that 'the ones with the most effect are those which talk about home, wives, family and children'. 'Soldiers eagerly read Russian leaflets even though they don't believe them,' admitted one German prisoner. Some 'cried when they saw a leaflet representing the corpse of a German soldier and an infant crying over it. On the other side were simple verses by the writer Erich Weinert.' The prisoner had no idea that Weinert, who had specially written the poem, 'Think of Your Child!', was very close by, attached to Don Front headquarters.

Perhaps the most effective piece of propaganda was to persuade German soldiers that they would not be shot on capture. Many of their officers had relied on the argument that surrender was out of the question because the Russians would kill them. One leaflet ended with a declaration by Stalin which began to convince even junior commanders that Soviet policy had changed: ' "If German soldiers and officers give themselves up, the Red Army must take them prisoner and spare their lives." (From Order No. 55 by the People's Commissar for Defence, J. Stalin.)'

The first encirclement of a large German army, trapped far from home, ordered to stay put and finally abandoned to its fate, has naturally created an intense debate over the years. Many German participants and historians have blamed Paulus for not having dis-obeyed orders, and broken out. Yet if anybody was in a position to give Paulus, who was deprived of vital information, a lead in the matter, it should have been his immediate superior, Field Marshal von Manstein.

'Can one serve two masters?' Strecker noted when Hitler rejected

Operation Thunderclap, the breakout plan to follow Operation Winter Storm. But the German Army only had a single master. The servile record since 1933 of most senior officers had left it both dishonoured and politically impotent. In fact, the disaster and humiliation of Stalingrad were the price which the army had to pay for its hubristic years of privilege and prestige under the National Socialist umbrella. There was no choice of master, short of joining the group round Henning von Tresckow and Stauffenberg.

Much time has been spent debating whether a breakout was feasible in the second half of December, yet even panzer commanders acknowledged that 'the chances of a successful breakout diminished with every week'. The infantry had even fewer illusions. 'We survivors', a corporal wrote home, 'can hardly keep going owing to hunger and weakness.' Dr Alois Beck, quite rightly, disputed the 'legend' that 'a breakout would have succeeded'. The Russians would have shot the 'half-frozen soldiers down like hares', because the men in their weakened state could not have waded through over a foot of snow, with its crust of ice on the surface, carrying weapons and ammunition. 'Every step was exhausting,' observed a staff officer from Sixth Army headquarters. 'It would have been like the Berezina.'

The whole 'Breakout or Defence' debate is thus a purely academic diversion from the real issues. In fact one suspects that the formidably intelligent Manstein recognized this at the time. He made a great play of sending Major Eismann, his intelligence officer, into the *Kessel* on 19 December to prepare the Sixth Army for Operation Thunderclap. Yet Manstein knew by then that Hitler, who had again reaffirmed his determination not to move from the Volga, would never change his mind.

In any case, Manstein must have realized by then that the relief attempt was doomed. Hoth's panzer divisions were being fought to a standstill on the Myshkova, with heavy casualties, even before the bulk of Malinovsky's 2nd Guards Army had deployed. And Manstein, who had kept himself well informed of developments within the *Kessel* and the state of the troops, must have realized that Paulus's men could never have walked, let alone fought, for between forty and sixty miles through the blizzards and deep frosts. The Sixth Army, with fewer than seventy under-supplied tanks, stood no chance of breaking through the 57th Army. Most important of all, Manstein knew by 19 December that Operation Little Saturn, with three Soviet armies breaking through into his rear, was changing the whole position irrevocably.

Quite simply, Manstein sensed that, in the sight of history and the German Army, he had to be seen to make every effort, even if he believed, quite correctly, that the Sixth Army's only chance of saving itself had expired almost a month earlier. His apparently uneasy conscience after the event must have been due to the fact that, with Hitler's refusal to withdraw from the Caucasus, he had needed the Sixth Army to tie down the seven Soviet armies surrounding it. If Paulus had attempted a breakout so few of his men would have survived, and in such a pitiable condition, that they would have been of no use to him in the moment of crisis.

19

'Christmas in the German Way'

The argument about breaking out of the *Kessel* in the second half of December also overlooked one curiously important psychological factor. Christmas was coming. No formation in the Wehrmacht was more preoccupied with the subject than the beleaguered Sixth Army. The quite extraordinary efforts devoted to its observance in bunkers below the steppe hardly indicated an impatience to break out. Lethargy from malnutrition combined with escapist daydreaming no doubt played a part, and probably so did the 'Fortress' mentality which Hitler helped to cultivate. But none of these entirely explain the almost obsessive emotional focus which the prospect of Christmas held for those trapped so far from home.

Preparations began well before Hoth's panzer divisions advanced north to the Myshkova river, and never seem to have slackened, even when soldiers became excited by the sound of approaching gunfire. From quite early in the month, men started to put aside tiny amounts of food, not in preparation for a breakout across the snow, but for a Christmas feast or for gifts. A unit in 297th Infantry Division slaughtered a packhorse early so as to make 'horse sausage' as Christmas presents. Advent crowns were fashioned from tawny steppe grass instead of evergreen, and little Christmas trees were carved out of wood in desperate attempts to make it 'just like at home'.

The sentimentality was by no means restricted to soldiers. General Edler von Daniels decorated his newly dug bunker with a Christmas tree and underneath a cradle with a snapshot of his 'Kesselbaby', born soon after their encirclement. He wrote to his young wife describing his plans to celebrate Christmas Eve 'in the German way, although in far-off Russia'. The military group had clearly become the surrogate family. 'Each man sought to bring a little joy to another,' he wrote after visiting his men in their bunkers. 'It was really uplifting to experience this true comradeship of the front line.' One festive banner proclaimed 'Comradeship through Blood and Iron', which, however appropriate to the circumstances, rather missed the message of Christmas.

One person who certainly did not miss the message was Kurt Reuber, the doctor in the 16th Panzer Division. The thirty-six-year-old Reuber, a theologian and friend of Albert Schweitzer, was also a gifted amateur artist. He converted his bunker in the steppe north-west of Stalingrad into a studio and began to draw on the back of a captured Russian map – the only large piece of paper to be found. This work, which today hangs in the Kaiser Wilhelm memorial church in Berlin, is the 'Fortress Madonna', an embracing, protective, almost womb-like mother and child, joined with the words of St John the Evangelist: 'Light, Life, Love'. When the drawing was finished, Reuber pinned it up in the bunker. Everyone who entered, halted and stared. Many began to cry. To Reuber's slight embarrassment – no artist could have been more modest about his own gifts – his bunker became something of a shrine.

There can be little doubt about the genuine and spontaneous generosity of that Christmas. A lieutenant gave out the last of his cigarettes, writing paper and bread as presents for his men. 'I myself had nothing,' he wrote home, 'and yet it was one of my most beautiful Christmases and I will never forget it.' As well as giving their cigarette ration, men even gave their bread, which they sorely needed. Others laboriously carved equipment racks for each other.

On Christmas Eve, Reuber's pianist battalion commander gave his last bottle of sparkling wine to the soldiers in the sickbay, but just after all the mugs were filled, four bombs exploded outside. Everyone flung themselves to the floor, spilling all the Sekt. The medical officer grabbed his first-aid bag and ran from the bunker to see to the casualties – one killed and three wounded. The dead man had been singing the Christmas carol '*O du fröhliche*'. The incident, not surprisingly, put an end to their celebrations. In any case, both the 16th Panzer and the 60th Motorized Infantry Division soon found themselves under full attack in the early hours of Christmas morning.

The traditional, and favourite, song that night was '*Stille Nacht, heilige Nacht*', which soldiers sang 'with husky voices' in bunkers by the light of hoarded candle stubs. There were many stifled sobs as men thought of their families at home. General Strecker was clearly moved when he made a tour of front-line positions. 'It is a "Stille Nacht" amid the turmoil of war . . . A Christmas that shows the true brotherhood of soldiers.' Visits by senior officers were also appreciated for their accompanying benefits. An NCO in a panzer division recorded that 'the divisional commander gave us a swig from his bottle and a bar of chocolate'.

In positions which were not attacked, men crowded into a bunker which had a wireless to hear 'the Christmas broadcast of Grossdeutsche Rundfunk'. To their astonishment, they heard a voice announce: 'This is Stalingrad!', answered by a choir singing '*Stille Nacht, heilige Nacht*', supposedly on the Volga front. Some men accepted the deception as necessary in the circumstances, others were deeply angered. They felt it was tricking their families and the German people as a whole. Goebbels had already proclaimed that this should be a 'German Christmas', a definition intended to convey notions of duty and austerity, and perhaps already a way of preparing the nation for news of the tragedy of Stalingrad.

At seven o'clock on Christmas morning, the Sixth Army war diary recorded: 'No supply flights arrived in the last forty-eight hours [a slight exaggeration]. Supplies and fuel coming to an end.' Later that day, Paulus sent a warning signal to Army Group Don to be passed back to General Zeitzler. 'If we do not receive increased rates of supplies in the next few days, we must expect a greatly increased death rate through exhaustion.'

Although they realized that the snowstorms of the previous day must have hindered flying, they had not been informed that Badanov's tanks had stormed on to Tatsinskaya airfield the previous morning. Manstein's headquarters did not even pass on the news that the Soviet counter-attack with four armies against Hoth's panzer divisions on the Myshkova river had been launched. When 108 tons of supplies finally arrived on 26 December, Sixth Army headquarters discovered that they had been sent ten tons of sweets for Christmas, but no fuel.

Most men, when they had the opportunity, sat apart to write a Christmas letter home in which they expressed their longing. 'In our hearts we all keep hoping', wrote a doctor with the 44th Infantry Division, 'that everything will change.' He spoke for many, but the better-informed commander-in-chief of the Sixth Army was not among them. 'Christmas naturally was not very joyful,' Paulus wrote to his wife a few days later. 'At such moments, festivities are better avoided . . . One should not, I believe, expect too much from luck.'

Not surprisingly, the contrast between German and Russian letters home during the Christmas period becomes even more marked than usual. While German letters tended to be sentimental, aching for home and family, the Russian letters that have survived clearly reveal an inexorable logic that the Motherland took priority. 'Darling!' wrote a soldier to his wife on Christmas Eve. 'We are pushing the serpents back to where they came from. Our successful advance brings our next meeting closer.' 'Hello Mariya,' wrote a soldier called Kolya. 'I've been fighting here for three months defending our beautiful [deleted by censor]. We have started pressing the enemy strongly. Now we have encircled the Germans. Every week a few thousand are taken prisoner and several thousand are destroyed on the field of battle. There are just the most stubborn SS soldiers left. They have fortified themselves in bunkers and shoot from them. And now I'm going to blow up one of those bunkers. Goodbye. Kolya.'

The temperature on Christmas Day fell to minus twenty-five degrees. The water in shell holes, however deep, was frozen solid. Flurries of snow hid much of the squalor in the *balkas*. Chaplains held field mass or communion in the snow to the sound of tarpaulins and tent canvas flapping and cracking in the wind, with half circles of men round a makeshift altar. In some cases, spiritual comfort and ideological justification became confused, as when Christian Germany was contrasted with godless Russia.

Even within the *Kessel*, Christmas did not prove entirely a season of goodwill. Dr Renoldi, the Sixth Army's surgeon-general, forbade the evacuation by air of frostbite casualties, on the grounds that their injuries might have been self-inflicted to avoid combat. And worst of all, virtually no food, apart from some rotting corn from the Stalingrad grain elevator, had been given to the 3,500 Russian prisoners of war in the camps at Voroponovo and Gumrak, because they did not feature on any ration strength. This partly bureaucratic atrocity led to a death rate of twenty a day by Christmas, and it soon escalated dramatically. The quartermaster responsible for feeding them claimed that typhus was the cause, but when an officer from Sixth Army headquarters asked whether there had been deaths from undernourishment, he was evasive. 'After reflecting for a moment, he denied it,' wrote the officer. 'I knew what he meant. Among our troops one was beginning to see similar things.' But linking their fate with that of German soldiers was a worse evasion. The inmates had no choice – they could not surrender. Even when desperate prisoners began to resort to cannibal-ism, nothing was done to improve their conditions, because that meant 'taking food from German soldiers'.

Christmas night was 'a beautiful starry night' and the temperature fell even further. Fighting, however, continued the next morning in the north-eastern sector of the *Kessel* defended by 16th Panzer Division and 60th Motorized Infantry Division. 'Thus a dozen of our units', reported the latter's divisional chaplain, 'were sent out to counter-attack in icy winds and thirty-five degrees of frost.' The two divisions, despite the terrible conditions and shortages of ammunition, managed to destroy some seventy tanks.

On that same morning of 26 December, Paulus sent another signal to Manstein, which began: 'Bloody losses, cold and insufficient supplies have reduced fighting strength of divisions severely.' He warned that if the Russians brought back their forces fighting Hoth's divisions, and redeployed them against the Sixth Army, 'it would not be possible to withstand them for long'.

An unexpected opportunity then arose. General Hube, the commander of XIV Panzer Corps, received an order to fly out of the *Kessel* on 28 December to Manstein's headquarters at Novocherkassk. An aircraft would take him on to East Prussia to receive the Swords to his Knight's Cross with Oak Leaves from the Führer in person. Paulus told Schmidt to give him 'all the necessary documents' on all matters from fuel levels to shortages of medical equipment. The hopes of generals and staff officers leaped at the news of his visit to Rastenburg. Hube, the blunt, one-armed veteran, was one of the few generals whom the Führer respected. They still could not believe 'that Hitler would abandon the Sixth Army'.

Hitler had no doubt convinced himself that he was doing everything to save the Sixth Army, but his grasp of reality had not improved. That day his headquarters signalled to Army Group Don, promising that in spite of the bad transport situation, it would be reinforced with '372 tanks and assault guns'. Manstein knew that this was wishful thinking.

In the city of Stalingrad, meanwhile, the remnants of Seydlitz's divisions were on the defensive. They had to conserve ammunition to repel attacks. They sheltered deep in cellars and bunkers, for warmth as well as safety from the Soviet artillery. 'There they sit like hairy savages in stone-age caves,' wrote Grossman, 'devouring horseflesh in smoke and gloom, amidst the ruins of a beautiful city that they have destroyed.'

The phrase 'strong enemy storm troop activity' appeared frequently in the Sixth Army war diary. Hans Urban, a twenty-eight-year-old police-station sergeant from Darmstadt, serving with the Hessian 389th Infantry Division, later provided a detailed report of this fighting in northern Stalingrad at the end of December.

> The enemy used to attack at dawn and at dusk, after a heavy artillery and mortar preparation. If they captured two or three bunkers from us, we would try to get them back later. On 30 December, after many of these attacks, I was ordered to take my rapid-fire group forward. My nine men with their machine-guns were able to hold

off the next attack by about 300 men from Spartakovka. The twenty infantrymen left on this sector were so exhausted from all the attacks that they could not offer much help. Most were ready to abandon their positions. I had with my two machine-guns no field of fire. The enemy were able to make use of the terrain and the ruins. We had to let the Russians get to within twenty yards before opening rapid fire. At least twenty-two were left dead in front of our positions. The surviving Russians tried to flush us out with grenades. The Russians attacked again on the same sector at daybreak on New Year's morning with three companies. It's hard to make an accurate estimate because they were shooting from holes in the ground, from behind collapsed walls or piles of rubble. We got them in a cross-fire from the two machine-guns, and they suffered heavy casualties. A mortar-man was hit, and although I'd never trained with the weapon, we were able to use their own ammunition against them. After it was over, we were so weak and exhausted and there were so many dead lying around in the open frozen stiff, that we could not even bury our own comrades.

Paulus, in contrast to his strongly pessimistic signals to Army Group Don and the letter to his wife, signed a stirring New Year message to the Sixth Army: 'Our will for victory is unbroken and the New Year will certainly bring our release! When this will be, I cannot yet say. The Führer has, however, never gone back on his word, and this time will be no different.'

Thanks to Hitler's insistence on time zones, the Russian New Year arrived two hours earlier than the German. General Edler von Daniels's card game of 'Doppelknopf' was interrupted at ten o'clock by 'a powerful firework display', as the Soviet besiegers fired in their 'New Year greeting'.

Daniels appears to have been in a good mood at this time. He had just been promoted to Lieutenant-General and awarded the Knight's Cross. Then, as a New Year's present from Paulus, he unexpectedly received a bottle of Veuve-Cliquot 'Schampus'. Several of the Stalingrad generals still seemed to be almost more preoccupied with decorations and promotions than with the fate of the Sixth Army.

When German midnight arrived, only star shells were fired. High-explosive rounds could not be wasted. The very last bottles were opened in the *Kessel* for the toast: '*Prosit Neujahr!*' Soviet divisions, on the other hand, suffered few restrictions on ammunition and alcohol. 'Celebrating the New Year was good,' wrote Viktor Barsov, in the marine infantry. 'I drank 250 grams of vodka that night. The food wasn't bad. In the morning to avoid a headache I drank 200 grams more.'

German soldiers tried to make light of their misfortunes, with the idea that everything would change for the better with the passing of the old year. 'Dear Parents, I'm all right,' wrote one soldier. 'Unfortunately, I again have to go on sentry tonight. I hope that in this New Year of 1943, I won't have to survive as many disappointments as in 1942.'

An almost obsessive optimism was produced by Hitler's New Year message to Paulus and the Sixth Army. Only the more sceptical spotted that the text did not constitute a firm guarantee. 'In the name of the whole German people, I send you and your valiant army the heartiest good wishes for the New Year. The hardness of your perilous position is known to me. The heroic stand of your troops has my highest respect. You and your soldiers, however, should enter the New Year with the unshakeable confidence that I and the whole German Wehrmacht will do everything in our power to relieve the defenders of Stalingrad and that with your staunchness will come the most glorious feat in the history of German arms. Adolf Hitler.'

'*Mein Führer!*' Paulus replied immediately. 'Your confident words on the New Year were greeted here with great enthusiasm. We will justify your trust. You can be certain that we – from the oldest general to the youngest grenadier – will hold out, inspired with a fanatical will, and contribute our share to final victory. Paulus.' New Year letters from many soldiers in the *Kessel* reflected a new mood of determination. 'We're not letting our spirits sink, instead we believe in the word of the Führer,' wrote a captain. 'We are maintaining a firm trust in the Führer, unshakeable until final victory,' wrote an NCO. 'The Führer knows our worries and needs,' wrote a soldier, 'he will always – and I'm certain of this – try to help us as quickly as possible.' Even a sceptical general like Strecker seems to have been affected. 'New hope arises,' he wrote, 'and there is some optimism about the present and immediate future.'

Paulus, on the other hand, was concerned at this time by the growing success of Soviet propaganda. The 7th Department at Don Front headquarters in charge of 'operational propaganda' had followed up their identification of 44th Infantry Division and General Edler von Daniels's 376th Infantry Division as the formations on which they should concentrate their efforts

Early on the morning of 3 January, Paulus went to the Austrian 44th Infantry Division, 'following radio broadcasts by prisoners from the 44th Infantry Division'. They had spoken on the shortages of food and ammunition and about the heavy casualties. 'The commander-in-chief', stated the Sixth Army report, 'wanted warnings to be given about the consequences of partaking in such broadcasts. Any soldiers who did so should realize that their names would be known, and they would face court martial.' During Paulus's meeting with General Deboi, the divisional commander, there was yet another 'heavy attack with tanks'.

The very next morning, Paulus visited the Romanian commander in the 'Fortress area', whose soldiers had suffered serious frostbite casualties owing to clothing shortages, 'above all boots, trousers and socks'. The rising number of desertions prompted Paulus to conclude that: 'Counter-propaganda is necessary against Russian leaflets printed in Romanian.'

Battalions and companies were so weak that they had become meaningless designations. Out of over 150,000 soldiers left in the *Kessel*, less than one in five were front-line troops. Many companies were down to a dozen men fit for duty. Fragments of units were therefore increasingly amalgamated into battle groups. The surviving panzer grenadiers of Sergeant-Major Wallrawe's company found themselves mixed 'with Luftwaffe companies and Cossack platoons' and sent to defend a position near Karpovka. It was an unfortunate spot to be sent to. A glance at the map indicated that the 'nose' which formed the south-western extremity of the *Kessel* would be the Russians' first objective when they decided to finish off the Sixth Army.

There were a few days of comparatively mild, wet weather at the very start of the year. Russian soldiers hated the thaw. 'I don't like the weather in Stalingrad', wrote Barsov in the marine infantry. 'It changes often and this makes the rifles go rusty. When it becomes warmer, the snow starts to fall. Everything becomes moist. *Valenki* [felt snow-boots] become soaking wet and we don't get much chance to dry things.' He and his comrades were, no doubt, happier on 5 January, when the temperature dropped to minus thirty-five degrees.

Soviet forces adopted a deliberate tactic to exploit their superiority in winter equipment. 'The Russians began with probing attacks', wrote a Luftwaffe liaison officer. 'If they breached the line, none of our men were in a position to dig new fire trenches. The men were physically too weak owing to lack of food, and the ground was frozen rock-hard.' Stranded on the open steppe, even more would die. On 6 January, Paulus signalled to General Zeitzler: 'Army starving and frozen, have no ammunition and cannot move tanks any more.' The same day, Hitler awarded General Schmidt the Knight's Cross of the Iron Cross.

Now that the fate of the Sixth Army was certain, Soviet journalists were brought to Don Front headquarters at Zavarykino. A delegation of Soviet writers came down from the capital to visit the 173rd Rifle Division, which had been raised from the Kievsky district of Moscow, and contained many intellectuals. 'From the command post of 65th Army, writers Aleksandr Korneychuk and Wanda Vasilevskaya' watched the division attack the Kazachy Kurgan, a Tartar burial mound on the north-west of the *Kessel*.

Even before Hoth's rescue attempt had been crushed on the Myshkova river, Stalin was harrying his generals to produce plans for the annihilation of the Sixth Army. On the morning of 19 December, he had telephoned Voronov, the *Stavka* representative overseeing Operation Little Saturn, and told him to move to Don Front headquarters. Voronov installed himself close to Rokossovsky's 'residenz', spread across the adjoining villages of Zavarykino and Medvedevo, where the accommodation for each general, or department, consisted of a 'five-walled' peasant *izba*, a log cabin with a dividing wall down the middle. American Willys staff cars, with Soviet markings, lurched in and out of the frozen ruts, taking generals off on tours of inspection to galvanize subordinate commanders in their efforts.

Voronov rapidly assembled a planning staff to study the options. He insisted, despite Stalin's insistence on having the results in two days, on first inspecting the terrain for himself. His visit to 57th Army headquarters took place on a clear day. He observed a group of Junkers transports that appeared overhead at about 9,000 feet without a fighter escort. The Russian anti-aircraft batteries grouped in the area opened fire too late; Soviet fighters also arrived too late to intercept. Not a single Junkers had been brought down. Voronov was even more furious when he discovered how little coordination there was between ground observers, anti-aircraft batteries and the fighter squadrons. The major-general in charge of anti-aircraft operations was terrorized into feverish activity.

Back at Zavarykino, Voronov again examined the figures. In spite of the strong German resistance put up early in December, Colonel I. V. Vinogradov, the chief intelligence officer of the Don Front, had not greatly revised his estimate of soldiers trapped in the *Kessel*. He now put them at 86,000, when asked to be precise. It was a figure which was to embarrass Red Army intelligence, especially when their NKVD rivals made sarcastic allusions later.

The draft plan for Operation Ring was at last ready on 27 December, and flown to Moscow. The next day Voronov was told to rewrite it. Stalin insisted that the first phase of the attack, focused on the Karpovka–Marinovka nose in the south-west, should come from the north-west and be coordinated with another operation at the opposite corner of the *Kessel*, cutting off the factory district of Stalingrad and the northern suburbs.

Stalin observed at a meeting of the State Defence Committee that the rivalry between Yeremenko, the commander of the Stalingrad Front, and Rokossovsky, the commander of the Don Front, had to be resolved before Operation Ring began. 'Whom shall we make responsible for the final liquidation of the enemy?' he asked. Somebody mentioned Rokossovsky. Stalin asked Zhukov what he thought.

'Yeremenko will be very hurt', Zhukov observed.

'We are not high-school girls', Stalin retorted. 'We are Bolsheviks and we must put worthwhile leaders in command.' Zhukov was left to pass on the unwelcome news to Yeremenko.

Rokossovsky, the commander-in-chief responsible for the *coup de grâce* on the Sixth Army, was allowed 47 divisions, 5,610 field guns and heavy mortars and 169 tanks. This force of 218,000 men was supported by 300 aircraft. But Stalin's impatience again built up, just as he was planning a strike against the Hungarian Second Army. To his fury, he was told that transport difficulties had slowed the delivery of reinforcements, supplies and ammunition. Voronov demanded yet another delay of four days. Stalin's sarcasm was bitter. 'You'll be sitting around there until the Germans take you and Rokossovsky prisoners!' With great reluctance, he agreed to the new date of 10 January.

German officers outside the *Kessel* had been wondering what would happen next. General Fiebig, the commander of VIII Air Corps, wondered after a long conversation with Richthofen: 'Why don't the Russians crush the *Kessel* like a ripe fruit?' Red Army officers on the Don Front were also surprised about the delay, and wondered how long it would be before they received their orders to attack. Voronov, however, had received another call from Moscow now telling him that an ultimatum to the Sixth Army must be prepared.

Voronov, in that first week of January 1943, wrote a draft addressed personally to Paulus. Constant calls from Moscow, with Stalin's amendments, were necessary. When finally approved, it was translated at Don Front headquarters by 'German anti-fascists from the group headed by Walter Ulbricht'. Meanwhile, NKVD representatives and Colonel Vinogradov of Red Army intelligence, displaying their usual rivalry, had begun to search for suitable officers to act as truce envoys. In the end, a compromise was reached. Late in the afternoon of 7 January, Major Aleksandr Mikhailovich Smyslov of army intelligence and Captain Nikolay Dmitrevich Dyatlenko of the NKVD, were selected to go together. Vinogradov, when interviewing Dyatlenko, suddenly asked: 'Are you a *khokhol*?' *Khokhol*, or 'tufty', was the insulting term for a Ukrainian, because Russians were often rude about their traditional style of haircut.

'No, Comrade Colonel,' replied Dyatlenko stiffly. 'I'm a Ukrainian.'

'So you're just like a Russian,' Vinogradov laughed. 'Well done. You are a suitable representative of the Red Army to meet the fascists.'

Smyslov and Dyatlenko were then briefed by General Malinin, the chief-of-staff, and by Voronov himself. One might have thought that Stalin was looking over their shoulder from the way both generals kept asking the envoys whether they fully understood the instructions from Moscow. In fact nobody really had a clear idea of the rules and ritual of a truce envoy. Dyatlenko admitted that his only knowledge came from the play *Field Marshal Kutuzov* by Solovyov.

'So lads,' said Voronov, 'will you fulfil your mission?'

'We will fulfil it, Comrade Colonel-General!' they chanted as one.

Malinin then ordered the front quartermaster-in-chief to kit out the two officers in the smartest uniforms available. The Germans had to be impressed. The quartermaster promised to have them 'dressed like bridegrooms', and winked 'like a magician' at the two envoys. With Voronov's backing, he had every general's aide at front headquarters on parade in his department. He ordered them all to strip, so that Dyatlenko and Smyslov could try on their uniforms and boots. The two envoys soon found themselves in a Willys staff car, with Colonel Vinogradov. Their destination, they were told, was Kotluban station on 24th Army's sector.

Russian troops in the area had received the order to cease firing from dusk. Then, all through the night, Red Army loudspeakers broadcast a message prepared by Ulbricht's anti-fascists, telling the Germans to expect truce envoys. By the next dawn, 8 January, firing had ceased. Smyslov and Dyatlenko were allotted a tall corporal, equipped with a white flag and a three-note trumpet. 'It was unusually quiet on the snow-covered plain' when they advanced to the very front trenches. The corporal blew the trumpet call: 'Attention! Attention! Everybody listen!' They advanced for about a hundred yards, then firing broke out. The three men were forced to dive for cover behind a low rampart made in the snow by Russian reconnaissance groups for night observation. The 'bridegroom' uniforms soon looked less smart; they also offered little protection from the intense cold.

When the firing died away, Smyslov and Dyatlenko rose to their feet and cautiously recommenced their advance. The corporal also stood up, waving the flag and blowing his trumpet. Once again, the Germans opened fire, but without shooting directly at them. It was clear that they wanted to force the truce envoys to retreat. After several more attempts, a furious Vinogradov sent a message forward to call off this dangerous version of grandmother's footsteps.*

Smyslov and Dyatlenko returned to Front headquarters to report, ashamed at the failure of their mission. 'Why are your noses hanging down, Comrades?' asked Voronov. 'The situation is such that it is not we who should ask them to accept our proposals, but vice versa. So we'll give them some more fire, and they will themselves come begging for them.' During that night, Russian aircraft flew over German positions, dropping leaflets printed with the ultimatum to Paulus, and a message addressed to '*Deutsche Offiziere, Unteroffiziere und Mannschaften!*', both signed by Voronov and Rokossovsky. To underline the message, 'they supported the words with bombs'. Red Army radio stations also broadcast the text, read by Erich Weinert, on the frequencies most used by the Germans, and a number of German wireless operators acknowledged. The leaflets were certainly read. A captain in the 305th Infantry Division admitted after capture that officers as well as soldiers had read the Soviet leaflets in secret, despite the penalties, 'because forbidden fruit is sweet'. Sometimes they showed leaflets in Russian to a trusty Hiwi and asked him to translate. 'Everyone knew about the ultimatum,' he said.

Smyslov and Dyatlenko had slept for only a couple of hours at front headquarters when they were woken at around midnight. A staff car was outside waiting for them by the time they had dressed in their old uniforms (the ADCs had immediately reclaimed their property). When they reached the intelligence department, they discovered that Colonel Vinogradov had been promoted to Major-General and that they had been awarded the Order of the Red Star. Vinogradov, having joked that he had been promoted 'for all the trousers he had worn out during his service', added that Smyslov and

---

* Paulus later claimed that he had never issued an order to open fire on any Russian flag of truce, but Schmidt might well have done.

Dyatlenko would receive an even more important medal if they managed to carry out their mission at a second attempt.

The two envoys were told to climb into a staff car with Vinogradov and the officer appointed to replace him as chief of intelligence. As they drove through the night again, the two newly promoted generals sang songs and 'kept interrupting each other with generals' anecdotes'. (Although Dyatlenko's respectful account does not say that they were drunk, they certainly appear to have been celebrating their promotions.) The rhythm of the songs was continually broken, as the staff car lurched in and out of huge potholes along the frozen dirt roads. It was a long journey round the southern side of the *Kessel*, crossing the Don westwards, then back across again at Kalach to the sector covered by 21st Army. Shortly before dawn, they reached the headquarters of the 96th Rifle Division, a few miles to the west of Marinovka.

Rather like condemned prisoners, Smyslov and Dyatlenko were given breakfast, boosted 'by a Narkom's [government minister's] ration'. Vinogradov put a stop to a second helping, and told them to get ready. They then suddenly realized that they had handed the white flag back to the quartermaster at front headquarters. A new one had to be made, using one of the divisional commander's sheets nailed crudely to a branch from an acacia.

The staff car drove them to the front line and parked in a *balka*, from where the party proceeded forwards on foot. Smyslov and Dyatlenko were joined by an elderly warrant officer, with a trumpet, who introduced himself as: 'Commander of the musical platoon Siderov'. A lieutenant also stepped forward and offered to escort them through the minefields – 'because my life is not worth as much as yours,' he explained.

The three envoys put on camouflage suits just behind the front trenches, then set off across the white expanse which blurred into a heavy mist. Some two dozen humps of snow ahead were frozen bodies. General Vinogradov and the other two generals climbed on to a burnt-out Russian tank to watch proceedings. Siderov blew the trumpet. The call 'Attention! Attention!' sounded, in Dyatlenko's ears, more like 'The Last Post'.

As they came closer to the German lines, they saw figures moving. It looked as if the front-line bunkers and trenches were being reinforced. Siderov waved the flag and blew the trumpet again urgently. 'What do you want?' a warrant officer called.

'We are truce envoys from the commander of the Red Army,' Dyatlenko shouted back in German. 'We are on our way to your commander-in-chief with a message. We ask you to receive us according to international law.'

'Come here then,' he said. Several more heads popped up and guns were levelled at them. Dyatlenko refused to advance until officers were called. Both sides became nervous during the long wait. Eventually, the warrant officer set off towards the rear to fetch his company commander. As soon as he had left, German soldiers stood up and started to banter. '*Rus! Komm, komm!*' they called. One soldier, a short man, bundled in many rags, clambered up on to the parapet of the trench and began to play the fool. He pointed to himself in an operatic parody. '*Ich bin Offizier,*' he sang.

'I can see what sort of an officer you are,' Dyatlenko retorted, and the German soldiers laughed. The joker's companions grabbed his ankles and dragged him back into the trench. Smyslov and Siderov were laughing too.

Finally, the warrant officer returned, accompanied by three officers. The most senior of them asked politely what they wanted. Dyatlenko explained, and asked if they would be received according to international convention, with guarantees for their safety. Complicated discussions followed on detail – whether they should remove their snow suits and have their eyes bandaged – before they were allowed forward. After the officers on both sides had exchanged salutes, Smyslov showed the oilskin packet, addressed to Colonel-General Paulus. The German officers whispered urgently among themselves. The senior lieutenant then agreed to take the Soviet representatives to their regimental commander. The black blindfolds issued by the front quartermaster the day before had been handed back with the white flag, so they had to improvise with handkerchiefs and belts. All Siderov could offer was the blouse of his snowsuit, and when that was fastened round his head, the German soldiers watching from their bunker entrance burst out laughing. 'Bedouin! Bedouin!' they called.

The senior lieutenant led Dyatlenko by the hand. After a few steps, he asked, 'with a smile in his voice', what was written in the message to Paulus. 'That we should surrender?'

'I am not ordered to know,' Dyatlenko replied, using the formula of the Tsarist army. They changed the subject.

'Tell me please,' said the lieutenant, 'if it is true that a German writer called Willi Bredel has been in Platonovsky? He has been addressing my soldiers on the radio for ten or maybe fourteen days. He appealed to them to surrender, and swore that their lives would be spared. Of course, my soldiers just laughed at him. But was he really here? It was clear from his accent that he was from Hamburg. So was it really him or a record of his voice?'

Dyatlenko longed to reply. Bredel was indeed one of the Germans working for his section and he got on well with him. But if he gave any hint, then the lieutenant would have understood immediately what his 'real job' was. An unplanned diversion occurred at that moment. The ice on which they were walking was both uneven from shell fire, yet also polished by the passage of boots wrapped in rags. Dyatlenko fell, knocking down the lieutenant. Smyslov, hearing the commotion, shouted in alarm. Dyatlenko reassured Smyslov and apologized to the lieutenant. He was not afraid of a trick. 'About a thousand prisoners of war had passed through my hands by then,' he wrote afterwards. 'I knew their psychology sufficiently well as a result, and I knew that these men would not harm me.'

German soldiers who came to lift the two fallen men slipped over in their turn, making a sprawling mass of bodies. Dyatlenko compared it to the Ukrainian children's game called 'A little heap is too little: someone is needed on top.'

The lieutenant kept up his questioning when the blindfold march resumed, then returned to the question of Bredel. Dyatlenko was less than frank. He said that the name was known to him and he had even read some of his books. Finally, the lieutenant warned him that they were coming to some steps.

The three truce envoys found themselves, when their blindfolds were removed, in a well-built bunker lined with tree-trunks. Dyatlenko noticed two sacks with spoiled grey grain, which they were trying to dry out. 'That serves you right, you snakes,' Dyatlenko thought. 'You burned the Stalingrad grain elevator and now you have to dig food for yourselves out from under the snow.' He also observed the coloured postcards and Christmas paper decorations still in place.

A senior German officer entered and demanded to know the authority for their mission. 'The *Stavka* of the Red Army command,' replied Dyatlenko. The senior officer then left the bunker, presumably to telephone. During the colonel's absence, the German officers and Dyatlenko discussed Christmas celebrations. They then discussed pistols and the Germans admired Dyatlenko's Tokarev. He rapidly surrendered it when the Russian truce envoys realized, to their great embarrassment, that according to international convention they should have left behind their personal weapons.

To maintain the fairly cordial atmosphere, Siderov opened the packet of 'Lux' cigarettes – what Dyatlenko called 'general's cigarettes' – which had been specially issued to them to impress the German officers. 'With great dignity, Siderov offered the packet to the Germans as if he had always smoked the best, and not *makhorka*.' He asked Dyatlenko to tell them that this was his third war: he had fought in 'the Imperialist War, the Civil War and now the Great Patriotic War'. Dyatlenko expected him to add 'against German fascist invaders', but in fact Siderov smiled and said: 'And during all these three wars, I have never had the chance to talk to the enemy so peacefully.' The German officers agreed and added that this little assembly consisted of the most peaceful people on the whole front. Conversation rather came to a halt after that. In the ensuing silence, they heard heavy firing. The Russians were horrified. One of the Germans dashed out of the bunker to discover what was happening. He returned with the accusation: 'It was your people.' Fortunately, the firing soon ceased. (The truce envoys discovered later that it had been Russian anti-aircraft batteries unable to resist the temptation when German transport aircraft appeared overhead.)

Tension rose during the long wait for the colonel's return. But when he came, it was not to announce as expected that a staff car had been sent from Sixth Army headquarters. He had, in Dyatlenko's words, 'a very different expression – like a beaten dog'. The junior officers, guessing what had happened, rose to their feet 'as if a sentence was about to be pronounced on all of them'.

'I am ordered', the colonel announced to the Russians, 'not to take you anywhere, not to accompany you, nor to receive anything from you, only to cover your eyes again, to lead you back, to return your pistols and to guarantee your safety.'

Dyatlenko protested most volubly. He offered, even though it was against his instructions, to give the oilskin packet to a specially authorized officer in return for a receipt.

'I am ordered to take nothing from you,' replied the German colonel.

'Then we ask you to write on the package that you, in accordance with orders received from higher command, refuse to accept the letter addressed to your army commander.' But the colonel refused even to touch the packet. There was nothing left, Smyslov and Dyatlenko concluded, but to allow themselves to be blindfolded again and escorted back. The same senior lieutenant guided Dyatlenko back.

'How old are you?' Dyatlenko whispered after they had set off.

'Twenty-four,' he replied. There were only a few years between them.

'This war between our peoples is a tragic mistake,' Dyatlenko said after a short pause. 'It will finish sooner or later and it would be good for me to meet you on that day, wouldn't it?'

'There is no room for illusions in my heart,' said the German lieutenant, 'because before a month is up, both you and I will be dead.'

'Did you Germans really think', said Dyatlenko, 'that Russia would let you spend a peaceful winter in warm bunkers?'

'No, it was possible to assume from the experience of the past winter that you would launch an offensive. But nobody expected it on such a scale or in such a way.'

'You told me earlier that your soldiers just laugh at the appeals of Willi Bredel.' Out of professional curiosity, Dyatlenko could not resist ignoring his instructions to avoid topical issues. 'But wasn't he right when he spoke about your hopeless situation. Weren't his appeals serious?'

'Everything he said was right,' the lieutenant replied. 'But don't forget one thing. When a war of two world outlooks is going on, it is impossible to persuade enemy soldiers by throwing words across the front lines.'

On reaching the trenches, the eyes of the three Russian officers were uncovered. Their pistols and snow suits were handed back. The two groups of officers faced each other and saluted, then the Russians, under Siderov's flag, returned 'through the white silence' to General Vinogradov who was still waiting by the burnt-out tank.

Vinogradov led them back to the *balka*. The commander of divisional reconnaissance lost no time. 'Siderov,' he said, 'quickly draw me a map of their defences.' The other two truce envoys followed them into a bunker dug into the side of the *balka* and watched 'our old man who spoke to the enemy so peacefully', draw a map of their fire points perfectly. 'I don't know if he had been given this mission from the start,' wrote Dyatlenko afterwards, 'or whether it was just his skill, but it transpired that he had been remembering everything.' Dyatlenko and Smyslov then returned to front headquarters in the Willys staff car with the two generals, 'sad and tired' because their mission had been a failure and many men were to die for no purpose.

Part Five

THE SUBJUGATION OF THE SIXTH ARMY

20

The Air-Bridge

'The misty cloud hung low,' wrote Hans Dibold, a doctor with the 44th Infantry Division, 'it all but touched one's head. In that cloud the engine of a lost transport plane wailed forlornly.'

The term 'air-bridge' was seldom used in the theatre of operations. The idea of a permanent link over the heads of the Russians gratified the illusionists looking at maps and charts in Berlin and Rastenburg. Hitler would suddenly demand information, so every general and staff officer, desperate to have the figures to hand, constantly badgered airfield commanders for the latest statistics and proof of action. This compulsive interference from above only made things worse. Luftwaffe generals in Germany had leaped to obey Hitler's decision to resupply the Sixth Army by air, allocating thoroughly unsuitable aircraft like the Ju-86, an aeroplane used for training pilots, to make the numbers look better. Even the use of gliders was considered until somebody observed that Russian fighters would destroy them with ease.

Chaos was also caused by rear airbase commanders sending forward Junkers 52s before they had been adapted for winter operations, simply to prove that they were reacting to the Führer's call quickly. The mass of transport aircraft arriving without warning had caused chaos, particularly since an air-supply operations group was not in place to take control. At the end of November, General Fiebig and the staff of VIII Air Corps took over responsibility, and the situation greatly improved, even though fundamental flaws in the whole project condemned it to failure from the start.

General von Richthofen had warned that they would need six full-sized airfields within the *Kessel*, not just one, and also properly trained ground staff. His fear about the shortage of runways was rapidly justified under bad weather conditions. The best day had been 19 December, when 154 aircraft landed with 289 tons, but good flying days were rare indeed. Weather was not the only problem. The airfield at Pitomnik attracted all the enemy's attention, so shot-up and crashed aircraft frequently made it unusable for short periods. Their burnt-out metal carcasses were pushed out into the snow beside the runway, forming a 'widely strewn machine graveyard'. Landing by night was doubly dangerous. The air-defence batteries at Pitomnik had an almost impossible balance to maintain. They needed to use searchlights to pick out Soviet night bombers, but the base of their beams provided a target for Russian artillery.

The strain on Luftwaffe aircrew was intense. 'Young and inexperienced aircrews were badly shaken' by the sights at Pitomnik, above all the miserable condition of the wounded waiting by the side of the runway for evacuation, and the piles of frozen corpses, left by the field hospital there because the ground was frozen too hard to bury them.

Whatever the Sixth Army's gratitude for the Luftwaffe's efforts, exasperation was inevitable. When one consignment was opened and found to contain only marjoram and pepper, Lieutenant-Colonel Werner von Kunowski, the Sixth Army's Quartermaster, exploded: 'Which ass was responsible for this load?' An officer with him joked that at least the pepper could be used in close-quarter combat.

After the Soviet attack on Tatsinskaya, the transport fleet was greatly reduced, leaving a much smaller pool from which serviceable aircraft could be tasked. Also, the new Ju-52 airbase at Salsk, just over 200 miles from Pitomnik, was close to the maximum operational range, so any aircraft whose engines burned up oil could not be used. In desperation, some of the Luftwaffe's largest four-engined aircraft – the Focke-Wulf 200 Condor, which could take up to six tons, and the Junkers 290, which could manage a load of up to ten tons – were brought into service, but they were vulnerable and lacked the solidity of the old 'Tante Ju' trimotor. Once Salsk also came under threat, in mid-January, the remaining Ju-52s had to move north-west to Zverevo north of Shakhty. This new airfield consisted of a packed-snow runway on open agricultural land. There was no accommodation, so ground crew, control staff and aircrew lived in igloos and tents.

Icing became an even greater problem in the air, while on the ground, engines became harder and harder to start. Heavy snowfalls often brought bases to a halt, since every plane had to be dug out of drifts. There were few anti-aircraft defences at Zverevo, and on 18 January, Soviet fighters and bombers, coming in eighteen waves during the course of the day, managed to destroy another fifty Ju-52s on the ground. This was one of the few really effective operations by Red Army aviation, whose pilots still lacked confidence.

Richthofen and Fiebig had felt from the beginning that they had no choice but to make the best of a doomed job. They expected little understanding from above. 'My trust in our leadership has rapidly sunk below zero', Richthofen told General Jeschonnek, the Luftwaffe chief-of-staff, on 12 December. A week later, on hearing that Goering had told Hitler that the supply situation in Stalingrad was 'not so bad', he had written in his diary: 'Apart from the fact that it would do his figure a power of good to spend a little time in the *Kessel*, I can only assume that my reports either are not read or are given no credence.'

While Goering did nothing to stint his appetite, General Zeitzler, in a gesture of solidarity with the starved troops in Stalingrad, reduced his own rations to their level. According to Albert Speer, he lost twenty-six pounds within two weeks. Hitler, informed of this diet by Martin Bormann, ordered Zeitzler to return to normal eating. As a concession, Hitler banned champagne and brandy at Führer head-quarters 'in honour of the heroes of Stalingrad'.

The vast majority of civilians in Germany had little idea of how close the Sixth Army was to final defeat. 'I hope that you'll break the encirclement soon,' a young woman wrote to her soldier penfriend in mid-January, 'and when you do, you'll be given leave straight away.' Even the Nazi Party chief of Bielefeld wrote in mid-January to General Edler von Daniels to congratulate him on the birth of his child, his Knight's Cross and promotion and said that he looked forward to seeing him 'very soon back amongst us again'.

The atmosphere of unreality pervaded the most senior government circles in Berlin. Speer, deeply disturbed by the situation at Stalingrad, accompanied his wife, 'who like everybody else still suspected nothing untoward', to a performance of *The Magic Flute* at the opera. 'But sitting in our box, in those softly upholstered chairs among this festively attired audience, all I could think of was that same kind of crowd at the Paris Opera when Napoleon was retreating in Russia, and of the now identical suffering of our own soldiers.' He fled back to his ministry, seeking escape in work, and tried to suppress his 'horrible feelings of guilt' towards his brother, a private in the Sixth Army at Stalingrad.

Speer's parents had recently rung him in panic. They had just heard that their youngest son Ernst was lying in 'a primitive field hospital' in a stable, 'only partly roofed and without walls' suffering from jaundice with fever, swollen legs and kidney pains. Speer's mother sobbed on the telephone: 'You can't do this to him.' And his father said: 'It's impossible that you, you of all people, can't do something to get him out.' Speer's sense of helplessness and guilt was compounded by the fact that the year before, following Hitler's order that senior officials must not use influence on behalf of relatives, he had fobbed off his brother with a promise to get him transferred to France once the campaign was over. Now the last letter from Ernst in Stalingrad said that he could not stand watching his fellow patients die in the field hospital. He had rejoined his comrades in the front line, despite his grotesquely swollen limbs and pathetic weakness.

Within the *Kessel*, as the Sixth Army waited for the final Russian offensive, stories spread not just of an SS Panzer Corps approaching, which Hitler had promised for mid-February, but even of an air-transported division being flown into the *Kessel* to bolster their defences.

Some rumours lost all touch with reality. Darker spirits claimed that the Fourth Panzer Army had got to within a dozen miles of their lines, but Paulus had then told General Hoth not to advance any further. Some soldiers even convinced themselves later that Paulus, as part of a secret deal with the Russians, had betrayed them. According to another story, 'the Russians have issued an order, that anyone who shoots a [captured] German pilot will be severely punished, because they were needed to fly transport planes in the rearmost areas, such was the shortage of Soviet aircrew'.

Rumours were bound to spread in their strange communities, whether the encampments round the airfields, or dugouts in *balkas* on the steppe, grouped together like a troglodyte village. If there was any wood to burn in the small bunker stoves, smoke emerged from little chimney stacks, made from empty food tins rammed together. Duckboards, tables, even bunks as men died, were broken up as fuel. The only substitute for real warmth was a fug, created with packed bodies and tarpaulins, but men still shivered uncontrollably. The comparative heat did little more than stir their lice into activity, and drive them wild with itching. They often slept two to a bunk with a blanket over their heads in a pathetic attempt to share body heat. The rodent population swelled rapidly on a diet of dead horses and humans. Out in the steppe, mice became voracious in their search for food. One soldier reported that mice had 'eaten two of his frozen toes' while he was asleep.

When rations arrived, on a sledge pulled by a starved pony, stiff, ungainly figures, wrapped in rags, emerged to hear the latest rumours. There was no fuel to melt snow for washing or shaving. Their hollow-cheeked faces were waxen and unshaven – the beards pathetically straggly from calcium deficiency. Their necks were thin and scrawny like those of old men. Their bodies crawled with lice. A bath and clean underwear were as distant a dream as a proper meal. The bread ration was now down to under 200 grams per day, and often little more than 100 grams. The horseflesh added to '*Wassersuppe*' came from local supplies. The carcasses were kept fresh by the cold, but the temperature was so low that meat could not be sliced from them with knives. Only a pioneer saw was strong enough.

The combination of cold and starvation meant that soldiers, when not on sentry, just lay in their dugouts, conserving energy. The bunker was a refuge which they could hardly face leaving. Often, their minds went blank because the chilling of their blood slowed down both physical and mental activity. Books had been passed round until they disintegrated or were lost in the mud or snow, but now few had the energy left to read. In a similar way, Luftwaffe officers running Pitomnik airfield had given up chess in favour of skat because any effort of concentration was beyond them. In many cases, however, the lack of food led not to apathy but to crazed illusions, like those of ancient mystics who heard voices through malnutrition.

It is impossible to assess the numbers of suicides or deaths resulting from battle stress. Examples in other armies, as already mentioned, rise dramatically when soldiers are cut off, and no army was more beleaguered than the Sixth Army at Stalingrad. Men raved wildly in their bunks, some lay there howling. Many, during a manic burst of activity, had to be overpowered or knocked senseless by their comrades. Some soldiers feared breakdown and madness in others as if it were contagious. But the greatest alarm was provoked when a sick comrade had dilated nostrils and black lips and the whites of his eyes turned pink. The fear of typhus seemed curiously atavistic, almost as if it were a medieval plague.

The sense of approaching death could also stimulate an intense awareness of all that they were about to lose. Tough men dreamed feverishly of images of home, and wept silently at the idea of never seeing wife or children again. More reflective characters re-examined memories, or studied the world about them, especially their comrades, with a new interest. Some even had enough emotion left to feel sorry for the starving horses gnawing desperately at a piece of wood.

For the first week or ten days in January, before the Soviet offensive broke, men tried not to let their true degree of wretchedness show in letters home. 'I received a quarter litre of vodka and thirteen cigarettes for the New Year,' wrote a soldier called Willy to his parents in a letter which never reached them, 'but all the food I've got now is a piece of bread. I've never missed you more than today when we were singing the "*Wolgalied*". I'm sitting in a cage here – it's not made of gold but of the Russian encirclement.' Many soldiers camouflaged the truth even further. 'We can only count upon the fact that spring will start soon,' a soldier called Seppel wrote home. 'The weather is still bad, but the main thing is to be healthy and have a good stove. The Christmas holidays passed well.' Others, however, did not try to conceal their feelings: 'The only thing left to me is to think about the three of you,' a soldier wrote to his wife and children.

Some desperate to escape considered self-inflicted wounds. Those who went through with it did not just risk execution. Even if no suspicions were aroused, they risked death from their own action. A light flesh wound was not enough to earn a flight out of the *Kessel*. A shot through the right hand was too obvious, and with so few soldiers left in the front line, the wound had to be disabling if they were to be released from combat duties. But once the final Soviet advance began, even 'a light wound which hindered movement, practically signified death'.

From early January, an increasing number of German soldiers began to surrender without resistance or even to desert to the enemy. Deserters tended to be infantrymen at the front, partly because they had more opportunity. There were also cases of officers and soldiers who refused evacuation, out of bravery and an almost obsessive sense of duty. Lieutenant Löbbecke, the commander of a company of tanks in 16th Panzer Division, had lost an arm in the fighting, but soldiered on without having the wound properly treated. His divisional commander could not persuade him to go for treatment. Eventually, General Strecker got hold of him.

'I request permission to stay with my men,' Löbbecke said immediately. 'I cannot leave them now when the fighting is so desperate.' Strecker, presumably from the smell, realized that the stump of Löbbecke's arm was putrefying. He had to order him on to an aircraft out of the *Kessel* to a base hospital.

For the truly incapacitated, the only hope of evacuation back to a field hospital was by sled or in an ambulance. Their drivers were already recognized as 'steering-wheel heroes', because of the very high casualty rate. A moving vehicle – and ambulances were among the very few allowed any fuel – immediately attracted Russian ground fire or air attack.

Walking wounded and sick made their own way to the rear through the snow. Many stopped to rest and never rose again. Others arrived in spite of appalling wounds or advanced frostbite. 'One day somebody knocked at our bunker,' remembered a Luftwaffe lieutenant at Pitomnik. 'Outside stood an older man, a member of the Organisation Todt engaged on road repair. Both his hands were so badly swollen from frostbite that he would never be able to use them again.'

Reaching the general hospital by the airfield was still far from a guarantee of evacuation or even treatment in the large tents, which did little to keep out the cold. Wounds and frostbite represented only a small part of the workload, which threatened to overwhelm doctors. There was a jaundice epidemic, dysentery and all the other sicknesses, accentuated by undernourishment and often dehydration, since there was no fuel to melt the snow. The wounded were also far more exposed to Soviet air attack than they had been at the front. 'Every half-hour Russian aircraft attacked the airfield,' reported a corporal later. 'Many comrades who were just about to be saved, having been loaded into aircraft, and were waiting to take off, lost their lives at the very last moment.'

The evacuation by air of the wounded and sick was just as unpredictable as the incoming supply flights. On three days, 19 and 20 December and 4 January, over a thousand were taken on each occasion, but the overall average, including days when no flights were possible, between 23 November and 20 January came to 417.

Selection for the aircraft was not made by the severity of wounds. It developed into a ruthless triage due to the shortage of aircraft space. 'Only the lightly wounded, those able to move themselves, could hope to get away,' recounted an officer courier. 'There was enough room for only about four stretchers inside a Heinkel fuselage, but you could pack in nearly twenty walking wounded. So if you had been severely hit, or were so sick that you could not move, you were as good as dead.' Luck, however, could still intervene. By pulling rank, this officer managed to get an infantry non-commissioned officer, who had been lying at the airfield for three days with a bullet lodged in his back, on to his aircraft. 'How this man had got to the airfield, I never knew.' He also pulled another NCO, an elderly man with a high fever, on board.

The Feldgendarmerie, hated by the troops and known as the 'chain dogs' because of the metal crescent gorget, hung on a chain, which they wore round their necks, guarded access to the runway, checking papers minutely to make sure that no malingerers got through. As hope of escape diminished in January, they resorted more and more to their sub-machine-guns to hold back the wounded and malingerers.

Many more wounded fitted into the giant, four-engined Focke-Wulf Condors, of which a few were used from the second week of January. They were, however, exceptionally vulnerable if overloaded. One sergeant in the 9th Flak Division watched the lumbering acceleration of a Condor on to which two of his wounded comrades had just been loaded. As the aircraft rose steeply after take-off to gain height, the helpless human cargo inside must have shifted or rolled towards the back, because the tail suddenly dropped. The engines screamed as the nose pointed almost vertically into the sky, then the whole aircraft fell back to the ground just beyond the perimeter and exploded in a fireball with a 'deafening sound'.

Further out, soldiers at the west end of the *Kessel* witnessed the fate of Junkers transports, knowing full well that their heavy outbound loads consisted of wounded comrades. Often these aircraft 'could not gain height quickly enough and ran into heavy flak, thus coming to a terrible end. I saw from my trench on several occasions this apocalyptic fate and was very, very depressed.'

As well as flying out wounded, couriers and certain specialists, the aircraft still brought in some officers and men who had gone on leave just before the *Kessel* was closed. Because of the news blackout in Germany, many of them had no idea of what had happened in their absence until their train reached Kharkov. Manstein's aide, Alexander Stahlberg, described how his twenty-one-year-old cousin by marriage, Gottfried von Bismarck, arrived at Army Group Don headquarters at Novocherkassk on 2 January after Christmas leave at home in Pomerania. He had received an order to fly into the *Kessel* to rejoin the 76th Infantry Division. Manstein, on discovering the circumstances, invited him to his table for dinner, where conversation was unrestrained. Both Manstein and Stahlberg greatly admired the way the young man, with no complaint, upheld the Potsdam tradition of the

9th Infantry Regiment by returning to a lost battle, not for Hitler, but out of a Prussian devotion to duty. Bismarck himself, however, put it in less glorious terms. 'I was a soldier, I had received an order and was obliged to accept the consequences.'

General Hube, when he returned to the *Kessel* on 9 January, the eve of the Soviet offensive, told Paulus and Schmidt that Hitler simply refused to acknowledge the possibility of defeat at Stalingrad. He had not listened to his account of conditions in the *Kessel*, instead he had tried to convince him that a second relief attempt might well be brought forward.

Some of Hube's officers were downcast that he, of all people, seemed to have been taken in by one of Hitler's performances of mesmerizing optimism – the 'sun-ray cure'. 'I was deeply disappointed', recorded Hube's intelligence officer, Prince Dohna, 'how easily such a brave and upright soldier could be persuaded.' Others, however, heard that Hube had even dared 'to advise Hitler to try to finish the war', and when Hube died in a plane crash the following year, rumours spread that Hitler might have had a hand in it. In a way, both sides were right. When Hube had reported to Army Group headquarters before flying back into the *Kessel*, Manstein certainly believed that he had been taken in by one of Hitler's displays of confidence. On the other hand, he subsequently discovered that Hube had dared suggest to Hitler that he might do better to hand over supreme command of the army to a general, so that he would not be damaged personally if the Sixth Army were lost.

Hube had been one of the Führer's favourite commanders, but his evident belief that the Sixth Army was doomed only confirmed Hitler's suspicion that all generals were infected with pessimism. Paulus recognized this. He came to the conclusion that only a highly decorated young warrior might appeal to Hitler's romantic notions and thus be in a better position to persuade him to listen to the truth.

Paulus had an obvious candidate for this mission in the form of Captain Winrich Behr, whose black panzer uniform with the Knight's Cross was likely to produce the right effect on the Führer. And Behr, responsible for updating not only the situation map, but also all the facts and figures in reports, was one of the best-briefed officers at Sixth Army headquarters.

Behr received so little warning of his mission on the morning of 12 January, two days after the start of the Soviet offensive, that he did not have time to offer to take letters home from his colleagues. He bundled up the Sixth Army war diary in his belongings to take it to safety, then hurried to Pitomnik. The runway was already under fire from heavy mortars as well as artillery. As Behr ran to the Heinkel 111, filling with wounded, the Feldgendarmerie armed with sub-machine-guns had to hold back hundreds of others trying to rush, or even crawl, to the plane.

The flight to Taganrog took one and a half hours. To his surprise, it was even colder down by the Sea of Azov than at Stalingrad. A staff car was waiting for him and he was taken to Field Marshal von Manstein's headquarters. Manstein assembled some of his officers and asked Behr to report on the situation. Behr described everything: the famine; the casualty rates; the exhaustion of the soldiers; the wounded lying in the snow, waiting for evacuation, their blood frozen; the pitiful shortage of food, fuel and ammunition. When Behr had finished, Manstein told him: 'Give Hitler exactly the same description as you gave me.' An aeroplane had been ordered for the next morning to take him to Rastenburg. The Führer was expecting him.

The following morning was just as cold, even though the bright sun gave a deceptive impression of warmth. At the airfield the Luftwaffe officer assigned to fly Behr to East Prussia did not bother to take his gloves with him when he went out to warm up the motors. When he returned to the building he had no skin left on his hands from touching frozen metal. Another pilot had to be found.

Behr finally reached the *Wolfsschanze* in the early evening. His belt and pistol were taken from him at the guardroom. From there, he was escorted to the operations room, where eighteen months later Stauffenberg brought his briefcase filled with explosives. There were between twenty and twenty-five senior officers present. After ten minutes, the doors opened and Hitler appeared. He greeted the young panzer captain.

'*Heil Herr Hauptmann!*'

'*Heil mein Führer!*' replied Behr, rigidly at attention in his black uniform, with the Knight's Cross at the neck. Behr already knew from his brother-in-law, Nicolaus von Below, who was Hitler's Luftwaffe adjutant, what the Führer's tactics were when a 'Cassandra' brought bad news. He always tried to control the conversation, imposing his version of events, and overwhelming his interlocutor, who knew only about a single sector of the front, with a powerful impression of the overall situation. This was exactly what happened.

When Hitler had finished recounting his plans for Operation Dietrich, a great counter-attack with SS panzer divisions turning defeat into victory, he said to Behr: 'Herr Hauptmann, when you return to General Paulus, tell him this and that all my heart and my hopes are with him and his Army.' But Behr, well aware that this was Hitler's 'trick', knew that he must not allow himself to be silenced.

'Mein Führer,' he answered. 'My commander-in-chief gave me the order to inform you of the situation. Please now give me permission to deliver my report.' Hitler, in front of so many witnesses, could not refuse.

Behr began to speak, and Hitler, rather to his surprise, made no attempt to interrupt him. He did not spare his audience any detail, including the growing desertions of German soldiers to the Russians. Field Marshal Keitel, unable to bear such frankness in the Führer's presence, shook his fist at Behr from behind Hitler's back in an attempt to silence him. But Behr continued relentlessly with his description of the exhausted, starving and frozen army, faced by overwhelming odds, and without the fuel or ammunition to repulse the new Russian offensive. Behr had all the figures of the daily deliveries by air in his head. Hitler asked if he was certain of these statistics, and when Behr replied that he was, he turned to a senior Luftwaffe officer and asked him to explain the discrepancy.

'Mein Führer,' replied the Luftwaffe general, 'I have here the list of planes and cargoes dispatched per day.'

'But mein Führer,' Behr interrupted. 'For the Army, what is important is not how many planes were sent out, but what we actually receive. We are not criticizing the Luftwaffe. Their pilots really are heroes, but we have received only the figures I have told you. Perhaps some companies retrieved odd canisters and kept them, without notifying their headquarters, but not enough to make a difference.'

Some senior officers tried to deflect Behr's criticisms with 'idiotic questions', but Hitler proved surprisingly helpful, probably because he wanted to appear to defend the interests of the *Stalingradkämpfer* against the general staff. But when Behr came to the situation facing the Sixth Army, Hitler turned back to the great map dotted with little flags as if nothing had changed. Behr knew that these flags, 'the same as months before', now represented 'divisions with only a few hundred men left'. Yet Hitler once again resorted to his message of reversing the whole situation by a brilliant counterstroke. He even proclaimed that a whole SS Panzer Army was already grouping round Kharkov, poised to strike towards Stalingrad. Behr knew from Field Marshal von Manstein that the SS formations being brought eastwards would need several more weeks. 'I saw then that he had lost touch with reality. He lived in a fantasy world of maps and flags.' For Behr, who had been an enthusiastic and 'nationalistic young German officer', the revelation came as a shock. 'It was the end of all my illusions about Hitler. I was convinced that we would now lose the war.'

Behr was not sent straight back to the *Kessel* as planned. He saw Hitler again the next day at noon, with Field Marshal Milch, who was ordered to galvanize Luftwaffe relief efforts to Stalingrad. Behr was later summoned by Hitler's senior military aide, General Schmundt, and subjected to a long and searching, although friendly, interview. Schmundt, one of Hitler's most loyal admirers (he was to die eighteen months later from Stauffenberg's bomb), quickly sensed that the young panzer captain had lost his faith. Behr admitted this openly when the question was put. Schmundt therefore decided that he should not be sent back to Paulus, in case he passed on his misgivings. Behr would return to the Black Sea coast, and work there at Melitopol as part of the new 'Special Staff' to be set up under Field Marshal Milch to help Fortress Stalingrad hold out to the last.

At Rastenburg, General Stieff and also Lieutenant-Colonel Bernhard Klamroth, who knew Behr well from before the war, took him aside and asked – 'in a coded manner' – whether he would join a movement to oust Hitler. Behr, who had only just seen the truth

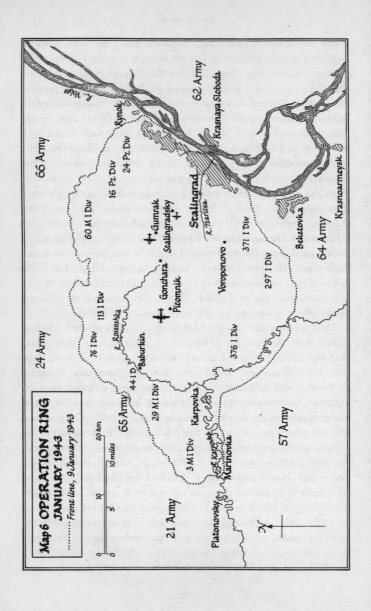

Map 6 OPERATION RING JANUARY 1943

······ Front line, 9 January 1943

R. Volga

66 Army

Rynok

24 Pz Div

16 Pz Div

60 MI Div

62 Army

Krasnaya Sloboda

Stalingrad

24 Army

113 I Div

76 I Div

Rossoshka

Baburkin

44 I D

Gonchara

Pitomnik

Gumrak

Stalingradsky

R. Tsaritsa

371 I Div

Voroponovo

297 I Div

64 Army

Beketovka

Krasnoarmeysk

376 I Div

65 Army

29 MI Div

Karpovka

57 Army

3 MI Div

R. Karpovka

Marinovka

21 Army

Platonovsky

20 km

10 miles

0   5   10   20

N

about Hitler's disastrous leadership, felt that he could not do a complete about-turn. Klamroth understood, but warned him to be careful with Manstein. 'At table he is very much against Hitler, but he just shoots his mouth off. If Hitler were to order him to turn left or right, he would do exactly what he was told.'

Klamroth's criticism was not exaggerated. For all the disrespect Manstein showed for the Führer in private among trusted subordinates and with his dachshund's trick of raising its paw in the Nazi salute, he did not want to risk his own position. In his memoirs, he used what might be called the stab-in-the-back argument: a *coup d'état* would have led to an immediate collapse of the front and chaos inside Germany. He was still part of the officer class, whose anti-Bolshevik loathing had been moulded by the 1918 mutinies and revolution. Behr took Klamroth's advice, and was cautious when he reported back to Army Group Don.

Manstein's fear of Hitler was soon demonstrated. The frank discussions among his own officers about responsibility for the Stalingrad disaster unnerved him so much that he issued an order to his chief of staff that 'Discussions about the responsibility for recent events must cease' because 'they can do nothing to change the facts of the matter and can only cause damage by undermining confidence'. Officers were also strictly forbidden to discuss 'the causes for the destruction of the Sixth Army' in their personal correspondence.

The Führer now wanted, whatever the outcome, a heroic example for the German people. On 15 January, he awarded Paulus the Oak Leaves to his Knight's Cross and announced 178 other important decorations for members of the Sixth Army. Many recipients still failed to recognize how double-edged these honours were.

Manstein, on the other hand, while despising Hitler's motives, knew that he too needed to prolong the agony of the Sixth Army. Every extra day that it held on gave him more time to pull the two armies in the Caucasus back to a defensible line. Hitler, through one of his grotesque twists of logic, could now argue that his decision to order Paulus to maintain his position had been correct.

The madness of events seems to have become slightly infectious.

Max Plakolb, the Luftwaffe officer in charge of the radio operators at Pitomnik, recorded several strange messages of exhortation they received from their own senior commanders. On 9 January, the day that the Soviet ultimatum was proclaimed, Plakolb and another member of his team received orders to fly out of the *Kessel*. 'Taking leave of those staying behind was hard. Each one wrote a letter home, which we took with us.' But like almost everyone escaping the Stalingrad *Kessel* at that time, he experienced a sensation of being born again. 'Thus did this 9 January become my second birthday.' Those escaping, however, were bound to undergo some form of survivor guilt. 'We never heard anything more of those comrades left behind.'

Everyone who had the chance entrusted last letters or small important possessions to comrades allotted a place on the aircraft. The piano-playing battalion commander from 16th Panzer Division had fallen sick, so Dr Kurt Reuber persuaded him to take the 'Fortress Madonna' with him. Reuber also managed to finish a last picture for his wife when his commanding officer's departure was delayed by a day because of bad weather. His last letter to her from Stalingrad went with it. He saw no point in shrinking from the reality of what they faced. 'Scarcely an earthly hope remains . . .'

It was some time before soldiers realized that the Christmas post delivered on 22 December was probably the last they would receive from the outside world. Odd batches came through afterwards, one as late as 18 January, but the regular *Luftpost* effectively ceased after 13 January, when soldiers were told that they had a last chance to write home. Many mentioned in their letters that they only had time 'to scribble a couple of lines'. As a doctor observed in a letter to his father, 'The mood here is very mixed. Some take it very badly, others lightly and in a composed way. It is an interesting study in character.'

The main contrast seems to be between those who wrote to impress their family with the patriotic symbolism of their approaching death, and those who wrote out of love. The latter, unlike the fervent nationalists, usually started their letter as gently as possible: 'Perhaps this will be the last letter from me for a long time.'

A Major von R. wrote to his wife: 'You are always my first and last thought. I am certainly not abandoning hope. Things are, however, so serious, that one does not know whether we will see each other again. Our men have been and still are achieving the impossible. We must not be less brave than them.'

The word 'fate' seems to be about the only word shared equally. 'Dear parents,' wrote a corporal. 'Fate has decided against us. If you should receive the news that I have fallen for Greater Germany, then bear it bravely. As a last bequest, I leave my wife and children to your love.'

Those most devoted to the regime focused far more in a self-important way on national honour and the great struggle, than on family farewells. They wrote of the 'fateful battle of the German nation', while still maintaining that 'our weapons and our leadership are still the best in the world'. In an attempt to derive a meaning from the grotesque tragedy, they buoyed themselves up with the idea that future generations would see them as the defenders of Europe from Asiatic bolshevism. 'This is a heroic struggle, the like of which the world has never experienced in such cold,' wrote a sergeant. 'German heroes guarantee Germany's future.'

These letters were never delivered. Captain Count von Zedtwitz, the chief of Fourth Panzer Army's field-post censorship, had been given the task of studying letters from the Stalingrad *Kessel*, to report on morale and feelings towards the regime. Although his reports bent over backwards to avoid sounding defeatist, it appears that Goebbels ordered that this last collection of post should be held back and eventually destroyed. The above quotations come from a sample apparently copied by Heinz Schröter, a junior officer formerly attached to the Sixth Army's propaganda company, who had been commissioned by the propaganda ministry to write an epic account of the battle.*

Other letters had already been intercepted in a very different way. General Voronov recorded that, on 1 January, 'we heard in the evening

---

* The examples published in an anonymous collection entitled *Last Letters from Stalingrad*, which had a powerful emotional effect when published in 1954, are now considered forgeries.

that a German transport plane had been shot down over our positions. About 1,200 letters were discovered in the wreckage.'

At Don Front headquarters, the department run by Captain Zabashtansky and Captain Dyatlenko went to work with every spare interpreter as well as all the German 'anti-fascists' on the mailbags for three days. They included letters in diary form from General Edler von Daniels to his wife. According to Voronov and Dyatlenko, the latest letter of 30 December revealed much about the weak defences of the 376th Infantry Division on the south-western flank, which tied in with what the NKVD interrogators had managed to find out from prisoners.

Until the final Soviet offensive began on 10 January, the main preoccupation of the Sixth Army remained the same. 'Enemy No. 1 is and always remains hunger!' wrote a doctor. 'My dear parents,' a corporal wrote home pathetically, 'if it's possible, send me some food. I'm so ashamed to write this, but the hunger is too much.'

German soldiers started to take great risks, venturing forward into no man's land to search the corpses of Russian soldiers for a crust of bread or a bag of dried peas, which they would boil in water. Their greatest hope was to find a twist of paper containing salt, for which their bodies ached.

The hunger pains of German soldiers in the *Kessel* were indeed bad, but others suffered far more. The 3,500 Russian prisoners of war in the camps at Voroponovo and Gumrak were dying at a rapidly accelerating rate. Several German officers were deeply shocked to discover during January that these prisoners were reduced to cannibalism, and made verbal reports. When Russian troops reached the camps at the end of January, the Soviet authorities claimed that only twenty men remained alive out of the original 3,500.

The spectacle which greeted the Russian soldiers – to judge by the film taken by newsreel cameras rushed to the spot – was at least as bad as those seen when the first Nazi death camps were reached. At Gumrak, Erich Weinert described the scene: 'In a gully, we found a large heap of corpses of Russian prisoners, almost without clothes, as thin as skeletons.' The scenes, particularly those of the 'Kriegsgefangen-Revier' filmed at Voropovono, may have done much to harden the hearts of the Red Army towards the new defeated.

Many of the thousands of Hiwis still attached to German divisions were starving too. Girgensohn, after carrying out an autopsy on one corpse, told the German officer in charge that this particular Hiwi had indeed died of hunger. This diagnosis 'left him completely astonished'. He claimed that his Hiwis received the same rations as German soldiers.

Many were treated quite well by their German officers, and there are numerous accounts demonstrating mutual trust during the last battle. But by then Russians in German uniform knew that they were doomed. There were no places for them on the aircraft flying out, and the encircling Soviet armies were accompanied by NKVD troops waiting to deal with them.

21

'Surrender Out of the Question'

The front out in the steppe had been comparatively quiet during the first week in January. Most of the time, there had been little more than the dull crack of a sniper's rifle, the odd burst of machine-gun fire, and the distant whistle at night of a signal flare going up: altogether what a lieutenant called 'the usual melody of the front'. After the broadcast and leaflet drops on 9 January, German soldiers knew that the final offensive was imminent. Sentries, shivering uncontrollably, had an even stronger reason to stay awake.

One soldier remarked to a chaplain on his rounds just before the offensive: 'Just a little bit more bread, Herr Pfarrer, then come what may.' But the bread ration had just been reduced to seventy-five grams. They all knew that they would have to face the Soviet onslaught weak from hunger and disease and with little ammunition, even if they did not entirely understand the reason.

There was both a fatalism – 'one spoke about death just like about a breakfast' – yet also a will to believe. Ordinary soldiers believed the stories of the SS Panzer Corps and reinforcements landing by air. In the 297th Infantry Division, soldiers continued to be convinced, 'that the relief force has already reached Kalach . . . the *Grossdeutschland* and the *Leibstandarte* divisions'. A star shell seen to the west was instantly interpreted as a signal from them. Even junior officers were misinformed by their superiors, as a lieutenant told his NKVD interrogator. Right into the first week of January, his regimental commander in the 371st Infantry Division was still telling them: 'Help is close.' The shock was great when they heard 'through informal sources' (presumably Luftwaffe personnel) about the failure of the attempt to rescue them and Army Group Don's retreat to the west.

The NKVD, on the other hand, was soon shaken to discover the number of Russians now fighting for the Germans in the front line at Stalingrad, not just labouring as unarmed Hiwis. German accounts certainly seem to indicate that a considerable proportion of the Hiwis attached to Sixth Army divisions in the *Kessel* were now fighting in the front line. Many officers testified to their skill and loyalty. 'Especially brave were the Tartars,' reported an officer in the factory district of Stalingrad. 'As anti-tank gunners using a captured Russian weapon, they were proud of every Soviet tank they hit. These fellows were fantastic.' Lieutenant-Colonel Mäder's battle group, based on two grenadier regiments from the 297th Infantry Division at the southernmost point of the *Kessel*, contained no fewer than 780 'combat-willing Russians', nearly half his force. They were entrusted with key roles. The machine-gun company had twelve Ukrainians 'who conducted themselves really well'. Their worst problem, apart from lack of food, was the shortage of ammunition. The battle group's nine field guns were rationed to an average of one and a half shells per gun per day.

Operation *Koltso*, or 'Ring', began early on Sunday, 10 January. Rokossovsky and Voronov were at the headquarters of 65th Army when the order 'Fire!' was given over the radio at five past six, German time. Guns roared, bouncing on their chassis from the recoil. *Katyusha* rockets screamed into the sky leaving dense trails of smoke. The 7,000 field guns, launchers and mortars continued for fifty-five minutes in what Voronov described as 'an incessant rolling of thunder'.

Black fountains appeared all over the snow-covered steppe, obliterating the white scene. The bombardment was so intense that Colonel Ignatov, an artillery commander, remarked with grim satisfaction: 'There are only two ways to escape from an onslaught of this character – either death or insanity.' In an attempt to be nonchalant, General Edler von Daniels described it as a 'very unpeaceful Sunday' in a letter to his wife. The grenadier regiment from his division in the front line was in no mood for levity, finding itself extremely vulnerable in its hastily prepared positions. 'The enemy munition reserves', wrote their commander, 'were so huge, that we had never experienced anything like it.'

The south-western protuberance of the *Kessel*, the 'Marinovka nose', defended by the 44th, 29th Motorized and the 3rd Motorized Infantry Divisions, was strengthened at the last moment by part of the 376th. Every regiment was desperately under strength. The 44th Infantry Division had to be reinforced with artillerymen and even personnel from construction battalions. Several tanks and heavy weapons were allotted to the sector. Just behind the pioneer battalion's position were two self-propelled assault guns and an 88-mm anti-aircraft gun. But in the bombardment, the pioneers saw their own battalion headquarters blasted to pieces. 'Nobody came out,' wrote one of them. 'For an hour, a hundred guns of various calibres and Stalin Organs fired away,' wrote a lieutenant in the same division. 'The bunker swayed continually under the bombardment. Then the Bolsheviks attacked in terrifying masses. Three waves of men rolled forward, never flinching. Red banners were borne aloft. Every fifty to a hundred yards there was a tank.'

The *Landsers*, their fingers so swollen from frostbite that they could hardly fit inside the trigger guard, fired from shallow fox-holes at the riflemen advancing across the snowfields with long spike bayonets fixed. Russian T-34s, some carrying infantry like monkeys on the backs of elephants, lurched across the steppe. The high winds which cut through clothing had blasted away the snow, exposing the top of the colourless steppe grass. Mortar shells rebounded off the frozen earth and exploded as air bursts, causing far more casualties. The defences of the 44th Infantry Division were soon smashed, and its survivors, once in the open, were at the mercy of the enemy as well as the elements.

During the afternoon, the 29th and 3rd Motorized Infantry Divisions in the main protuberance of the nose started to find themselves outflanked. In the 3rd Motorized Infantry Division, the replacement soldiers were apathetic. 'Some of them were so exhausted and sick,' wrote an officer, 'and thought only of slipping away to the rear at night, that I could only keep them in their positions at pistol point.' Other accounts suggest that many summary executions were carried out during this last phase, but no figures are available.

Sergeant-Major Wallrawe's scratch company of panzer grenadiers, Luftwaffe troops and 'Cossacks' held out until ten o'clock on the first night, when they received the order to pull back because the enemy had broken past them. They managed to take up a position north of Karpovka station, but were soon pushed back again. 'From this day on, we had neither warm bunker nor warm food nor any peace!' wrote Wallrawe.

These weakened divisions, with little ammunition, stood no chance against the mass attacks of the Soviet 21st and 65th Armies, backed by the ground-attack aircraft of the 16th Air Army. The Germans had fortified Marinovka and Karpovka on the south side of the nose with pillboxes and gun emplacements, but this was of little use with the main thrusts coming from the bridge of the nose. German attempts to counter-attack with odd groups of their remaining tanks and weakened infantry were doomed. The Russians used heavy mortar fire to separate the infantry from tanks, then obliterated the survivors in the open. The Don Front political department hammered home the slogan: 'If the enemy does not surrender, he must be destroyed!'

While the 65th and 21st Armies attacked the 'Karpovka nose' on that first day, the 66th Army attacked the 16th Panzer and the 60th Motorized Infantry Divisions at the northernmost point, where the undulating hills were stained a blackish yellow colour, burned bare by Soviet trench mortars. The remaining tanks of the 2nd Panzer Regiment once again scored hit after hit on waves of T-34s charging across the open, and forced the survivors to withdraw.

Meanwhile, on the southern sector, the 64th Army began to bombard the 297th Infantry Division and the 82nd Romanian Regiment attached to it. Soon after the shelling began, Colonel Mäder received a call from a divisional staff officer: 'Those pigs of Romanians have made a run for it.' The furthest battalion had retreated, leaving a hole half a mile wide on the flank of his battle group. The Russians, spotting the opportunity, sent in tanks, and pushed a hole deep into the line. The position of the whole division was at risk, but its pioneer battalion, led by Major Götzelmann in a semi-suicidal counter-attack, managed to seal the gap for a time.

This partly Austrian division, which had not suffered like those withdrawn across the Don, managed to maintain a robust defence. Over the next two days, it continued to fight off the 36th Guards Rifle Division, the 422nd Rifle Division, two brigades of marine infantry and part of the 13th Tank Corps. When a soldier 'with previous convictions' tried to desert to the Russians, he was shot down by his own comrades before he reached enemy lines. But within a few days, after intense propaganda attempts, more than forty others deserted to the enemy.

The main Soviet effort was concentrated on the advance from the west. By the end of the second morning, 11 January, Marinovka and Karpovka were captured. The victors counted 1,600 German corpses.

As soon as the fighting was over, peasant women appeared as if from nowhere and rushed over to the German trenches to search for blankets, either for their own needs, or as currency. Erich Weinert, accompanying the advancing troops, saw Russian soldiers throwing the files off the backs of trucks captured at a headquarters so that they could use the vehicles themselves. 'Karpovka looks like an enormous jumble sale,' he wrote. But amid the chaos of abandoned and destroyed military material, he saw the results of the terrible opening bombardment. 'The dead are lying, grotesquely twisted, their mouths and eyes still wide open with horror, frozen stiff, with their skulls torn open and their bowels hurled out, most of them with bandages on their hands and feet, still soaked with yellow anti-frostbite ointment.'

The Sixth Army's resistance, when one considers its physical and material weakness, was astonishing. The most telling measure lies in the casualties it inflicted during the first three days. The Don Front lost 26,000 men and over half its tank force. Soviet commanders made little attempt to reduce casualties. Their men provided easy targets, advancing in extended line. Brown clumps of Russian dead littered the snow-covered steppe. (White camouflage suits were reserved mainly for reconnaissance companies and snipers.) The anger of Russian soldiers and officers was vented on their German prisoners, skeletal and lice-infested. Some were shot on the spot. Others died when they were marched off in small columns, and Soviet soldiers sprayed them with machine-gun fire. In one case, the wounded commander of a *shtraf* company forced a captured German officer to kneel before him in the snow, cried out the reasons why he was seeking revenge, then shot him.

During the early hours of 12 January, the Soviet 65th and 21st Armies reached the west bank of the frozen Rossoshka river, thus eliminating the Karpovka nose. Those troops who withdrew, still intending to fight, had to manhandle their anti-tank guns with them. In some cases, Russian prisoners were again used as draught animals, and worked to death. It was so cold and the ground was frozen so hard, General Strecker noted, that 'instead of digging trenches, our soldiers build up defensive snow banks and snow bunkers'. The panzer grenadiers of 14th Panzer Division, 'resisted bitterly, even though they had virtually no more ammunition, out in the open on the frozen steppe'.

Few members of the Sixth Army felt like celebrating Goering's fiftieth birthday that day. The shortage of fuel and ammunition was catastrophic. Sixth Army headquarters was not exaggerating in its signal to General Zeitzler the next morning. 'Munitions coming to an end.' When Wallrawe's mixed group, occupying old Russian positions dug the previous summer, faced another major attack the following morning they could 'open fire only at the closest range because of the lack of ammunition'.

The lack of fuel in this retreat made the evacuation of the wounded more difficult than ever. Incapacitated patients who had been piled in trucks, which then ground to a halt, just froze to death in the open. Those 'soldiers with blue-black faces' who reached Pitomnik airfield were shaken by the scene. 'The airfield', noted a young officer, 'was in chaos: heaps of corpses, which men had carried out of the bunkers and tents which house the wounded, and dumped; Russian attacks; bombardments; Junkers transport planes landing.'

Lightly wounded soldiers and malingerers, appearing like a horde of beggars in rags, tried to rush the aircraft as they landed, in an attempt to board. Unloaded cargo was thrown aside or ransacked for food. The weakest in these hordes were trampled underfoot. The Feldgendarmerie, rapidly losing control of the situation, opened fire on numerous occasions. Many of the badly wounded with legitimate exit passes doubted that they would ever escape from this hell.

Sergeant-Major Wallrawe, meanwhile, had received a shot in the stomach. This was usually a death sentence in the *Kessel*, but he saved himself through determination. Two of his corporals carried him back from their position, and put him on a truck with other wounded. The driver headed straight for Pitomnik airfield. With only two miles left to go, they ran out of fuel. The driver was under orders to destroy the vehicle in such circumstances. He could do nothing for the wounded, who were 'left to their fate'. Wallrawe, despite the intense pain from his wound, knew that he would die unless he made it on to a plane. 'I had to crawl the rest of the way to the airfield. By then night had fallen. In a huge tent I received some medical help. Bombs from a sudden air raid fell among the hospital tents, destroying a number of them.' In the chaos which ensued, Wallrawe managed to get himself on to an outbound 'Ju' at three in the morning.

At Pitomnik a chance coincidence might save a wounded man's life, while hundreds of others were left to die in the snow. Alois Dorner, a gunner with the 44th Infantry Division who had been wounded in the left hand and left thigh by shell splinters, was appalled by the scenes at Pitomnik. 'Here was the greatest misery that I have seen in my whole life. An endless wailing of wounded and dying men . . . most of them had received nothing to eat for days. No more food was given out to the wounded. Supplies were reserved for fighting troops.' (It is hard to tell how far this was official policy. Senior officers at Sixth Army headquarters have strongly denied it, but some subordinate commanders appear to have instituted it on their own authority.) Dorner, who had not eaten since 9 January, was also expecting to die, when in the night of 13 January, the Austrian pilot of a Heinkel 111 passed by and happened to ask where he came from. 'I'm from near Amstetten,' he replied. His fellow Austrian called over another member of his crew, and together they carried Dorner to the plane.

On the northern flank, 16th Panzer and 60th Motorized Infantry Divisions had been beaten back, leaving a dent in that sector, while in Stalingrad itself, Chuikov's 62nd Army attacked the 100th Jäger and the 305th Infantry Divisions, retaking several blocks. Meanwhile, the main Soviet advance from the west continued through driving snow, crushing in the western side of the *Kessel*. The 29th Motorized Infantry Division was effectively wiped out. A lack of fuel forced the 3rd Motorized Infantry Division to abandon their vehicles and heavy weapons and retreat on foot through the thick snow. There was little hope of establishing a new defence line on the open steppe when soldiers did not have the strength to dig in.

The Soviet 65th and 21st Armies pushed on towards Pitomnik, assisted by the 57th and 64th Army's breakthroughs on the southern flank, where the 297th Infantry Division, including Mäder's battle group, was forced backwards. Their right-hand neighbour, Edler von Daniels's 376th Infantry Division, was cut off. Early in the afternoon of 14 January, Sixth Army headquarters signalled: '376 Infantry Division is destroyed. It is probable that Pitomnik airfield will only be usable until 15 January.'

News of Soviet tank attacks now caused 'panzer-fright' in German ranks. There were hardly any anti-tank guns left with ammunition. Nobody had time to reflect on the way they had despised the Romanians for just such a reaction two months before.

At this rather late stage in the battle, Hitler decided that the Sixth Army must be given more help to hold out. His motives were almost certainly mixed. He may have been genuinely shocked to find from Captain Behr how little help was getting through, but he must also have wanted to make sure that Paulus had no excuse for surrender. His solution – a characteristic move triggering great activity for little tangible result – was to establish a 'Special Staff' under Field Marshal Erhard Milch to oversee the air-supply operation. One member of Milch's staff described this belated move as 'Hitler's excuse to be able to say that he had tried everything to save the soldiers in the *Kessel'*.

Albert Speer accompanied Milch to the airfield, when he was setting off to take up his new role. Milch promised to try to find his brother and have him flown out of the *Kessel*, but neither Ernst Speer, nor even the remains of his unit, could be found. They had all disappeared, 'missing presumed dead'. The only trace, Speer recorded, was a letter which came out by air, 'desperate about life, angry about death, and bitter about me, his brother'.

Milch and his staff reached Taganrog believing that they could achieve a great deal, but, as a senior Luftwaffe transport officer wrote, 'one look at the actual situation was enough to convince them that nothing more could be done with the inadequate resources available'.

The morning of 15 January, their first day of work, did not mark an encouraging start. Milch received a telephone call from the Führer demanding that the Stalingrad airlift be increased. As if to underline his efforts, Hitler that day awarded Paulus the Oak Leaves to his Knight's Cross. At lunchtime Goering rang Milch to forbid him to fly into the *Kessel*. Fiebig then reported that Pitomnik had fallen to the Russians (in this he was slightly premature), and that the radio beacons in Gumrak had not yet been set up, which meant that transport aircraft should not be dispatched.

The remaining Messerschmitt 109s flew out of Pitomnik soon after dawn the next morning, when the advancing Russians were in view. Those which diverted to Gumrak airfield landed to find heavy snow, which had not been cleared. At midday, Gumrak also came under artillery bombardment, and the Messerschmitts and Stukas there flew out of the *Kessel* for the last time on Richthofen's orders. Paulus protested in vain.

That day a battalion of the 295th Infantry Division surrendered en bloc. Voronov's leaflet promising correct treatment of prisoners appears to have had some effect. 'It was senseless to run away,' the battalion commander said during his interrogation by Captain Dyatlenko. 'I told my men that we would surrender in order to save lives.' This captain, who had been an English teacher, added, 'I feel very bad because this is the first case of a whole battalion of German troops surrendering.'

Another battalion commander who surrendered later, this one with the 305th Infantry Division in Stalingrad, spoke of the 'unbearable conditions in our battalion'. 'I could not help my men and I avoided meeting them. Everywhere in our regiment I heard soldiers talk of the suffering from cold and hunger. Every day our medical officer received dozens of frostbite casualties. Because the situation was so catastrophic, I considered that surrendering the battalion was the best way out.'

Pitomnik airfield and its field hospital were abandoned with great suffering. Those who could not be moved were left behind in the care of a doctor and at least one orderly, the standard practice in a retreat. The rest of the wounded either limped, crawled or were dragged on sledges along the pitted road of iron-hard ice which led over eight miles to Gumrak. The few trucks left with any fuel were frequently stormed, even when they were already full of wounded. A Luftwaffe captain reported on conditions along the route on 16 January, the day Pitomnik fell: 'Heavy one-way traffic consisting of retreating soldiers, who appear like complete down and outs. Feet and hands are wrapped in strips of blanket.' In the afternoon he recorded a 'considerable increase in stragglers from various arms who had supposedly lost contact with their units, begging for food and shelter'.

At times the sky cleared completely, and the sun on the snow was blinding. As evening fell, the shadows became steel blue, yet the sun on the horizon was a tomato red. The condition of almost all soldiers, not just the wounded, was terrible. They limped on frost-bitten feet, their lips were cracked right open from frost, their faces had a waxen quality, as if their lives were already slipping away. Exhausted men slumped to the snow and never rose again. Those in need of more clothes stripped corpses of clothing as soon as they could after the moment of death. Once a body froze, it became impossible to undress.

Soviet divisions were not far behind. 'It is severely cold,' Grossman noted as he accompanied the advancing troops. 'Snow and the freezing air ice up your nostrils. Your teeth ache. There are frozen Germans, their bodies undamaged, along the road we follow. It wasn't us who killed them. The cold did. They have bad boots and bad coats. Their tunics are thin and look like paper . . . There are footprints all over the snow. They tell us how the Germans withdrew from the villages along the roads, and from the roads into the ravines, throwing their arms away.' Erich Weinert, with another unit, observed crows circling, then landing, to peck out the eyes of corpses.

At one point, on approaching Pitomnik, Soviet officers started to check their bearings, because far ahead they had sighted what appeared to be a small town on the steppe, yet none was marked on their maps. As they came closer, they saw that it consisted of a huge military junkyard, with shot-up panzers, trucks, wrecked aircraft, motor cars, assault guns, half-tracks, artillery tractors and almost every other conceivable item of equipment. The greatest satisfaction for Russian soldiers came from seeing abandoned and shot-up aircraft by the airfield at Pitomnik, especially the giant Focke-Wulf Condors. Their advance eastwards towards Stalingrad produced constant jokes about being 'in the rear of the Russians'.

During this stage of the retreat, German hopes of SS panzer divisions and air-landed reinforcements finally expired for most men. Officers knew that the Sixth Army was indeed doomed. 'Several commanders', recorded a doctor, 'came to us and begged for poison to commit suicide.' Doctors were also tempted by the idea of oblivion, but as soon as they considered it carefully, they knew that their duty was to stay with the wounded. Of the 600 doctors with the Sixth Army, none capable of working flew out.

Casualty clearing stations at this time were so overcrowded that patients shared beds. Often when a severely wounded man was carried in by comrades, a doctor would wave them away because he already had too many hopeless cases. 'Faced with so much suffering,' recorded a Luftwaffe sergeant, 'so many men in torment, so many dead and convinced that there was no possibility of help, without a word we carried our lieutenant back with us. Nobody knows the names of all those unfortunate men who, huddled together on the ground, bleeding to death, frozen, many missing an arm or a leg, finally died because there was no help.' The shortage of plaster of paris meant that doctors had to bind shattered limbs with paper. 'Cases of post-operative shock soared,' recorded a surgeon. Diphtheria cases also increased greatly. The worst part was the growth of lice on the wounded. 'On the operating table we had to scrape lice off uniforms and skin with a spatula and throw them into the fire. We also had to remove them from eyebrows and beards where they were clustered like grapes.'

The 'so-called hospital' at Gumrak was even worse than that at Pitomnik, largely because it was swamped by the influx. 'It was a form of hell,' reported a wounded officer who had retreated from the Karpovka nose. 'The corpses lay in heaps beside the road, where men had fallen and died. Nobody cared any more. There were no bandages. The airfield was under bombardment, and forty men were packed into a bunker dug for ten, which shook with every explosion.' The Catholic chaplain at the hospital was known as the 'Death king of Gumrak' because he was giving extreme unction to over 200 men a day. Chaplains, after closing the eyes of the dead, used to snap off the bottom half of the identity disk as official proof of death. They soon found their pockets heavy.

Doctors nearby also worked in the 'death ravines', with the wounded lying in the tunnels dug out of the side for horses. For one doctor, the place, with its cemetery just above, was Golgotha. This central dressing station and centre for cranial injuries had to be abandoned, with the most severely wounded left behind. When the Russians arrived a few days later, they machine-gunned most of the bandaged figures. Ranke, a divisional interpreter, suffering from a head wound, rose up and yelled at them in Russian. In astonishment, the soldiers stopped shooting and took him to their commissar, who in turn sent him on behind the retreating Germans to demand surrender.

If Russian soldiers were in a mood for vengeance, then the frozen corpses of Red Army prisoners in the open camp nearby provided much to fire their anger. The survivors were so badly starved that when their rescuers gave them bread and sausage from their rations, most died immediately.

*

The *Kessel* would have collapsed far more rapidly if some men had not retained a hard core of belief in the cause for which they were fighting. A Luftwaffe sergeant with the 9th Flak Division wrote home: 'I am proud to number myself among the defenders of Stalingrad. Come what may, when it is time for me to die, I will have had the satisfaction of having taken part at the most eastern point of the great defensive battle on the Volga for my homeland, and given my life for our Führer and for the freedom of our nation.' Even at this late stage, most fighting units continued to show dogged resistance, and there were examples of outstanding courage. General Jaenecke reported that 'an attack by twenty-eight Russian tanks near Bassagino station was halted by a Lieutenant Hirschmann, operating an anti-aircraft gun entirely on his own. He destroyed fifteen T-34s in this engagement.' At this closing stage of the battle, leadership made more difference than ever. Apathy and self-pity were the greatest dangers, both to military order and to personal survival.

On the sectors which had not yet been broken, starving men were too exhausted to go outside the bunker to hide their tears from their comrades. 'I am thinking about you and our little son,' wrote an unknown German soldier in a letter which never reached his wife. 'The only thing I have left is to think of you. I am indifferent to everything else. Thinking about you breaks my heart.' Out in the fire-trenches, men were so cold and weak that their slow, uncoordinated movements made them appear as if they were drugged. Yet a good sergeant would keep a grip on them, making sure that rifles were still cleaned and grenades stocked ready to hand in excavated shelves.

On 16 January, just after the capture of Pitomnik, Sixth Army headquarters sent a signal, complaining that the Luftwaffe was only parachuting supplies. 'Why were no supplies landed tonight at Gumrak?' Fiebig replied that landing lights and ground-control radios were not working. Paulus seemed to be unaware of the chaos at the airfield. The unloading parties were badly organized and the men too weak to work properly – 'completely apathetic', was the Luftwaffe's opinion. Discipline had broken down among the lightly wounded as well as stragglers and deserters drawn to the airfield and its promise of salvation. The Feldgendarmerie 'chain dogs' were starting to lose control over the mobs of starving soldiers, desperate to get away. According to Luftwaffe reports, many were Romanians.

By 17 January, the Sixth Army had been forced back into the eastern half of the *Kessel*. There was comparatively little fighting over the next four days, as Rokossovsky redeployed his armies for the final push. While most German regiments at the front followed orders, disintegration accelerated in the rear. The chief quartermaster's department recorded that 'the Army is no longer in any position to supply its troops'. Almost all the horses had been eaten. There was almost no bread left – frozen solid, it was known as '*Eisbrot*'. Yet there were stores full of food, held back by overzealous quartermasters, which the Russians captured intact. Some of those in authority, perhaps inevitably, exploited their positions. One doctor later described how one of his superiors, right in front of his eyes, 'fed his dog with thickly buttered bread when there was not a single gram available to the men in his dressing station'.

Paulus, convinced that the end was near, had sent a signal on 16 January to General Zeitzler recommending that units which were still battleworthy should be allowed to break out southwards, because to stay in the *Kessel* meant either imprisonment or death through hunger and cold. Even though no immediate reply was obtained from Zeitzler, preparatory orders were issued. The following evening, 17 January, a staff officer with the 371st Infantry Division told Lieutenant-Colonel Mäder that: 'On the codeword "Lion" the whole *Kessel* would fight its way out on all sides. Regimental commanders were to assemble fighting groups of around two hundred of their best men, inform the rest of the line of march, and break out.'

A number of officers had already started to 'consider ways to escape Russian captivity, which seemed to us worse than death'. Freytag-Loringhoven in 16th Panzer Division had the idea of using some of the American jeeps captured from the Russians. His idea was to take Red Army uniforms and some of their very reliable Hiwis, who wanted to escape the vengeance of the NKVD, in an attempt to slip through enemy lines. This idea spread to the staff of the division, including its commander, General Angern. Even their corps commander, General Strecker, was briefly tempted when he heard about it, but as an officer with strong traditional values, the idea of leaving his soldiers was out of the question. One group from XI Corps subsequently made the attempt, and a number of other small detachments, some on skis, broke out to the south-west during the last days of the *Kessel*. Two staff officers from Sixth Army headquarters, Colonel Elchlepp and Lieutenant-Colonel Niemeyer, the chief of intelligence, died out in the steppe.

Paulus clearly never considered the idea of abandoning his troops. On 18 January, when a last post from Germany was distributed in some divisions, he wrote just one line of farewell to his wife, which an officer took out for him. His medals, wedding ring and signet ring were also taken out, but these objects were apparently seized by the Gestapo later.

General Hube received orders to fly out from Gumrak early the next morning in a Focke-Wulf Condor to join Milch's Special Staff. On 20 January, after his arrival, he in turn sent a list of 'trusted and energetic officers' to be sent out to join him. Perhaps unsurprisingly, the majority were not specialists in supply or air transport, but officers from his own panzer corps, especially his old division. Hube, no doubt, felt justified, since Sixth Army headquarters had stipulated that panzer specialists were among those entitled to evacuation by air.

General-Staff-trained officers were also included in the specialist category, but the most curious priority of all was what might best be described as the Sixth Army's Noah's Ark. Sergeant-Major Philipp Westrich from 100th Jäger Division, a tilelayer by trade, was 'flown out of the *Kessel* on 22 January 1943 on the orders of Sixth Army, which requested one man from each division'. Lieutenant-Colonel Mäder and two NCOs were selected from the 297th Infantry Division, and so the list went on, division by division. Hitler, having given up Paulus's Sixth Army for dead, was already considering the idea of rebuilding another Sixth Army – a phoenix's egg snatched from the ashes. On 25 January, the idea became a firm plan. Hitler's chief adjutant, General Schmundt, recorded: 'The Führer decreed the reforming of the Sixth Army with a strength of twenty divisions.'

Officer couriers, taking out vital documents, had been selected on compassionate grounds. Prince Dohna-Schlobitten, who left on 17 January, was given the job for XIV Panzer Corps headquarters, not because he was the chief intelligence officer, but because he had the most children of any officer on the staff. Soon afterwards, Sixth Army headquarters insisted that officers flown out as specialists should double as couriers. Captain von Freytag-Loringhoven, selected because of his record as the commander of a panzer battalion, was ordered first to collect dispatches and other documents from army headquarters. There he saw Paulus, who 'seemed absolutely bent under the responsibility'.

At Gumrak airfield, after a long wait, he went out to one of five Heinkel bombers, escorted by Feldgendarmerie, who had to force back the wounded and sick at the point of their sub-machine-guns. At the moment of leaving the *Kessel*, he inevitably had mixed feelings. 'I felt very badly about leaving my comrades. On the other hand it was a chance to survive.' He had tried to get Count Dohna (a distant cousin of Prince Dohna) out as well, but he had been too sick. Although securely packed into the aircraft, with some ten wounded soldiers, Freytag-Loringhoven could see that they were not out of danger. Their Heinkel remained stationary beside the runway while the other four took off. A pump had jammed during refuelling. Artillery shells began to fall closer. The pilot threw aside the pump, and ran back to the cockpit. They took off, lifting slowly, with their heavy load of wounded, into the low cloud base. At about six thousand feet, the Heinkel suddenly came up out of the cloud and into 'wonderful sunshine', and Freytag-Loringhoven was another who felt as if he 'had been reborn'.

When they landed at Melitopol, ambulances from the base hospital were waiting for the wounded, and a staff car took Freytag-Loringhoven to Field Marshal Manstein's headquarters. He had no illusions about his appearance. He was in 'a very bad state'. Although a tall, well-built man, his weight had fallen to 120 pounds. His cheeks were cavernous. Like everyone in the *Kessel*, he had not shaved for many days. His black panzer overalls were dirty and torn, and his fieldboots were wrapped in rags as a protection against frostbite. Stahlberg, Manstein's ADC, immaculate in his field-grey uniform, was clearly taken aback. 'Stahlberg looked at me and I saw him wondering, "Does he have lice?" – and I certainly did have lice – and he shook hands very cautiously with me.'

Stahlberg took him straight in to see Manstein, who gave him a much more friendly welcome. The field marshal immediately got up from his desk and came round to shake hands without any apparent qualms. He took the dispatches and questioned the young captain closely about conditions in the *Kessel*. Yet Freytag-Loringhoven felt that he was essentially 'a cold man'.

Manstein told Freytag-Loringhoven that he would be attached to Field Marshal Milch's Special Staff established to improve the airlift. He reported first to Colonel-General von Richthofen, who just acknowledged his arrival and said that he was too busy to see him. Field Marshal Milch on the other hand, 'an old Nazi' whom he had not expected to like, proved 'much more human'. He was horrified by Freytag-Loringhoven's appearance. 'My God, look at the state of you!' After asking about the conditions in Stalingrad, Milch said: 'Now you must have good food.'

He gave orders that Freytag-Loringhoven should receive special rations of meat, butter and even honey. The exhausted young panzer commander was then shown to one of the sleeping compartments on the luxury train. 'It was the first time that I had seen a bed in nine months. I did not care about my lice. I threw myself into the white linen and decided to postpone my visit to the delousing station until first thing the next morning. The comfort and the warmth – it was minus twenty-five degrees outside – was an unbelievable contrast.'

Those officers coming out to work on Milch's Special Staff were disorientated at first by their transformation to another world of plenty and possibility. But they still had no clear idea of what could and could not be expected of an airlift. 'Is it possible to fly in tanks one by one?' was one of Hube's questions at his first meeting with Milch.

Milch himself, like anybody who had not set foot inside the *Kessel*, still could not grasp how truly terrible conditions were within. On receiving Paulus's signal on 18 January that the Sixth Army would be able to hold out for only a few days more because they were virtually out of fuel and ammunition, he told Goering in a telephone conversation: 'Those in the Fortress appear to have lost their nerve.' Manstein was of the same opinion, he added. They both seem to have instinctively adopted a policy of personal sympathy for individuals at the same time as they distanced themselves from the horrors suffered by the abandoned army.

The wider implications of the impending disaster were left to Führer headquarters and the propaganda ministry in Berlin. 'The Stalingrad *Kessel* is approaching the end,' Goebbels had declared at his ministerial conference three days before. 'The German press must prepare appropriate coverage of the victorious outcome of this great battle in Stalin's city – if necessary with supplements.' The 'victory' was supposedly one of moral symbolism.

Helmuth Groscurth, Strecker's chief of staff and the most active member of the opposition to the regime in the *Kessel*, was determined that the facts of the disaster be communicated to senior officers to provoke them into action. He arranged a passage out for one of his trusted colleagues, Major Count Alfred von Waldersee. Waldersee was to go straight to army headquarters, at the Bendlerstrasse in Berlin, to see General Olbricht, a senior member of the opposition, and then the retired General Beck, with the message that 'only an immediate strike' against Hitler could now save the Sixth Army. Beck asked Waldersee to go straight to Paris to see General von Stülpnagel and Field Marshal von Rundstedt. Rundstedt's reply was 'so depressing' that Waldersee lost all hope of achieving anything.

Groscurth sent a last letter to his brother on 20 January, the birthday of his daughter Susi – 'who soon will have a father no more, like thousands of other children', he wrote. 'The torment goes on and will get worse by the hour. We are pushed back into the narrowest area. We will, however, fight on to the last round, as ordered, particularly since we are told that the Russians have been killing all prisoners, which I doubt . . . People have no idea what's going on here. Not a single promise is kept.'

Sixth Army headquarters sensed that Milch's staff did not appreciate how bad things were. 'There is not a single healthy man left at the front,' it reported that day, 'everyone is at least suffering from frostbite. The commander of the 76th Infantry Division on a visit to the front yesterday came across many soldiers who had frozen to death.'

The Soviet offensive began again with renewed force on that morning of 20 January. The 65th Army broke through north-west of Gonchara, which was captured that night. Gumrak, only a few miles away, was the main objective.

The evacuation of the airfield and nearby headquarters the following evening was chaotic as *Katyusha* batteries opened up. That night, Milch's staff received a signal from Sixth Army headquarters: 'Gumrak airfield unusable from 22 January at 04.00 hours. At that time the new airfield of Stalingradsky will be clear for landing.' This was optimistic. The landing strip at Stalingradsky was incapable of taking large aircraft. General Paulus was by then entirely fatalistic, and almost certainly suffering from deep depression. A Luftwaffe major just returned from the *Kessel* reported to Field Marshal Milch that Paulus had told him: 'Whatever help arrives from now on will be too late. We have had it. Our men have no strength left.' When the major tried to brief him on the general situation to the west facing Army Group Don, he had replied: 'Dead men are no longer interested in military history.'

Because of the lack of fuel, 500 wounded men were left in the field hospital at Gumrak. As dawn rose on the morning of 22 January, Russian infantry could be seen in the distance, advancing in extended line 'as if on a hare shoot'. As the enemy approached to within rifle range, officers from 9th Flak Division who had been responsible for the airfield packed into the last vehicle, a staff car. A hundred yards down the road they found a soldier from the field hospital, both of whose legs had been amputated, trying to propel himself along on a sled. The Luftwaffe officers stopped, and tied his sled to the back of the car as he requested, but it overturned almost as soon as they started again. One lieutenant suggested that he cling on to the front, since there was no room left inside. The wounded man refused to hold them up any longer. They were by then within range of the Russian infantry. 'Leave me!' he shouted. 'I haven't got a chance anyway.' The Luftwaffe officers knew that he spoke the truth. Anybody who could not walk at this point was already as good as dead. They drove on and the crippled soldier sat slumped in the snow by the side of the icy track, waiting for the Russians to arrive and finish him off.

He may well have been shot, like many wounded by the wayside. The Communist writer, Erich Weinert, attempted to claim that 'abandoned cripples' trying to hobble after their comrades had got in the way of 'the gunfire of the advancing Red Army'. The truth was that the Red Army, like the Wehrmacht, made little provision for enemy wounded. Reports that the 500 left behind in the field hospital at Gumrak in the care of two sick orderlies and a divisional chaplain were massacred are, however, inaccurate. The Red Army just left them to fend for themselves on 'water from snow and horse carcasses'. Those who survived were moved to the camp at Beketovka ten days later.

The spectacle of defeat grew more terrible the closer retreating soldiers came to Stalingrad. 'As far as the eye can see, lie soldiers crushed by tanks, helplessly moaning wounded, frozen corpses, vehicles abandoned through lack of fuel, blown-up guns and miscellaneous equipment.' Meat had been hacked from the flanks of a dead horse beside the road. Men dreamed of coming across a parachute container, packed with supplies, but they had been either seized on landing, or lost in the snowfields.

Although the collapse in the centre could not be stemmed, in many sectors German battle groups carried out a dogged fighting retreat. Early in the morning of 22 January, the remnants of the 297th Infantry Division were pushed back from the Voroponovo sector towards the southern outskirts of Stalingrad. Major Bruno Gebele and the survivors of his battalion awaited the next onslaught. Their only artillery support consisted of several mountain howitzers commanded by a sergeant, who was told to hold his fire until the Russians were between 200 and 250 yards away. Shortly before seven o'clock, as the remnants of Gebele's battalion sheltered from artillery fire in their bunkers, a sentry gave the alert: '*Herr Major, sie kommen!*'

Gebele had time only to yell '*Raus!*' His soldiers threw themselves into their fire positions. A mass of snow-suited infantry was charging towards them, baying '*Urrah! Urrah! Urrah!*' The first ones were only forty yards away when the German grenadiers opened fire with light machine-guns, rifles and machine pistols. The Russians suffered terrible losses. 'The first wave was killed or left lying there, the second also, and then a third wave came. In front of our position the Soviet dead piled up and served as a sort of sandbag wall for us.'

The Russians did not abandon the attack. They simply changed its direction, and concentrated against the flanking detachments. At nine-thirty, they broke through the Romanians over to the left. An anti-tank round hit Gebele's second-in-command, who was standing next to him, killing him instantly. Gebele himself then felt a massive blow to his left shoulder. A bullet from the same burst of machine-gun fire had also killed his chief clerk, Feldwebel Schmidt, having gone straight through his steel helmet. The enraged Gebele, resting a carbine on the snow wall in front of him, was able to get off a few shots, using his good arm and shoulder.

Another wave of Russian infantry came at them. Gebele screamed to his surviving men to open fire again. A staff sergeant tried firing a light mortar, but the range was so short that the headwind made a couple of the bombs fall on their own positions. Eventually, having held out for seven hours, Gebele saw that a Russian flag had appeared on a water tower to their rear. They had been outflanked. He gathered the last survivors of his battalion, and led them back towards the centre of Stalingrad. Inside the city, they were shaken by the scenes of destruction and military collapse. 'It was bitterly cold,' wrote one of them, 'and surrounded by such chaos, it felt as if the world was coming to an end.'

That 22 January – the day after Goebbels had prepared the stage-management of the Stalingrad tragedy by calling for 'total war' – Sixth Army received the signal from Hitler which sealed its fate. 'Surrender out of the question. Troops fight on to the end. If possible, hold reduced Fortress with troops still battleworthy. Bravery and tenacity of Fortress have provided the opportunity to establish a new front and launch counter-attacks. Sixth Army has thus fulfilled its historical contribution in the greatest passage in German history.'

22

'A German Field Marshal Does Not Commit Suicide with a Pair of Nail Scissors!'

Whenever Luftwaffe planes flew over, men looked up longingly, and continued to stare at the sky well after the tiny dot had disappeared. 'With heavy hearts', wrote one soldier, 'we gazed after the German aircraft and thought how wonderful it would be to be able to fly away, out of this inferno in which we had been abandoned.' After the capture of Gumrak airfield early on the morning of 22 January, only a handful of planes had managed to land at the small Stalingradsky landing strip. The 'air-bridge', and thus the last line of escape, had collapsed.

Resupply now depended on canisters dropped by parachute, 'the supply bombs', but despite Sixth Army's requests for red canopies, the Luftwaffe continued to use white. The system of drops became even more hit-and-miss, because few units had any recognition panels left and VIII Air Corps lost radio contact with Sixth Army head-quarters on 24 January. Hube had a message dropped telling soldiers in the ruins of Stalingrad that, on hearing aero-engines, they should lie down on the snow-covered ground in the form of a cross to signify 'German soldiers here'. When the light or visibility was bad, they fired signal flares into the air to direct aircraft as they approached, but the Russians all around would immediately shoot flares of similar colour into the sky to confuse the pilots. Strong winds also blew many loads across the rapidly changing front lines into enemy hands. Some men were so desperate that they risked trying to retrieve canisters right out in the open. Russian snipers picked them off with ease. In the ruins of Stalingrad, starving German soldiers attempted to ambush Soviet soldiers just to get their bread bag.

The fall of Gumrak had meant yet another terrible journey for the wounded, many of whom had already been transferred from Pitomnik, having failed to find a place on an aeroplane there. 'Exhausted wounded men dragged themselves to the ruins of the town', one survivor reported, 'crawling like wild animals on all fours, in the hope of finding some sort of help.'

The conditions in Stalingrad in the makeshift hospitals were even more appalling than at Gumrak, with around 20,000 wounded packed into cellars under the ruins of the city, to say nothing of the sick, which may well have brought the total to 40,000. Some 600 badly wounded men filled the cellars of the Stalingrad theatre, with no light and no sanitation. 'Moans, calls for help and prayers', wrote a doctor from the 60th Motorized Infantry Division, 'were mixed with the thunder of the bombardment. A paralysing smell of smoke, blood and the stench of wounds filled the room.' There were no more bandages, no medicine, and no clean water.

A number of doctors from front-line units received orders to help out in the network of tunnels in the Tsaritsa ravine. This complex, like galleries in a mine, now contained over 3,000 seriously wounded or seriously ill soldiers. Dr Hermann Achleitner, on arriving for duty, was reminded immediately of the phrase: 'Abandon hope all ye who enter here.' The piles of frozen corpses outside shocked him deeply. Inside, the image of hell was increased by improvised oil lamps as the only source of light. The fetid, deoxygenated air was disgusting to breathe. He was greeted by pitiful cries of 'Give us something to eat!' The patients received only one thin slice of stale bread per day. The doctors turned this into a sort of soup, which was hot and made it go a little further. The lack of bandages was serious for the cases of severe frostbite. 'Often', he noted, 'toes and fingers stayed behind in the filthy old bandages, when we changed them.' Delousing was impossible. Medical orderlies changing bandages found a grey mass of lice crawling on to their own wrists and arms from the patient. When a man died, the lice could be seen leaving his body en masse in search of living flesh. The doctors did what they could to isolate cases of typhus as soon as it was diagnosed, but they knew that it would not be long before they had an epidemic on their hands. A young German soldier, surveying the misery around, was heard to murmur: 'They must never know at home what is happening here.'

The retreat from the steppe, as the *Kessel* was crushed by Rokossovsky's armies, brought the number of Germans crowded into the ruined city to over 100,000 men. Many, if not most, of them were suffering from dysentery, jaundice and other sicknesses, their faces tinged a greenish yellow.

The reactions of Stalingrad civilians were not always hostile, as wounded men from the 297th Infantry Division discovered. 'Two Stalingrad women rubbed my frozen legs for an hour to prevent the effects of severe frostbite,' wrote an officer. 'Again and again, they looked at me with compassion and said: "So young and yet he must already be dying!"' The same group of soldiers, to their astonishment, found several Russian women in a partly wrecked house. They had just baked some bread, and agreed to exchange a loaf for a hunk of frozen horsemeat.

Regiments and divisions were utterly meaningless. The 14th Panzer Division had fewer than eighty men still able to fight. Hardly a single tank or heavy weapon with ammunition remained. In such a hopeless situation, discipline was starting to break down. Resistance continued largely through fear of Russian revenge, following Paulus's rejection of surrender.

Unthreatened by anti-tank guns, Soviet T-34s crushed German weapon pits and gunners alike under their tracks. Bunkers and fortified buildings were destroyed with a field gun wheeled up to almost point-blank range. German soldiers now suffered a terrible sense of powerlessness, unable to do anything for their wounded comrades or even for themselves. Their own merciless advances of the previous summer seemed to belong to an entirely different world. On 25 January, Paulus and Colonel Wilhelm Adam, one of his senior staff officers, received light head wounds from a bomb explosion. General Moritz von Drebber surrendered with part of the 297th Infantry Division three miles south-west of the mouth of the Tsaritsa. The

Soviet colonel who came to take his surrender is said to have demanded: 'Where are your regiments?' Moritz von Drebber, according to this version broadcast two days later on Soviet radio by the novelist Theodor Plievier, another German Communist of the 'Moscow Emigration', glanced around at the remaining handful of men, broken by exhaustion and frostbite, and replied: 'Do I really have to explain to you, Colonel, where my regiments are?'

The chief medical officer of the Sixth Army, General Renoldi, was one of the first generals to give himself up. (Red Army intelligence first heard as a result of his interrogation that Paulus was in a state of collapse.) Some generals, however, took an active role. Hube's replacement, General Schlömer, was shot in the thigh, and General von Hartmann of the 71st Infantry Division was killed by a bullet through the head. General Stempel, the commander of the 371st Infantry Division, shot himself, as did a number of other officers as the enemy seized the south of Stalingrad up to the Tsaritsa river.

On 26 January at dawn, tanks of the 21st Army met up with Rodimtsev's 13th Guards Rifle Division north of the Mamaev Kurgan, near the Red October workers' settlements. The scenes were predictably emotional, especially for Chuikov's 62nd Army, which had been fighting on its own for almost five months. 'The eyes of the hardened soldiers who met were filled with tears of joy,' wrote Chuikov. Bottles were passed back and forth in fierce celebration. The Stalingrad *Kessel* was split in two, with Paulus and most of the senior officers bottled up in the smaller, southern pocket, and General Strecker's XI Corps in the northern part of the city round the Stalingrad tractor factory. His only link with the outside world was the 24th Panzer Division's radio set.

Over the next two days, German and Romanian stragglers, the wounded and shell-shocked, as well as still-active combat groups, all withdrew into the ever-diminishing southern pocket, where Paulus and Schmidt had set up new headquarters, under the Univermag department store on Red Square. The last symbol of German occupation was the swastika banner hanging from a makeshift flagpole fastened to the balcony above the main entrance. The remains of Colonel Roske's 194th Grenadier Regiment provided its defending force. Roske was promoted to General as the new commander of the extinct 71st Infantry Division.

The increasing number of senior officers who were surrendering meant that Don Front's 7th Department, responsible for 'operational propaganda', was busier than ever. So many prisoners had been brought in for interrogation since the offensive started that it had been hard to select the 'more interesting' ones.

Captain Dyatlenko received a signal ordering him to return immediately to Don Front headquarters. Another captured German general had already been brought in for interrogation. Dyatlenko knew it was worth spending time on this new arrival, General Edler von Daniels. The search through the mailbags of the crashed transport aeroplane at the beginning of the month had produced the letters in the form of a diary which Daniels had written to his wife. Daniels, like most newly captured prisoners, was in a vulnerable state. As an experienced interrogator, Dyatlenko knew that the best tactic was the least expected one. He questioned his prisoner obliquely about his 'Kessel-baby', then took him off balance by suddenly producing the letters and papers which Daniels thought were safely back in Germany.

'Herr General,' Dyatlenko records having said to him. 'Please have your papers back. This is your property and you can put it in your family archive when you return home after the war.' Apparently Daniels was overcome with gratitude. He accepted tea and biscuits and Russian cigarettes, and then 'answered our questions'. Dyatlenko kept at him until evening. After a break for dinner, he carried on until midnight.

On many occasions, such a refined approach was not necessary. The psychological confusion and the anger of defeat, produced docility if not cooperation from officers who felt both personally betrayed, and also guilty towards their own men for having assured them of the Führer's promises of salvation. During interrogation, they often made a point of uttering derogatory remarks against Hitler and the regime. They called Goebbels 'the lame duck' and bitterly regretted that the overweight Goering had not undergone a 'Stalingrad diet'. But it certainly appeared to their Russian captors that these generals had recognized the real character of their Führer only when they experienced the treacherous way in which he had behaved towards them and the Sixth Army. Few of them had described him or his policies as criminal when they were advancing deep into Russia and atrocities were being committed so close behind their front lines that they must have been aware of them, if not in some cases directly responsible.

From these interviews with captured officers, Don Front headquarters formed the firm impression that Paulus 'was under great strain, playing a role that had been forced on him'. They were increasingly convinced that Paulus was virtually a prisoner in his own headquarters, guarded by his chief of staff. Dyatlenko had no doubt that Schmidt was 'the eyes and hand of the Nazi Party' in the Sixth Army, because captured officers reported that 'Schmidt was commanding the Army and even Paulus himself'.

Colonel Adam, when interrogated later by Dyatlenko, told him that Schmidt had been the one who gave the order for the truce envoys to be sent back. (Dyatlenko did not reveal that he had been one of them.) The senior officers at Sixth Army headquarters had apparently been well aware of the contents of the oilskin pouch. On that morning of 9 January, when Dyatlenko and Smyslov waited in the bunker, they had read during breakfast the leaflets dropped by Russian planes with the text of the ultimatum. That same morning, General Hube had flown back into the *Kessel* from his visit to Hitler. He had brought the order that there was to be no surrender. According to Adam, this had strengthened General Schmidt's intransigent position at Sixth Army headquarters.

On 29 January, the eve of the tenth anniversary of Hitler's accession to power, Sixth Army headquarters sent a signal of congratulation from its ruined cellar. 'To the Führer! The Sixth Army greet their Führer on the anniversary of your taking power. The swastika flag still flies over Stalingrad. May our struggle be an example to present and future generations never to surrender in hopeless situations so that Germany will be victorious in the end. *Heil mein Führer!* Paulus.'

This signal, grotesque in the circumstances, seems more likely to have been drafted and sent by General Schmidt. The words certainly had his ring to them. Paulus, at that stage, was ill from dysentery, shaken by events and demoralized, so it is not hard to imagine him just giving a nod of approval when shown the message form. Groscurth, for example, had reported in a letter not long before: 'Paulus is in a state of physical and moral disintegration.'

On 30 January, the anniversary itself, Goering made a broadcast from the air ministry, comparing the Sixth Army to the Spartans at Thermopylae. This speech was not well received in Stalingrad, where it was listened to on radios. The fact that it was Goering, of all people, who was delivering 'our own funeral speech', heaped insult upon injury. Gottfried von Bismarck described the effect as 'macabre'. In the theatre cellars in Stalingrad, which were packed with wounded, Goering's voice was instantly recognized. 'Turn it up!' somebody shouted. 'Switch it off!' yelled others, cursing him. The broadcast finished with Bruckner's Fifth Symphony. Some officers joked bitterly that the 'suicide of the Jews' on the top of Masada might have been a more appropriate comparison than Thermopylae. They did not realize quite how accurate they were. Hitler was indeed counting on a mass suicide, above all of senior officers.

Hitler's own speech was delivered by Goebbels later on that anniversary day, having been delayed by RAF bombers. It rang with bitter defiance, but the streak of self-justification was too raw to be hidden. He devoted only a single sentence to Stalingrad, the disaster which cast such a shadow over the regime's day of celebration: 'The heroic struggle of our soldiers on the Volga should be an exhortation to everyone to do his maximum in the struggle for Germany's freedom and our nation's future, and in a wider sense for the preservation of the whole of Europe.' It was the first admission that from then on the Wehrmacht would be fighting to stave off defeat.

The next day, Hitler, as if to offset any sense of disaster, created no fewer than four new field marshals, including Paulus. It was the largest group of senior promotions since the victory over France. When the signal came through announcing his promotion to General Field Marshal, Paulus guessed immediately that he had been presented with a cup of hemlock. He exclaimed to General Pfeffer at his last generals' conference: 'I have no intention of shooting myself for this Bohemian corporal.' Another general told his NKVD interrogator that Paulus had said: 'It looks like an invitation to commit suicide, but I will not do this favour for him'. Paulus instinctively disapproved of suicide. When he heard that some of his men were choosing a 'soldier's suicide' – standing on top of their trenchworks waiting to be shot down by the enemy – he gave orders to forbid the practice.

Hitler was not, of course, concerned with saving lives, he was interested only in creating potent myths. He clearly hoped that senior army officers would follow the example of Admiral Lütjens on the *Bismarck*, a fantasy no doubt encouraged by news of the deaths of Generals von Hartmann and Stempel.

The reduction of the southern pocket continued rapidly. By 30 January, Soviet troops had penetrated right to the very centre of the city. In the cellars where the main mass of Germans sheltered from the cold and the artillery fire, there was a mood of despair and dread anticipation. In the old NKVD headquarters, the winter sky was visible through the smashed dome. The stone floor was covered with rubble and fallen masonry, and the cage-like structure of stairs and railings was twisted. A red-cross flag outside the entrance enraged a German infantry officer, who saw it as a signal of surrender. He went down to the cellar, where the doctors continued to operate in the light of a field-hospital gas-lamp, while they waited for the Russians to arrive. Gaunt and wild-eyed, the officer threatened them with his sub-machine-gun. 'What's going on here? There'll be no surrender! The war goes on!' Many men were unbalanced by battle stress or hallucinations due to severe malnutrition. The cellars were filled with men raving in delirium. Dr Markstein, a Danziger, just shrugged. 'This is a dressing station,' he said. The deranged warrior did not shoot them, he disappeared ghost-like back into the gloom without another word.

When General von Seydlitz, in the same building, released his divisional commanders on 25 January to decide for themselves whether or not to surrender, Paulus relieved him of his command. He placed all of Seydlitz's divisions under General Walter Heitz, the commander of VIII Corps. Heitz then issued an order that anyone who attempted to surrender should be fired upon. When Seydlitz and over a dozen other officers surrendered – they included Generals Pfeffer, Korfes and Sanne – bursts of machine-gun fire were aimed at them from German lines as the Russians led them away. Seydlitz claimed later that two German officers were mortally wounded as a result of Heitz's 'apocalyptic order'.

General Heitz, however, having given the order 'We fight to the last bullet but one', does not appear to have included himself and his headquarters in this rhetorical flourish. An officer under his command remarked that his staff, almost certainly with his knowledge, had already prepared white flags.

Colonel Rosenfeld, the Luftwaffe commander of 104th Flak Regiment, adopted the rhetoric expected by the regime. 'The swastika flag flies above our heads,' he signalled on the evening of 30 January. 'The order of our supreme commander-in-chief will be followed to the last. Long live the Führer.' That night Sixth Army headquarters sent a signal, warning that individual commanders were surrendering because their troops had no more ammunition, but also adopted similar flourishes to those of Rosenfeld, claiming that they were 'listening to the national anthem for the last time with arms raised in the German salute'. Again, this sounds more like Schmidt's style than that of Paulus. Whatever the truth, few soldiers had either the wish or the energy to share such emotions. 'During that night of 30 January', recorded a sergeant, 'each man was preoccupied with his own thoughts, with gnawing uncertainty, with painful wounds and frostbite, with thoughts of home, and with our fate.' Officers especially expected execution. Many removed their badges of rank.

In the middle of that same night, General Voronov in his *izba* at Don Front headquarters awoke in a panic from a restless sleep. The idea had suddenly come to him that Paulus might escape on an aircraft landing on the ice of the Volga. Stalin's reaction to the loss of such a prize was evidently not hard to imagine. He jumped out of bed at once and telephoned to give orders for guns along the east bank at Stalingrad to be trained on the ice as a precaution.

By early next morning, 31 January 1943, Shumilov's 64th Army had secured virtually all of the centre of Stalingrad. Ruined buildings and cellars had been cleared with grenade and flame-thrower. Red Square was subjected to an intense mortar and artillery bombardment, before Russian soldiers moved in on the Univermag department store. Roske's remaining grenadiers above Paulus's headquarters in the basement finally laid down their weapons. At 7.35 a.m., Captain Behr on Milch's staff received the signal: 'Russians at the entrance. We are preparing to surrender.' Ten minutes later, as Senior Lieutenant Fyodor Ilchenko went down into the packed and stinking basement, came the signal: 'We are surrendering.' Behr then passed on the message to Manstein's headquarters at Army Group Don. Back in Germany, the official communiqué announced: 'In Stalingrad the situation is unchanged. The defenders' spirit is unbroken.'

Staff officers from General Shumilov's headquarters arrived to discuss surrender terms with General Schmidt in the basement. Paulus remained in an adjoining room, while Adam kept him informed of every step. Whether this was a ploy to allow Paulus to distance himself from the surrender, or a further example of Schmidt handling events because Paulus was in a state of virtual collapse, is not clear. Finally, two hours after Lieutenant Ilchenko's appearance, General Laskin arrived to take Paulus's formal surrender, before he, Schmidt and Adam, were taken to Shumilov's headquarters by staff car, as General Roske had apparently insisted. Like their men, the three men who emerged into the sunlight had incipient beards, even if their faces were not quite as cadaverous as those of their soldiers. Colonel Adam, Vasily Grossman noted, had the flaps of his *ushanka* fur hat down 'like the ears of a pedigree dog just out of the water'. Newsreel cameramen were waiting to record the event.

Those still in the cellars of the city centre waited until Red Army soldiers appeared. Waving the barrels of their sub-machine-guns, they ordered the Germans to throw their weapons in a corner and file out. The defeated made ready for captivity by wrapping the rags from torn-up uniforms round their boots. Some German soldiers called out *'Hitler kaputt!'* as a signal of surrender. Russian soldiers might reply '*Kameraden, Krieg kaputt! Paulus kapituliert!*', but mostly they shouted '*Faschist!*' or '*Fritz! Komm! Komm!*'

When Soviet troops entered the theatre cellars, they gave the order: 'Whoever's capable of walking, get outside to be marched to a prison camp.' Those who set off assumed that the wounded left behind would be looked after. They discovered only later that the Red Army operated on the principle that those prisoners who could not march were finished off where they lay.

In one or two cases, rage and despair produced an explosive mixture. In the NKVD building, every German expected to be shot in reprisal, after an officer, who had concealed his pistol, suddenly shot a Russian major at point-blank range, then turned the gun on himself. Somehow the moment of anger among the Russian troops passed, and the prisoners were spared.

The surrender at Stalingrad produced a volatility in which the fate of a German was utterly unpredictable. Soviet soldiers, whether deliberately or by accident, set fire to the improvised hospital full of wounded in the pioneer barracks by the airfield. Two Luftwaffe flak officers, who had been escorted to an upstairs room by Russian soldiers, in the belief that the red patches on their collars signified high rank, escaped by jumping out of a shattered window. They landed by the latrine, and when soldiers appeared ready to shoot them, the younger lieutenant saved both their lives by quick thinking and acute psychology. He told his companion to pull down his trousers. The Russians laughed and spared them. They could not shoot men with their trousers down.

The NKVD Special Department groups were searching for Hiwis and also for 'fascist dogs', by which they meant 'SS, Gestapo, panzer troops, and Feldgendarmerie'. A number of German soldiers, wrongly identified as SS, who laughed at the suggestion, were pushed to one side and executed with sub-machine-guns. Apparently Red Army soldiers from a Siberian division turned away in disgust from the spectacle. The same account, based on the interrogation six months later of a woman Soviet intelligence officer by the Secret Field Police, records the execution of a group of twenty-three Hiwis.

The NKVD's search for Hiwis was relentless. Any man not in full

German uniform risked being shot on the spot, as one battalion commander from the 297th Infantry Division discovered. 'Soviet soldiers suddenly stopped us, and because of my lack of uniform and cap, wanted to shoot me as a "Hiwi". Only a doctor's knowledge of Russian saved me.'

A considerable number of Hiwis proved loyal to the Germans right to the end. In the ruins of Stalingrad just before the surrender, some soldiers from the 305th Infantry Division were starving. The Hiwis with them disappeared, and they thought that they had seen the last of them, but the Russians returned with food for them. Where they had found it, they would not say. The loyalty of these Russians was not always reciprocated, however. Shortly before the surrender, one officer was asked by his warrant officer: 'What shall we do with our eight Hiwis? Should I shoot them?' The lieutenant, taken aback at such cold-bloodedness, rejected the idea. He told the Hiwis to hide or slip out as best they could. They were on their own.

The fate of the Hiwis rounded up at the end of the battle of Stalingrad is still unclear, partly because the files of the 10th NKVD Division remain firmly closed. There is no way of knowing how many had died during ten weeks of encirclement and the last three weeks of intense fighting. Some were shot on capture, a handful were used as interpreters and informers, then almost certainly killed later, but most were marched off by the NKVD. Even members of Red Army intelligence did not know what happened to them afterwards. They may well have been massacred – there were accounts later of captured Hiwis being beaten to death, rather than shot, to save ammunition – but in the early part of 1943 the Soviet regime wanted to increase its force of slave labour, especially when it was transferring Gulag prisoners to *shtraf* companies. A solution of working Hiwis to death certainly offered a more vicious revenge since it would have protracted their suffering. On the other hand, both Stalin and Beria were so obsessed with treason that only instant death might have satisfied them.

During the last few days of the battle, the Soviet military authorities were increasingly anxious to prevent small groups escaping their net.

Three German officers in Red Army uniform, led by a lieutenant-colonel, were captured on 27 January. A Russian lieutenant from a tank regiment cornered another two officers, and was wounded when they fired at him. Of the nine or ten groups of Germans estimated to have broken out of the ring, none of them appear to have escaped, but by then Army Group Don had been forced back beyond the river Donets, over 200 miles from the *Kessel*. There is, however, an unconfirmed and unconvincing story of a soldier who did make it, but was killed next day when a bomb hit the field hospital in which he was being treated for exhaustion and frostbite. Others are said to have tried to escape southwards out into the steppe and seek shelter with the Kalmyks, who had been friendly, but the Kalmyks themselves, like numerous other peoples from the southern regions of the Soviet Union, soon attracted the revenge of Beria's NKVD.

Russian soldiers from front-line units, especially Guards divisions, are said to have been more correct in their treatment of the vanquished than second-line units. But some drunken soldiers, celebrating victory, shot prisoners, despite orders to the contrary. Even members of elite formations rapidly stripped their captives of watches, rings and cameras, as well as the Wehrmacht's highly prized mess tins in aluminium. Many of these items would then be bartered for vodka. In some cases a decent pair of jackboots would be seized off a prisoner, who would be thrown the Russian's decrepit cast-offs in return. One doctor lost his prized copy of *Faust*, a small leather-bound edition printed on onion paper, which a Russian soldier wanted for rolling *makhorka* cigarettes. Blankets were also snatched off backs, sometimes just for the satisfaction of revenge because the Germans had taken the warm clothes of so many Russian civilians.

As the gaunt prisoners stumbled out of cellars and bunkers, their hands held high in surrender, their eyes searched for a piece of wood that could serve as a crutch. Many were suffering from such bad frostbite that they could hardly walk. Almost everyone had lost toenails, if not toes. Soviet officers observed that the Romanian soldiers were in an even worse state than the Germans. Apparently their rations had been cut off earlier in an attempt to maintain German strength.

The prisoners kept their eyes down, not daring to look at their guards or the ring of emaciated civilians who had emerged from the ruins in such astonishing numbers. All around, odd shots broke the silence of the former battlefield. Those in bunkers sounded muffled. Nobody knew whether each report signified the end of a soldier found hiding, of one who had offered resistance in some way, or of a severely wounded soldier receiving the *coup de grâce*.

These defeated remnants of the Sixth Army, without weapons or helmets, wearing woollen caps pulled down or even just rags wrapped round their heads against the hard frost, shivering in their inadequate greatcoats fastened with signal cable as a belt, were herded into long columns of march. A group of survivors from the 297th Infantry Division was confronted by a Russian officer, who pointed at the ruins around and yelled at them: 'That's how Berlin is going to look!'

Field Marshal Paulus, accompanied by Lieutenant Lev Bezyminsky of Red Army intelligence, was driven from 64th Army headquarters in his own staff car to Don Front headquarters outside Zavarykino, some fifty miles from Stalingrad. Schmidt and Adam followed under escort in another car. They were shown to their quarters, another five-walled *izba*. A permanent guard detachment under Lieutenant C. M. Bogomolov awaited them. The other 'Stalingrad generals' were brought to another *izba* close by, where they were watched by Lieutenant Spektor and a platoon of men.

Bogomolov and his men, keenly conscious of the historic moment, eyed their charges with fascination. The tall Paulus had to duck low on entering. Following Adam's example, he had abandoned his dress cap for an *ushanka* fur hat. He still wore the uniform of a colonel-general. Paulus was followed by General Schmidt and Colonel Adam, who impressed the guards by his 'rather good command of Russian'. Paulus's soldier driver came last carrying their heavy suitcases. The Mercedes staff car was promptly appropriated by General W. I. Kazakov, the Front artillery commander.

Paulus and Schmidt occupied the inner room of the *izba*, while Colonel Adam and the escort were quartered in the outer room. They were joined by two NKVD agents sent from Moscow by Beria. Late in the evening, General Malinin, the front chief of staff, and Colonel Yakimovich, a senior staff officer, arrived. Bezyminsky, acting as interpreter, informed Paulus and Schmidt that their task was to search their luggage for 'forbidden articles', which included all sharp metal objects. Schmidt exploded. 'A German Field Marshal', he yelled, 'does not commit suicide with a pair of nail scissors!' Paulus, who was exhausted, signalled to him with a wave of the hand not to bother, and handed over his shaving kit.

Shortly before midnight, Paulus was told that the Red Army commanders were now assembled and waiting to interview him. Lieutenant Yevgeny Tarabrin, the German-speaking NKVD officer sent to escort him everywhere, heard Paulus whisper to Schmidt, as he helped him into his overcoat: 'What should I say?'

'Remember you are a General Field Marshal of the German Army,' Schmidt is said to have hissed back. More surprising, and most significant to the ears of Red Army intelligence, the Russian officer reported that Schmidt used the *du* intimate form of address to his superior.*

Only half an hour before the meeting began, Captain Dyatlenko of the NKVD received orders to report to the *izba* used by Marshal Voronov, who had just been promoted by Stalin. 'So Captain,' Voronov greeted him affably. 'You no doubt remember the time the old man didn't want to receive you. Well, now he's visiting us himself. And you're going to receive him.'

Voronov was sitting at the table with General Rokossovsky, the front commander, and General K. F. Telegin, the front commissar. A photographer appeared wearing a fur-lined flying jacket. To Dyatlenko's astonishment, he treated Voronov with relaxed familiarity. It transpired that this was the famous documentary film-maker Roman Karmen, who had become friendly with Voronov during the Spanish Civil War. Karmen lined up the chair destined for Paulus, to get the right shot through the door from Voronov's bedroom. He knew that

---

* Winrich Behr, who knew Schmidt well, thinks this use of *du* highly unlikely although he considered that 'there is no doubt that General Schmidt built up a strong influence over Paulus'.

the result was to be used to tell the world of the Soviet Union's great victory.*

The atmosphere was tense in Voronov's *izba* when their 'guest' arrived. The tall, thin, stooping Paulus presented a grey figure, with his 'mouse-coloured' uniform and face ashen from nervous strain. His hair was turning to 'pepper and salt', and even the growth of beard was black and white. Only when Paulus approached the table did Voronov indicate the empty chair. 'Sit down, please,' he said in Russian. Dyatlenko jumped to his feet, and interpreted. Paulus made a half-bow and sat down. Dyatlenko then introduced the two Soviet commanders. 'The Representative of the *Stavka*, Marshal of Artillery Voronov! Commander of the Don Front, Colonel-General Rokossovsky!' Paulus jerked to his feet and made half-bows in each man's direction.

Voronov began to speak, pausing every few moments for Dyatlenko to translate. 'Herr Colonel-General, it is rather late and you must be tired. We have also been working a lot during the last few days. This is why we will now discuss just one problem which is urgent.'

'Excuse me,' Paulus broke in, taking Dyatlenko off balance. 'But I am not a colonel-general. The day before yesterday, my headquarters received a signal saying that I had been promoted to general field marshal. It is also written in my military identity papers.' He touched the breast pocket of his tunic. 'It was not possible, however, to change my uniform in the circumstances.'

Voronov and Rokossovsky exchanged glances of ironical amusement. General Shumilov had already informed Don Front headquarters of Paulus's last-minute promotion.

---

* Karmen's photograph was doctored in Moscow. General Telegin was removed from the print because Stalin considered him insufficiently important for such a historic occasion. (Even Dyatlenko's promotion to major was accelerated for the release of the photograph.) This incident developed into one of those grotesque farces of the Stalinist era. When the photograph appeared across the front of *Pravda*, with his face removed, Telegin was terrified that someone had denounced him for a chance remark. Nothing happened, however, so he thought he was safe, but then, in 1948, he was suddenly arrested on the orders of Abakumov (the head of SMERSH) for no apparent reason.

'So, Herr General Field Marshal', Voronov resumed, 'we are asking you to sign an order addressed to the part of your army which still resists, telling them to surrender to prevent the useless loss of life.'

'It would be unworthy of a soldier!' Paulus burst out before Dyatlenko had finished his translation.

'Is it possible to say', asked Voronov, 'that to save the lives of your subordinates is behaviour unworthy of a soldier when the commander himself has surrendered?'

'I didn't surrender. I was taken by surprise.'

This 'naive' reply did not impress the Russian officers, who were well aware of the circumstances of the surrender. 'We are talking of a humanitarian act,' Voronov continued. 'It will take us only a couple of days or even just a few hours to destroy the rest of your troops who continue to fight on. Resistance is useless. It will only cause the unnecessary deaths of thousands of soldiers. Your duty as an army commander is to save their lives, and this is even more the case because you yourself saved your life by surrendering.'

Paulus, who had been playing nervously with the packet of cigarettes and ashtray laid on the table for his use, shirked the question by sticking to formulae. 'Even if I did sign such an order, they won't obey. If I have surrendered, I automatically cease to be their commander.'

'But a few hours ago you were their commander.'

'Since my troops were split into two groups,' Paulus persisted, 'I was the commander of the other pocket only in theory. Orders came separately from Führer headquarters and each group was commanded by a different general.'

The argument went 'round and round in circles'. Paulus's nervous tic was even more pronounced, and Voronov too, knowing that Stalin was waiting in the Kremlin to hear the result, began to show the strain. His upper lip twitched, the legacy of a car crash in Belorussia. Paulus, in his blocking tactics, even claimed that if he did sign the paper, it would be regarded as a forgery. Voronov replied that, in that case, they would have one of his own generals brought over to witness the signature, and he would be sent into the north *Kessel* with the paper to guarantee its authenticity. But Paulus, however lame his arguments sounded, stuck to his refusal to sign. Voronov finally had to accept that any further attempt to persuade him was useless.

'I must inform you, Herr General Field Marshal,' Dyatlenko translated, 'that by your refusal to save the lives of your subordinates, you are taking on a heavy responsibility for the German people and the future of Germany.' Paulus stared at the wall, depressed and silent. In this 'tormented pose' only the tic in his face indicated his thoughts.

Voronov then brought the interview to a close by asking Paulus if his lodging was satisfactory, and whether he needed a special diet because of his illness. 'The only thing I would like to request,' Paulus replied, 'is to feed the many prisoners of war, and to give them medical attention.' Voronov explained that 'the situation at the front made it difficult to receive and cope with such a mass of prisoners', but that they would do all they could. Paulus thanked him, stood up and gave another half-bow.

Hitler heard the news at the heavily guarded *Wolfsschanze* deep in the East Prussian forest, a place once described by General Jodl as a cross between a monastery and a concentration camp. He did not bang the table this time, he stared silently into his soup.

His voice and anger returned the next day. Field Marshal Keitel and Generals Jeschonnek, Jodl and Zeitzler were all summoned to the Führer's midday conference. 'They have surrendered there formally and absolutely,' said Hitler in angry disbelief. 'Otherwise they would have closed ranks, formed a hedgehog, and shot themselves with their last bullet. When you consider that a woman has the pride to leave, to lock herself in, and to shoot herself right away just because she has heard a few insulting remarks, then I can't have any respect for a soldier who is afraid of that and prefers to go into captivity.'

'I can't understand it either,' replied Zeitzler, whose performance on this occasion makes one wonder about his assurances to Manstein and others that he had done everything to convince the Führer of the true situation regarding the Sixth Army. 'I'm still of the opinion that it might not be true; perhaps he is lying there badly wounded.'

Hitler kept coming back again and again to Paulus's failure to commit suicide. Clearly, it had entirely sullied the myth of Stalingrad in his imagination. 'This hurts me so much because the heroism of so many soldiers is nullified by one single characterless weakling . . . What is Life? Life is the Nation. The individual must die anyway . . . What hurts me most, personally, is that I still promoted him to field marshal. I wanted to give him this final satisfaction. He could have freed himself from all sorrow and ascended into eternity and national immortality, but he prefers to go to Moscow.'

The northern pocket, with the remnants of six divisions under General Strecker, still held out. Strecker, with the headquarters of XI Corps in the Stalingrad tractor plant, signalled: 'Troops are fighting without heavy weapons or supplies. Men collapsing from exhaustion. Freezing to death still holding weapons. Strecker.' His message was robust, but conspicuously avoided Nazi clichés. Hitler, who received the signal after the meeting with Zeitzler, replied late in the afternoon: 'I expect the north *Kessel* to hold out to the last.' To emphasize the point still further, he issued a Führer directive a short time later: 'XI Army Corps must resist to the last to tie down as much enemy strength as possible to facilitate operations on other fronts.'

The four Soviet armies had redeployed rapidly to crush the last pocket. With a concentration of 300 field guns to just over half a mile, the factory district was smashed once again. Any surviving bunkers were destroyed at point-blank range, some with field guns, some with flame-throwers, sometimes with tanks driving right up and sticking their barrel into an embrasure.

Strecker believed that, purely to help Manstein, there was a military purpose served by fighting on, but he utterly rejected any idea of self-destruction for propaganda purposes. In his mind, there was no doubt where the duties of an officer lay, as a conversation with a regimental adjutant shortly before the end showed.

'When the time comes,' the adjutant assured him, 'we will commit suicide.'

'Suicide?' exclaimed Strecker.

'Yes, Herr General! My colonel will also shoot himself. He believes we should not allow ourselves to be captured.'

'Well let me tell you something. You will not shoot yourself, nor will your colonel shoot himself. You will go into captivity along with your men and will do everything you can to set a good example.'

'You mean . . .', the young officer's eyes lit up, 'I don't have to shoot myself.'

Strecker spent most of the night of 1 February at the regimental headquarters of an old friend, Colonel Julius Müller. A single candle burned in one corner of the bunker as the small group present talked about the recent fighting, past friends and the imprisonment ahead. 'No one mentions all the suffering,' Strecker noted, 'no one speaks bitterly.' In the early hours of the morning, Strecker stood up. 'Müller, I have to go,' he said. 'May you and your men go with God.' Strecker was greatly taken with Thomas Carlyle's description of God as 'the true Field Marshal'. No doubt, his vision of heaven was a place of perfect military order.

'We will do our duty, Herr General,' Müller replied as the two men shook hands.

Strecker had already rejected the requests of his divisional commanders to surrender, but at four in the morning of 2 February, Generals von Lenski and Lattmann asked Strecker once more for permission. Strecker refused again. Lenski then said that one of his officers had already left to negotiate terms with the Russians. Strecker saw no point in continuing. He and Groscurth drafted their final signal. 'XI Army Corps has with its six divisions performed its duty down to the last man in heavy fighting. Long live Germany!' It was received by Army Group Don. Strecker asserted later that he and Groscurth had deliberately omitted any acclamation of Hitler, but the version recorded and then sent on to East Prussia ended with 'Long live the Führer!' Somebody must have thought it politic to make the signal more palatable at the *Wolfsschanze*.

When two Russian soldiers appeared looking rather hesitant at the entrance of the command bunker, Groscurth shouted at them to fetch a general. Strecker wrote afterwards that many of their own soldiers were 'only barely alive'.

Foreign journalists were taken on a tour of the factory district a few days later. 'What the normal relief of the terrain had been no one could tell,' wrote the British correspondent, Alexander Werth. 'You wound your way up and down, up and down; what was a natural slope, or what was the side of a dozen bomb-craters that had merged into one, no one could say. Trenches ran through the factory yards; through the workshops themselves; at the bottom of the trenches there still lay frozen green Germans and frozen grey Russians and frozen fragments of human shape, and there were tin helmets, German and Russian, lying among the brick debris, and the helmets were half-filled with snow. There was barbed wire here, and half-uncovered mines, and shell cases, and more rubble, and fragments of walls, and tortuous tangles of rusty steel girders. How anyone could have survived here was hard to imagine.'

The morning of 2 February began with a thick mist, which was later dispersed by sun and a wind which whipped up the powdery snow. As news of the final surrender spread among the 62nd Army, signal flares were fired into the sky in an impromptu display. Sailors from the Volga flotilla and soldiers from the left bank crossed the ice with loaves of bread and tins of food for the civilians who had been trapped for five months in cellars and holes.

Groups and individuals walking about embraced those they met in wonder. Voices were subdued in the frozen air. There was no shortage of figures in the colourless landscape of ruins, yet the city felt deserted and dead. The end was hardly unexpected, or even sudden, yet the Russian defenders found it hard to believe that the battle of Stalingrad had finally come to an end. When they thought about it, and remembered the dead, their own survival astonished them. Out of each division sent across the Volga, no more than a few hundred men survived. In the whole Stalingrad campaign, the Red Army had suffered 1.1 million casualties, of which 485,751 had been fatal.

Grossman looked back over the last five months. 'I thought of the wide dirt road leading to the fishermen's village on the bank of the Volga – a road of glory and death – and the silent columns marching along it in the choking dust of August, in the moonlit nights of September, in the drenching rains of October, in the snows of November. They had marched with a heavy step – anti-tank men, machine-gunners, simple infantrymen – they had marched with a grim and solemn silence. The only sound that had come from their ranks was the clank of their weapons and their measured tread.'

Very little that was recognizable remained from the city which had existed before Richthofen's bombers appeared on that August afternoon. Stalingrad was now little more than a battered and burned skeleton. About the only landmark left standing was the fountain with statues of little boys and girls dancing round it. This seemed an unsettling miracle after so many thousands of children had perished in the ruins all around.

23

'Stop Dancing! Stalingrad Has Fallen'

At midday on 2 February a Luftwaffe reconnaissance aircraft circled over the city. The pilot's radio message was immediately passed to Field Marshal Milch: 'No more sign of fighting in Stalingrad'.

After Voronov and Rokossovsky's first interview with Paulus, Captain Dyatlenko returned to interrogating the other captured generals. Contrary to his expectations, they reacted in very different ways. General Schlömer, who had taken over command of XIV Panzer Corps from Hube, arrived limping on a stick and wearing a Red Army padded jacket. He won over his interrogator with an easy charm and remarks about 'the Corporal uneducated in military problems' and the 'untalented careerists in his entourage'. General Walther von Seydlitz, on the other hand, whom the NKVD 'later discovered to be the most energetic defender of disobedience to the Führer during the encirclement', conducted himself 'in a very reserved way'.

For Stalin, 91,000 prisoners, including twenty-two German generals, were better trophies than flags or guns. Paulus, still in a state of shock, at first refused to appear in front of the journalists brought down from Moscow. 'We have our own rules,' retorted Colonel Yakimovich of Don Front headquarters, with Lieutenant Bezyminsky interpreting. 'You are to do what you are told.' One compromise was, however, permitted. Paulus would not have to answer questions from the journalists, he only had to show himself to prove that he had not committed suicide.

The foreign correspondents were rather surprised by the appearance of the German generals. 'They looked healthy, and not in the least undernourished,' wrote Alexander Werth. 'Clearly, throughout the agony of Stalingrad, when their soldiers were dying of hunger, they were continuing to have more or less regular meals. The only man who looked in poor shape was Paulus himself. He looked pale and sick, and had a nervous twitch in his left cheek.'

Attempts to put questions were not very successful. 'It was rather like being at the zoo,' wrote Werth, 'where some animals showed interest in the public and others sulked.' General Deboi was clearly keen to please, and immediately told the foreign journalists – 'as if to ask us not to be frightened' – that he was Austrian. General Schlömer was the most relaxed. He turned to one of his captors and, patting the officer's shoulder boards, which had just been reintroduced by Stalin, exclaimed with a comic look of surprise: 'What – new?' General von Arnim, on the other hand, was chiefly preoccupied with the fate of his luggage and what he thought of Red Army soldiers as a result. 'The officers behave very correctly,' he announced, but the soldiers he described as 'impudent thieves!'

The strain of capture also made for undignified behaviour in the two peasant houses at Zavarykino. Adam deliberately provoked Senior Lieutenant Bogomolov one morning with a Nazi salute and a 'Heil Hitler'. Schmidt, however, was the officer most disliked by the Russians. Bogomolov forced him to apologize to a mess waitress whom he had reduced to tears as she served their lunch. A few days later, trouble broke out across the way in the *izba* which housed the other generals. Lieutenant Spektor of guard group No. 2 telephoned Bogomolov, begging him to come quickly. A fight had broken out. 'When I opened the door of the house,' wrote Bogomolov, 'I saw that a German general was grasping the wrist of a Romanian general. When the German saw me, he let go, and then the Romanian hit him in the mouth. It turned out that the quarrel was about the Romanian's knife, fork and spoon, which he claimed that the German had tried to take.' Bogomolov, in contemptuous disbelief, sarcastically warned Lieutenant Spektor 'that if he allowed such behaviour to continue, he too would have his spoon confiscated'.

Latent rivalries and dislikes between generals had come out into the open. Heitz and Seydlitz loathed each other even more after Seydlitz had allowed his divisional commanders to make their own decisions about surrender. Heitz, who had ordered his soldiers to fight to 'the last cartridge but one', had himself surrendered, and then accepted dinner from General Shumilov at 64th Army head-quarters. He also spent the night there. When he finally joined the other captured generals at Zavarykino, there was an uproar because he arrived with several suitcases packed ready for imprisonment. When tackled about his order to fight to the end, he replied that he would have committed suicide, but his chief of staff had prevented him.

For the Wehrmacht, it was a time of counting the cost. Field Marshal Milch's staff estimated that they had lost 488 transport planes and 1,000 crew members during the airlift. The 9th Flak Division was destroyed, along with other ground personnel, to say nothing of Fourth Air Fleet's losses in bombers, fighters and Stukas, during the campaign.

The army's exact losses are still uncertain, but there was no doubt that the Stalingrad campaign represented the most catastrophic defeat hitherto experienced in German history. The Sixth Army and the Fourth Panzer Army had effectively been destroyed. In the *Kessel* alone some 60,000 had died since the start of Operation Uranus and around 130,000 had been captured. (Again the confusion over statistics appears to be due mainly to the numbers of Russians in German uniform.) These figures do not take into account the losses in and around Stalingrad between August and November, the destruction of four allied armies, the defeat of Manstein's rescue attempt and the losses inflicted by Operation Little Saturn. Altogether, the Axis must have lost over half a million men.

Presenting such a catastrophe to the German people was a challenge to which Goebbels had risen with frenetic energy, using all his talent for shameless distortion. The regime had not admitted that the Sixth Army was encircled until 16 January, when it spoke of 'our troops who for several weeks have been heroically fighting enemy attacks on all sides'. Now, it chose entirely the opposite direction, claiming that not a single man had survived.

Goebbels mobilized wireless stations and press to unite the country in martial grief. His instructions to newspapers on how they were to portray the tragedy poured forth. They must remember that every word about this dramatic struggle would go down in history. The press must always employ the word Bolshevik, not Russian. 'The whole of German propaganda must create a myth out of the heroism of Stalingrad which is to become one of the most treasured possessions in German history.' The Wehrmacht communiqué, in particular, must be phrased in a way 'which will move hearts for centuries to come'. It had to rank with Caesar's address to his troops, with Frederick the Great's appeal to his generals before the battle of Leuthen and with Napoleon's call to his imperial guard.

The communiqué was broadcast as a special announcement on the wireless twenty-four hours after Strecker's surrender. 'From Führer headquarters, 3 February 1943. The supreme command of the Wehrmacht announces that the battle of Stalingrad has come to an end. True to its oath of allegiance, the Sixth Army under the exemplary leadership of Field Marshal Paulus has been annihilated by the overwhelming superiority of enemy numbers . . . The sacrifice of the Sixth Army was not in vain. As the bulwark of our historic European mission, it has held out against the onslaught of six Soviet armies . . . They died so that Germany might live.'

The regime's lies proved counter-productive, especially the idea that every member of the Sixth Army had died. No reference was made in any announcement to the 91,000 prisoners already proclaimed by the Soviet government, an item of news that had been rapidly broadcast all round the world. Inevitably, many more people than usual tuned into foreign stations.

A period of three days' national mourning was ordered, with places of entertainment closed and all wireless stations playing solemn music, yet the newspapers were forbidden black margins and no flags were to be flown at half mast.

The Security Service of the SS did not underestimate the effect on civilian morale. They also knew that letters from the *Kessel*, describing the horror and the squalor, fundamentally contradicted the regime's heroic treatment of the disaster. 'The farewell letters of Stalingrad combatants', ran one report, 'spread great spiritual distress not only to relatives but also to a wider circle of the population, the more so because the content of these letters was passed round rapidly. The description of the suffering during the last weeks of fighting haunts relatives day and night.' Goebbels had, in fact, foreseen this problem much earlier, and decided to intercept postcards from those taken prisoner. In his diary on 17 December he wrote: 'In future, cards to relatives should no longer be delivered, because they offer an access door to Germany for Bolshevik propaganda.'

Soviet efforts proved too energetic to stop. The NKVD's prison camps provided postcards, but because the German authorities would not allow them in, their contents were printed in small type, many to a sheet, and dropped over German lines as propaganda leaflets. When these were dropped, German soldiers at the front picked them up, although they risked severe punishment, and sent anonymous letters to the addresses on the list to say that their man was alive. They signed themselves 'a compatriot' or just 'xxx'. Sometimes, to the horror of the Nazi authorities, families even received a copy of the Soviet leaflet and contacted others in the same situation.

Paulus himself seems to have sensed before the surrender that the regime might try to twist the Stalingrad disaster into a new version of the stab-in-the-back myth. (Whether this influenced his decision to refuse the surrender terms on 9 January is impossible to say.) This time, however, the scapegoats for defeat would not be Communists and Jews as in 1918, but the general staff and the aristocracy, still closely associated in the popular mind. Those about to come into the line of fire had an inkling of the storm ahead.

Otto, Fürst von Bismarck, the German minister at the embassy in Rome, slipped away with his wife for a holiday at the end of January to avoid the official celebrations of the Nazi regime's tenth anniversary. Like most German diplomats away from Berlin, he had little idea of the true horrors of the Stalingrad debacle. On the evening of 31 January, they were in the Palace Hotel in St Moritz when an urgent telephone call from the German ambassador in Berne was put through. 'Stop dancing!' the ambassador warned. 'Stalingrad has fallen.' They both knew that St Moritz had become the favourite resort of senior officers from the SS. Nothing more needed to be said.

The propaganda ministry's party line about general and grenadier fighting shoulder to shoulder soon changed. On 18 February, Goebbels organized a mass rally in the Berlin Sportpalast, with the theme 'Total War – Shortest War!' A huge banderol carried the great call of 1812: 'Let Our War-Cry be: Now the People Rise Up and Storm Break Loose'. The very different historical contexts made this glaringly inappropriate to all but the most committed supporter of the regime.

'Do you want total war?' Goebbels yelled from the podium. His audience bayed its response. 'Are you determined to follow the Führer and fight for victory whatever the cost?' Once again the party faithful roared.

Goebbels, during the weeks following Stalingrad, set the agenda. He demanded an end to half-measures, with mass mobilization, yet symbolism was almost more important in the rash of measures. The copper cladding over the Brandenburg Gate was removed for use in war industry. Professional sporting events were banned. Luxury shops, including jewellers, were closed. All fashion magazines were to cease publication. Goebbels even organized a campaign against fashion, with the notion that women did not need to dress up, because they would please 'victorious homecoming soldiers just as much in patches'. Rumours spread that permanent waving would be forbidden. Hitler, who passionately believed that it was the duty of womankind to be decorative, objected to this, and Goebbels was forced to announce that 'there is no need for a woman to make herself ugly'. Barter, that first sign of a siege economy, spread rapidly. Scrubbing-brushes, for example, were soon exchanged for tickets to a Furtwängler concert.

Nightclubs and luxury restaurants, such as Horcher and the Quartier Latin, Neva Grill, Peltzers Atelier and the Tuskulum in the Kurfürstendamm, were closed. When they reopened, customers were to be encouraged to restrict themselves to *Feldküchengerichte* – 'field kitchen dishes' – as an act of solidarity with the soldiers in Russia, quite probably an idea inspired by Zeitzler's forbidden fast. Goering, however, arranged that Horcher, his favourite restaurant, was reopened as an officers' club for the Luftwaffe.

The barely veiled message that corrupt, upper-class generals had betrayed the Nazi ideal was conveyed in numerous ways. Not long afterwards, all members of German royal families serving in the armed forces were told to resign their commissions. Even riding in the Tiergarten was stopped.

More and more Nazi propaganda slogans appeared on walls, but cynical Berliners preferred the graffiti: 'Enjoy the war, the peace will be much worse.' 'Hold out' became the most overused word in the propaganda lexicon. A fear grew for the future, above all of Russia's determination to wreak a violent revenge. An innkeeper from the Black Forest on leave from the *Ostfront* said to Christabel Bielenberg: 'If we are paid back one quarter of what we are doing in Russia and Poland, Frau Doktor, we will suffer, and we will deserve to suffer.'

Germans who did not admire the Nazis recognized the grotesque paradox only too clearly. The invasion of the Soviet Union had forced the Russians to defend Stalinism. Now the threat of defeat forced Germans to defend Hitler's regime and its ghastly failure. The difference was that the Russians had had a vast land mass into which to retreat, while Germany faced war on two fronts, massive bombing raids and a blockade. To make matters worse, Roosevelt and Churchill at Casablanca had declared their intention to fight on until the unconditional surrender of the Axis. This strengthened Goebbels's hand immeasurably.

The opposition, for a variety of reasons ranging from irresolution and disagreement to sheer bad luck, had not managed to act in time. It was already far too late to convince the Allies that there was a democratic alternative to the Nazi regime, as opposed to a palace coup by generals afraid of defeat. Its members, although well aware of this, still hoped that Stalingrad would at least provide the trigger for revolt, but no army group commander was prepared to move. Less senior, but much more determined, officers were ready to take huge risks, if necessary to lose their own lives in the attempt, but Hitler, who seemed to possess an almost feral nose for danger, was too well guarded, and constantly changed his plans at the last moment.

The only overt sign of disaffection following the collapse at Stalingrad came from a small group of Munich students, known as the White Rose. Their ideas spread to other students in Hamburg, Berlin, Stuttgart and Vienna. On 18 February, after a campaign of leaflets and slogans painted on walls calling for the overthrow of Nazism, Sophie Scholl and her brother Hans were arrested after scattering more handbills at the Ludwig-Maximilian University in Munich. Tortured by the Gestapo, then sentenced to death by Roland Freisler at a special session of the People's Court in Munich, brother and sister were beheaded. A number of other members of their circle, including the professor of philosophy, Kurt Huber, suffered similar fates.

Soon after the final surrender at Stalingrad, Hitler saw Field Marshal von Manstein, the first senior officer from outside his immediate circle. Manstein outlined the measures he had been forced to take to avoid total collapse in southern Russia. Hitler wanted to order him not to withdraw any further, but Manstein knew that, in the circumstances, he could set the terms. During their discussions, Hitler said that he alone took the responsibility for Stalingrad, then promptly sidestepped his own confession by adding that he could put some of the blame on Goering, but since he had appointed the Reichsmarschall to be his successor, he could not hold him responsible for Stalingrad. No mention was made of his own confused strategy and attempts to control operations from afar. His greatest recriminations were still reserved for Paulus. He told Goebbels that after the war he would have Paulus and his generals court-martialled for failing to carry out his explicit order to resist to the last bullet.

Hitler now seldom held forth at table, as had been his habit. He preferred to eat alone. Guderian found him greatly changed: 'His left hand trembled, his back was bent, his gaze was fixed, his eyes protruded but lacked their former lustre, his cheeks were flecked with red.' But when Hitler met Milch, he showed no regret for the vast waste of life at Stalingrad. He could think only of raising the stakes once again, throwing away even more lives. 'We will end the war this year,' he told him. 'I have accordingly decided on a gigantic mobilization of all German popular strength.'

In Russia, the fierce exultation over the victory was spontaneous as well as orchestrated. The Kremlin bells rang out news of Paulus's surrender. Rousing martial music was broadcast over the radio and communiqués were published across the front of every newspaper. They lauded the 'stern lesson in history' administered to the 'adventurers of the German General Staff' by the Red Army's own Hannibals in this modern battle of Cannae. Stalin was portrayed as the wise leader and great architect of victory.

Morale in the Soviet Union genuinely soared. Throughout the battle people everywhere had asked each other for the latest news of the fighting on the Volga. When victory came after such a terrible battle, people kept telling each other: 'You cannot stop an army which has done Stalingrad.' They joked too in delight at the expense of the defeated enemy. 'I wonder how it feels to be a field marshal caught in a cellar?' was a popular remark. 'After Stalingrad, not a single soldier had a single doubt about the outcome of the war,' said an officer wounded there. Stalingrad divisions were distributed to different armies and fronts to raise morale still further.

Stalin was soon appointed Marshal of the Soviet Union by the Presidium of the Supreme Soviet of the USSR, a touch which was marginally more modest than Napoleon crowning himself. The history of the war was suddenly refashioned. The disasters of 1941 were made to appear as if they were all part of a cunning plan devised by Stalin. Stalin's picture and name had been kept out of the press during the bad periods, but now 'the great captain of the Soviet people', 'the genius organizer of our victories' was back to the fore. All disasters and all evils were attributed to others, rather as courtiers were blamed in tsarist times. Ilya Ehrenburg, with breathtaking cynicism, remarked that the people 'needed to believe'. Even prisoners in the Gulag wrote to the Great Father of the People, convinced that he would step in to correct a terrible miscarriage of justice, unthinkable under Communism. No leader had a more effective lightning conductor than Beria.

Red Army generals were conspicuously rewarded. The recent suspension of dual command with commissars was crowned with the formal reinstatement of the rank and description of 'officer'. The euphemism 'commander' was dropped. As General Schlömer had noted with amusement, shoulder boards – symbols of privilege which some Bolshevik lynch mobs in 1917 had nailed to the bodies of their tsarist wearers – were reinstated. (Gold braid had been secretly ordered from Great Britain, to the astonishment and disapproval of officials there.) One soldier in a Guards division heard the news about shoulder boards from an old man polishing boots in a railway station: 'They're starting these gold shoulder boards once more,' the man told him in angry disbelief. 'Just like in the White Army.' His fellow soldiers too were amazed when he told them the news on returning to the train: 'Why in the Red Army?' they asked. Such mutterings were ignored. The new decorations for the Great Patriotic War – the Orders of Suvorov and of Kutuzov – were also distributed to senior commanders in the campaign.

The greatest propaganda success, however, extended far beyond Soviet frontiers. The story of the Red Army's sacrifice had a powerful effect across the world, especially within occupied Europe. Its effect on resistance movements everywhere and thus its influence on the politics of post-war Europe were considerable. The triumph of the Red Army boosted the status of the Party member and attracted fellow-travellers in droves. Even conservatives could not avoid praising the heroism of the Red Army. In Britain, King George VI commissioned a Sword of Stalingrad to be forged for presentation to the city. The morale of civilians and soldiers alike was boosted by newsreels lauding the victory, with flickering footage of Paulus and the long columns of prisoners of war, snaking across the snow-covered landscape. Everyone knew that the Russians were taking the brunt of the German onslaught, and that the Eastern Front was bleeding the Wehrmacht to death far more surely than any western theatre. The Red Army would push on, as the officer had shouted at the prisoners of war, until Berlin looked like the ruined city of Stalingrad.

24

The City of the Dead

The silence that fell on 2 February in the ruined city felt eerie for those who had become used to destruction as a natural state. Grossman described mounds of rubble and bomb craters so deep that the low-angled winter sunlight never seemed to reach the bottom, and 'railway tracks, where tanker wagons lie belly up, like dead horses'.

Some 3,500 civilians were put to work as burial parties. They stacked frozen German corpses like piles of timber at the roadside, and although they had a few carts drawn by camels, most of the removal work was accomplished with improvised sleds and handcarts. The German dead were taken to bunkers, or the huge anti-tank ditch, dug the previous summer, and tipped in. Later, 1,200 German prisoners were put to work on the same task, using carts, with humans instead of horses pulling them. 'Almost all members of these work parties', reported a prisoner of war, 'soon died of typhus.' Others – 'dozens each day' according to an NKVD officer in Beketovka camp – were shot on the way to work by their escorts.

The grisly evidence of the fighting did not disappear swiftly. After the Volga thawed in spring, lumps of coagulated blackened skin were found on the river bank. General de Gaulle, when he stopped in Stalingrad on his way north to Moscow in December 1944, was struck to find that bodies were still being dug up, but this was to continue for several decades. Almost any building work in the city uncovered human remains from the battle.

More astonishing than the number of dead was the capacity for human survival. The Stalingrad Party Committee held meetings in all districts 'liberated from fascist occupation', and rapidly organized a census. They found that at least 9,796 civilians had lived through the fighting, surviving in the battlefield ruins. They included 994 children, of whom only nine were reunited with their parents. The vast majority were sent off to state orphanages or given work clearing the city. The report says nothing of their physical or mental state, witnessed by an American aid worker, who arrived very soon after the fighting to distribute clothes. 'Most of the children', she wrote, 'had been living in the ground for four or five winter months. They were swollen with hunger. They cringed in corners, afraid to speak, to even look people in the face.'

The Stalingrad Party Committee had higher priorities. 'Soviet authorities were immediately reinstalled in all districts of the city', it reported to Moscow. On 4 February, Red Army commissars held a political rally for the 'whole city', both civilian survivors and soldiers. This assembly, with its long speeches in praise of Comrade Stalin and his leadership of the Red Army, was the Party's version of a service of thanksgiving.

The authorities did not at first allow civilians who had escaped to the east bank to return to their homes, because of the need to clear unexploded shells. Mine-clearance teams had to prepare a basic pattern of 'special safe paths'. But many soon managed to slip back over the frozen Volga without permission. Messages appeared chalked on the side of ruined buildings, testifying to the numbers of families broken up by the fighting: 'Mama, we are all right. Look for us in Beketovka. Klava.' Many people never discovered which of their relatives were alive or dead until after the war was over.

A large contingent of German prisoners, many of whom were too weak to stand, were also forced to attend a political rally in the centre of Stalingrad, and listen to long harangues from three of the leading German Communists: Walter Ulbricht, Erich Weinert and Wilhelm Pieck.

The state of most prisoners at the time of the surrender was so pitiful, that a considerable death rate was predictable in the weeks and months to follow. How far this was exacerbated by ill-treatment, casual brutality, and above all logistic deficiencies is impossible to calculate. Of the 91,000 taken prisoner at the end of the battle, almost half had died by the time spring arrived. The Red Army itself acknowledged in subsequent reports that orders for the care of prisoners had been ignored, and it is impossible to tell how many Germans were shot out of hand during or soon after their surrender, often as vengeance for the deaths of relatives or comrades.

The death rate in the so-called hospitals was terrifying. The tunnel system in the Tsaritsa gorge, redesignated 'Prisoner of War Hospital No. 1', remained the largest and most horrific, only because there were no buildings left offering any protection against the cold. The walls ran with water, the air was little more than a foul, sickly recycling of human breath, with so little oxygen left that the few primitive oil lamps, fashioned from tins, flickered and died constantly, leaving the tunnels dark. Each gallery was not much wider than the casualties lying side by side on the damp beaten earth of the tunnel floor, so it was difficult, in the gloom, not to step or trip on feet suffering from frostbite, provoking a hoarse shriek of pain. Many of these frostbite victims died of gangrene, because the surgeons could not cope. Whether they would have survived amputation in their weakened state and without anaesthetic is another matter.

The condition of many of the 4,000 patients was pitiful in the extreme, and the doctors were helpless as fungus spread on rotten flesh. They had almost no bandages left and no medicaments. Ulcers and open sores provided easy entry points for tetanus from the filth around. Sanitary arrangements, which consisted of a single bucket to scores of men suffering from dysentery, were unspeakable, and at night there were no lamps. Many men were too weak to raise themselves from the ground and there were not enough orderlies to answer the constant cries for help. The orderlies, already weak from undernourishment and soon fever-ridden themselves, had to carry polluted water up from the ravine.

The doctors did not even have a reliable list of patients' names, let alone proper medical notes. Second-line Russian troops, and also members of ambulance units, had stolen their medical equipment and drugs, including analgesics. The Protestant chaplain of the 297th Division was shot in the back of the neck by a Soviet major when he bent over to help a wounded man.

Russian medical officers were appalled by the conditions. Some were sympathetic. The Russian commandant shared out his cigarettes with German doctors, but other Soviet personnel traded bread for any watches which had survived the earlier rounds of looting. Dibold, the doctor from the 44th Infantry Division, described how when a woman army surgeon, jolly and with the strong red face of peasant ancestors, came in to bargain for watches, a young Austrian from a poor family produced a silver pocket watch. He handed over this heirloom, no doubt given to him on going off to war, and in return he received half a loaf. This he divided among the other men, keeping the smallest portion for himself.

Misery also brought the scum to the surface. Certain individuals exploited the helplessness of former comrades with a previously unimaginable shamelessness. Thieves robbed from corpses and from the weakest patients. If anyone had a watch, wedding ring or other valuable left, it was soon snatched in the dark. But nature had its own form of poetic justice. The robbers of the sick rapidly became typhus victims from infected lice transferred with the booty. One interpreter, infamous for his activities, was found to have a large bag of gold rings hidden on him when he died.

At first, the Soviet authorities provided no rations at all. NKVD and Red Army files now show that, even though surrender was known to be imminent, virtually no preparation had been made to guard, let alone to feed, the prisoners. The German Communist, Erich Weinart, claimed that heavy snow had hampered the transport of supplies, but this is unconvincing. The real problem was a mixture of brutal indifference and bureaucratic incompetence, above all a lack of coordination between army and NKVD.

There was also a deep reluctance to allow German prisoners rations when the Soviet Union was so desperately short of food. Many Red Army soldiers were badly undernourished, to say nothing of civilians, so the idea of giving any food at all to invaders who had plundered their country seemed almost perverse. Rations finally started to arrive after three or four days, by which time many men had eaten virtually nothing in almost two weeks. Even for the sick there was little more than a loaf of bread between ten men, plus some soup made from water with a few millet seeds and salted fish. It would have been unrealistic to expect better treatment, especially when one considers the Wehrmacht's record on the treatment of its own prisoners, both military and civilian, in the Soviet Union.

The greatest fear of doctors for their patients, however, was not death by starvation but a typhus epidemic. Many had expected an outbreak in the *Kessel* when the first cases appeared, but had not dared voice their concerns in case it started a panic. In the tunnel system, they continued to isolate the different diseases as they appeared, whether diphtheria or typhus. They begged the authorities to provide delousing facilities, but many Red Army soldiers and almost all the civilians in the region were themselves still infested.

It was not surprising that so many died. There seemed to be little reason left to fight for life. The prospect of seeing families again was remote. Germany was so far away that it could have been another world, a world which now seemed to have more to do with pure fantasy. Death promised a release from suffering, and towards the end, drained of pain as well as strength, there was no more than a sense of floating weightless. The ones most likely to survive seemed to be those who fought on, either through religious faith, or an obstinate refusal to die in such squalor, or out of a determination to live for their family's sake.

A will to live played just as important a part in those marched off to prison camps. What Weinert described as 'limping and shuffling ghosts in rags' followed the back of the man in front. As soon as the exertion of the march warmed their bodies, they could feel the lice become more active. Some civilians grabbed blankets from their backs, spat in their faces and even threw stones. It was best to be close to the front of the column and, safest of all, to stay near one of the escorts. Some soldiers whom they passed, contrary to Red Army orders, took pot shots for fun at the columns of prisoners, just as German soldiers had fired at columns of Red Army prisoners in 1941.

The luckier ones were marched straight to one of the designated collection camps in the area, although they varied greatly in distance. Those from the northern pocket, for example, were marched over twelve miles to Dubovka, north of Stalingrad. It took two days. During the night, they were shepherded into the roofless remains of buildings – destroyed by the Luftwaffe, as their guards did not fail to remind them.

Thousands, however, were taken on what can only be described as death marches. The worst, without food or water in temperatures of between twenty-five and thirty degrees below zero, followed a completely zigzag route from the Tsaritsa ravine, via Gumrak and Gorodishche, finally ending up on the fifth day at Beketovka. From time to time, they heard shots in the freezing air, as another victim collapsed in the snow, unable to walk any further. Thirst was as great a threat as weakness from hunger. Although surrounded by snow, they suffered the fate of the Ancient Mariner, knowing the dangers of consuming it.

Shelter was seldom available at night, so the prisoners slept in the snow together. Many woke to find close comrades dead and frozen stiff beside them. In an attempt to prevent this, one of the group was designated to stay awake ready to wake the others after half an hour. Then they would all move as briskly as they could to reactivate the circulation. Others did not even dare to lie down. Hoping to sleep like horses, they stood together in a group with a blanket over their heads to keep in some warmth from their breath.

Morning brought not relief, but dread of the march ahead. 'The Russians had very simple methods,' observed a lieutenant who survived. 'Those who could walk, were marched off. Those who could not, either through wounds or sickness, were shot or left without food to die.' Having quickly grasped this brutal logic, he was prepared to barter his woollen pullover for milk and bread from a Russian peasant woman at the night stop, because he knew that otherwise he would collapse from weakness the next day.

'We set out with 1,200 men,' recounted a soldier from the 305th

411

Infantry Division, 'and only a tenth, about 120 men, were left alive by the time we reached Beketovka.'

The gateway to the main camp at Beketovka was another entrance which deserved the superscription: 'Abandon hope all ye who enter here.'

On their arrival, the guards searched prisoners for valuables once again, then made them stand for 'registration'. The prisoners soon discovered that standing out in the freezing weather for hours and hours, parading in groups of fives for 'counting parade', would be a daily penance. Finally, after the NKVD had carried out an initial processing, they were led off to the wooden huts, where they were packed in, forty or fifty men to a room, 'like herrings in a barrel', recorded a survivor. On 4 February, an NKVD officer complained to Don Front headquarters that the situation was 'extremely critical'. The camps at Beketovka had received 50,000 prisoners, 'including also sick and wounded'.

The NKVD camp authorities were overwhelmed. They had no motor transport at all and tried to beg the army for a single truck. Water was eventually brought to the camp in iron barrels on carts towed by camels. A captured Austrian doctor noted his first impression: 'Nothing to eat, nothing to drink, filthy snow and urine-yellow ice offered the only relief for an unbearable thirst . . . Every morning more corpses.' After two days, the Russians provided some 'soup', which was no more than a sack of bran tipped into warm water. Anger at the conditions led to prisoners scraping handfuls of lice off their own bodies and throwing them at their guards. Such protests provoked summary execution.

Right from the start, the Soviet authorities set out to divide the prisoners of war, first on national lines, then political. Romanian, Italian and Croat prisoners of war were given the privilege of working in the kitchens, where the Romanians in particular set out to gain revenge on their former allies. The Germans had not only got them into this hell, they believed, they had also cut off their supplies in the *Kessel* to feed their own troops better. Gangs of Romanians attacked individual Germans collecting food on behalf of their hut and seized it. The Germans retaliated, by sending escorts to guard their food carriers.

'Then came another shock,' recorded a Luftwaffe sergeant-major. 'Our Austrian comrades suddenly ceased to be Germans. They called themselves "Austritsy", hoping to secure better treatment – as indeed happened.' Germans felt bitter that 'all the guilt of the war was heaped on those of us who remained "Germans",' particularly since Austrians, with an interesting turn of logic, tended to blame Prussian generals, rather than the Austrian Hitler, for their predicament.

The struggle to stay alive remained paramount. 'The dead each morning were laid outside the barrack block,' wrote a panzer officer. These naked, frozen corpses were then stacked by working parties in an ever-extending line down one side of the camp. A doctor estimated that at Beketovka the 'mountain of bodies' was 'about a hundred yards long and six feet high'. At least fifty to sixty men died every day, estimated the Luftwaffe warrant officer. 'We had no tears left,' he wrote later. Another prisoner used as an interpreter by the Russians later managed to get a look at the 'death register'. He noted down that up to 21 October 1943, 45,200 died in Beketovka alone. An NKVD report acknowledges that in all the Stalingrad camps, 55,228 prisoners had died by 15 April, but one does not know how many had been captured between Operation Uranus and the final surrender.

'Hunger', observed Dr Dibold, 'changed the psyche and character, visibly in behaviour patterns and invisibly in men's thoughts.' German as well as Romanian soldiers resorted to cannibalism to stay alive. Thin slices of meat cut from frozen corpses were boiled up. The end product was offered round as 'camel meat'. Those who ate it were quickly recognizable, because their complexion acquired a hint of red, instead of the grey-green pallor of the majority. Cases were reported from other camps in and around Stalingrad, even in a camp housing prisoners captured during Operation Uranus. One Soviet source claims that 'only at gunpoint could prisoners be forced to desist from this barbarism'. The authorities ordered more food, but incompetence and corruption in the system blunted any measure.

The accumulated effect of exhaustion, cold, sickness and starvation dehumanized prisoners in other ways. With dysentery rife, those who collapsed and fell into the hell-hole of the latrines were left to drown, if still alive. Few had the strength or the will to pull them out. Their terrible fate below was ignored. The need of others suffering from dysentery to use the latrine was far too urgent.

Curiously, the latrine saved one starving young lieutenant, a count whose family owned several castles and estates. He overheard a soldier say something in the unmistakable dialect of his district, and quickly called out, asking where he was from. The soldier gave the name of a small village nearby. 'And who are you and where do you come from?' he asked in return. The officer told him. 'Oh yes,' the soldier laughed. 'I know. I used to see you go past in your red Mercedes sports car, off to shoot hare. Well, here we are together. If you are hungry, perhaps I can help.' The soldier had been chosen as a medical orderly in the prison hospital, and because so many of the inmates died before they had a chance to eat their bread ration, he managed to accumulate a bag of leftover crusts to share with others after each spell of duty. This utterly unexpected intervention saved the young count's life.

Survival often ran counter to expectation. The first to die were generally those who had been large and powerfully built. The small thin man always stood the best chance. Both in the *Kessel* and later in the prison camps, the equally minute ration scales were almost bound to reverse the normal survival of the fittest, because they made no allowance for the size of the individual. It is interesting that in Soviet labour camps, only horses were fed according to their size.

When spring arrived, the Soviet authorities began to reorganize the prisoner-of-war population in the region. Altogether some 235,000 former members of the Sixth Army and the Fourth Panzer Army, including those captured during Manstein's attempted relief operation in December, as well as Romanians and other allies, had been held in around twenty camps and prison hospitals in the region.

The generals were the first to leave. Their destination was a camp near Moscow. They departed in what junior officers cynically dubbed the 'White Train', because its carriages were so comfortable. Great bitterness was caused by the fact that those who had given orders to fight to the end had not just outlived their own rhetoric, but now enjoyed incomparably better conditions than their men. 'It is the duty of a general to stay with his men,' remarked one lieutenant, 'not to go off in a sleeping-car.' Chances of survival proved brutally dependent on rank. Over 95 per cent of soldiers and NCOs died, 55 per cent of junior officers and just 5 per cent of senior officers. As the foreign journalists had noted, few of the senior officers had shown signs of starvation just after the surrender, so their defences were not dangerously weakened in the same way as their men's. The privileged treatment which the generals received, however, was a revealing testimony to the Soviet Union's sense of hierarchy.

Small numbers of officers were sent to camps in the region of Moscow, such as Lunovo, Krasnogorsk and Suzdal. Those selected for 'anti-fascist education' were sent to the fortified monastery of Yelabuga, east of Kazan. Conditions of transport were most certainly not up to those provided for the generals. Out of one convoy of 1,800 men in March, 1,200 died. In addition to typhus, jaundice and diphtheria, scurvy, dropsy and tuberculosis had now emerged. And as soon as spring arrived properly, the number of cases of malaria rose rapidly.

The diaspora of soldiers and junior officers was considerable, with 20,000 sent to Bekabad, east of Tashkent, 2,500 to Volsk, north-east of Saratov, 5,000 down the Volga to Astrakhan, 2,000 to Usman, north of Voronezh, and others to Basyanovsky, north of Sverdlovsk, Oranky near Gorky, and also to Karaganda.

When prisoners were registered before departure, many put down 'agricultural labourer' as their profession in the hope of being sent to a farm. Hardened smokers collected camel dung and dried it to have something to smoke on the journey. After the experience of Beketovka, they were certain that the worst must be over, and the prospect of movement and change had its own appeal, but they soon discovered their mistake. Each railway wagon, with up to a hundred men forced into each one, had a single hole in the middle of the floor as a latrine. The cold was still terrible, but thirst was again the worst affliction, for they were given dried bread and salt fish to eat, but little water.

So desperate did they become, that they licked the condensation frozen to metal parts inside the truck. At stops men allowed out often could not resist seizing handfuls of snow and forcing it into their mouths. Many died as a result, usually so silently that their comrades only realized that they had gone much later. Their corpses were then stacked by the sliding door of the wagon, ready for unloading. '*Skolko kaputt?*' Soviet guards would shout out in their pidgin-German at stops. 'How many dead?'

Some journeys lasted up to twenty-five days. The transports via Saratov, then across Uzbekistan to Bekabad, were among the worst. In one wagon only eight men remained alive out of 100. When prisoners finally reached the reception camp in sight of the Pamir mountains, they discovered that it had been established for the construction of a nearby hydroelectric dam. Their relief to hear that they were to be deloused, at last, soon turned to dismay. They were clumsily shaved all over, which could 'only be compared to sheep-shearing', then sprayed with powder. A number died from the primitive chemicals used.

There were no huts to live in, only earth bunkers. But the worst surprise was a German corporal who had joined the Soviets as a guard commander. 'No Russian ever treated me with such brutality,' wrote the same prisoner.* Fortunately, movement between camps in this parallel Gulag was frequent. From Bekabad, many went to Kokant or, best of all, to Chuama, where there were much better medical facilities, and even a crudely improvised swimming pool. The Italian prisoners there were already well organized, catching sparrows to supplement the soup.

Those left behind in Stalingrad found that the collection camp at Krasnoarmeysk had been turned into a labour camp. The food at least improved with *kasha* (buckwheat porridge) and fish soup, but

---

* German guards were also used in other camps. The worst were some two hundred Germans (most appear to have been Saxons for some reason) who had deserted from punishment battalions. Armed with wooden clubs, and granted the designation of 'Fighters against Fascism', they refused to allow soldiers to fall out to relieve themselves during roll-call, even though the overwhelming majority were suffering from dysentery.

the work was often dangerous. When spring arrived, many of them were put to work retrieving Volga river craft sunk by the Luftwaffe and the German Army. One Russian shipyard manager, shaken by the number of prisoners who died on this work, swore his daughter to secrecy before telling her about it.

The NKVD's grip on Stalingrad had not slackened. German prisoners working from both banks of the Volga had noticed that the first building in the city to be repaired was the NKVD headquarters, and almost immediately there were queues of women outside with food parcels for relatives who had been arrested. Former Sixth Army soldiers guessed that they too would be prisoners there for many years. Molotov later confirmed their fears, with his declaration that no German prisoners would see their homes until Stalingrad had been rebuilt.

25

The Sword of Stalingrad

In November 1943, one year after Operation Uranus, a Douglas transport plane flew low over Stalingrad. The Soviet diplomats on board were on their way from Moscow to meet the American and the British leaders at Tehran. One of the passengers was Valentin Berezhkov, who had been Dekanozov's interpreter in Berlin on the eve of Barbarossa.

'We pressed to the windows in silence,' he wrote later. 'First individual houses scattered in the snow came into view, and then a kind of unbelievable chaos began: lumps of walls, boxes of half-ruined buildings, piles of rubble, isolated chimneys.' They could, however, distinguish signs of life. 'Visible against the snow were the black figures of people and every now and then there was evidence of new buildings.' Out over the steppe again, they spotted the rusty skeletons of tanks.

At the Tehran conference, Churchill presented the Sword of Stalingrad to 'the Soviet people'. The blade bore the engraved dedication: 'To the steelhearted citizens of Stalingrad, a gift from King George VI as a token of the homage of the British people.' Churchill made the ceremony memorable by his oratory. Stalin, who accepted the sword with both hands, lifted it to his lips to kiss the scabbard. He then passed it to Marshal Voroshilov, who clumsily let the sword slide out of the scabbard. It clattered loudly on the floor.

That evening, Stalin raised his glass after dinner. 'I propose a salute', he said, 'to the swiftest possible justice for all Germany's war criminals . . . I drink to our unity in dispatching them as fast as we catch them, all of them, and there must be quite a few of them.' Some sources say that he proposed the execution of 50,000 Wehrmacht officers to destroy German military power for good. Churchill stood up angrily and declared that the British people would never 'stand for such mass murder'. Nobody should be shot without a proper trial. He walked out. Stalin, amused at the reaction he had provoked, went after him. Placing both hands on his shoulders, he claimed that he had been joking and cajoled Churchill into returning.

The Tehran conference determined Allied strategy for the rest of the war. Churchill's plan for an invasion through the Balkans was vetoed for sound military reasons. The Western Allies' main effort had to be devoted to north-west Europe. But this strategic logic left the fate of eastern and central Europe entirely in Stalin's hands. Churchill, with a strong inkling of the consequences, could do nothing. Red Army sacrifices and the terrible suffering of Russian civilians allowed Stalin to manipulate the Western Allies through a sort of blood guilt because their losses had been minimal in comparison. Several historians charting the Soviet Union's rise to superpower status have rightly pointed to the victory at Stalingrad as the basis for Stalin's success at Tehran.

Stalin, capitalizing on his new aura of great statesman, and as a deliberate sop to Roosevelt, had announced the abolition of the Comintern on 15 May 1943. It was an easy pawn to pretend to sacrifice. Georgi Dimitrov stayed in place, running a rump Comintern under a different name: the International Section of the Central Committee. Meanwhile, the Soviet victory at Stalingrad had been the greatest boost imaginable to Communist propaganda throughout the world. It was an inspiration even to those who had lost their faith after the Stalinist inquisition in the Spanish Civil War or the Nazi–Soviet Pact of 1939. The story roused left-wing sculptors, painters, novelists and poets, such as Pablo Neruda, who in his *Nuevo Canto de Amor a Stalingrado* wrote a poem of international love to a city whose name had brought hope to the world.

*

For the German prisoners captured at Stalingrad, the future was correspondingly bleak. Some, still dreaming of great counter-attacks which would free them, became convinced at night that they could hear the guns of an advancing army. They were the least likely to survive the years ahead in the prisoner-of-war camps, constructed according to NKVD standards with perimeter fences consisting of ten horizontal strands of barbed wire.

Captivity was almost as uncertain a fate as fighting. It also had its share of the ironies of war. Dibold, the Austrian doctor from the 44th Infantry Division, was astonished when three new patients reached his prison hospital. This trio, who looked Jewish, wore German uniforms with eagles and swastikas. One of them smiled at his confusion. 'Doctor, the miracle of the twentieth century: a Jew as one of Adolf Hitler's soldiers.' They were from a Hungarian labour battalion. Their Russian captors had clothed them from captured stores.

Although prison camp rations had improved in the summer of 1943, they were still uneven, varying from camp to camp. Rations were often stolen by corrupt quartermasters who exchanged them for vodka, or by guards whose own families received little more than the German prisoners. Most of the ill-treatment came from a lack of imagination, monumental incompetence, and above all, that Russian tolerance of suffering which Marxist-Leninist doctrine had managed to exploit so successfully. Nothing, however, was predictable. Prisoners testified how guards, on seeing a photograph of their children, would soften. At a prison hospital outside Stalingrad, after inmates had become used to the idea of men being shot or left to die on the march, Russian guards inexplicably spared three prisoners recaptured after a futile attempt to escape.

Even when conditions improved in the spring of 1943, the death rate in most prison hospitals was at least one per cent per day. The problems were still enormous, especially in the Stalingrad region, with pellagra, tuberculosis, dropsy and scurvy added to the other diseases. A Soviet woman doctor told her German counterparts that Stalingrad civilians were suffering more from scurvy than the German prisoners, but she gave permission for foraging parties to be sent out to collect herbs and other greenstuff, from which the German doctors, in their dispensary, made vitamin concentrates. The inventiveness of prisoner-of-war doctors produced brilliant improvisations. One created out of scrap metal a sphygmomanometer for testing blood pressure. Doctors manufactured their own inoculation against typhus, which consisted of injecting an extract of lice guts. Any article of silk was unpicked to provide surgical thread and scalpels were made out of sharpened tin lids.

Prisoners, suddenly transformed into an underclass, had to learn quickly. They pilfered and fashioned numerous ingenious gadgets. They also learned to make the most of their rations, for example, roasting fish bones from the soup on the stove, and then crushing them up. Some made terrible mistakes. At Ilmen, prisoners reduced to eating reeds and water-hemlock died rapidly as a result. And one prisoner who managed to grab a handful of butter in the kitchen died in agony because his stomach was so unused to fats.

The bad diet on top of the weeks of starvation in the *Kessel* was the main reason for patients in the prison hospitals failing to recover. They lost nearly all their hair, and their neck muscles became too feeble to raise their heads. Those dying shunned the daylight, as if preparing themselves for perpetual darkness.

Death could often be a deliverance, almost like sleep for the exhausted. A number slipped away quite suddenly, just when doctors thought them over the worst. Sick men would share beds for warmth, even though a number woke up to find themselves next to a corpse. Some had succumbed rapidly. Helmuth Groscurth died of typhus on 7 April 1943 in the officers' camp of Frolovo where 4,000 inmates died out of 5,000. It was three years before his family received news of his death. Kurt Reuber died on 20 January 1944, in Yelabuga camp only a few weeks after he had drawn another Madonna for Christmas with the same words: 'Light, Life, Love'.

A few, after having survived the worst, suddenly killed themselves unexpectedly. In a prison hospital, one officer woke to find a friend in the next bed sitting up motionless. He had managed to kill himself by 'thrusting a long thin shard of glass from a broken window straight up into the heart'.

Even the comparatively healthy had little hope of surviving. Their rations – such as unground millet which ran right through the stomach – gave them little strength for the heavy work which the NKVD intended to extract from them through Stakhanovite work programmes. Materialism, as one of them put it, meant that 'man was just another material' to be used and discarded. Prisoners were used as pack animals. They first had to build their own camps in almost virgin forest. They were not allowed huts, but underground bunkers, which flooded in spring and autumn. Once the camp was established, their life was one of heavy labour, cutting and dragging timber, and sometimes peat-cutting for winter fuel. Those kept in the Stalingrad area, rebuilding the city and recovering sunken ships from the Volga, were later put to work, along with other Gulag prisoners, digging that Stalinist showpiece, the Volga–Don canal.

Soon after its triumph at Stalingrad, the Soviet state made plans to undermine the Nazi regime and replace it with a puppet Communist state. Prisoners of all ranks were to be divided into 'anti-fascists' and 'fascists'.

In the spring and summer of 1943, senior officers were moved from a camp at Krasnogorsk to the monastery at Suzdal, and then to what became their semi-permanent base: Camp 48 at Voikovo, an old inn and health spa, which was dubbed 'the Castle', because of its relative luxury. The NKVD moved the implacable Schmidt away from Paulus, because he was seen as a bad influence.

The NKVD department in charge of prisoners of war first organized an umbrella organization, the National Committee for Free Germany. To run it, Beria's men used their tame German Communists. Two months later, another group, the League of German Officers, was set up to attract anti-Nazis unwilling to support the National Committee.

Major-General Melnikov, the vice-chief of the department, controlled these activities. Although very much part of Beria's empire, Melnikov also worked closely with the International Section of the Central Committee. Dmitry Manuilsky, Stalin's former spy on the Comintern with special responsibility for German affairs, had been given another watching brief, which may explain his curious visit to Stalingrad during the latter part of the battle, when Chuikov refused him permission to cross to the west bank.

On 19 August 1943, three Stalingrad generals, Seydlitz, Lattmann and Korfes, who had been identified from interrogations as likely collaborators, were taken from Voikovo to a 're-education centre' at Lunovo. Seydlitz appears to have been emotionally overwhelmed by what he believed was a collective change of heart of many officers, all wanting to save Germany from the Hitlerian apocalypse. He saw himself as their natural leader.

Early in September, Melnikov sent Seydlitz, Korfes and Lattmann back to Voikovo to win over the other Stalingrad generals. Their arrival late at night brought the generals out of their rooms in their pyjamas, intrigued to hear what all the excitement was about. But when Seydlitz announced melodramatically that this was the day of the 'new Tauroggen', General Strecker turned away angrily. And next day, when Seydlitz and Lattmann urged them to join in calling for a revolt against Hitler's regime, Strecker, Sixt von Arnim, Rodenburg and Pfeffer accused them angrily of treason. Seydlitz and his colleagues did, however, win over Generals Edler von Daniels, Drebber and Schlömer.

Seydlitz, in his moral outrage against Hitler and conviction that they had to join the tide of history to save Germany, failed to recognize the dangers. They had left their opposition to the Nazi regime so late that the Allies would never listen to them or give them any say in the fate of their country. Meanwhile, their organizers (he does not even appear to have realized that Melnikov belonged to the NKVD) would simply exploit them for Soviet interests.

Soviet documents show that on 17 September 1943 Seydlitz, as president of the League of German Officers, presented a plan to General Melnikov which proposed raising an army corps of 30,000 men from those captured at Stalingrad. 'According to Seydlitz's idea,' Melnikov reported back to Beria, 'this corps will be the base for the new government after Hitler is overthrown.'

'Seydlitz', Melnikov added, 'considers himself a candidate for the job of chief commander of the armed forces of Free Germany in the future.' He apparently also promised to prepare a plan for a press and radio propaganda campaign, 'sending men to the German rear to win over formation commanders to our side and to organize joint action against Hitler's regime'. Seydlitz would send messages to 'his personal friends, the commander of the Central Front, von Kluge, and General Thomas who is responsible for Hitler's headquarters staff'.

Seydlitz, accompanied by Generals Lattmann and Korfes, and Colonel Günter van Hooven, presented his plan on 22 September. He expected the Soviet authorities to help them form 'a small army from prisoners of war which could be used by a new German government to seize power.' They called for one army staff, two corps staffs, four full divisions, and a supporting aviation force with three bomber squadrons, four fighter squadrons and an air reconnaissance group: in all seven generals, 1,650 officers and 42,000 soldiers. Seydlitz appears to have had no idea of the death rate of Stalingrad prisoners after the surrender.

At a subsequent meeting, Seydlitz recommended 'that all the contingents should be flown into Germany, perhaps Berlin'. The NKVD officer present pointed out 'the technical difficulties of flying such a number of troops into Germany but von Seydlitz replied that it was up to the Russians to sort out the details'. General Korfes, however, did not conceal his exasperation with such a pipe dream. 'It's utterly Utopian', he said, 'to think that all the units could be carried by air.' He added: 'Russian air force commanders would consider such a proposal to be proof that German generals are fantasists.'*

Seydlitz appears to have been oblivious to the anger and ill-feelings which he and his colleagues stirred up. Officers bitterly opposed to the anti-fascists set up a court of honour, sentencing those who collaborated with the Russians to be shunned in perpetuity. As a

---

* It is, of course, possible that General von Seydlitz secretly saw this operation as a chance of tricking the Soviets into sending him and thousands of Sixth Army prisoners home. But if this had been the case, one would have expected him to mention the episode after the war when he faced such heavy condemnation from former colleagues for having collaborated with Stalin's regime.

gesture of defiance, they began to use the raised-hand salute. This polarization made life very hard for those who wanted nothing to do either with 'anti-fascists' or with Hitler loyalists. One lieutenant found himself forced to sleep on the floor for weeks because the rival groups would not allow him a bunk.

In February 1944, Russian aircraft started dropping leaflets over Germany and front-line troops, signed by Seydlitz and his colleagues. The Gestapo provided an urgent report for Himmler verifying that Seydlitz's signature was genuine. General Gille of the Waffen SS, whose troops in the Cherkassy salient were showered with leaflets from the National Committee, sent copies back to Germany. He also passed back personal letters addressed to him from Generals Seydlitz and Korfes, who had been sent to his part of the front by Shcherbakov. The handwriting was again analysed by the Gestapo and confirmed as accurate.

The leaflets caused panic. Hitler summoned Himmler for a meeting, then sent General Schmundt off with a declaration of loyalty for field marshals to sign. Even this was not enough to reassure him. On 19 March, Rundstedt, Rommel, Kleist, Busch, Weichs and Manstein were summoned from their duties to the Berghof to read out a message condemning General von Seydlitz-Kurzbach, 'the contemptible traitor to our holy cause', and emphasizing their support for Hitler.

Melnikov's department, on the other hand, started to have doubts. Recruitment had tailed away, while the propaganda efforts had not won over a single major unit, even when the Wehrmacht was suffering massive defeats. Seydlitz attributed 'the absence of significant success' to 'the lack of inclination in Germans for revolution, a system of police violence and the complete suppression of opinion, the absence of any capable resistance organization, and the total fear of defeat and its consequences, fanned for so long by the fear of bolshevism'. Despite these failures, he still wanted the Soviet Union to 'recognize officially' the National Committee as a government in waiting. But Dmitry Manuilsky, in a typically Stalinist twist, warned that Seydlitz's memorandum, 'compiled in a devious way', was a 'provocative attempt' to 'exacerbate our relations with our allies'. 'There is no doubt', he wrote, 'that the recognition of the National Committee by the Soviet government would provoke in Great Britain and the United States a whole campaign directed to show the position of the Soviet Union as pro-German.' The Molotov–Ribbentrop Pact clearly cast long shadows in Soviet memories. Manuilsky suspected that Seydlitz was being manipulated by General Rodenburg and the 'former military intelligence chief', Colonel van Hooven (who was in fact a signals officer).

Stalinist paranoia became worse. In May 1944, Weinert, the President of the National Committee, sent three German officers to the Leningrad Front to carry out propaganda for the Red Army. Two of the officers, Captain Stolz and Lieutenant Willimzig, refused to do what they were ordered. They were brought back to Moscow under close escort to be interrogated by Weinert, Ulbricht, General von Seydlitz and General Lattmann. After four days they are said to have confessed to being 'members of an illegal fascist organization inside the League of German Officers'. Both men were arrested by the NKVD as double agents working for the Nazis, and taken away for further interrogation. Other German officers, including General Rodenburg, were arrested and 'confessed' in their turn. Manuilsky, pretending that his earlier suspicions of a plot were now justified, immediately gave the order that all German officers should be removed from propaganda duties at the front. Clearly Stalin had decided that these unsuccessful efforts were simply not worth provoking any trouble with the Western Allies at such a stage of the war, when he needed all their help.

Seydlitz at this time suffered bouts of severe depression. In an attempt to bolster his morale, NKVD officers organized a birthday cake for him with four red marzipan roses to represent his four daughters. But like all manic-depressives, he also underwent irrational bursts of optimism. The assassination attempt against Hitler on 20 July may have been a failure, but the ensuing Gestapo repression revealed the degree of opposition within the German Army at home. Even Strecker, on hearing of the execution of Field Marshal von Witzleben, was persuaded to sign an appeal against Hitler, but he still despised Seydlitz.

On 8 August 1944, Beria reported triumphantly to Stalin that Paulus had finally signed a declaration to the German people. Paulus's subsequent appeal to Army Group North to surrender was entirely drafted by the NKVD 'on Comrade Shcherbakov's instructions', and signed on 21 August by Paulus and twenty-nine captured generals.

Paulus's declarations triggered Hitler's rage again at having made him a field marshal. The Führer's suspicion that he would give in to his Soviet captors appeared to be confirmed. Yet clearly, Paulus, after nearly a year and a half of imprisonment, had not made his decision on the spur of the moment. His son Friedrich, a captain, had been killed at Anzio in February 1944, and he had no doubt come to see his duty differently. He wanted to help shorten a lost war and diminish the number of senseless deaths. His other son, Ernst Alexander, also a captain, was subsequently arrested under the *Sippenhaft* decree. That autumn, their Romanian mother, Elena Constance Paulus, who had always distrusted the Nazis, was told by Gestapo officers that she would be spared if she renounced his name. She is said to have turned her back on them scornfully. She was arrested and held in a camp.

Paulus, cut off from reliable news, requested meetings with a member of the Central Committee 'who could explain the principles of Soviet policy towards a conquered Germany'. He 'and the other generals held prisoner bore a heavy responsibility calling for the overthrow of Hitler's government, and therefore had a moral right to know the position of the Soviet government towards Germany'.

He expressed his hopes that Germany might be saved from annihilation during a series of interviews in February 1945, with Lieutenant-General Krivemko, the chief of the NKVD Department for Prisoners of War, and Amyak Zakharovich Kobulov, who ran the Third Directorate of the Ministry of State Security. (Kobulov, the NKVD resident in Berlin just before the launch of Operation Barbarossa, had operated Dekanozov's torture and execution chamber within the Soviet Embassy.) 'It should be mentioned', Krivemko and Kobulov wrote in their report to Beria, 'that with military operations carried on to German territory, the mood among German general prisoners of war is severely depressed. General of Artillery von Seydlitz was greatly upset by news of the meeting of leaders of the Three Powers [at Yalta]. Seydlitz declared that Germany looked as though it was going to be divided between the USA, Great Britain, the USSR and France. Germany will be left in shreds and the best way out would be to join the USSR "as the seventeenth Soviet Republic".'

When news of Germany's unconditional surrender broke in Moscow on 9 May 1945, and a thousand-gun salute boomed out monotonously from the Kremlin, Strecker recorded how he and his colleagues suffered 'spiritual depression . . . listening to the victorious Russian announcements and the songs of drunken Soviet soldiers'.

For Russians, on the other hand, it was the proud yet sad end of a nightmare which had begun almost four years before and cost the Red Army nearly 9 million dead and 18 million wounded. (Only 1.8 million prisoners of war returned alive out of more than 4.5 million taken by the Wehrmacht.) Civilian casualties are much harder to assess, but they are thought to run to nearly 18 million, bringing the total war dead of the Soviet Union to over 26 million, more than five times the total of German war dead.

In 1946, Paulus appeared as a witness at the Nuremberg tribunal. The Soviet Press referred to him as 'the ghost of Stalingrad'. Afterwards, he was lodged in a villa in Moscow, where he played cards and wrote his version of events. He had aged rapidly and his tic was worse than ever. In 1947 his wife died in Baden-Baden, without having seen her husband again. One can only speculate as to her feelings about the disaster which the battle of Stalingrad signified for Romania, the country of her birth, as well as for her own family.

In November 1947, when the Cold War was rapidly intensifying, the Soviet authorities decided that those deemed guilty of war crimes under the ukase of 13 April 1943, 'irrespective of their physical condition', would be sent on forced labour to Vorkhuta at the northern end of the Urals. Former members of the SA, the SS, camp guards, the Secret Field Police and the Feldgendarmerie – in some cases even the Hitler Youth – were transferred to 'special regime' camps. The definition of war crimes extended from atrocities against civilians to the looting of chickens and fodder for horses.

As the future structure of the German Democratic Republic (the

DDR) began to be assembled in the Soviet-occupied zone of Germany, some senior officers from Stalingrad, including Lattmann, Korfes, Müller and Steidle were allotted roles, several joining the Volkspolizei. General Arno von Lenski's conversion to Communism led to his being chosen as a member of the Politburo. Colonel Adam, still a fellow traveller, was appointed to a post in the tame Social Unity Party. General von Seydlitz, however, lost out in every direction.

In 1949, another wave of Stalinist purges swept the Soviet Union. German prisoners of war suddenly faced manufactured 'war crimes' trials. The Cold War, following the siege of West Berlin, was at its most volatile stage. The fighter ace, Erich Hartmann, was charged with destroying aircraft, the property of the Soviet government. General Strecker was taken back to Stalingrad, where a court martial found him guilty of destroying the tractor factory, even though his corps had been nowhere near the place until the very end of the battle, by which time it had long been a ruin. Like the majority accused in this wave, he received a death sentence, automatically commuted to twenty-five years' imprisonment. Lieutenant Gottfried von Bismarck was condemned to twenty-five years' hard labour because Russian prisoners of war had worked on his family's estate in Pomerania. In July 1950, the thoroughly disillusioned and embittered General von Seydlitz was arrested and sentenced to twenty-five years' imprisonment as a war criminal and 'revanchist reactionary general'.

Less controversial prisoners found peace of a sort, often thanks to the compassion of Russian women. In some cases, it formed part of an old tradition. Past the prison camp of Kamshkovo, between Moscow and Gorky, ran the Vladimirskaya, the old road along which tsarist exiles were marched to Siberia. Peasants had come out to give them water or even to carry their burdens along the road for them. A similar humanity, untouched by ideology, still existed.

The Austrian doctor, Hans Dibold, was deeply moved by the sympathy of Russians when one of their most respected medical officers, Dr Richard Speiler, from the Weizsäcker hospital in Heidelberg, fell ill suddenly in the early spring of 1946. He had survived typhus, typhoid and diphtheria in the Ilmen camp. His colleagues were convinced at first that he had malaria. In fact it was blood poisoning picked up during his work. His colleagues were tormented by the idea that their misdiagnosis was leading to his death. They gave him sulphonamides and the last of their penicillin. The two Russian dispensary assistants also handed over the last of their penicillin, which had been allocated for Russian patients, but he died just the same.

The hospital cemetery was approached by a track with low pines and juniper bushes on each side. Behind lay the forest. The Russian doctors paid their respects and the commandant allowed Speiler's colleagues to organize his funeral in the forest cemetery exactly as they wished. Speiler had returned to the Christian faith in his last few days. The Russian doctors, paying no heed to the possible reactions of a commissar, also attended the funeral service, conducted by a tall, frail pastor. For survivors of the Sixth Army present that day, the service 'was valid not only for the one dead man there, but for all who lay outside, and all those others far to the south, in Stalingrad and in the steppe between the Don and the Volga, and whom no Christian word had accompanied to their last rest'.

Since 1945, some 3,000 or so of the Stalingrad prisoners had been released, either individually or in batches and allowed home, usually because they were deemed unfit for labour. In 1955 there were still 9,626 German prisoners of war, or 'convicted war criminals' as Khrushchev described them, of whom some 2,000 were survivors of Stalingrad. These prisoners were finally set free after Chancellor Konrad Adenauer's visit to Moscow in September 1955. They included Generals Strecker, Seydlitz, Schmidt and Rodenburg, and Lieutenant Gottfried von Bismarck, who, almost thirteen years before, had flown into the *Kessel* to rejoin his unit after that dinner with Field Marshal von Manstein. Just to have survived, he wrote, was 'sufficient reason to be thankful in the face of fate'.

Seydlitz, when their journey ended in Friedland bei Göttingen, knew that he faced a difficult future in the atmosphere of the Cold War. In April 1944, he had been condemned *in absentia* as a traitor, and all his possessions were confiscated. This ruling was overturned by a court in 1956, but the new Bundeswehr refused to restore his rank and pension. The fact that he had cooperated with the Communist enemy put him, in the eyes of many, in a different league from those officers who tried to assassinate Hitler, even though General Achim Oster, one of the few survivors of the July Plot, recognized Seydlitz as belonging to their ranks. He died, like his cavalry ancestor, 'a very unhappy man'.

As the historical events were raked over in the post-war years, the mutual recriminations over responsibility for the sacrifice of the Sixth Army became increasingly bitter. Schmidt, who contrary to Hitler's expectations had always refused to cooperate with his captors, remained ferociously hostile to officers in the Free Germany movement. Colonel Adam, who had accused him of forcing Paulus to fight to the end, was treated witheringly in return as a 'pensioner of the Soviet-occupied zone'.

Paulus, in East Germany, tried vainly to defend himself from accusations of having been subservient to Hitler and indecisive. After his release from captivity in the autumn of 1953, he lived in the Soviet zone, where he wrote paper after paper explaining the situation he had faced. A long, painful illness led to his death in Dresden in 1957. His body was brought to the west, and buried next to that of his wife, in Baden-Baden.

His opponent at Stalingrad, General Chuikov, whose 62nd Army had followed the long road to Berlin as the 8th Guards Army, became commander of the occupation forces, a Marshal of the Soviet Union and deputy minister of defence under Khrushchev, who had appointed him on that September night of crisis by the Volga. The thousands of Soviet soldiers executed at Stalingrad on his orders never received a marked grave. As statistics, they were lost among the other battle casualties, which has a certain unintended justice.

APPENDIX A

German and Soviet Orders of Battle, 19 November 1942

WEHRMACHT

SIXTH ARMY	General of Panzer Troops Paulus
	Major-General Schmidt
Ia Operations:	Colonel Elchlepp†
Ib Quartermaster:	Major von Kunowski
Ic Intelligence:	Lieutenant-Colonel Niemeyer†
IIa Adjutant:	Colonel W. Adam
Chief of Artillery:	Major-General Vassoll
Chief of Signals:	Colonel Arnold* (replaced by Colonel van Hooven‡)
Chief of Engineers:	Colonel H. Selle* (replaced by Colonel Stiotta*)
Chief of Medical Corps:	General Renoldi
OKH liaison officer:	Lieutenant-Colonel von Zitzewitz*

ARMY TROOPS: MAJOR UNITS

Mortar regiments: 51st, 53rd
Nebelwerfer regiments: 2nd, 30th
Artillery regiments: 4th, 46th, 64th, 70th
Artillery battalions: 54th, 616th, 627th, 849th
Heavy-artillery battalions: 49th, 101st, 733rd
Pioneer battalions: 6th, 41st

IV CORPS	General of Pioneers Jaenecke*
	Colonel Crome
29th Motorized Infantry Division	Major-General Leyser
297th Infantry Division	Lieutenant-General Pfeffer
371st Infantry Division	Lieutenant-General Stempel†
VIII CORPS	General of Artillery Heitz
	Colonel Schildknecht
76th Infantry Division	Lieutenant-General Rodenburg
113th Infantry Division	Lieutenant-General Sixt von Arnim
XI CORPS	Lieutenant-General Strecker
	Colonel Groscurth‡
44th Infantry Division	Lieutenant-General Deboi
376th Infantry Division	Lieutenant-General Freiherr Edler von Daniels
384th Infantry Division	Lieutenant-General Freiherr von Gablenz*
XIV PANZER CORPS	General of Panzer Troops Hube*
	Colonel Thunert*
3rd Motorized Infantry Division	Lieutenant-General Schlömer
60th Motorized Infantry Division	Major-General Kohlermann*
16th Panzer Division	Lieutenant-General Angern†
LI CORPS	General of Artillery von Seydlitz-Kurzbach
	Colonel Clausius
71st Infantry Division	Lieutenant-General von Hartmann†
79th Infantry Division	Lieutenant-General Graf von Schwerin*
94th Infantry Division	Lieutenant-General Pfeiffer*
100th Jäger Division	Lieutenant-General Sanne
295th Infantry Division	Major-General Doctor Korfes
305th Infantry Division	Major-General Steinmetz*

389th Infantry Division   Major-General Magnus
14th Panzer Division   Major-General Lattmann
24th Panzer Division   Lieutenant-General von Lenski

LUFTWAFFE GROUND TROOPS
9th Flak Division   Major-General Pickert*

LUFTWAFFE AIR SUPPORT
4th Air Fleet   Colonel-General Freiherr von Richthofen

VIII AIR CORPS   General Fiebig

* flown out of the *Kessel* before the final surrender
† died before or just after the final surrender
‡ died in captivity

RED ARMY ON THE 'STALINGRAD AXIS'

REPRESENTATIVES OF THE *STAVKA*:
Army General G. K. Zhukov
Colonel-General of Artillery N. N. Voronov
Colonel-General A. M. Vasilevsky

Stalingrad Front   Colonel-General A. I. Yeremenko
     N. S. Khrushchev

62ND ARMY   General V. I. Chuikov
Rifle Divisions: 13th Guards (A. I. Rodimtsev), 37th Guards (V. G.

Zholudev), 39th Guards (S. S. Guriev), 45th, 95th (V. A. Gorishny),
112th, 138th (I. I. Lyudnikov), 193th (F. N. Smekhotvorov), 196th,
244th, 284th (N. F. Batyuk), 308th (L. N. Gurtiev); 10th NKVD Rifle
Division (Rogatin)
Marine Infantry Brigade: 92nd
Special Brigades: 42nd, 115th, 124th, 149th, 160th
Tank Brigades: 84th, 137th, 189th

64TH ARMY   General M. S. Shumilov
Rifle Divisions: 36th Guards, 29th, 38th, 157th, 204th
Marine Infantry Brigade: 154th
Special Brigades: 66th, 93rd, 96th, 97th
Tank Brigades: 13th, 56th

57TH ARMY   General F. I. Tolbukhin
Rifle Divisions: 169th, 422nd
Special Brigade: 143rd
Tank Brigades: 90th, 235th

*13th Mechanized Corps (T. I. Tanashchishin)

51ST ARMY   General N. I. Trufanov
Rifle Divisions: 15th Guards, 91st, 126th, 302nd
Special Brigade: 38th
Tank Brigade: 254th

*4th Mechanized Corps (V. T. Volsky)
*4th Cavalry Corps (Shapkin)

28TH ARMY
Rifle Divisions: 34th Guards, 248th
Special Brigades: 52, 152, 159
Tank Brigade: 6th Guards

Stalingrad Front Reserve: 330th Rifle Division; 85th Tank Brigade

8TH AIR ARMY   General T. T. Khryukin

Don Front   Colonel-General K. K. Rokossovsky

66TH ARMY   Major-General A. S. Zhadov
Rifle Divisions: 64th, 99th, 116th, 226th, 299th, 343rd
Tank Brigade: 58th

24TH ARMY   General I. V. Galanin
Rifle Divisions: 49th, 84th, 120th, 173rd, 233rd, 260th, 273rd
Tank Brigade: 10th

16th Tank Corps

65TH ARMY   Lieutenant-General P. I. Batov
Rifle Divisions: 4th Guards, 27th Guards, 40th Guards, 23rd, 24th, 252nd,
   258th, 304th, 321st
Tank Brigade: 121st

16TH AIR ARMY   Major-General S. I. Rudenko

South-West Front   General N. F. Vatutin

21ST ARMY   General I. M. Chistyakov
Rifle Divisions: 63rd, 76th, 96th, 277th, 293rd, 333rd
Tank Regiments: 1st, 2nd, 4th Guards

*4th Tank Corps (A. G. Kravchenko)
*3rd Guards Cavalry Corps (P. A. Pliev)

5TH TANK ARMY   General P. L. Romanenko
Rifle Divisions: 14th Guards, 47th Guards, 50th Guards, 119th, 159th, 346th

*1st Tank Corps (V. V. Butkov)
*26th Tank Corps (A. G. Rodin)
*8th Cavalry Corps

1ST GUARDS ARMY   General D. D. Lelyushenko
Rifle Divisions: 1st, 153rd, 197th, 203rd, 266th, 278th

Front Reserve: 1st Guards Mechanized Corps

2ND AIR ARMY

17TH AIR ARMY   Major-General S. A. Krasovsky

* First-wave breakthrough formations for Operation Uranus

APPENDIX B

The Statistical Debate:
Sixth Army Strength in the Kessel

The variety of figures cited for the strength of the encircled Sixth Army requires at least an attempt at clarification. Estimates of the strength of the Sixth Army within the *Kessel* on 19 November 1942 range widely, mainly it seems because there were so many Russians incorporated in the ranks of the Sixth Army that they had been included on the German ration strength and not cited separately. Some of the figures of Manfred Kehrig, the author of *Stalingrad: Analyse und Dokumentation einer Schlacht*, the magisterial volume published in 1974 under the auspices of the Militärgeschichtlichen Forschungs-samt, have recently been challenged by Rüdiger Overmans. Overmans, work-ing mainly from Wehrmacht retrospective estimates (basically an attempt later to calculate from personnel records who had been trapped inside the *Kessel*), puts the figure of surrounded Germans as low as 195,000, the Hiwis at 50,000 and the Romanians at 5,000, a total of approximately 250,000. Kehrig had estimated 232,000 Germans, 52,000 Hiwis and 10,000 Romanians, a total of approximately 294,000. Another more recent study estimates a total on 18 December of 268,900, of which 13,000 were Romanians and Italians, and 19,300 Hiwis.

This latest breakdown, allowing for the difference in dates and consequent casualty figures, tallies fairly closely with the total compiled on 6 December by the Sixth Army's Oberquartiermeister. This 'Sixth Army ration strength in the *Kessel*' gave a total of 275,000 men, including 20,300 Hiwis and 11,000 Romanians. (Romanian army sources assert that they had 12,600 men in the *Kessel*. There were also several hundred Italians.) If one adds to these figures the 15,000 men lost 'only inside the *Kessel*' between 21 November and

6 December, that would mean that almost 290,000 men had been surrounded on 22 November.

All writers are agreed that around 25,000 wounded and specialists were flown out, but there is little certainty over the numbers killed or taken prisoner. The truth will never be known in the chaos after the Soviet offensive of 10 January 1943 to crush the *Kessel*. All that we can be fairly sure of is that just under 52,000 members of the Sixth Army had died between 22 November and 7 January, but it is not stated how many of these were Hiwis. The Soviet figure of prisoners taken between 19 November and 31 January – 111,465 as well as 8,928 in hospitals – does not specify how many were German nor, more important, how many belonged to the encircled troops, as opposed to those captured during Operations Winter Storm and Little Saturn.

The Soviet onslaught of Operation Ring on 10 January 1943, added to the effects of disease, cold, starvation, exhaustion and summary execution, suggests that losses soared – they may well have doubled to around 100,000, including Hiwis. Both Kehrig and Overmans estimate German losses from 22 November until the surrender at close to 60,000. They naturally make no attempt to estimate the number of Hiwis who died during the fighting. One can only assume that very few got away with their lives afterwards.

References

ARCHIVAL SOURCES

AMPSB	Arkhiv Muzeya Panorami Stalingradskoy Bitvi (Archive of the Panoramic Museum of the Battle of Stalingrad), Volgograd
APRF	Arkhiv Prezidiuma Rossiyskoy Federatsii (Archive of the Presidium of the Russian Federation), Moscow
BA-MA	Bundesarchiv-Militärarchiv, Freiburg im Breisgau
BZG-S	Bibliothek für Zeitgeschichte – Sammlung Sterz, Stuttgart
GARF	Gosudarstvennyy Arkhiv Rossiyskoy Federatsii (State Archive of the Russian Federation), Moscow
MGFA-P	Militärgeschichtliches Forschungsamt library, Potsdam
ÖStA-AdR	Österreichisches Staatsarchiv – Archiv der Republik, Vienna
ÖStA-KA	Österreichisches Staatsarchiv – Kriegsarchiv, Vienna
PRO	Public Record Office, Kew (UK)
RGALI	Rossiyskiy Gosudarstvennyy Arkhiv Literaturi i Iskusstva (Russian State Archive of Literature and the Arts), Moscow
RGVA	Rossiyskiy Gosudarstvennyy Voennyy Arkhiv (Russian State Military Archive), Moscow
RTsKhIDNI	Rossiyskiy Tsentr Khraneniya i Izucheniya Dokumentov Noveyshey Istorii (Russian Centre for the Conservation and Study of Documents of Contemporary History), Moscow
TsAMO	Tsentralnyy Arkhiv Ministerstva Oborony (Central Archive of the Ministry of Defence), Podolsk
TsKhIDK	Tsentr Khraneniya i Izucheniya Dokumentalnikh Kollektsiy

References

(Centre for the Conservation and Study of Historic Document Collections), Moscow

TsMVS   Tsentralnyy Muzey Vooruzhyonnykh Sil (Central Museum of the Armed Forces), Moscow

VOTsDNI   Volgograd Oblast, Tsentr Dokumentov Noveyshey Istorii (Volgograd Regional Centre for Documents of Contemporary History)

(NB. German documents cited from Russian archives are, unless otherwise stated, Russian translations of captured papers.)

INTERVIEWS AND UNPUBLISHED ACCOUNTS

Yelena Filippovna Albert (Stalingrad anti-aircraft defences); Winrich Behr (Hauptmann, HQ Sixth Army and Sonderstab Milch); Lev Aleksandrovich Bezyminsky (Senior Lieutenant, Red Army Intelligence, Don Front HQ); Gottfried von Bismarck (Leutnant, 76th Infantry Division); C. M. Bogomolov (Lieutenant, NKVD, Don Front HQ); Alexander Fürst zu Dohna-Schlobitten (Rittmeister, HQ XIV Panzer Corps); Nikolay Dmitrevich Dyatlenko (Major, NKVD, Don Front HQ); Josef Farber (Soldat, 305th Infantry Division); Generalleutnant a.D. Bernd Freiherr von Freytag-Loringhoven (Hauptmann, 16th Panzer Division and Sonderstab Milch); Zinaida Georgevna Gavrielova (Lieutenant, Medical Services, 62nd Army); Prof. Dr Hans Girgensohn (pathologist, Sixth Army); Aleksandr Vladimirovich Glichov (Lieutenant, 24th Army, then 65th Army); Professor Nikolay Viktorovich Goncharov (Stalingrad civilian); Nina Grigorevna Grebennikova (Stalingrad civilian); Dr Yevgeny Aleksandrovich Grigorev (Stalingrad civilian); Klemens Graf von Kageneck (Hauptmann, 3rd Panzer Division); Viktor Ivanovich Kidyarov (Sergeant, 62nd Army); Lazar Ilich Lazarev (Lieutenant, Marine Infantry); Henry Metelmann (Soldat, 22nd Panzer Division); Valentina Ivanovna Nefyodova (Stalingrad civilian); Oberstleutnant a.D. Gert Pfeiffer (Hauptmann, 60th Motorized Infantry Division); Hans Schmieder (Hauptwachtmeister, 9th Flak Division, Luftwaffe); Aleksandr Sergeevich Smirnov (Sergeant, 64th Army); Klavdia Vasilevna Sterman (Private, Red Army Aviation); Aleksandr Vasilevich Tsygankov (Lieutenant, 62nd Army); Boris Nikolaevich Ulko (Corporal, 1st Guards Army); Heinz Wischnewski (Leutnant, 22nd Infantry Division)

Three other veterans wanted their contributions to remain anonymous.

Source Notes

PREFACE

p. xiv 13,500 executions, Institute of Military History, 21 Jan. 1993, quoted in Erickson, 'Red Army battlefield performance', p. 244

p. xiv 'former Russians', Dobronin to Shcherbakov, 8 Oct. 1942, TsAMO 48/486/24, p. 81

CHAPTER I

p. 3 'an important clarification', Berezhkov, *In diplomatischer Mission bei Hitler*, p. 63

p. 3 'thirty-nine aircraft . . .', Maslennikov, RGVA, 38652/1/58

p. 4 'is not here . . .', Berezhkov, op. cit., p. 64

p. 5 'Disinformation has . . .', quoted in Andrew and Gordievsky, p. 212

p. 6 'In the course . . .', quoted in Erickson, *The Road to Stalingrad*, p. 110

p. 6 'Reichsminister von Ribbentrop . . .', Berezhkov, op. cit., p. 65

p. 7 'barely five feet tall . . .', Andrew and Gordievsky, p. 195

p. 7 'like a caged . . .', 'statesmanlike . . .', 'The Führer . . .', Schmidt, pp. 212, 234

p. 7 'His face was scarlet . . .', Berezhkov, op. cit., p. 67

p. 8 'The Soviet Government's . . .', Schmidt, pp. 234–5

p. 8 'The Führer . . .', Berezhkov, op. cit., p. 67

p. 8 'You'll regret . . .', Berezhkov, op. cit., p. 68

p. 9 'Even if you retreat . . .', Volkogonov, p. 413

p. 10   'It was as if . . .', Gavrielova, conversation, 22 Nov. 1995

p. 10   'fought in four wars', Goncharov, conversation, 23 Nov. 1995

p. 10   'We thought . . .', Nefyodova, conversation, 22 Nov. 1995

p. 11   'Propaganda fell . . .', Grigorev, conversation, 22 Nov. 1995

CHAPTER 2

p. 12   'Nothing is impossible . . . !' Reichstag speech of 4 May 1941, *Völkischer Beobachter*, 5 May 1941

p. 12   'to establish a defence . . .', Führer Directive No. 21, 18 Dec. 1940

p. 13   'The war with Russia . . .', Gefreiter, 24th Pz. Div., interrogation, 12 Aug. 1942, TsAMO 48/453/13, p. 32

p. 13   305th Inf. Div. motor transport, BA-MA, RH19 VI/1, p. 129

p. 14   'Our optimism . . .', Freytag-Loringhoven, conversation, 23 Oct. 1995

p. 14   'the final encounter . . .', IMT ND-447-PS

p. 14   'that the downfall of 1918 . . .', BA-MA, RW4/577

p. 14   'That would be . . .', Stahlberg, p. 159

p. 15   'battle between . . .', quoted in Messerschmidt, p. 214

p. 16   'Many tens of millions . . .', IMT ND 221-L

p. 16   'It makes one's hair . . .', Hassell, 8 Apr. 1941, p. 173

p. 16   'The annihilation of those same Jews . . .', quoted in Jürgen Förster, 'Motivation and indoctrination in the Wehrmacht, 1933–1945', in Addison and Calder, p. 270

p. 17   'The jewish-bolshevik . . .', 11th Army HQ, 20 Nov. 1941, quoted in Klee and Dressen, pp. 41–44

p. 17   'The generals . . .', Paulus, 21 July 1951, 'Das Verhalten der Generalität unter Hitler', BA-MA, N372/9, p. 1

p. 17   'For us . . .', Edgar Klaus, p. 36, and *Beiträge zur Geschichte der 60. Infanterie Division (mot.)*, TS, MGFA-P, 1979, p. 3

p. 17   'Instead of . . .', Kroll, conversation, 6 May 1996

p. 18   'Within the regiment . . .', Kageneck, conversation, 24 Oct. 1995

p. 18   'of the three . . .', Dr Alois Beck, ÖStA-AdR 522

p. 18   'You could not . . .', anonymous conversation, 16 May 1996

p. 18   'the Wehrmacht should not . . .', Theo Schulte, 'The German soldier in occupied Russia', in Addison and Calder, p. 279

p. 18   'shocked by . . .', Dohna-Schlobitten, pp. 213–14, and conversation, 16 Oct. 1995

p. 19   'handed over . . .', RGVA, 38652/1/8

p. 19   'The bombs were falling . . .', Col. I. T. Starinov, 'The frontier aflame', in Bialer, p. 225

p. 20   'Of course I'll be there . . .', Schmidt, p. 233

p. 20   'approximately 160 . . .', quoted in Domarus, vol. ii, p. 1731

p. 20   'European Crusade . . .', *Völkischer Beobachter*, 28 June 1941

CHAPTER 3

p. 21   'I know! It has already . . .', Starinov, op. cit., in Bialer, p. 222

p. 22   'impetuous dash . . .', Erich von Manstein, *Lost Victories*, p. 187

p. 22   'Our pilots feel . . .', 4 Oct. 1942, TsAMO 48/486/24, p. 48

p. 23   'The Germans are coming . . .', Erickson, *The Road to Stalingrad*, p. 121

p. 23   'the study of the . . .', Erickson, 'The development of Soviet military doctrine', p. 7

p. 24   'political demands . . .', captured document, APRF 3/58/451

p. 25   'I was with the troops . . .', Starinov, op. cit., in Bialer, p. 237

p. 25   'a number of conclusions', APRF, 45/1/478

p. 26   'I am dying . . .', TsMVS

p. 26   'nearly always stubborn . . .', APRF, 3/58/451

p. 27   'shocking and incomprehensible', Gavrielova, conversation, 22 Nov. 1995

p. 27   'The hatred Fascism . . .', Grossman, *Life and Fate*, p. 34

p. 27   'The Motherland Calls!', TsMVS

p. 28   'Our aim is to defend . . .', quoted in N. D. Dyatlenko MS.

p. 28   'Tomorrow, or . . .', Ehrenburg collection, RGALI 1204/2/3453

p. 29   'the greatest battle . . .', Sommerfeldt, pp. 95–6

p. 30   'Look closely . . .', Malaparte, p. 61

CHAPTER 4

p. 31   'The vastness . . .', 12 August 1941, quoted in Messenger, p. 150

p. 32   'up to forty miles . . .', Gottfried von Bismarck MS.

p. 32   'the knights of modern warfare', Podewils, p. 32

p. 35   'What a great . . .', letter, 11 Oct. 1941, quoted in Paulus, p. 144

p. 35   'Strong-point after . . .', letter, Lt-Gen. Himer, 2 Oct. 1941, quoted in Paulus, p. 143

p. 37   'rubbish', quoted in Volkogonov, p. 422

p. 38   'with his impassive . . .', Werth, *The Year of Stalingrad*, p. 104
p. 38   'Was the military parade . . .', conversation, Ulko, 22 Nov. 1995
p. 39   'If they want a war of extermination . . .', Werth, *Russia at War*, p. 246
p. 39   'There can be . . .', Erickson, *The Road to Stalingrad*, p. 258
p. 40   'Many of the men . . .', Gen. d. Pz. Tr. Rudolf Schmidt, XXXIX Panzer Corps, 13 Nov. 1941, quoted in Paulus, p. 145
p. 40   'This is no longer . . .', quoted in Bartov, *Hitler's Army*, p. 41
p. 44   'a small army . . .', Melnikov to Beria, 25 Sept. 1943, TsKhIDK, 451p/2/6
p. 44   'The German people . . .', Hitler, quoted in Seydlitz, p. 114
p. 44   'You could see . . .', Pabst, p. 54
p. 44   'photographing of executions . . .', German reference: W 283/11.41c, 28 Nov. 1941, RTsKhIDNI 17/125/96
p. 45   'destroy and burn to ashes', quoted in Volkogonov, p. 456
p. 45   'Suicide in . . .', order entitled 'Suicide and Attempted Suicide' of 17 Jan. 1942, TsAMO 48/453/21, p. 29
p. 45   'Christmas will not take place . . .', TsAMO 206/294/48, p. 468
p. 46   'You are under . . .', TsAMO 206/294/48, p. 346
p. 46   'Notes for Those . . .', TsAMO 206/294/48, pp. 471–4
p. 47   'We want to return . . .', Reichenau to XXIX Army Corps, 25 Dec. 1941, 01348/41, RTsKhIDNI 17/125/96
p. 47   'Front Letter No. 3', TsAMO 206/294/12, pp. 17–19

CHAPTER 5

p. 52   'roughneck . . .', quoted in Messenger, p. 61
p. 53   'more like a scientist . . .', Kageneck, conversation, 24 Oct. 1995
p. 54   'Even his . . .', letter, 11 Feb. 1942, quoted in Paulus, p. 164
p. 54   'punitive measures', VOTsDNI 113/14/306, quoted in Epifanov, p. 135
p. 55   SS–Obersturmführer August Häfner, quoted in Klee and Dressen (eds.), p. 111
p. 55   'In various places . . .', reproduced in Heer (ed.), p. 75
p. 55   'dishonourable for officers . . .', Paget, p. 173
p. 56   'We cannot . . .', quoted in Groscurth, p. 91
p. 56   'You should bring with you . . .', quoted in Heer, p. 78
p. 56   more than 30,000, R. W. M. Kempner, *SS im Kreuzverhör*, Munich, 1964, p. 29
p. 56   Reichenau's order, quoted in Klee and Dressen (eds.), p. 39

p. 57   village of Komsomolsk, TsAMO 206/294/48

p. 57   'Interrogations should end . . .', TsAMO 48/453/21, p. 32

p. 57   'The Landsers go . . .', 5 July 1942, TsAMO 206/294/48, p. 485

p. 58   'Führer's Birthday' and other examples all in BA-MA, N395/10

p. 58   'dead men lying . . .', Kageneck, p. 30

p. 59   'We were afraid . . .', Kageneck, pp. 32–3

p. 59   'Most of them . . .', Malaparte, p. 121

p. 59   600 Soviet prisoners, Goldhagen, p. 157

p. 59   'should be left to starve', BA-MA, N159/4, quoted in Messerschmidt, pp. 221–2

p. 59   'of cold, of starvation . . .', Erickson, *The Road to Stalingrad*, p. 328

p. 59   Maximov, NKVD report, 4 Mar. 1943, TsAMO 226/335/7, p. 364

p. 60   'Their information on . . .', 29 Mar. 1942, RTsKhIDNI 17/125/96

p. 60   'work only if . . .', 16 Mar. 1942, RTsKhIDNI 17/125/96

p. 60   'My ambulance had . . .', Dr Hans Heinz Schrömbgens, quoted in Schneider-Janessen, p. 136

p. 61   Feodosia, BA-MA, RW2/v. 151, 152, quoted in de Zayas, p. 181

p. 62   'Morale was . . .', Freytag-Loringhoven, conversation, 23 Oct. 1995

p. 62   'Just be happy . . .', Bruno Gebele, in Beck, p. 102

p. 63   'qualitative superiority . . .', Förster, 'Evolution and development of German doctrine 1914–1945', p. 7

p. 63   'My great concern . . .', Bock diary, 8 May 1942, quoted in Paulus, p. 176

p. 63   'that it was a farewell . . .', Seydlitz, p. 147

p. 63   'The buildings . . .', Seydlitz, p. 148

p. 65   'shells bounced . . .', Kageneck, conversation, 24 Oct. 1995

p. 66   'The fighting methods . . .', Uffz. Hans Urban, 389th I.D., BA-MA, RW4/v 264, p. 89

p. 67   'the German searchlights . . .', MS. by unknown soldier in Ehrenburg papers, RGALI 1204/2/3453

p. 67   'the success . . .', 20 May 1942, quoted in Paulus, p. 166

p. 67   'How refreshing it is . . .', 12 July 1942, quoted in Paulus, p. 168

CHAPTER 6

p. 69   'If we don't take . . .', Paulus, p. 157

p. 71   'the fateful place', Podewils, p. 29

p. 73   'The Russian tanks . . .', Podewils, pp. 47–8

p. 73   'shot them . . .', TsAMO 230/586/1, p. 78

p. 74 'During the . . .', Bock diary, 3 July 1942, Paulus, p. 185

p. 75 'As far as the eye . . .', Podewils, p. 47

p. 75 'It was almost . . .', Kageneck, conversation, 24 Oct. 1995

p. 76 'an ocean that . . .', Strecker, 19 July 1942, Haller, p. 44

p. 76 'Black figures . . .', Podewils, p. 44

p. 77 'A really small boy . . .', 5 July 1942, Bähr and Bähr, p. 137

p. 77 'Germany, I have not . . .', Bähr and Bähr, p. 139

p. 77 'Our lads have . . .', Cpl István Balogh, diary entry, 24 July 1942, RTsKhIDNI 17/125/97

p. 78 'We were starved . . .', TsAMO 206/294/47, p. 147

p. 80 Rattenhuber's interrogation by SMERSH on 28 Nov. 1945, *Voennye Arkhivi Rossii*, No. 1, 1993, p. 357

p. 81 'The constant . . .', Halder, 23 July 1942, p. 489

p. 81 'a sun-ray cure', quoted in Stahlberg, p. 308

p. 81 'absolute League of Nations army', quoted in Messenger, p. 149

p. 82 'amid silent people . . .', RTsKhIDNI 17/125/97

p. 82 'enough to buy . . .', interrogation 26 Sept. 1942, TsAMO 206/294/47, p. 561

p. 82 'A man went to . . .', RTsKhIDNI 17/125/97

p. 83 98,000 casualties, Mark Axworthy, 'The Romanian soldier at the siege of Odessa', in Addison and Calder, p. 227

p. 83 'The habit of looting . . .', RTsKhIDNI 17/125/97

CHAPTER 7

p. 84 'They've forgotten . . .', TsAMO 3/11 556/9, Volkogonov, p. 459

p. 84 'anyone who removes . . .', Order 270 of 16 Aug. 1941, TsAMO 298/2526/5a, quoted in Volkogonov, p. 427

p. 85 'Panic-mongers . . .', 16 Aug. 1942, TsAMO 48/486/28, p. 8

p. 85 'to combat cowardice', Zhukov to Stalin, quoted in Volkogonov, p. 469

p. 85 'traitor to the . . .', RTsKhIDNI 17/43/1774

p. 85 422,700 Red Army men, Erickson, 'Red Army battlefield performance', in Addison and Calder, p. 236

p. 85 'atone with . . .', TsAMO 48/486/28, p. 15

p. 85 'already wounded . . .', Dobronin to Shcherbakov, 29 Oct. 1942, TsAMO 48/486/24, p. 315

p. 86 'pale because they . . .', Nikolay Filin, 'Kak i pochemu ya byl agentom SMERSh', *Vechernyaya Moskva*, 25 Nov. 1995

p. 86 'It is very difficult . . .', Ehrenburg papers, RGALI 1284/2/3466

p. 86 'of the treatment . . .', order from Second Panzer Army, 9 Feb. 1942, RTsKhIDNI 17/125/96

p. 87 'Most of the soldiers . . .', 10 Aug. 1942, TsAMO 48/453/13, p. 10

p. 87 'a sin against . . .', TsAMO 48/453/13, pp. 4–7

p. 87 'as hot . . .', letter, 9 July 1942, quoted in Haller, p. 192; '53 degrees in the sun', Groscurth, p. 527

p. 87 'The Russians have . . .', Gefr. H. S., 389th I.D., 10 Aug. 1942, BZG-S

p. 87 'Soviet bombers . . .', BA-MA, RH27-16/42

p. 88 'the plague of flies . . .', Dr Günther Diez, quoted in Schneider-Janessen, p. 130

p. 88 'To be honest . . .', 19 July 1942, TsAMO 206/294/48, p. 485

p. 89 horsebrush, TsAMO 48/486/28, p. 15

p. 89 'about this senseless task', Podewils, p. 98

p. 90 'hiding in a ditch', 31 July 1942, TsAMO 206/294/47, p. 251

p. 90 'They had a longer range . . .', Freytag-Loringhoven, conversation, 23 Oct. 1995

p. 91 'They would have quickly . . .', Simonov, *Raznye dni voiny*, p. 180

p. 92 'Russians resisting . . .', 2, 3, 5 and 6 Aug. 1942, TsAMO 206/294/48, p. 486

p. 92 night-fighter regiment, Sterman, conversation, 7 Nov. 1995

p. 94 'Papa Hube', BA-MA, RH27-16/42

p. 94 'consuming so many . . .', Behr, conversation, 25 Oct. 1995

p. 94 'old warhorse', Dohna-Schlobitten, conversation, 16 Oct. 1995

p. 94 'too pessimistic', Freytag-Loringhoven, conversation, 23 Oct. 1995

p. 94 'Not an encouraging sight . . .', Podewils, p. 85

p. 95 'whenever a Russian . . .', Metelmann, conversation, 12 Apr. 1996

p. 95 'an enormous herd of elephants', Seydlitz, p. 158

p. 96 'The Russians are . . .', quoted Paulus, p. 187

p. 96 '*höchst primitiv*', Podewils, p. 95

p. 96 181st Rifle Division, conversation, Tsygankov, 22 Nov. 1995

p. 97 'the many, many . . .', Sold. H. R., 9 Aug. 1942, 389th I.D., BZG-S

p. 97 seventy-two corpses, 24 Sept. 1942, TsAMO 62/335/7

p. 97 'The Russians can . . .', Gefr. W. V., 9 Aug. 1942, 305th I.D., BZG-S

p. 97 'The only consolation . . .', Sold. B. B., 389th I.D., 14 Aug. 1942, BZG-S

p. 97 'workers' columns', RTsKhIDNI 17/43/1773

p. 98 petroleum-storage tanks, Nefyodova and Grebennikova, conversation, 23 Nov. 1995

p. 98 'Do you want to defend . . . ?' Albert, conversation, 23 Nov. 1995

p. 98 high-school pupils, RTsKhIDNI 17/43/1774

p. 99 'Traitor to the Party . . .', RTsKhIDNI 17/43/1774

p. 99 'special attention to the investigation . . .', Dobronin to Shcherbakov, 18 Nov. 1942, TsAMO 48/486/25, p. 240

p. 99 'advising him to . . .', RTsKhIDNI 17/43/1774

p. 99 'political and moral degeneracy . . .', RTsKhIDNI 17/43/1774

p. 100 'the end of the world . . .', Lazarev, conversation, 13 Nov. 1995

p. 100 'After the Don . . .', TsAMO 206/294/48, p. 485

CHAPTER 8

p. 103 'a very exhilarating . . .', Freytag-Loringhoven, conversation, 23 Oct. 1995

p. 103 'General Paulus . . .', Richthofen diary, 20 Aug. 1942, Paulus, p. 188

p. 103 'to cripple . . .', Richthofen diary, 23 Aug. 1942, Paulus, p. 188

p. 103 'Make use of today!' Podewils, p. 107

p. 104 'in tightly packed groups', BA-MA, RH27-16/42

p. 104 'Stalingrad, the city of Stalin . . .', BA-MA, RH20-6/216

p. 104 'a day which . . .', Gavrielova, conversation, 22 Nov. 1995

p. 104 'Comrades, an air-raid . . .', Nekrassov, p. 82

p. 104 'not just industrial . . .', Grigorev, conversation, 22 Nov. 1995

p. 105 'literally had to drag . . .', Nefyodova, conversation, 22 Nov. 1995

p. 105 'Before filling in . . .', Goncharov, conversation, 23 Nov. 1995

p. 106 1,600 sorties, 1,000 tons, Plocher, p. 231

p. 106 'No one bothered . . .', Goncharov, conversation, 23 Nov. 1995

p. 106 'Around Gumrak . . .', BA-MA, RH27-16/42

p. 107 'seemed to think . . .', Albert, conversation, 22 Nov. 1995

p. 107 'Oh, they're finished now!' Grossman papers, RGALI 618/2/108

p. 107 'the soldiers . . .', BA-MA, RH27-16/42

p. 107 'We had started . . .', Freytag-Loringhoven, conversation, 23 Oct. 1995

p. 107 'The Volga is reached!' BA-MA, RH20-6/216

p. 107 'a feeling of . . .', Langsdorff, p. 194

p. 108 'We looked at the . . .', Freytag-Loringhoven, conversation, 23 Oct. 1995

p. 108 'the girls refused . . .', Grossman papers, RGALI 618/2/108

p. 108 'stayed at her post . . .', Goncharov, conversation, 22 Nov. 1995

p. 108 'Right until the late . . .', BA-MA, RH27-16/42

p. 108 'It is completely . . .', BA-MA, RW4/v. 264

p. 109 'We shall never surrender . . .', TsMVS

p. 109 'deserted his post', RTsKhIDNI 17/43/1773

p. 110 'Yesterday we reached . . .', Gefr. E. R. 16th Pz. Div., 25 Aug. 1942, BZG-S

p. 110 '*mit Eleganz*', Gefr. B. G., 2 Sept. 1942, BZG-S

p. 111 'gunboats', BA-MA, RH27-16/42

p. 111 'We know how . . .', Podewils, p. 117

p. 112 'like a calm lake', Podewils, p. 105

p. 112 'Soon we too will . . .', Gefr. B. G., 24 Aug. 1942, BZG-S

p. 112 'The song will really . . .', Uffz. W. W., 27 Aug. 1942, BZG-S

p. 112 'You can't imagine . . .', Sold. H. R., 389th I.D., 28 Aug. 1942, BZG-S

p. 113 'very nervous', Richthofen diary, Paulus, p. 188

p. 113 'the closer the . . .', Strecker, Haller, p. 89

p. 113 'We will not abandon . . .', 26 Aug. 1942, TsMVS

p. 114 'Many men have . . .', Dobronin to Shcherbakov, 29 Oct. 1942, TsAMO 48/486/24, p. 308

p. 114 'Concentration of enemy . . .', ÖStA-KA B/1540

p. 115 'led a battalion . . .', Dobronin to Shcherbakov, 8 Oct. 1942, TsAMO 48/486/24, p. 78

p. 115 'This silver streak . . .', Podewils, p. 119

p. 115 'Gentlemen, flying for fun . . .', Einsiedel, p. 12

p. 116 'This shitty Russia', Uffz. H. T., 71st I.D., 30 Aug. 1942, BZG-S

p. 117 'worried and angry', Glichov, conversation, 6 Nov. 1995

p. 117 'What's the matter . . .', Volkogonov, p. 461

p. 118 'Delay at this moment', Erickson, *The Road to Stalingrad*, p. 384

p. 118 The Germans also suffered . . ., BA-MA, RH27-16/43

p. 118 'Hello, my dear ones!' V. M. Kovalov, 2 Sept. 1942, AMPSB 258/4904

p. 118 'the Volga was the last line . . .', Glichov, conversation, 6 Nov. 1995

p. 119 'but Stalingrad will . . .', Gefr. B. G., 3 Sept. 1942, BZG-S

p. 119 'According to . . .', Sold. W. W., 305th I.D., 2 Sept. 1942, BZG-S

p. 119 'The ring round . . .', BA-MA, RH20-6/216

p. 119 'Here, everyone . . .', letter, 23 Aug. 1942, quoted in Paulus, p. 169

CHAPTER 9

p. 121 'the fateful city', letter, 3 Dec. 1942, Groscurth, p. 530

p. 123 'satisfying progress . . .', Halder, 7 Sept. 1942, p. 518

p. 123 'That is a lie!' quoted in Domarus, vol. ii, p. 1908

p. 123 'long stare . . .', Warlimont, p. 269

p. 124 'a completely new . . .', Below, p. 315

p. 124 'The tanks are no good . . .', BA-MA, RH27-16/43

p. 124 'The Russians attacked . . .', Freytag-Loringhoven, conversation, 23 Oct. 1995

p. 124 'As far as the eye . . .', Gefr. O. K., 13 Sept. 1942

p. 125 'What if your beloved . . .', *Stalinskoe znamia*, 8 Sept. 1942

p. 125 'Do not count days . . .', Zayas, p. 169

p. 125 'sad smell of . . .', Simonov, *Raznye dni voiny*, vol. ii, pp. 175–6

p. 127 'Comrade Chuikov . . .', Chuikov, p. 84

p. 128 'Time is blood', Chuikov, p. 89

p. 128 'to get across the Volga . . .', Chuikov, p. 93

p. 128 'experienced traitor . . .', 8 Oct. 1942, TsAMO 48/486/24, p. 77

p. 129 'every German must . . .', Chuikov, p. 80

p. 129 'strong positions . . .', BA-MA, RH20-6/216

p. 129 'then fourteen days . . .', Halder, p. 521

p. 129 'A mass of Stukas . . .', Gefr. H. S., 389th I.D., BZG-S

p. 131 'Yeremenko says . . .', Zhukov, p. 143

p. 131 'Both divisions . . .', BA-MA, RH20-6/216

p. 133 'Major Stalin', S. D. Lugansky, 'Malenkov', in Bialer, p. 455

p. 134 'the kites perched . . .', Grossman papers, RGALI 618/2/108

p. 135 'flowed from Rodimtsev . . .', conversation, Kidyarov, 22 Nov. 1995

p. 135 'Since yesterday . . .', anon., 29th I.D. (mot.), 15 Sept. 1942, BZG-S

p. 136 'he was afraid of . . .', 8 Oct. 1942, TsAMO 48/486/24, p. 77

p. 136 'Instead of taking . . .', 8 Oct. 1942, TsAMO 48/486/24, p. 77

p. 137 'did not agree . . .', 8 Oct. 1942, TsAMO 48/486/24, p. 78

p. 137 'These clouds of earth . . .', Grossman, *Life and Fate*, p. 35

p. 138 'Stalingrad has been taken . . .', TsAMO 3/11 556/10, quoted in Volkogonov, pp. 474–5

p. 138 'Whenever an Me-109 . . .', 4 Oct. 1942, TsAMO 48/486/24, p. 48

p. 138 'As soon as Stuka . . .', Max Plakolb, ÖStA-KA B/1540; Kalb interrogation, TsAMO 48/453/13, p. 70

p. 139 'Attack target area . . .', Herbert Pabst, letters, quoted in Bähr and Bähr, pp. 186–8

p. 139 'The soldiers' . . .', Dr Günther Diez, Schneider-Janessen, p. 130

p. 141 'Each Guards soldier . . .', conversation, Kidyarov, 22 Nov. 1995

p. 142 'The air is filled . . .', BA-MA, RH27-16/42

p. 142 'It's not a human . . .', Podewils, p. 115

p. 142 'Home is so far . . .', Herbert Pabst, quoted in Bähr and Bähr, p. 184

p. 142 'Hello, my dear Palina!', AMPSB 22789

p. 142 'The Germans won't . . .', AMPSB 752-/5.481
p. 143 'left the line of defence . . .', Dobronin to Stalingrad Front Military
Council, 3 Oct. 1942, TsAMO 48/486/24, pp. 9, 30–32

CHAPTER 10

p. 145 'necessity of indoctrinating . . .', Halder, p. 528
p. 145 'The general staff . . .', 19 Aug. 1942, Groscurth, p. 548
p. 146 'ready to film . . .', Dohna-Schlobitten, p. 246
p. 146 'the battle flag . . .', BA-MA, RH20-6/216, p. 51
p. 146 'in much too rosy . . .', quoted in Boelcke, p. 365
p. 146 'from morning . . . highly nervous', 29 Aug. 1942, Groscurth, p. 550
p. 148 'fighting in the . . .', Grossman papers, RGALI 618/2/108
p. 148 'like a layered cake', Goncharov, conversation, 25 Nov. 1995
p. 148 'an aberration in the art of war', Förster, 'Evolution and development
of German doctrine . . .', p. 2
p. 149 'The enemy is . . .', Strecker, Haller, p. 90
p. 149 'Not a house is left . . .', Lt Anselm Radbruch, letter, 26 Sept. 1942,
Bähr and Bähr, p. 174
p. 149 'The defenders have . . .', Max Plakolb, ÖStA-KA B/1540
p. 149 'Make a mistake . . .', Smirnov, conversation, 22 Nov. 1995
p. 150 'If only you could . . .', Grossman papers, RGALI 1710/1/100
p. 150 25 million rounds, BA-MA, RH20-6/216, p. 58
p. 150 'The Russkies . . .', Gefr. O. K., Pion. Bt 45, 16 Sept. 1942, BZG-S
p. 151 'We lie exhausted . . .', Klaus, p. 20
p. 151 'The Russians' unchallenged . . .', Sixth Army war diary, 15 Nov.
1942, BA-MA, RH20-6/221
p. 152 'in Stalingrad . . .', Tsygankov, conversation, 22 Nov. 1995
p. 152 'On the other side . . .', Grossman papers, RGALI 681/2/108
p. 153 'Vanyusha . . .', Tsygankov, conversation, 22 Nov. 1995
p. 153 'Further weapon training . . .', 3 Oct. 1942, TsAMO 48/486/24, p. 10
p. 154 'the gaunt and melancholy', Grossman papers, RGALI 618/2/108
p. 154 'Look after your . . .', TsAMO 48/486/39, p. 21
p. 155 'covered in icicles . . .', Tsygankov, conversation, 22 Nov. 1995
p. 155 'Shells exploding . . .', Col. Vishnevsky, 17 Nov. 1942, AMPSB 602/
10343
p. 157 'every imaginable sort . . .', Lazar Ilich Lazarev, conversation, 13 Nov.
1995
p. 157 'military tribunal of NKVD Forces', RTsKhIDNI 17/43/1773

p. 157 'physically and spiritually . . .', Gavrielova, conversation, 22 Nov. 1995

p. 157 'brought over a hundred . . .', and 'threw grenades . . .', TsMVS

p. 157 Kochnevskaya, 21 Nov. 1942, TsAMO 48/486/25, p. 268

p. 158 'thousands of wounded . . .', Sterman, conversation, 7 Nov. 1995

p. 158 'They often closed . . .', Professor Krimskaya, quoted in Schneider-Janessen, p. 134

p. 158 Yekaterina Petlyuk, John Erickson, 'Soviet women in war', in Garrard and Garrard (eds.), p. 66

p. 158 'I had never seen . . .', Simonov, *Raznye dni voiny*, p. 187

p. 159 'In hospital . . .', Grossman papers, RGALI 1710/1/100

p. 159 'socialist competition', Dobronin to Shcherbakov, 28 Oct. 1942, TsAMO 48/486/24, pp. 297–8

p. 159 'If they don't . . .', 4 Nov. 1942, TsAMO 48/486/25, p. 47

p. 160 'it seemed as though . . .', Maj. V. Velichko, 'The 62nd Army', in USSR, *Stalingrad*, p. 148

p. 161 'white symmetrical . . .', Nekrassov, p. 82

p. 162 'Russian women . . .', Uffz. Hans Urban, BA-MA, RW4/v. 264, p. 89

p. 162 'One more battle . . .', Chuikov, p. 167

p. 162 'You can't imagine . . .', Gefr. H. S., 389th I.D., BZG-S

p. 163 'the confusing . . .', Viktor Kainzer, Jäg.-Rgt 54, *Stalingradbund Österreich*, May 1984

p. 164 'Where are you?' Chuikov, p. 184

p. 164 'For the defenders . . .', 17 Nov. 1942, TsAMO 48/486/25, p. 216

p. 165 'no man will shift . . .', quoted in Domarus, vol. ii, pp. 1914, 1916

CHAPTER 11

p. 166 'We Russians were . . .', Smirnov, conversation, 22 Nov. 1995

p. 166 'In the blazing city . . .', Chuikov, p. 223

p. 166 'Those who do not . . .', *Stalinskoe znamia*, 4 Sept. 1942

p. 166 'the defeatist mood . . .', 8 Oct. 1942, TsAMO 48/486/24, p. 74

p. 167 German tanks protect deserters, TsAMO 48/486/24, p. 20

p. 167 Deserters from 124th Special Brigade, 3 Oct. 1942, Dobronin to Stalingrad Front Military Council, TsAMO 48/486/24, p. 8

p. 167 'Since their last . . .', BA-MA, RH27-16/43

p. 167 'he was arrested . . .', BA-MA, RH27-16/43

p. 167 'Morale among . . .', Uffz. J. Sch., 79th I.D., 22 Sept. 1942, BZG-S

p. 168   178th Reserve Rifle Regt, Dobronin to Shcherbakov, 21 Oct. 1942, TsAMO 48/486/24, p. 239

p. 168   'citizens of Stalingrad . . .', 13 Nov. 1942, TsAMO 48/486/25, p. 162; 8 Oct. 1942, TsAMO 48/486/24, p. 77

p. 168   'A shortage of . . .', 8 Oct. 1942, TsAMO 48/486/24, p. 77

p. 168   'It was impossible . . .', 26 Nov. 1942, TsAMO 48/486/25, pp. 317–18

p. 169   'If I am sent to the . . .', 16 Nov. 1942, TsAMO 48/486/25, p. 209

p. 169   'the carelessness . . .', 13 Nov. 1942, TsAMO 48/486/25, p. 165

p. 169   'an extreme measure . . .', 15 Nov. 1942, TsAMO 48/486/25, p. 201

p. 169   'During the night . . .', 13 Nov. 1942, TsAMO 48/486/25, p. 165

p. 170   'It is hard for them . . .', 11 Nov. 1942, TsAMO 48/486/25, pp. 138–9

p. 170   'received such . . .', 14 Nov. 1942, TsAMO 48/486/25, p. 183

p. 170   'To indoctrinate . . .', 14 Nov. 1942, TsAMO 48/486/25, p. 185

p. 170   'He announced that . . .', 15 Oct. 1942, TsAMO 48/486/24, p. 176

p. 170   'It is very difficult . . .', 13 Nov. 1942, TsAMO 48/486/25, p. 163

p. 170   'In battle conditions . . .', TsAMO 48/486/24, p. 79

p. 171   'criminal disorder . . .', 23 Nov. 1942, TsAMO 48/486/25, p. 292

p. 171   446 desertions, TsAMO 48/486/29, p. 49

p. 171   'a protective zone . . .', 15 Oct. 1942, TsAMO 48/486/24, p. 187

p. 171   'tried to hide . . .', 8 Oct. 1942, TsAMO 48/486/24, p. 82

p. 171   'Eleven soldiers . . .', 25 Oct. 1942, TsAMO 48/486/24, p. 259

p. 172   'a sign of cowardice . . .', 7 Nov. 1942, TsAMO 48/486/25, p. 106

p. 172   'men found with . . .', 18 Nov. 1942, TsAMO 48/486/25, p. 240

p. 172   'discredited the leaders . . .', 8 Oct. 1942, TsAMO 48/486/24, pp. 82–3

p. 172   'When soldiers mutter . . .', Nikolay Filin, 'Kak i pochemu ya byl agentom SMERSh', *Vechernyaya Moskva*, 25 Nov. 1995

p. 173   'nine grams of lead', TsAMO 48/486/24, p. 162

p. 173   'thanks to . . .', Dobronin to Shcherbakov, 8 Oct. 1942, TsAMO 48/486/24, p. 76; 18 Nov. 1942, TsAMO 48/486/25, p. 236

p. 173   'To be honest . . .', quoted in Garrard and Garrard, p. 155

p. 173   'cemented the stones . . .', Maj. V. Velichko, 'The 62nd Army', in USSR, *Stalingrad*, p. 145

p. 174   'Life is not easy . . .', Grossman papers, RGALI 1710/1/100

p. 175   'only fifty yards out . . .', Goncharov, conversation, 24 Nov. 1995

p. 175   'Today I saw . . .', Uffz. H. D., 295th I.D., 6 Nov. 1942, BZG-S

p. 176   'We crossed a bridge . . .', Simonov, 25 Sept. 1942, in USSR, *Stalingrad*, p. 60

p. 176   'these things cannot be helped . . .', Simonov, 25 Sept. 1942, in USSR, *Stalingrad*, p. 64

p. 177 'The enemy . . .', 5 Nov. 1942, TsAMO 48/486/25, p. 63

p. 177 'suitable', VOTsDNI, 113/14/306L, quoted in Epifanov, p. 136

p. 178 'the majority aged between . . .', from the interrogation of Mikhail Bulanov, 3 Dec. 1943, quoted in Klee and Dressen (eds.), p. 95

p. 178 'in hopeless cases . . .', Podewils, p. 131

p. 178 'a huge black crowd', Nefyodova, conversation, 23 Nov. 1995

p. 179 'no one knows how', Goncharov, conversation, 24 Nov. 1995

p. 179 'signalling to the enemy . . .', Dobronin to Stalingrad Front Military Council, 3 Oct. 1942, TsAMO 48/486/24, pp. 9, 32

p. 179 270,000 Ukrainians, BA-MA Wi ID/33, in Sergei Kudryashov, 'The hidden dimension', in Erickson and Dilks, p. 242

p. 179 800 Ukrainian youths, VOTsDNI, 113/14/306, pp. 75–90, Epifanov, p. 153

p. 180 Stalingrad campaign interrogations of German and allied PoWs, TsAMO 62/335/7, 48/453/13, 206/294/12, 206/294/47, 206/294/48, 226/335/7

p. 180 'Older soldiers . . .', captured 16 Sept. 1942, TsAMO 48/453/13, p. 36

p. 180 Kaplan interrogations, TsAMO 48/453/13, pp. 75, 46, 48

p. 181 'very energetic measures . . .', 7 Aug. 1942, 14th Pz. Div., RTsKhIDNI 17/125/96

p. 181 'How can we possibly . . .', RTsKhIDNI 17/125/97

p. 182 'God keep me alive . . .', RTsKhIDNI 17/125/97

p. 182 'God, don't let . . .', RTsKhIDNI 17/125/97

p. 182 'You should . . .', 30 July 1942, TsAMO 206/294/48, p. 466

p. 183 'We did not fire . . .', TsAMO 206/294/47, p. 251

p. 183 991 Special Strafbattalion, RTsKhIDNI 17/125/97

p. 183 'Russian agents . . .', TsAMO 48/453/21, p. 96

p. 184 'lords and vassals', Klaus, p. 23

p. 184 'Above all . . .', Stolberg report, BA-MA, RW4/v. 264, p. 161

p. 184 'one for officers . . .', BA-MA, RW4/v. 264, p. 156

p. 184 'To avoid in future . . .', 19 Sept. 1941, 3rd Rom. Army to 13th Rom. I.D., RTsKhIDNI, 171/125/96

p. 184 'It is disturbing . . .', 25 Oct. 1942, Groscurth, p. 552

p. 184 50,000 Russian auxiliaries, Kehrig, pp. 662–3; see also Rüdiger Overmans, 'Das andere Gesicht des Krieges', in Förster (ed.), *Stalingrad*, p. 441

p. 184 'Russians in the German . . .', 4 Mar. 1943, TsAMO 226/335/7, p. 364

p. 185 'We believed the leaflets . . .', RTsKhIDNI 17/125/97

p. 186 'Ivan', conversation, Henry Metelmann, 12 Apr. 1996
p. 186 'On some parts . . .', 8 Oct. 1942, TsAMO 48/486/24, p. 81

CHAPTER 12

p. 187 'Will Stalingrad . . .', letter to his brother, Groscurth, p. 528
p. 187 'the dark towering bulk . . .', Grossman papers, RGALI, 628/2/108
p. 188 'The Russians made . . .', Uffz. Philipp Westrich, 100th Jäger Division, BA-MA, RW4/v. 264, p. 86
p. 189 'dogged, rugged . . .', Grossman papers, RGALI 618/2/108
p. 190 'As soon as dusk falls . . .', Grossman papers, RGALI 618/2/108
p. 191 overloaded boat, 15 Oct. 1942, TsAMO 48/486/24, p. 162
p. 191 'encircle minefields . . .', TsAMO 48/486/25, p. 66
p. 191 'drunk themselves out . . .', TsAMO 48/486/39, p. 22
p. 191 'the infantry company . . .', Dobronin to Shcherbakov, 15 Oct. 1942, TsAMO 48/486/24, p. 188, and 48/486/28, p. 216
p. 192 'which signifies . . .', Sixth Army war diary, 10 Oct. 1942, BA-MA, RH20-6/221
p. 192 'The whole sky . . .', Gefr. H. S., 389th I.D., 14 Oct. 1942, BZG-S
p. 193 'The fighting assumed . . .', Maj. V. Velichko, 'The 62nd Army', in USSR, *Stalingrad*, p. 149
p. 193 'Those of us . . .', Dobronin to Shcherbakov, 15 Oct. 1942, TsAMO 48/486/24, p. 189
p. 193 'Our support . . .', Uffz. H. G., 305th I.D., 24 Oct. 1942, BZG-S
p. 193 'It was a terrible . . .', Grams, p. 54
p. 194 'The major part . . .', Sixth Army war diary, BA-MA, RH20-6/221
p. 194 'more than thirty medium . . .', TsAMO 48/486/35, pp. 212–13
p. 194 'Guns destroyed . . .', TsAMO 48/486/35, p. 214
p. 194 'real mass heroism', TsAMO 48/486/24, p. 200
p. 195 'Factory walls . . .', Strecker, quoted in Haller, p. 90
p. 195 'Our General . . .', Sold. H. R., 389th I.D., 14 Oct. 1942, BZG-S
p. 195 'The help of our fighter . . .', TsAMO 48/486/35, p. 212
p. 195 'I cannot understand . . .', Herbert Pabst, 18 Oct. 1942, Bähr and Bähr, p. 188
p. 196 'hundreds of wounded . . .', Chuikov, p. 203
p. 197 'exceptional cowardice', Koshcheev to Shcherbakov, 9 Nov. 1942, TsAMO 48/486/25, p. 117
p. 198 'Communist-infected circles', Boelcke, p. 384
p. 199 'Hello, Shura!' RGALI 1284/2/3466

p. 199 'I'm getting along . . .', Grossman papers, RGALI 618/2/108

p. 199 'we are constantly . . .', 12 Oct. 1942, AMPSB 7555/13530

p. 199 'Mariya . . .', 23 Oct. 1942, AMPSB 7555/13530

p. 200 'People might reproach me . . .', AMPSB, quoted in Volgograd University history department project

p. 200 'I often ask myself . . .', Leutnant Otten, AMPSB, quoted in Volgograd University history department project

p. 200 'I can't stop worrying . . .', to Josef Joffner from his wife in Nuremberg, AMPSB N45079A

p. 200 'Aunt Lyuba . . .', 11 Nov. 1942, TsAMO 48/486/25, p. 139

p. 200 'the wounded caught . . .', 7 Nov. 1942, TsAMO 48/486/25, p. 117

p. 201 'In 62nd Army alone . . .', 11 Nov. 1942, TsAMO 48/486/25, pp. 138–9

p. 201 'In the occupied . . .', 11 Nov. 1942, TsAMO 48/486/25, p. 151

p. 202 'absolutely incorrect attitude' and 'unnecessary appendix', 14 Nov. 1942, Koshcheev to Shcherbakov, TsAMO 48/486/25, p. 179

p. 202 'Without my permission . . .', Koshcheev to Shcherbakov, 21 Nov. 1942, TsAMO 48/486/25, p. 262

p. 202 'because now that they . . .', 14 Nov. 1942, TsAMO 48/486/25, pp. 179–80

p. 202 'a counter-revolutionary statement', Dobronin to Shcherbakov, 18 Oct. 1942, TsAMO 48/486/24, p. 249

p. 202 'They've invented the Orders . . .', Dobronin to Shcherbakov, 15 Oct. 1942, TsAMO 48/486/24, p. 162

p. 202 'criminal carelessness', 15 Oct. 1942, TsAMO 48/486/24, p. 344

p. 202 medal in vodka, Lazarev, conversation, 13 Nov. 1995

p. 203 'a new wave of . . .', 4 Nov. 1942, TsAMO 48/486/25, pp. 176–7

p. 203 'noble sniper', 10 Nov. 1942, TsAMO 48/486/25, p. 122

p. 204 *Rus, komm, komm!*' 6 Nov. 1942, TsAMO 48/486/25, pp. 76–7

p. 204 'Fascists should know . . .', 4 Nov. 1942, TsAMO 48/486/25, p. 58

p. 204 'learned the dark sides of life', Grossman papers, RGALI 618/2/108

p. 205 Manenkov, 17 Nov. 1942, TsAMO 48/486/25, p. 216

p. 205 'still the best . . .', 12 Nov. 1942, TsAMO 48/486/25, p. 144

p. 205 'In war . . .', Grossman papers, RGALI, 1710/1/100

p. 206 'formerly workers . . .', 4 Nov. 1942, TsAMO 48/486/25, p. 52

p. 206 'so close to the . . .', Hptm. Kempter, quoted in Hauck, pp. 74–5

p. 206 'the dogs fight . . .', Gefr. H. S., 389th I.D., 5 Nov. 1942, BZG-S

p. 207 'We felt at home in the dark', Chuikov, p. 211

p. 207 'Father . . .', Gefreiter Gelman to his family, AMPSB, quoted in Volgograd University history department project

p. 207 'Don't worry . . .', Grossman papers, RGALI 1710/1/100
p. 207 'Here a saying . . .', Sold. K. H. 113th I.D., 27 Oct. 1942, BZG-S

CHAPTER 13

p. 208 Munich *Oktoberfest*, BA-MA, N395/9
p. 208 'It's not an . . .', Sold. K. H., 113th I.D., 27 Oct. 1942, BZG-S
p. 208 'We really need . . .', Uffz. H. D., 295th I.D., 6 Nov. 1942, BZG-S
p. 209 'a highly *active* defence', 14 Oct. 1942, BA-MA, RH20-6/220
p. 209 *How to Construct* . . ., BA-MA, RH20-6/238, p. 197
p. 209 'The Führer has . . .', 7 Nov. 1942, Groscurth, p. 529
p. 209 'rises and falls . . .', Uffz. W. B. 371st I.D., 26 Oct. 1942, BZG-S
p. 209 'Here one must . . .', Uffz. A. R., 60th I.D. (mot.), 19 Nov. 1942, BZG-S
p. 209 'most beautiful festival . . .', Uffz. H. B., 371st I.D., 28 Oct. 1942, BZG-S
p. 209 'requirements for . . .', 3 Nov. 1942, BA-MA, RH27-24/3
p. 210 'who have been in the . . .', AOK 6, 29 Oct. 1942, BA-MA, RH20-6/220
p. 210 'It's a typically German affair . . .', Pabst, p. 121
p. 210 'For the time being . . .', Uffz. A. R., 60th I.D. (mot.), 19 Nov. 1942, BZG-S
p. 210 'Jaundice especially . . .', Klaus, p. 21
p. 211 '*Fieberkurve*' and 'the troops' reduced . . .', Dr Dormanns, 28 Jan. 1943, quoted in Schneider-Janessen, p. 132
p. 211 'fearless commander . . .', Koshcheev to Shcherbakov, 4 Nov. 1942, TsAMO 48/486/25, pp. 61–2
p. 211 'The effect of massed . . .', KTB AOK 6, BA-MA, RH20-6/221
p. 212 'In the last two days . . .', 6 Nov. 1942, TsAMO 48/486/25, p. 69
p. 212 'to install . . .', 7 Nov. 1942, TsAMO 48/486/25, p. 101
p. 212 'heavy enemy night bombing . . .', Sixth Army war diary, 1 Nov. 1942, BA-MA, RH20-6/221
p. 212 'Along the whole . . .', 7 Nov. 1942, Groscurth, p. 529
p. 212 'exceeding . . .', 6 Nov. 1942, TsAMO 48/486/25, p. 70
p. 212 'out of 1,697 Komsomol . . .', TsAMO 48/486/10, p. 275
p. 212 'got drunk', report of 11 Nov. 1942, TsAMO 48/486/25, p. 142
p. 213 'anti-chemical liquids', 23 Nov. 1942, TsAMO 48/486/25, pp. 291–3
p. 213 'I wanted to reach . . .', quoted in Domarus, vol. ii, pp. 1937–8
p. 214 'Hitler refused outright . . .', Below, p. 322

p. 214 'The ice floes collide . . .', Grossman papers, RGALI 618/2/108

p. 214 Volga steamers, Grossman papers, RGALI 618/12/21

p. 215 347th Rifle Regt, 7 Nov. 1942, TsAMO 48/486/25, p. 101

p. 215 signal flares, 10 Nov. 1942, TsAMO 48/486/25, p. 122

p. 215 '*Rus!* Don't shoot!', 7 Nov. 1942, TsAMO 48/486/25, p. 115

p. 215 'it was noticed . . .', 10 Nov. 1942, TsAMO 48/486/25, p. 122

p. 216 'army conventionality', Richthofen diary, 1 Nov. 1942, Paulus, p. 190

p. 217 'hurricane of fire', and 'Begin shelling . . .', 15 Nov. 1942, TsAMO 48/486/25, pp. 197–8

p. 217 'If they can't . . .', Richthofen diary, 16 Nov. 1942, in Paulus, p. 191

p. 218 'Hitler was obsessed . . .', Behr, conversation, 25 Oct. 1995

p. 218 '42 per cent of his battalions . . .', Philippi and Heim, p. 177

p. 218 'all the trials . . .', Seydlitz, p. 164

p. 218 'These were different . . .', Glichov, conversation, 6 Nov. 1995

p. 219 'not in the air, but at the Germans', 13 Nov. 1942, TsAMO 48/486/25, p. 155

CHAPTER 14

p. 220 'And what . . .', Zhukov, p. 140; Erickson, *The Road to Stalingrad*, p. 389

p. 221 'shift the strategic . . .', Zhukov, p. 140

p. 221 'deep operations', Erickson, 'The development of Soviet military doctrine', p. 5

p. 222 'a regime of the strictest secrecy', Vasilevsky, p. 189

p. 223 'but Zhukov was Zhukov', Glichov, conversation, 6 Nov. 1995

p. 223 Soviet tank production figures, Erickson, *The Road to Stalingrad*, p. 375

p. 224 'fighters in overalls', quoted in John Erickson, 'Soviet women at war', in Garrard and Garrard, p. 50

p. 224 'What was Your Help to the Front?', TsMVS

p. 224 'For the death of enemies . . .' and '4,363 . . .', Ehrenburg papers, RGALI 1204/2/3453

p. 225 'within fifteen miles . . .', RTsKhIDNI 17/43/1773

p. 227 'greatest feat was . . .', Glantz, *Soviet Military Deception in the Second World War*, p. 113

p. 227 'My dear friend . . .', Behr, conversation, 25 Oct. 1995

p. 230 'the Third Romanian . . .', Sixth Army war diary, BA-MA, RH20-6/221

p. 230 'On the Don . . .', Richthofen diary, 12 Nov. 1942, Paulus, p. 191

p. 230 'Weather . . .', Richthofen diary, 14 Nov. 1942, Paulus, p. 191

p. 230 Khrushchev and Yeremenko at Svetly-Yar, 18 Nov. 1942, TsAMO 48/486/25, p. 230

p. 231 'on a wild-goose chase', Metelmann, conversation, 12 Apr. 1996

p. 231 'Hitler was misinformed . . .', Below, p. 322

p. 232 'on receiving . . .', Sixth Army war diary, BA-MA, RH20-6/221

p. 232 81st Cavalry Division, 10 Nov. 1942, TsAMO 48/486/25, p. 123, and 21 Nov. 1942, TsAMO 48/486/25, p. 279

p. 232 'In the next few days . . .', 10 Nov. 1942, TsAMO 48/486/25, p. 129

p. 233 'We could tell . . .', Zhukov, p. 169

p. 233 'defeatism and . . .', Koshcheev to Shcherbakov, 28 Nov. 1942, TsAMO 48/486/25, pp. 355–6

p. 234 'knew something was . . .', Glichov, 6 Nov. 1995

p. 234 'I am well aware of the . . .', RTsKhIDNI 17/125/96

p. 235 119 field hospitals, Schneider-Janessen, p. 135

p. 235 'as a physician would . . .', Lt-Gen. A. Rodin, in USSR, *Stalingrad*, p. 109

p. 235 'Along the whole . . .', BA-MA, RH20-6/221

p. 235 '2,053 miles from the German . . .', Golovchanski, p. 133

CHAPTER 15

p. 239 'According to the statement . . .', BA-MA, RH20-6/221

p. 239 'as thick as milk', Lt-Gen. A. Rodin, in USSR, *Stalingrad*, p. 110

p. 240 'I have the impression . . .', Behr, conversation, 25 Oct. 1995

p. 240 'because the ground . . .', Dr Hans Heinz Schrömbgens, quoted in Schneider-Janessen, p. 135

p. 240 'I don't know', Glichov, conversation, 6 Nov. 1995

p. 240 'there will be a holiday . . .', quoted in Chuikov, p. 235

p. 241 'The attack . . .', Hptm. Krauss, BA-MA, RH19 VI/11, p. 251

p. 241 'Sappers, jump off!', Smirnov, conversation, 22 Nov. 1995

p. 244 'Once again . . .', Richthofen diary, 19 Nov. 1942, quoted in Paulus, p. 192

p. 244 'up to now . . .', Sixth Army war diary, BA-MA, RH20-6/221

p. 244 'an enemy . . .', 11.30, 19 Nov. 1942, BA-MA, RH20-6/221

p. 244 'boxes of files', Krauss, report, BA-MA, RH19 VI/11, p. 251

p. 246 'It is not even possible . . .', Richthofen diary, 19 Nov. 1942, quoted in Paulus, p. 192

p. 247 'Hopefully . . .', General von Richthofen diary, 19 Nov. 1942, Paulus, p. 192

p. 247 'Change of situation . . .', 22.00, 19 Nov. 1942, BA-MA, RH20-6/221

p. 247 'in whose ranks . . .', BA-MA, RH27-16/42

p. 247 'move out', Gefr. Joachim Grunow, Pz. Regt 2, report, 1 Aug. 1943, BA-MA, RH27-16/43

p. 248 'no particular . . .', quoted in Beck, pp. 169–70

p. 248 'masses of . . .', Gebele, quoted in Beck, p. 170

p. 249 13th Tank Brigade, 64th Army, TsAMO 48/486/25, p. 303

p. 249 'The Romanians . . .', Gebele, quoted in Beck, p. 170

p. 249 157th Rifle Division, 23 Nov. 1942, TsAMO 48/486/25, p. 290

p. 249 64th Army wounded, 25 Nov. 1942, TsAMO 48/486/25, p. 303

p. 249 'that the long-awaited . . .', 20 Nov. 1942, TsAMO 48/486/28, p. 275

p. 249 'happiest day of the whole war', Lazarev, conversation, 7 Nov. 1995

p. 249 'panzer-fright', quoted in Kehrig, p. 148

p. 250 '*Antonescu kaputt!*' 23 Nov. 1942, TsAMO 48/486/25, p. 287

p. 250 'cases of chaos . . .', TsAMO 48/486/25, p. 287

p. 251 'fleeing wildly . . .', report of Hptm. Gürtler, BA-MA, RW4/v. 264, p. 85

p. 251 'much material . . .', report, Lt Graf Stolberg, 17 Feb. 1943, BA-MA, RW4/v. 264, p. 157

p. 251 'The catastrophic . . .', 22 Nov. 1942, 24th Pz. Div., RH27-24/5

p. 252 'the road is strewn . . .', Grossman papers, RGALI 618/2/108

p. 252 'staff papers scattered . . .', USSR, *Stalingrad*, p. 112

p. 253 'a not unfavourable . . .', Kehrig, p. 160

p. 253 'Paulus and Schmidt had . . .', Behr, conversation, 25 Oct. 1995

p. 254 'for him an . . .', Richthofen diary, 23 Nov. 1942, Paulus, p. 225

p. 254 'Sixth Army stand . . .', 15.25, 21 Nov. 1942, Kehrig, p. 163

p. 255 'The first news . . .', report of Hptm. Wassermann, 16th Pz. Div., 2 Aug. 1943, RH27-16/43

p. 256 'We're surrounded!' Grams, p. 58

p. 256 'A sombre Totensonntag . . .', letter, 3 Dec. 1942, Bähr and Bähr, p. 189

p. 256 'We became very much . . .', Freytag-Loringhoven, conversation, 23 Oct. 1995

p. 256 'We will continue to fight . . .', quoted in Axworthy, p. 96

p. 257 '. . . is the offensive . . .', (original German), Ehrenburg papers, RGALI 1207/2/3477

p. 257 'as if it were 1870', Stolberg, 17 Feb. 1943, BA-MA, RW4/v. 264, p. 157

p. 257 'When the retreat started . . .', TsAMO 206/294/47, p. 147

p. 257 'Only two out of . . .', Werth, *The Year of Stalingrad*, p. 369

p. 258 'extraordinarily rapid', BA-MA, N395/11

p. 259 'The numerous Romanians', Dohna-Schlobitten, p. 256

p. 259 'especially the frantic . . .', Lt Walter Öhme, Pz. Regt 2, report, 28 July 1943, BA-MA, RH27-16/43

p. 260 'Here everything's . . .', Uffz. Römer, report, 23 May 1943, BA-MA, RH27-16/43

p. 261 'Right on towards the Don' (original German), Ehrenburg papers, RGALI 1207/2/3477

p. 261 'A number of tanks . . .', Gefr. Joachim Grunow, Panzer Regt 2, report, 1 Aug. 1943, BA-MA, RH27-16/43

p. 261 'last resort', Dohna-Schlobitten, p. 253

p. 262 'Everyone was running . . .', Uffz. Römer, report, 23 May 1943, BA-MA, RH27-16/43

p. 262 'all items . . .', Dohna-Schlobitten, p. 255

p. 262 'the very same bridge . . .', II./Pz. Gren. Rgt 64, BA-MA, RH27-16/43

p. 262 'very proud', report, Oberfeldwebel Wallrawe, BA-MA, RH27-16/43

p. 262 'I feel much better . . .', Dmitry Venkutov, 26 Nov. 1942, AMPSB 11480

p. 263 'The battles are strong . . .', AMPSB 602/10343

p. 263 'old women's kerchiefs . . .', Grossman papers, RGALI 1710/1/101

p. 263 450 collaborators, VOTsDNI 113/14/306, p. 94, quoted in Epifanov, p. 142

p. 264 'in a serious condition . . .', 25 Nov. 1942, TsAMO 48/486/25, p. 304

p. 264 'owing to . . .', Dohna-Schlobitten, p. 258

CHAPTER 16

p. 266 'I've got them!' Albert Speer, quoted in Sereny, p. 207

p. 266 'alarming news . . .', 19 Nov. 1942, KTB-OKW, vol. ii, 1942, p. 988

p. 267 'alterations to . . .', Bradley and Schulze-Kossens (eds.), p. 22

p. 267 'temporary encirclement', BA-MA, RH20-6/241

p. 267 'It's impossible . . .', General von Richthofen diary, Paulus, p. 224

p. 267 'We have nothing . . .', BA-MA, N601/v. 4, p. 3

p. 268 'Decision with reasons, please!' BA-MA, N601/v. 3, pp. 12, 13. This conversation was reconstructed and agreed by both Schmidt and Pickert, working together on 7 Jan. 1963, after they had consulted all the available documents to refresh their memories.

p. 269 wine and champagne, conversation, Behr, and BA-MA, N395/12

p. 269 'They all shared . . .', Schmidt, BA-MA, N601/v. 4, p. 7

p. 269 'Army surrounded', quoted in Kehrig, pp. 559–60

p. 269 'The Sixth Army is . . .', BA-MA, RH20-6/238

p. 270 'We've found . . .', Zeitzler, Kehrig, p. 196

p. 270 'whatever the circumstances', Kehrig, p. 562

p. 270 'highly paid NCOs', 25 Nov. 1942, Paulus, p. 227

p. 271 'completely unthinkable', Seydlitz, p. 193

p. 271 'Already the minor . . .', 25 Nov. 1942, BA-MA, N372/12, p. 2

p. 271 'In thousands of . . .', Toepke, p. 44

p. 272 'Now that you have . . .', conversation, 25 Oct. 1995

p. 272 'According to a Führer decree . . .', Sixth Army, 6 Dec. 1942, BA-MA, RH20-6/239, p. 135

p. 272 propaganda leaflets, 23 Nov. 1942, TsAMO 48/486/25, p. 277

p. 272 'The Führer ordered . . .', Bradley and Schulze-Kossens, p. 26

p. 272 'the grateful army . . .', letter, 15 Nov. 1942, Groscurth, p. 530

p. 274 'And be warned . . .', Stahlberg, p. 212

p. 274 'When we entered . . .', Stahlberg, p. 217

p. 275 'the troops in the area . . .', BA-MA, RW4/v. 264

p. 275 'The whole Sixth Army . . .', Henry Holze, in Kruse, p. 14

p. 275 'Yesterday and today . . .', 26 Nov. 1942, BA-MA, RW4/v. 264

p. 275 'the most difficult question . . .', Strecker, quoted in Haller, p. 96

p. 276 'Such an action . . .', BA-MA, N601/v. 4, p. 13

p. 276 'I know that . . .', Paulus, p. 83

p. 276 'Prussian field marshals . . .', Rudolph-Christoph Freiherr von Gersdorff, *Soldat im Untergang: Lebensbilder*, p. 134

p. 276 'march out . . .', Behr, conversation, 25 Oct. 1995

p. 276 'Hold on . . .', Paulus, order, 27 Nov. 1942, BA-MA, RH20-6/238

p. 276 Schmidt denial, BA-MA N601/v. 10, p. 12

p. 277 'We're never going . . .', Klaus, p. 35

CHAPTER 17

p. 278 'A systematic withdrawal . . .', Wallrawe, BA–MA, RH27-16/43

p. 278 'artillery and infantry . . .', TsAMO 48/486/13, p. 472

p. 279 'The bolsheviks . . .', Stolberg, report, BA–MA, RW4/v. 264, p. 159

p. 279 'It is said . . .', TsAMO 206/294/47, p. 108

p. 279 'doubts about . . .', Oblt. v.d. Sode, 16th Panzer Division, report, 12 Aug. 1943, BA–MA, RH27-16/43

p. 280 'Since the . . .', Sold. K. P., 376th I.D., 14 Dec. 1942, BZG-S

p. 280 'Rations cut . . .', BA–MA, RH20-6/237

p. 280 'It was defeatism . . .', anonymous conversation

p. 281 'But surely it doesn't matter . . .', anonymous conversation

p. 281 forty-two air raids, Römer, report, 23 May 1943, BA–MA, RH27-16/43

p. 283 'The commanding officer . . .', Kurt Reuber, letter, 18 Dec. 1942, Bähr and Bähr, p. 192

p. 284 'Miserably frozen . . .' (original German), Ehrenburg papers, RGALI, 1207/2/3477

p. 284 'We squat . . .', Reuber, letter, 3 Dec. 1942, quoted in Bähr and Bähr, p. 190

p. 284 'The plague of lice . . .', report, OGefr. Heinrich, Pz. Regt 2, 28 July 1943, BA–MA, RH27-16/43

p. 284 'Underneath the lantern . . .' (original German), TsAMO 206/294/48, p. 452

p. 285 'Because of bad communications . . .', TsAMO 48/486/13, p. 472

p. 285 'The failure of officers and commissars . . .', TsAMO 48/486/13, p. 472

p. 286 'These Russians . . .', Einsiedel, *Tagebuch der Versuchung*, p. 110

p. 286 'a tremendous education for victory . . .', Zhukov, p. 151

p. 286 'The morale of . . .', Grossman papers, RGALI 1710/1/101

p. 287 'We were like gypsies . . .', Glichov, conversation, 6 Nov. 1995

p. 287 spotted 'a white mug with a rose', Glichov, conversation, 14 Nov. 1995

p. 288 'When I killed . . .', Lazarev, conversation, 13 Nov. 1995

p. 288 'A soldier felt . . .', Lazarev, conversation, 13 Nov. 1995

p. 289 'very difficult', Lazarev, conversation, 13 Nov. 1995

p. 290 'Listen, Herr General . . .', Strecker, quoted in Haller, p. 97

p. 290 'Things seem . . .', Groscurth, 3 Dec. 1942, p. 530

CHAPTER 18

p. 291 'I can't remain . . .', 11 Dec. 1942, BA-MA, RW4/v. 264, p. 212

p. 292 captured pilot, Obergefreiter Paul German (*sic*), TsAMO 48/453/13, p. 261

p. 293 'The trapped German forces . . .', Zhukov, 29 Nov. 1942, p. 178

p. 296 'cornerstone', quoted Paulus, p. 235

p. 296 'He described . . .', Raus bequest, ÖStA-KA B/186: III

p. 297 'Intention: Fourth . . .', BA-MA, RH19 VI, p. 60

p. 297 'Order for . . .', General Raus, ÖStA-KA B/186: III

p. 298 'Once a unit . . .', Gilbert (ed.), p. 17

p. 298 'a gigantic . . .', Raus, ÖStA-KA B/186: III

p. 300 'Around the runway . . .', Rohden, p. 46

p. 301 'Right down to . . .', General Raus, ÖStA-KA B/186: III

p. 302 'Yesterday and today . . .', Kolya Batyuk, 18 Dec. 1942, AMPSB 488/7955(5)

p. 303 'a steadily increasing . . .', Wolfgang Eckart, 'Von der Agonie einer missbrauchten Armee', in Wette and Ueberschär (eds.), p. 109

p. 304 'without having received . . .', Professor Dr Hans Girgensohn, 'Der Hungertod in Stalingrad: Die Geschichte seiner Entdeckung', privately published, 1992

p. 304 'The suspected causes . . .', Girgensohn, ibid.

p. 304 'a large-scale experiment . . .', 6 Jan. 1943, BA-MA, RH20-6/796

p. 304 'luxurious', Prof. Dr Hans Girgensohn, conversation, 22 Apr. 1996

p. 306 'stress illness', Girgensohn, conversation, 22 Apr. 1996

p. 306 rats deprived of sleep, Dr Susan Greenfield in the Royal Institution Christmas Lecture, 28 Dec. 1994

p. 306 'There's little new . . .', Lt W. M., 22 Dec. 1942, BZG-S

p. 306 'Slowly, our brave . . .', 30 Dec. 1942, BA-MA, RW4/v. 264

p. 307 'There stands a soldier . . .', Sepp Wirrer, 'Das Wolgalied', *Kameradschaft Stalingrad*, Aug./Sept. 1983

p. 307 German Communists, Korfes, undated MS. in MGFA-P; and Dyatlenko MS.

p. 308 'crackling sound of the propaganda voice', Hans Schmieder MS.

p. 308 'the ones with the . . .', 6 Dec. 1942, TsAMO 206/294/47, p. 102

p. 308 'Soldiers eagerly . . .', 16 Sept. 1942, TsAMO 48/453/13, p. 36

p. 308 ' "If German soldiers . . ." ', TsAMO 48/486/13, p. 488

p. 308 'Can one serve two masters?' Strecker, quoted in Haller, p. 97

p. 309 'the chances of a . . .', Freytag-Loringhoven, conversation, 23 Oct. 1995

p. 309 'We survivors . . .', BA-MA, RW4/v. 264

p. 309 'a break-out . . .', Beck, ÖStA-AdR 522

p. 309 'Every step was exhausting,' Behr conversation, 25 Oct. 1995

CHAPTER 19

p. 311 'just like at home', Kurt Reuber, letter, 25 Dec. 1942, quoted in Bähr and Bähr, p. 195

p. 312 'in the German way . . .', 24 Dec. 1942, BA-MA, N395/12

p. 313 *'O du fröhliche'*, Kurt Reuber, letter, 25 Dec. 1942, Bähr and Bähr, p. 195

p. 313 'with husky voices', Walter Kuber, 'Von Weihnachten 1942 bis zu meiner Gefangennahme am 31.1.1943', in Beck, p. 193

p. 313 'It is a . . .', Strecker, quoted in Haller, p. 102

p. 313 'the divisional commander . . .', Heinrich Simonmeier, Uffz., report, 29 July 1943, BA-MA, RH27-16/43

p. 313 'No supply flights . . .', BA-MA, RH20-6/236

p. 313 'If we do not receive . . .', BA-MA, RH20-6/240

p. 314 'In our hearts . . .', Oberstabarzt Dr Carl Otto Marckstadt, quoted in Schneider-Jancssen, p. 146

p. 314 'Christmas naturally . . .', letter, 28 Dec. 1942, quoted in Paulus, p. 89

p. 314 'Darling! . . .', Dmitry Venkutov to his wife, 24 Dec. 1942, AMPSB 11480

p. 314 'Hello Mariya', 24 Dec. 1942, AMPSB 739/13529

p. 315 'After reflecting . . .', Toepke, p. 83

p. 315 'Thus a dozen . . .', Hptm. d.R. Czygan, 8 Jan. 1943, BA-MA, RW4/v. 264, p. 205

p. 315 'Bloody losses . . .', BA-MA, RH20-6/237

p. 316 'all the necessary . . .', Adam, *Der schwere Entschluss*, p. 264

p. 316 'that Hitler . . .', Dohna-Schlobitten, conversation, 16 Oct. 1995

p. 316 '372 tanks . . .', BA-MA, RH19 VI/7, p. 59, and RH19 VI/8, p. 38

p. 316 'The enemy used . . .', Uffz. Hans Urban, BA-MA, RW4/v. 264, pp. 88–91

p. 317 'Our will for victory . . .', 31 Dec. 1942, BA-MA, RH20-6/240, p. 119

p. 317 'a powerful . . .', Daniels to wife, 1 Jan. 1943, BA-MA, N395/12

p. 318 'Celebrating the New Year . . .', letter, 9 Jan. 1943, Shindel', p. 45

p. 318 'Dear Parents, I'm all right . . .', AMPSB N45079A

p. 318 'In the name of . . .', BA-MA, RH20-6/236

p. 318 *'Mein Führer!'* 1 Jan. 1943, BA-MA, RH20-6/236

p. 318 'We're not . . .'; 'We are maintaining . . .'; 'The Führer knows . . .', BA-MA, RW4/v. 264

p. 319 'New hope arises . . .', Strecker, Haller, p. 102

p. 319 'following radio . . .', BA-MA, RH20-6/240, pp. 77, 86

p. 319 'with Luftwaffe . . .', Wallrawe, RH27-16/43

p. 320 'I don't like the . . .', V. Barsov, letter of 9 Jan. 1943, Shindel', p. 45

p. 320 'The Russians began . . .', Max Plakolb, ÖStA-KA B/1540

p. 320 'Army starving and frozen . . .', BA-MA, RH20-6/244D

p. 320 'From the command post . . .', *Opolchentsy v boyakh za Rodinu . . .*, p. 15

p. 321 'Whom shall we . . .', Zhukov, *Kakim my ego pomnim*, p. 245

p. 322 'You'll be sitting . . .', Marshal N. N. Voronov, 'Operation "Ring"', *Voenno-istoricheskii zhurnal*, 5 & 6, 1962

p. 322 'Why don't the Russians . . .', Martin Fiebig, 1 Jan. 1943, quoted in Kempowski (ed.), *Das Echolot . . .*, vol. i, p. 24

p. 322 'German anti-fascists . . .', Dyatlenko MS.

p. 324 'Everyone knew about . . .', TsAMO 226/335/7, p. 233

p. 324 'for all the trousers . . .', Dyatlenko MS.

CHAPTER 20

p. 333 'The misty cloud . . .', Dibold, p. 9

p. 334 'widely strewn . . .', Wieder, p. 45

p. 334 'Young and inexperienced . . .', Morzik, p. 188

p. 334 'Which ass . . .', Toepke, p. 69

p. 335 'My trust in . . .', 12 Dec. 1942, Paulus, p. 259, 19 Dec. 1942, p. 260

p. 335 'in honour of the heroes . . .', quoted in Sereny, p. 364

p. 335 'I hope that you'll break . . .', AMPSB, N677

p. 336 'very soon . . .', BA-MA, N395/13

p. 336 'who like everybody else . . .', Speer, quoted in Sereny, pp. 364–5

p. 337 'the Russians have . . .', Uffz. Hans Urban, 389th I.D., BA-MA, RW4/v. 264, p. 89

p. 337 'eaten two of his . . .', BA-MA, RW4/v. 264, p. 93

p. 338 'I received a quarter litre . . .', AMPSB, uncatalogued

p. 338 'We can only count . . .', 26 Dec. 1942, AMPSB N677

p. 339 'The only thing left . . .', 27 Dec. 1942, AMPSB N45079A

p. 339 'a light wound . . .', Kuber, in Beck, p. 195

p. 339 'I request permission . . .', Strecker, quoted in Haller, p. 104

p. 339 'steering-wheel heroes', Beck, p. 158

p. 340 'One day . . .', Plakolb, ÖStA-KA B/1540

p. 340 'Every half-hour . . .', Gefr. Joachim Grunow, Panzer Regt 2, report, 1 Aug. 1943, BA-MA, RH27-16/43

p. 340 'Only the . . .', Freytag-Loringhoven, conversation, 23 Oct. 1995

p. 341 'deafening sound', Hans Schmieder MS.

p. 341 'could not gain . . .', Siegfried Mühler, 44th I.D., ÖStA-KA B/1582

p. 342 'I was a soldier . . .', Gottfried von Bismarck, MS.

p. 342 'I was deeply . . .', Dohna-Schlobitten, p. 263

p. 342 'to advise . . .', Freytag-Loringhoven, conversation, 23 Oct. 1995

p. 343 'Give Hitler exactly . . .', Behr, conversation, 25 Oct. 1995

p. 345 'in a coded manner', letter from Winrich Behr to the author, 26 Feb. 1996

p. 347 'Discussions about the . . .', Manstein, 25 Jan. 1943, BA-MA, RH19 VI/12

p. 348 'Taking leave . . .', Max Plakolb, ÖStA-KA B/1540

p. 348 'Scarcely an earthly hope . . .', Reuber, 7 Jan. 1943, Bähr and Bähr, p. 205

p. 348 'to scribble . . .', BA-MA, RW4/v. 264, p. 95

p. 348 'The mood here . . .', 13 Jan. 1943, BA-MA, RW4/v. 264, p. 121

p. 348 'Perhaps this will . . .', 13 Jan. 1943, BA-MA, RW4/v. 264, p. 119

p. 348 'You are always . . .', 13 Jan. 1943, BA-MA, RW4/v. 264, p. 100

p. 349 'Fate has . . .', Gefreiter, BA-MA, RW4/v. 264, p. 96

p. 349 'fateful battle . . .', 13 Jan. 1943, BA-MA, RW4/v. 264, p. 118

p. 349 'This is a heroic struggle . . .', 13 Jan. 1943, BA-MA, RW4/v. 264, p. 99

p. 349 'we heard in . . .', Voronov, p. 18

p. 350 376th Infantry Division, Dyatlenko MS., and Voronov, p. 44

p. 350 'Enemy No. 1 is . . .' and 'My dear parents . . .', BA-MA, RW4/v. 264

p. 350 Cannibalism, Oberstleutnant a.D. Pfeifer, conversation, 20 Oct. 1995, and anonymous

p. 350 'In a gully . . .', Weinert, p. 122

p. 351 'left him completely . . .', Girgensohn, conversation, 22 Apr. 1996

CHAPTER 21

p. 352 'the usual melody . . .', Lt W. M., 15 Dec. 1942, BZG-S

p. 352 'Just a little . . .', 10 Jan. 1943, BA-MA, RW4/v. 264, p. 212

p. 352 'one spoke about death . . .', BA-MA, RW4/v. 264

p. 352 Ordinary soldiers, Freytag-Loringhoven, conversation, 23 Oct. 1995

p. 352 'that the relief force . . .', BA-MA, RW4/v. 264, p. 63

p. 353 'Help is close', interrogation, 16 Jan. 1943, TsAMO 226/335/7, p. 202

p. 353 'Especially brave were . . .', BA-MA, RW4/v. 264

p. 353 'who conducted themselves . . .', BA-MA, RW4/v. 264, p. 61

p. 353 'an incessant rolling . . .', Voronov, p. 27

p. 353 'There are only two . . .', Eugene Dolmatowsky, 27 Jan. 1943, 'The Ring closes in', in USSR, *Stalingrad*, p. 142

p. 353 'very unpeaceful Sunday', letter/diary to wife, 10 Jan. 1943, BA-MA, N395/12

p. 354 'The enemy munition . . .', Zank, p. 60

p. 354 'Nobody came out', Siegfried Mühler, ÖStA-KA B/1582

p. 354 'For an hour . . .', Stolberg, report, 17 Feb. 1943, BA-MA, RW4/v. 264, p. 160

p. 354 'Some of them . . .', *Stalingradbund Österreich*, August 1989

p. 355 'From this day on . . .', Wallrawe report, BA-MA, RH27-16/43

p. 355 'If the enemy . . .', TsAMO 206/294/18, p. 432

p. 355 'Those pigs of Romanians . . .', BA-MA, RW4/v. 264, p. 61

p. 356 'Karpovka looks . . .', Weinert, p. 34

p. 357 'instead of digging . . .', Strecker, quoted in Haller, p. 104

p. 357 'resisted bitterly . . .', Grams, p. 61

p. 357 'Munitions coming . . .', 13 Jan. 1943, BA-MA, RW4/v. 264

p. 357 'open fire only . . .', Wallrawe, BA-MA, RH27-16/43

p. 357 'soldiers with . . .', Klaus, p. 66

p. 358 'left to their fate', Wallrawe, BA-MA, RH27-16/43

p. 358 'Here was the greatest . . .', Alois Dorner, 'Meine Rettung aus dem Kessel von Stalingrad', *Kameradschaft Stalingrad*, Aug./Sept. 1989

p. 359 '376 Infantry Division . . .', 14 Jan. 1943, BA-MA, RW4/v. 264

p. 359 'Hitler's excuse . . .', Freytag-Loringhoven, conversation, 23 Oct. 1995

p. 360 'missing presumed dead', Speer, quoted in Sereny, p. 366

p. 360 'one look at the actual . . .', Morzik, p. 191

p. 360 'It was senseless to run away', TsAMO 206/294/47, p. 109

p. 361 'unbearable conditions . . .', interrogation, 2 Feb. 1943, TsAMO 226/335/7, p. 233

p. 361 'Heavy one-way traffic . . .', BA-MA, RL30/4

p. 361 'It is severely cold', Grossman papers, RGALI 1710/1/100

p. 362 'Several commanders . . .', Dr Günther Diez, Schneider-Janessen, p. 145

p. 362 'Faced with so much . . .', Schmieder MS.

p. 363 'Cases of post-operative . . .', Dr Günther Diez, Schneider-Janessen, p. 144

p. 363 'the so-called hospital', Freytag-Loringhoven, conversation, 23 Oct. 1995

p. 363 'It was a form of hell', Stolberg, report, 17 Feb. 1943, BA-MA, RW4/v. 264, p. 160

p. 363 'Death king of Gumrak', Seydlitz, p. 254

p. 364 'I am proud . . .', Hans Schmieder, 'Ein Überlebender aus dem Kessel von Stalingrad berichtet', *Deutsches Soldatenjahrbuch*, 1987

p. 364 'an attack by twenty-eight . . .', BA-MA, RW4/v. 264

p. 364 'I am thinking about . . .', letter from unknown German soldier, AMPSB, quoted in Volgograd University history department project

p. 364 'Why were no . . .', BA-MA, RL30/5

p. 364 'completely apathetic', BA-MA, RL30/6

p. 365 'the Army is no longer . . .', BA-MA, RH20-6/796

p. 365 'fed his dog with . . .', Dr Günther Diez, Schneider-Janessen, p. 143

p. 365 'On the codeword "Lion" . . .', BA-MA, RW4/v. 264

p. 365 'consider ways . . .', Freytag-Loringhoven, conversation, 23 Oct. 1995

p. 366 'trusted and energetic . . .', BA-MA, RH19 VI/11, p. 50

p. 366 'flown out of the . . .', BA-MA, RW4/v. 264, p. 86

p. 366 'The Führer decreed . . .', Bradley and Schulze-Kossens, p. 42

p. 367 'seemed absolutely bent . . .', Freytag-Loringhoven, conversation, 23 Oct. 1995

p. 368 'Is it possible . . .', BA-MA, RL30/6

p. 369 'Those in the Fortress . . .', 12.48, 18 Jan. 1943, BA-MA, RL30/6

p. 369 'The Stalingrad *Kessel* . . .', quoted in Boelcke, p. 369

p. 369 'only an immediate strike', Waldersee, quoted in Groscurth, p. 95

p. 369 'who soon will have no . . .', Groscurth, p. 553

p. 370 'There is not a single . . .', BA-MA, RL30/6, p. 73

p. 370 'Gumrak airfield . . .', BA-MA, RL30/6, p. 80

p. 370 'Whatever help . . .', Maj. Maes, 22 Jan. 1943, BA-MA, RL30/6, p. 83

p. 370 'as if on a hare shoot', and (p. 371) 'Leave me!', anonymous conversation

p. 371 'abandoned cripples', Weinert, p. 33

p. 371 'water from snow . . .', Böhme, p. 237

p. 371 'As far as the eye . . .', Hans Schmieder MS.

p. 372 '*Herr Major, sie kommen!*' Gebele, in Beck, p. 183

p. 372 'It was bitterly cold . . .', Kuber, in Beck, p. 194

p. 372 'Surrender out of . . .', 22 Jan. 1943, BA-MA, RH19 VI/12, p. 324

CHAPTER 22

p. 374 'With heavy hearts . . .', Kuber, in Beck, p. 196

p. 374 red parachutes, Winrich Behr, conversation, 25 Oct. 1995

p. 374 'German soldiers here', BA-MA, RH19 VI/12, p. 451

p. 375 'Exhausted wounded men . . .', BA-MA, RW4/v. 264

p. 375 'Moans, calls for help . . .', Dr Hubert Haidinger, in *Bund ehemaliger Stalingradkämpfer, Weihnachts Rundbrief*, 1992, p. 9

p. 375 'Abandon hope . . .', Dr Hermann Achleitner, 'Als Arzt in Stalingrad', in Beck, p. 199

p. 376 'Two Stalingrad women . . .', Gebele, in Beck, p. 186

p. 377 'Where are your regiments?' Theodor Plievier broadcast, BA-MA, RW4/v. 264, p. 227

p. 377 'The eyes of the hardened . . .', Chuikov, p. 279

p. 378 'more interesting', Dyatlenko MS.

p. 378 'Kessel-baby', Dyatlenko MS.; see also 'Das "Kesselkind" des Generals' in *Freiheit*, 7 Apr. 1965, and BA-MA, N395/12

p. 379 'the eyes and hand . . .', Dyatlenko MS.

p. 379 'To the Führer! . . .', BA-MA, RL30/5

p. 380 'Paulus is in a . . .', 20 Jan. 1943, Groscurth, p. 533

p. 380 'our own funeral speech', Wieder, *Stalingrad und die Verantwortung des Soldaten*, p. 100

p. 380 'macabre', Gottfried von Bismarck MS.

p. 380 'Turn it up!' Dr Hubert Haidinger, op. cit., p. 7

p. 380 'suicide of the Jews', anonymous conversation

p. 380 'The heroic . . .', quoted in Domarus, vol. ii, p. 1979

p. 381 'I have no intention . . .', quoted in Beck, p. 207

p. 381 'It looks like an invitation . . .', Dyatlenko MS.

p. 381 'What's going on here?' Dibold, pp. 24–5

p. 382 'apocalyptic order', Seydlitz, p. 250

p. 382 'We fight to the last bullet . . .', anonymous conversation

p. 382 'The swastika . . .', 30 Jan. 1943 at 19.50 hrs, BA-MA, RL30/5

p. 382 'listening to the . . .', BA-MA, RL30/5

p. 382 'During that night . . .', Schmieder MS.

p. 383 'Russians at the . . .', Sonderstab Milch, BA-MA, RL30/6, p. 83

p. 383 'In Stalingrad the situation . . .', BA-MA, RW4/v. 264

p. 383 'like the ears . . .', Grossman, *Life and Fate*, p. 801

p. 384 'Kameraden, Krieg kaputt!' Fritz Ecker, 'Ein weiter Weg', *Stalingradbund Österreich*, Jan. 1991

p. 384 'Whoever's capable . . .', Dr Hubert Haidinger, op. cit., p. 8

p. 384 'Fascist dogs', Klavdia Sveridovna Ribaltshenko (*sic*), interrogation by Gruppe Geheime Feldpolizei 626, 21 July 1943, BZG-S

p. 385 'Soviet soldiers . . .', Beck, p. 189

p. 385 'What shall we do with . . .', anonymous conversation

p. 387 'That's how Berlin . . .', Beck, p. 197

p. 387 'rather good command of Russian', C. M. Bogomolov MS.

p. 388 'A German Field Marshal . . .', Lev Bezyminsky, conversation, 10 Nov. 1995

p. 388 'there is no doubt that . . .', Winrich Behr, letter to the author, 26 Feb. 1996

p. 390 'round and round in circles', Bezyminsky, conversation, 10 Nov. 1995

p. 391 'I must inform you . . .', Dyatlenko MS.

p. 391 'They have surrendered . . .', 1 Feb. 1943, quoted in Gilbert (ed.), pp. 17–22; and Warlimont, pp. 319–23

p. 392 'Troops are fighting . . .', and 'I expect . . .', BA-MA, RL 30/5

p. 392 'XI Army Corps . . .', war diary Sonderstab Milch, BA-MA, RL 30/6, p. 151

p. 392 'When the time comes . . .', Strecker, Haller, p. 105

p. 393 'XI Army Corps . . .', BA-MA, RL 30/5

p. 393 'Long live Germany!' Haller, p. 107

p. 393 'What the normal . . .', Werth, *The Year of Stalingrad*, p. 463

p. 394 1.1 million casualties, of which 485,751, quoted by Erickson, in Erickson and Dilks, p. 264

p. 394 'I thought of the . . .', Grossman papers, RGALI, 1710/1/101

CHAPTER 23

p. 396 'No more . . .', BA-MA, RL 30/6

p. 396 'the Corporal uneducated . . .', Dyatlenko MS.

p. 396 'We have our own rules', Bezyminsky, conversation, 10 Nov. 1995

p. 397 'They looked healthy . . .', Werth, *The Year of Stalingrad*, p. 446

p. 397 'It was rather like . . .', Werth, *The Year of Stalingrad*, p. 444

p. 397 'When I opened . . .', Bogomolov MS.

p. 398 'our troops . . .', Boelcke, p. 408

p. 399 'which will move . . .', Boelcke, p. 430

p. 399 'From Führer headquarters . . .', Domarus, vol. ii, p. 1985

p. 400 'The farewell letters . . .', 18 Feb. 1943, Heinz Boberach (ed.),

Meldungen aus dem Reich 1938–1945, vol. xii, p. 4822, quoted in Wette and Ueberschär, p. 63

p. 400 'in future . . .', Boelcke, p. 411

p. 400 'Stop dancing!' Leopold Graf von Bismarck, conversation, 4 May 1996

p. 402 'If we are paid back . . .', Bielenberg, p. 135

p. 403 'We will end the war . . .', quoted Rohden, p. 127

p. 404 'You cannot stop . . .', 'I wonder how it feels . . .', Wettlin, pp. 86, 88

p. 404 'After Stalingrad . . .', Smirnov, conversation, 22 Nov. 1995

p. 404 'needed to believe', Ehrenburg, pp. 10–11

p. 405 'They're starting these gold . . .', Ulko, conversation, 21 Nov. 1995

CHAPTER 24

p. 406 'railway tracks, where . . .', Grossman papers, RGALI, 1710/1/101

p. 406 'Almost all members . . .', Beck, p. 191

p. 406 'dozens each day', Lt Medvedev to Maj. Demchenko, 9 March 1943, quoted in Epifanov, p. 241

p. 407 'liberated from fascist . . .', RTsKhIDNI 17/8/226

p. 407 'Most of the children . . .', Wettlin, p. 119

p. 407 'Soviet authorities . . .', RTsKhIDNI 17/8/226

p. 407 'special safe paths', Goncharov, conversation, 23 Nov. 1995

p. 407 'Mama, we are all right', quoted in Agapov, p. 11

p. 410 'limping and shuffling . . .', Weinert, p. 37

p. 411 'The Russians had very simple methods . . .', anonymous conversation

p. 411 'We set out with 1,200 men', Josef Farber, conversation, 16 Apr. 1996

p. 412 'like herrings . . .', Böhme, p. 237

p. 412 'extremely critical', TsAMO 62/355/1, p. 226, quoted in Epifanov, p. 235

p. 412 'nothing to eat . . .', Dr Hubert Haidinger, *Bund ehemaliger Stalingradkämpfer, Weihnachts Rundbrief*, 1992, p. 9

p. 413 'Then came another shock . . .', Schmieder MS.

p. 413 'The dead each . . .', Willi Lotz, 'Die Gefangenlager der Stalingrader: Erinnerungen an Beketowka', in *Kameradschaft Stalingrad*, Aug.–Sept. 1981

p. 413 'mountain of bodies', Dr Hubert Haidinger, in *Bund ehemaliger Stalingradkämpfer, Weihnachts Rundbrief*, 1992, p. 10

p. 413 'We had no tears left', Schmieder MS.

p. 413 'death register', Böhme, p. 237

p. 413   55,228 prisoners, TsKhIDK, 1e/1/9, p. 34, report by Capt. Kruglov, quoted in Epifanov, p. 47

p. 413   'Hunger . . .', Dibold, address to Bund ehemaliger Stalingradkämpfer, 18 Sept. 1976, Limburg

p. 413   'camel-meat', anonymous conversation

p. 413   'only at gunpoint . . .', A. Chuyanov, *Na Stremnina Veka*, Moscow, 1976, p. 264, quoted in Epifanov, p. 33

p. 414   'And who are you . . .', anonymous conversation

p. 415   'It is the duty of a general . . .', anonymous conversation

p. 416   'only be compared to sheep-shearing', Schmieder MS.

CHAPTER 25

p. 418   'We pressed to . . .', Berezhkov, *History in the Making*, p. 242

p. 418   'I propose a salute . . .', Berezhkov, op. cit., pp. 289–91

p. 420   'Doctor, the miracle . . .', Dibold, p. 170

p. 421   'thrusting a long thin shard . . .', anonymous conversation

p. 422   'man was just . . .', anonymous conversation

p. 423   'According to Seydlitz's idea . . .', 17 Sept. 1943, TsKhIDK, 451p/2/6

p. 425   'the contemptible . . .', quoted Seydlitz, p. 341

p. 425   'the absence of significant success', Melnikov, TsKhIDK, 451p/3/7

p. 425   'recognize officially', APRF 3/58/498

p. 425   'compiled in a devious way', APRF 3/58/497

p. 426   'members of . . .', 25 May 1944, Manuilsky to Shcherbakov, RTsKhIDNI 495/77/37, pp. 32–4

p. 427   'on Comrade Shcherbakov's . . .', GARF r-9401/2/66

p. 427   'who could explain the principles . . .', 20 Feb. 1945, Krivemko to Beria, GARF r-9401/2/92/322-4

p. 427   'It should be mentioned . . .', 20 Feb. 1945, Krivemko to Beria, GARF r-9401/2/92/322-4

p. 428   'spiritual depression . . .', Strecker, quoted in Haller, p. 214

p. 428   losses, G. F. Krivosheyev (ed.), *Grif sekretnosti sniat': Poteri vooruzhennykh sil SSSR v voinakh, boevykh deistviiakh i voennykh konfliktakh*, Moscow, Voenizdat, 1993, quoted in Erickson, 'Red Army battlefield performance', pp. 235–6

p. 428   'irrespective of their physical . . .', quoted in Epifanov, p. 163

p. 429   'revanchist reactionary general', RTsKhIDNI 495/77/37

p. 430   'was valid not only . . .', Dibold, p. 186

p. 430 'sufficient reason . . .', Gottfried von Bismarck MS.

p. 431 'a very unhappy man', Behr, conversation, 25 Nov. 1995

p. 431 'pensioner of the Soviet-occupied zone', BA-MA, N601/v. 9, p. 8

APPENDIX B

p. 439 195,000, Rüdiger Overmans, 'Das andere Gesicht des Krieges: Leben und Sterben der 6. Armee', in Förster (ed.), p. 442

p. 439 268,900, Peter Hild, 'Partnergruppe zur Aufklärung von Vermissten-schicksalen deutscher und russischer Soldaten des 2. Weltkrieges', in Epifanov, p. 29

p. 439 'Sixth Army ration strength in the Kessel', BA-MA, RH20-6/239, p. 226

p. 439 'only inside the Kessel', BA-MA, RH20-6/237, p. 129

p. 440 111,465, TsKhIDK, 1s/4/3, p. 16, quoted in Epifanov, p. 25

p. 440 Sixth Army losses: 15,000 to 6 December, then 36,859 between 6 December and 7 January, BA-MA, N601/v. 5

Select Bibliography

Achleitner, Dr Hermann, 'Als Arzt in Stalingrad', in Beck (ed.)
Adam, Wilhelm, *Stalingrad Mahnt*, Berlin, 1951
———, *Der schwere Entschluss*, Berlin, 1965
Addison, Paul, and Calder, Angus (eds.), *Time to Kill, The Soldier's Experience of War 1939–1945*, London, 1997
Agapov, Boris, *After the Battle*, Moscow, 1943
Andrew, Christopher, and Gordievsky, Oleg, *KGB, The Inside Story*, London, 1990
Andreyev, Catherine, *Vlasov and the Russian Liberation Movement*, Cambridge (UK), 1987
Axworthy, Mark, *Third Axis, Fourth Army*, London, 1995

Bähr, W., and Bähr, H. W. (eds.), *Kriegsbriefe gefallener Studenten 1939–1945*, Tübingen, 1952
Bartov, Omer, *The Eastern Front, 1941–1945, German Troops and the Barbarisation of Warfare*, London, 1985
———, *Hitler's Army: Soldiers, Nazis and War in the Third Reich*, Oxford, 1991
Beck, Alois (ed.), *Bis Stalingrad*, Ulm, 1983
Below, Nicolaus von, *Als Hitlers Adjutant 1937–1945*, Mainz, 1980
Berezhkov, Valentin M., *In diplomatischer Mission bei Hitler in Berlin 1940–1941*, Frankfurt am Main, 1967
———, *History in the Making*, Moscow, 1982
———, *Ich war Stalins Dolmetscher: Hinter den Kulissen der politischen Weltbühne*, Munich, 1991

Beyer, W. R., *Stalingrad. Unten, wo das Leben konkret war*, Frankfurt am Main, 1987

Bialer, Seweryn, *Stalin and His Generals: Soviet Military Commanders' Memoirs of World War II*, Boulder, Colo., 1984

Blank, Alexander, *Die deutschen Kriegsgefangenen in der UdSSR*, Cologne, 1979

Boddenberg, W., *Die Kriegsgefangenpost Deutscher Soldaten in Sowjetischem Gewahrsam und die Post von ihren Angehörigen während des II. Weltkrieges*, Berlin, 1985, MS. MGFA-P

Boelcke, W. A. (ed.), *'Wollt Ihr den Totalen Krieg?' Die Geheime Goebbels-Konferenzen*, Stuttgart, 1967

Böhme, K. W., *Die deutschen Kriegsgefangenen in sowjetischer Hand*, Munich, 1966

Bradley, Dermot, and Schulze-Kossens, Richard (eds.), *Tätigkeitsbericht der Chefs des Heerespersonalamtes General der Infanterie Rufolf Schmundt*, Osnabrück, 1984

Bullock, Alan, *Hitler and Stalin, Parallel Lives*, London, 1991

Carell, Paul (P. K. Schmidt), *Hitler's War on Russia*, London, 1964

Cassidy, H. C., *Moscow Dateline*, Boston, Mass., 1943

Chaney, Otto Preston, *Zhukov*, Oklahoma City, Okla., 1972

Chuikov, Vasili Ivanovich, *The Beginning of the Road: The Battle for Stalingrad*, London, 1963

Clark, Alan, *Barbarossa: The Russian–German Conflict 1941–1945*, London, 1996

Craig, William, *Enemy at the Gates: The Battle for Stalingrad*, New York, 1973

Dallin, Alexander, *German Rule in Russia 1941–1945*, London, 1981

Deist, Wilhelm (ed.), *The German Military in the Age of Total War*, Leamington Spa, War. (UK), 1985

Dettmer, Friedrich, *Die 44. Infanterie-Division*, Friedberg, 1979

Dibold, Hans, *Arzt in Stalingrad. Passion einer Gefangenschaft*, Salzburg, 1949

Dieckhoff, Gerhard, and Holzmann, M., *3. Infanterie-Division*, Friedberg, 1978

Doerr, Hans, *Der Feldzug nach Stalingrad*, Darmstadt, 1955

Dohna-Schlobitten, Alexander Fürst zu, *Erinnerungen eines alten Ostpreussen*, Berlin, 1989

Domarus, M., *Hitler, Reden und Proklamationen, 1932–1945*, Würzburg, 1962

Druzhinin, B. V., *Two Hundred Days of Fire*, Moscow, 1970

Dunn, Walter S., *Hitler's Nemesis: The Red Army*, Westport, Conn., 1994

Ebert, Jens, *Zwischen Mythos und Wirklichkeit. Die Schlacht um Stalingrad in deutsch-sprachigen authentischen und literarischen Texten*, Berlin, vols. i & ii, 1989 MS. MGFA-P

———, *Stalingrad – eine Deutsche Legende*, Reinbek bei Hamburg, 1992

Ehrenburg, Ilya, *Men, Years – Life: The War 1941–1945*, London, 1964

Einsiedel, Heinrich Graf von, *Tagebuch der Versuchung*, Berlin, 1950

———, *The Shadow of Stalingrad*, London, 1953

———, *Der Überfall*, Hamburg, 1984

Epifanov, A. E., *Die Tragödie der deutschen Kreigsgefangenen in Stalingrad*, Osnabrück, 1996

Erickson, John, *The Road to Stalingrad*, London, 1975 (*Stalin's War with Germany*, vol. 1)

———, *The Road to Berlin*, London, 1983 (*Stalin's War with Germany*, vol. 2)

———, 'The development of Soviet military doctrine', *The Origins of Contemporary Doctrine Conference, Larkhill*, 28 March 1996

———, 'Red Army battlefield performance, 1941–1945: The system and the soldier', in Addison and Calder (eds.)

Erickson, John, and Dilks, David (eds.), *Barbarossa, the Axis and the Allies*, Edinburgh, 1994

Fest, Joachim, *Hitler*, vol. ii, Frankfurt am Main, Ullstein, 1976

———, *Staatsstreich: Der lange Weg zum 20. Juli*, Berlin, 1994

Förster, Jürgen, *Stalingrad, Risse im Bündnis 1942/43*, Freiburg, 1975

———, 'Das Unternehmen "Barbarossa" als Eroberungs- und Vernicht-ungskrieg', in *Das deutsche Reich und der Zweite Weltkrieg*, vol. iv, Stuttgart, 1983

———, 'Evolution and development of German doctrine, 1914–1945', *The Origins of Contemporary Doctrine Conference, Larkhill*, 28 March 1996

——— (ed.), *Stalingrad: Ereignis, Wirkung, Symbol*, Munich, 1992

Garrard, C., and Garrard, J. (eds.), *World War II and the Soviet People*, New York, 1993

Gilbert, Felix (ed.), *Hitler Directs His War: The Secret Records of His Daily Military Conferences*, New York, 1951

Giulini, Udo, *Stalingrad und mein zweites Leben*, Neustadt/Weinstrasse, 1978

Glantz, David, *Soviet Military Deception in the Second World War*, London, 1989

————, *The Role of Intelligence in Soviet Military Strategy in World War II*, Novato, Calif., 1990

Glantz, David, and House, J. M., *When Titans Clashed*, Kansas City, 1995

Goellecke, Pontianus van, *Der Weg ins Leere*, Wolfenbüttel, 1974

Goldhagen, Daniel, *Hitler's Willing Executioners: Ordinary Germans and the Holocaust*, London, 1997

Golovchanski, A., *'Ich will raus aus diesem Wahnsinn.' Deutsche Briefe von der Ostfront*, Wuppertal, 1991

Götte, Franz, and Peiler, H., *Die 29. Infanterie-Division*, Friedberg, 1984

Grams, Rolf, *Die 14. Panzer-Division, 1940–1945*, Bad Nauheim, 1957

Groscurth, Helmuth, *Tagebücher eines Abwehroffiziers*, Stuttgart, 1970

Guderian, Gen. Heinz, *Panzer Leader*, London, 1952

Halder, Col.-Gen. Franz, *Kriegstagebuch*, vol. iii, Stuttgart, 1964

Haller, U. (ed.), *Lieutenant General Karl Strecker*, Westport, Conn., 1994

Harrison, Mark, *Soviet Planning in Peace and War, 1938–1945*, Cambridge (UK), 1985

Hassell, Ulrich von, *The von Hassell Diaries*, London, 1948

Hauck, Friedrich, *Eine deutsche Division in Russland: 305. Infanteriedivision*, Friedberg, 1975

Heer, Hannes (ed.), *Vernichtungskrieg. Verbrechen der Wehrmacht 1941 bis 1944, Ausstellungskatalog*, Hamburg, 1996

Heiber, H. (ed.), *Lagebesprechungen im Führerhauptquartier. Protokollfragmente aus Hitlers militärischen Konferenzen 1942–1945*, Munich, 1962

Himpe, Ullus, *Die 71. Infanterie-Division in Zweiten Weltkrieg*, Neckargemünd, 1973

Hoffmann, Kurt, *Beiträge zur Geschichte der 60. Infanterie-Division (mot.)*, MS. MGFA-P, 1979

Holl, Adalbert, *Was geschah nach Stalingrad?* Duisburg, 1964

Hoth, Hermann, *Panzer Operationen*, Heidelberg, 1956

Jacobsen, Hans-Adolf (ed.), *Generaloberst Halder: Kriegstagebuch*, 3 vols., Stuttgart, 1963

Jacobsen, Hans-Adolf, and Rohwer, J. (eds.), *Decisive Battles of World War II: The German View*, London, 1965

Jukes, Geoffrey, *Hitler's Stalingrad Decisions*, Berkeley, Calif., 1985

Kageneck, August von, *Examen de conscience*, Paris, 1996

Kehrig, Manfred, *Stalingrad: Analyse und Dokumentation einer Schlacht*, Stuttgart, 1974

Keitel, Wilhelm, *The Memoirs of Field Marshal Keitel*, New York, 1966

Kemmerich, P., *Im Vorfeld von Stalingrad. Tagebuchblätter*, Munich, 1964

Kempowski, Walter (ed.), *Das Echolot. Eine kollektives Tagebuch Januar und Februar 1943*, Munich, 1993

Kerr, Walter, *The Secret of Stalingrad*, London, 1979

Klaus, Edgar, *Durch die Hölle des Krieges, Erinnerungen eines deutschen Unternehmers an Stalingrad*, Berlin, 1991

Klee, E., and Dressen, W. (eds.), *Gott Mit Uns, Der deutsche Vernichtungskrieg im Osten*, Frankfurt am Main, 1992

Klee, Ernst; Dressen, Willi; and Riess, Volker (eds.), *Schöne Zeiten: Judenmord aus der Sicht der Täter und Gaffer*, Frankfurt am Main, 1988

Kluge, Alexander, *Schlachtsbeschreibung*, Freiburg, 1964

Konsalik, Heinz (ed.), *Stalingrad, Porträt einer Stadt, Inferno einer Schlacht, Protokoll eines Wahnsinns*, Bayreuth, 1968

Korfes, Dr Otto, *Zur Geschichte von Stalingrad, 1942–1943*, MGFA-P, undated MS.

Knight, Amy, *Beria, Stalin's First Lieutenant*, Princeton, NJ, 1993

Kruse, Martin (ed.), *Die Stalingrad-Madonna, das Werk Kurt Reubers als Dokument der Versöhnung*, Hanover, 1993

Krylov, Nikolai, *Stalingrad. Die entscheidende Schlacht des zweiten Weltkrieges*, Cologne, 1981

Kurowski, Franz, *Lüftbrucke Stalingrad: die Tragödie der Luftwaffe und der 6. Armee*, Voninckel, 1983

Langsdorff, Gero von, 'Jagdflieger in Stalingrad: Aus den Aufzeichnungen des Oberleutnant Kurt Ebener', *Deutsches Soldatenjahrbuch*, 1973, pp. 193–202

Lenz, Friedrich, *Stalingrad – der verlorene Sieg*, Heidelberg, 1956

Löser, Jochen, *Bittere Pflicht. Kampf und Untergang der 76. Berlin-Brandenburgischen Infanterie-Division*, Osnabrück, 1988

Lucke, Christian von, *Panzer-Regiment 2*, Kleve, 1953

Malaparte, Curzio, *The Volga Rises in Europe*, London, 1958

Manstein, FM Erich von, *Lost Victories*, London, 1959

———, *Aus einen Soldatenleben*, Bonn, 1985

Messenger, Charles, *The Last Prussian*, London, 1991

Messerschmidt, Manfred, *Was damals Recht war – NS-Militär und Strafjustiz im Vernichtungskrieg*, Essen, 1996

Metelmann, H., *Through Hell for Hitler*, London, 1990
Michalka, W. (ed.), *Der Zweite Weltkrieg*, Munich, 1989
Michel, Karl, *Es begann am Don*, Bern, 1946
Morzik, D. F., *German Air Force Airlift Operations*, New York, 1961
Mösch, Gerhard, *Stalingrad. Ein Erlebnis und seine Konsequenzen*, Kassel, 1946

Neidhardt, Hanns, *Mit Tanne und Eichenlaub, Kriegschronik der 100. Jäger-Division*, Graz, 1981
Noakes, Jeremy, and Pridham, Geoffrey (eds.), *Nazism 1919–1945*, 3 vols., Exeter, Devon (UK), 1988

Pabst, Helmut, *The Outermost Frontier*, London, 1957
Paget, R. T., *Manstein, His Campaigns and His Trail*, London, 1951
Paulus, Friedrich, *Ich stehe hier auf Befehl*, Frankfurt am Main, 1960
Philippi, Alfred, and Heim, Ferdinand, *Der Feldzug gegen Sowjetrussland 1941–1945*, Stuttgart, 1962
Piekalkiewicz, Janusz, *Stalingrad, Anatomie einer Schlacht*, Munich, 1977
Plocher, Hermann, *The German Air Force versus Russia, 1942*, New York, 1966
Plotnikov, Col. Y. V., *Die Stalingrader Schlacht*, Moscow, 1982
Podewils, Clemens, *Don und Volga*, Munich, 1952

Reinhardt, Dr Klaus, *Moscow: The Turning Point*, New York, 1992
Riedesser, Peter, *Maschinengewehre hinter der Front*, Frankfurt am Main, 1996
Robel, Gert, *Die deutschen Kriegsgefangenen in der Sowjetunion*, Munich, 1974
Rohden, Hans-Detlef Herhudt von, *Die Luftwaffe ringt um Stalingrad*, Wiesbaden, 1950
Rokossovsky, K. K., *A Soldier's Duty*, Moscow, 1970
Rotundo, Louis (ed.), *Battle for Stalingrad. The 1943 Soviet General Staff Study*, New York, 1989

Sadaranda, Dana, *Beyond Stalingrad: Manstein and the Operations of Army Group Don*, New York, 1990
Samsonov, A. M. (ed.), *Stalingradskaia bitva*, Moscow, 1968
Sapp, Franz, *Gefangen in Stalingrad*, Steyr, 1992
Scheibert, Horst, *Nach Stalingrad – 48 Kilometer*, Heidelberg, 1956
Schimak, Anton, Lamprecht, Karl and Dettmer, Friedrich, *Die 44 Infanterie-Division*, Vienna, 1969
Schmidt, Paul, *Hitler's Interpreter, The Secret History of German Diplomacy 1935–1945*, London, 1951
Schneider-Janessen, Karlheinz, *Arzt im Krieg*, Frankfurt am Main, 1993

Schramm, P. E., and Hillgruber, A. (eds.), *Kriegstagebuch des OKW der Wehrmacht*, Frankfurt am Main, 1963

Schröter, Heinz, *Stalingrad . . . bis zur lezte Patrone*, Lengerich, 1953

Schulte, Theo J., *The German Army and Nazi Policies in Occupied Russia*, Oxford, 1989

Sella, A., *The Value of Human Life in Soviet Warfare*, London, 1992

Selle, H., *Die Tragödie von Stalingrad*, Hanover, 1948

Sereny, Gitta, *Albert Speer: His Battle With Truth*, London, 1995

Seth, Ronald, *Stalingrad: Point of Return*, London, 1959

Sevryuk, Vladimir, *Moscow–Stalingrad*, Moscow, 1970

Seydlitz, Gen. Walther von, *Stalingrad, Konflikt und Konsequenz, Erinnerungen*, Oldenburg, 1977

Shindel', Aleksandr Danilovich (ed.), *Po obe storoni fronta*, Moscow, 1995

Shtemenko, S. M., *The Soviet General Staff at War*, Moscow, 1970

Shukman, H., *Stalin's Generals*, London, 1993

Simonov, Konstantin Mikhailovich, *Stalingrad Fights On*, Moscow, 1942

———, *Raznye dni voiny, Dnevnik pisatelia*, vol. ii, Moscow, 1978

Sommerfeldt, Martin, *Das Oberkommando der Wehrmacht gibt bekannt*, Frankfurt am Main, 1952

Stahlberg, Alexander, *Bounden Duty*, London, 1990

Steidle, Luitpold, *Entscheidung an der Wolga*, Berlin, 1970

Strassner, Peter, *Verräter: Das Nationalkomitee Freies Deutschland*, Munich, 1963

Stratowa, Wulf, *Kein Friede in Stalingrad: Feldpostbriefe 1941/1942*, Vienna, 1995

Streit, Christian, *Keine Kameraden: Die Wehrmacht und die sowjetischen Kriegsgefangenen*, Stuttgart, 1991

Toepke, Gunter, *Stalingrad, Wie es wirklich war*, Stade, 1949

Tuyll, H. Van, *Feeding the Bear: American Aid to the Soviet Union 1941–1945*, New York, 1989

Uberberschär, Gerd, and Wette, Wolfram (eds.), *'Unternehmen Barbarossa', der deutsche Überfall auf die Sowjetunion 1941*, Frankfurt am Main, 1993

USSR, *Stalingrad, an Eye Witness Account*, London, 1943

Vasilevsky, A. M., *A Lifelong Cause*, Moscow, 1978

Van Creveld, Martin, *Hitler's Strategy, the Balkan Clue*, Cambridge, 1973

———, *Fighting Power: German and US Army Performance 1939–1945*, London, 1983

Vogel, Detlef, and Wette, Wolfram, *Andere Helme – Andere Menschen?* Essen, 1995

Volkogonov, Dimitri, *Stalin: Triumph and Tragedy*, London, 1991

Voronov, N. N., 'Operation "Ring"', *Voenno-istoricheski zhurnal*, 5 & 6, 1962

Voss, Paul-Hans, *Freigegeben, Tagebuch Aufzeichnungen eines Funkers*, Rossdorf, 1982

Waasen, Heinrich Maria, *Was geschah in Stalingrad?* Zell am See, Salzburg, 1950

Warlimont, Walter, *Im Hauptquartier der deutschen Wehrmacht 1939–1945*, Frankfurt am Main, 1962

Wegner, Bernd, 'German perceptions of Soviet military and economic strength in preparation for Operation Blau', in C. Andrew and J. Noakes, *Intelligence and International Relations 1900–1945*, Exeter, Devon (UK), 1987

——, 'Der Krieg Gegen die Sowjetunion 1942/3', in Militärgeschichtliches Forschungsamt, *Das deutsche Reich und der Zweite Weltkrieg*, vol. vi, Stuttgart, 1990

Weinert, Erich, *Stalingrad Diary*, London, 1944

Werth, Alexander, *The Year of Stalingrad*, London, 1946

——, *Russia at War 1941–1945*, London, 1964

Werthen, Wolfgang, *Geschichte der 16. Panzerdivision*, Bad Nauheim, 1958

Wette, Wolfram, and Ueberschär, Gerd (eds.), *Mythos und Wirklichkeit einer Schlacht*, Frankfurt am Main, 1993

Wettlin, Margaret, *Russian Road*, London, 1945

Wich, Rudolph, *Baden-Württembergische Divisionen im 2. Weltkrieg*, Karlsruhe, 1957

Wieder, Joachim, *Die Tragödie von Stalingrad, Erinnerungen eines Überlebenden*, Deggendorf, 1955

——, *Stalingrad und die Verantwortung des Soldaten*, Munich, 1962

Yeremenko, A. I., *Tage der Entscheidung. Als Frontoberbefehlshaber in der Schlacht an der Wolga*, Berlin, 1964

Zank, Horst, *Stalingrad, Kessel und Gefangenschaft*, Herford, 1993

Zayas, Alfred M. de, *The Wehrmacht War Crimes Bureau, 1939–1945*, Lincoln, Neb., 1989

Zhilin, Lt-Gen. P. A., *They Sealed Their Own Doom*, Moscow, 1970

Zhukov, Georgi K., *Marshal Zhukov's Greatest Battles*, New York, 1969

——, *Kakim my ego pomnim*, Moscow, 1988

PERIODICALS, NEWSPAPERS, JOURNALS AND VETERANS' PUBLICATIONS

Bund ehemaliger Stalingradkämpfer, Weihnachts Rundbrief
Bundestreffen der Stalingradkämpfer
Deutsches Soldatenjahrbuch
Istoricheskii Arkhiv
*Kameradschaft Stalingrad: Mitteilungsblatt für die ehemaligen Stalingradkämpfer
und den Österreichischen Stalingradbund*
*Opolchentsy v boyakh za Rodinu. Boevoi put' divizii Narodnogo opolchenya
Kievskogo raiona g. Moskvy*, Moscow, 1981
Stalingradbund Österreich
Stalinskoe znamia
Voenno-istoricheskii zhurnal
Völkischer Beobachter

FICTION AND OTHER LITERARY WORKS

Anon., *Last Letters from Stalingrad*, London, 1956*
Bondarev, Yuri, *Heisser Schnee*, Berlin, 1972
Bredel, Willi, *Der Sonderführer*, Berlin, 1970
Grossman, Vasily, *The People Immortal*, London, 1943
———, *Stalingrad*, Moscow, 1946
———, *Life and Fate*, London, 1985
Konsalik, Heinz, *Der Arzt von Stalingrad*, Munich, 1956
Lazarev, L. (ed.), *Let the Living Remember*, Moscow, 1976
Nekrassov, Viktor Platonovich, *Front Line Stalingrad*, London, 1962
Neruda, Pablo, 'Canto a Stalingrado' and 'Nuevo Canto de Amor a Stalingrado', in *Tercera Residencia 1935–1945*, Barcelona, 1977
Plievier, Theodor, *Stalingrad*, Berlin, 1946
Simonov, Konstantin M., *Days and Nights*, New York, 1945

*This collection is listed under fiction as the authenticity of the letters is very much in doubt.

Index

ABOUT THE AUTHOR

Antony Beevor was educated at Winchester and Sandhurst. A regular officer in the 11th Hussars, he served in Germany and England. He has published several novels, while his works of non-fiction include *The Spanish Civil War*; *Crete: The Battle and the Resistance*, which won the 1993 Runciman Award; and *Berlin: The Downfall, 1945*. With his wife, the writer Artemis Cooper, he wrote *Paris After the Liberation: 1944–1949*. Antony Beevor is a Fellow of the Royal Society of Literature and a Chevalier de l'Ordre des Arts et des Lettres in France. Most of his titles are published by Penguin.

Stalingrad was awarded the Samuel Johnson Prize for Non-fiction, the Wolfson History Prize and the Hawthornden Prize in 1999. It became a number-one bestseller both in hardback and paperback, the UK edition alone selling half a million copies, and has been published around the world in eighteen translations.